WORKSHOP MANUAL

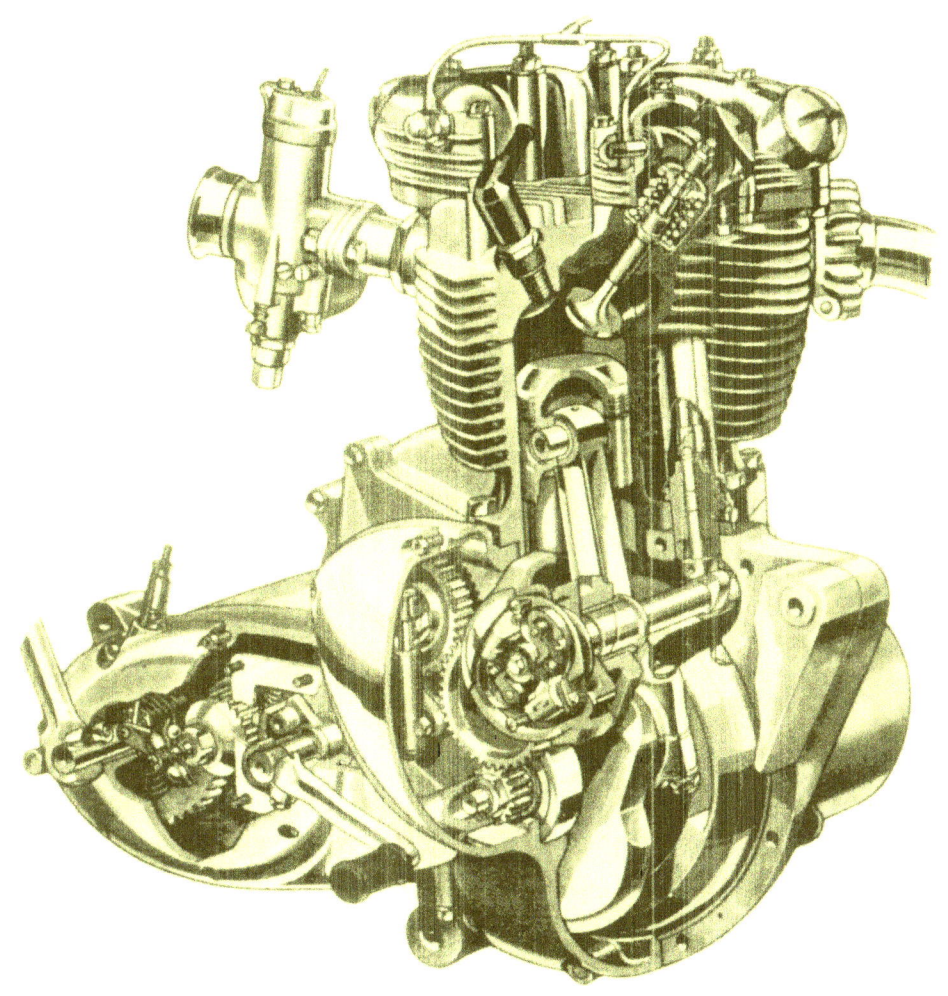

UNIT CONSTRUCTION 650 c.c. TWINS

T120 TR6 & 6T · FROM ENGINE No. DU.101
1963 to 1970

TRIUMPH ENGINEERING CO LTD

MERIDEN WORKS · ALLESLEY · COVENTRY · ENGLAND

TELEPHONE MERIDEN 331   TELEGRAMS "TRUSTY" COVENTRY

REF 99 – 0883/0889

IMPORTANT

PRIOR TO UNDERTAKING ANY MAINTENANCE OR REPAIR TASKS THE READER IS INSTRUCTED TO REVIEW THE INFORMATION REGARDING ENGINE NUMBERS ON THE REAR COVER OF THIS MANUAL.

INTRODUCTION

Welcome to the world of digital publishing ~ the book you now hold in your hand was printed using the latest state of the art digital technology. The advent of print-on-demand has forever changed the publishing process, never has information been so accessible and it is our hope that this book serves your informational needs for years to come. If this is your first exposure to digital publishing, we hope that you are pleased with the results. Many more titles of interest to the classic automobile and motorcycle enthusiast, collector and restorer are available via our website at www.VelocePress.com. We hope that you find this title as interesting as we do.

NOTE FROM THE PUBLISHER

The information presented is true and complete to the best of our knowledge. All recommendations are made without any guarantees on the part of the author or the publisher, who also disclaim all liability incurred with the use of this information.

TRADEMARKS

We recognize that some words, model names and designations, for example, mentioned herein are the property of the trademark holder. We use them for identification purposes only. This is not an official publication.

INFORMATION ON THE USE OF THIS PUBLICATION

This manual is an invaluable resource for those interested in performing their own maintenance. However, in today's information age we are constantly subject to changes in common practice, new technology, availability of improved materials and increased awareness of chemical toxicity. As such, it is advised that the user consult with an experienced professional prior to undertaking any procedure described herein. While every care has been taken to ensure correctness of information, it is obviously not possible to guarantee complete freedom from errors or omissions or to accept liability arising from such errors or omissions. Therefore, any individual that uses the information contained within, or elects to perform or participate in do-it-yourself repairs or modifications acknowledges that there is a risk factor involved and that the publisher or its associates cannot be held responsible for personal injury or property damage resulting from the use of the information or the outcome of such procedures.

WARNING!

One final word of advice, this publication is intended to be used as a reference guide, and when in doubt the reader should consult with a qualified technician.

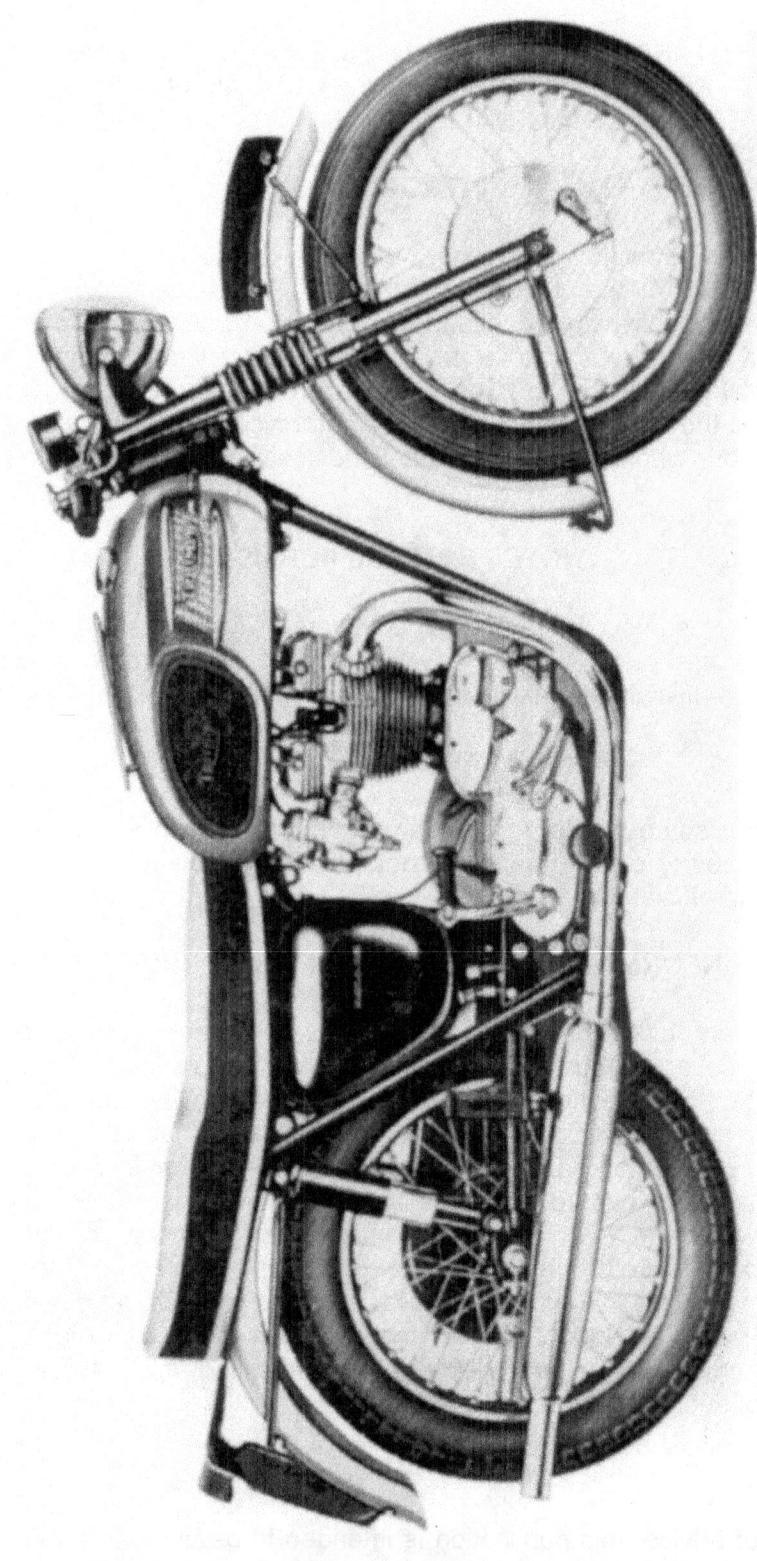

TRIUMPH 650 c.c. UNIT CONSTRUCTION TWINS

650 c.c. TRIUMPH BONNEVILLE 120 (T120)

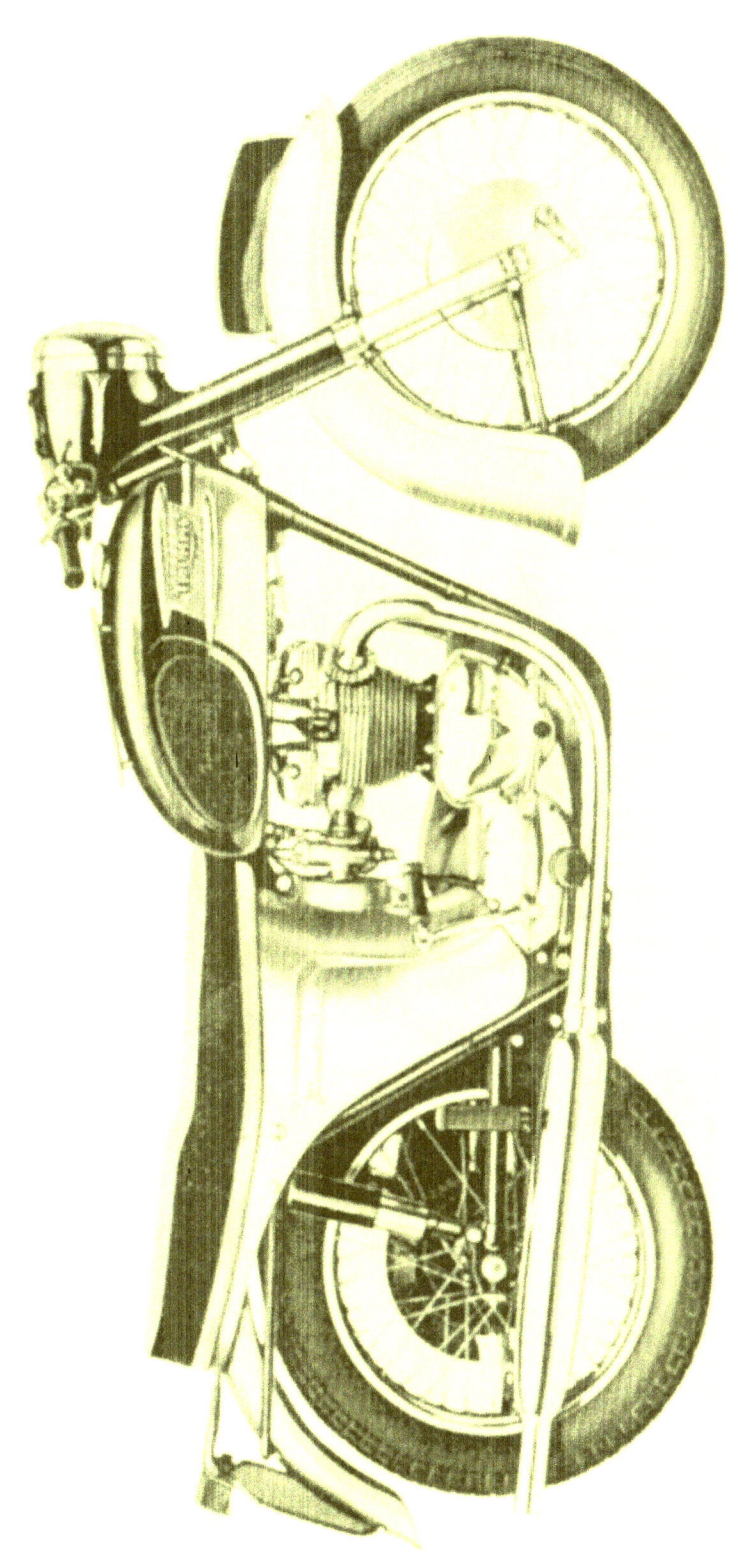

TRIUMPH 650 c.c. UNIT CONSTRUCTION TWINS

650 c.c. TRIUMPH THUNDERBIRD 6T.

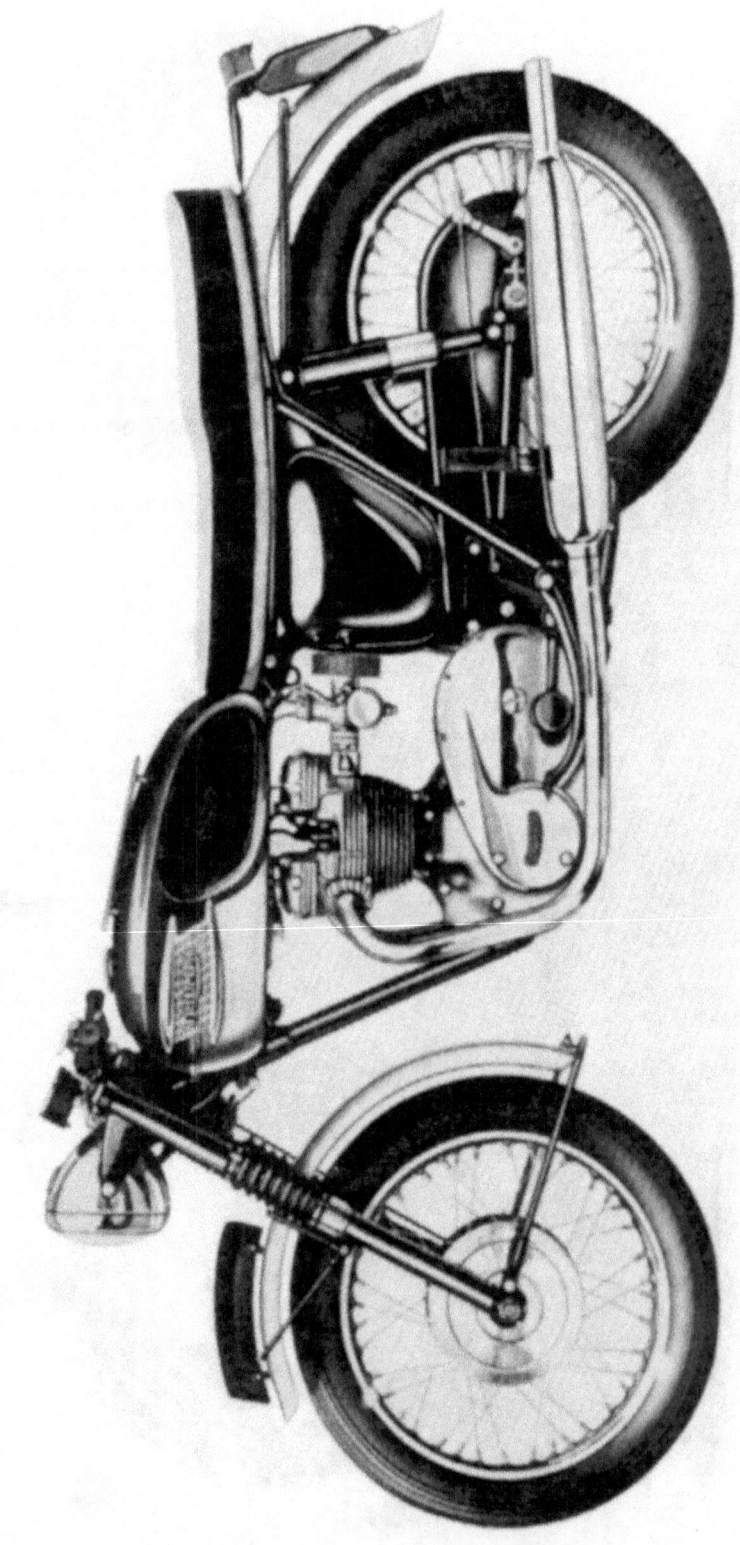

TRIUMPH 650 c.c. UNIT CONSTRUCTION TWINS

650 c.c. TRIUMPH TROPHY (TR6)

TRIUMPH 650 c.c. UNIT CONSTRUCTION TWINS

650 c.c. TRIUMPH BONNEVILLE 120 (T120)

TRIUMPH 650 c.c. UNIT CONSTRUCTION TWINS

650 c.c. (40 cu. in.) BONNEVILLE (T120R)

TRIUMPH 650 c.c. UNIT CONSTRUCTION TWINS

650 c.c. (40 cu. in.) TIGER 650 (TR6R)

TRIUMPH 650 c.c. UNIT CONSTRUCTION TWINS

650 c.c. TRIUMPH TROPHY (TR 6)

TRIUMPH 650 c.c. UNIT CONSTRUCTION TWINS

650 c.c. (40 cu. ins.) TROPHY (TR6R)

TRIUMPH 650 c.c. UNIT CONSTRUCTION TWINS

650 c.c. (40 cu. in.) TROPHY 650 (TR6C)

TRIUMPH 650 c.c. UNIT CONSTRUCTION TWINS

650 c.c. (40 cu. in.) BONNEVILLE T.T. SPECIAL (T120TT)
DISCONTINUED AFTER ENGINE NUMBER DU. 66245 (1967)

TRIUMPH 650 c.c. UNIT CONSTRUCTION TWINS

650 c.c. TRIUMPH THUNDERBIRD (6T)
DISCONTINUED AFTER ENGINE NUMBER DU. 44393 (1966)

CONTENTS

	SECTION
GENERAL DATA	
LUBRICATION SYSTEM	A
ENGINE	B
TRANSMISSION	C
GEARBOX	D
FRAME & ATTACHMENT DETAILS	E
WHEELS, BRAKES & TYRES	F
TELESCOPIC FORK	G
ELECTRICAL SYSTEM	H
SERVICE TOOLS	J
CONVERSION CHARTS	CT

UNIT CONSTRUCTION 650cc ENGINE/FRAME NUMBERS

1963	DU101 to DU5824
1964	DU5825 to DU13374
1965	DU13375 to DU24874
1966	DU24875 to DU44393
1967	DU44394 to DU66245
1968	DU66246 to DU85903
1969	DU85904 to DU90282

1969 & 1970 ALPHA NUMERIC ENGINE/FRAME NUMBERS

In 1969 Triumph introduced a new system of numbering engines and frames. There are two letters, a five digit number, and a model designation. The first letter represents the month, the second the model year, and a number which began at 00100 for each model year. Each model year usually started in August and ran until July of the next year. The year of manufacture is the model year. For example: ECXXXXX would be a 1969 model manufactured in May of 1969, and NCXXXXX would be a 1970 model manufactured in October of 1969. The letter "V" after the model designates a 5 speed gearbox.

MONTH	YEAR
A = JANUARY	C = 1969
B = FEBRUARY	D = 1970
C = MARCH	E = 1971
D = APRIL	G = 1972
E = MAY	H = 1973
G = JUNE	J = 1974
H = JULY	K = 1975
J = AUGUST	N = 1976
K = SEPTEMBER	P = 1977
N = OCTOBER	X = 1978
P = NOVEMBER	A = 1979
X = DECEMBER	B = 1980

GENERAL DATA

T120 Bonneville
TR6 Trophy
6T Thunderbird

Also: Alternative Fitments for TR6 and T120 Sports Models
USA variations T120R, T120TT, TR6R, TR6C
Miscellaneous data before engine number DU. 66246

Note:—Throughout this Section, read **All** Models as for T120 Bonneville, unless otherwise detailed under the particular Model

As the existing threaded parts on all Triumph motorcycles are gradually modified to a Unified thread, it becomes a matter of necessity to know the threads you are dealing with.

THREADS PER INCH

Size	Cycle Engineers Institute (C.E.I.)	UNIFIED Unified Fine (UNF)	Unified Coarse (UNC)	WHITWORTH British Standard Fine (BSF)	British Standard Whitworth (Coarse) (BSW)
$\frac{1}{4}"$	26	28	20	26	20
$\frac{5}{16}"$	26	24	18	22	18
$\frac{3}{8}"$	26	24	16	20	16
$\frac{7}{16}"$	26	20	14	18	14
$\frac{1}{2}"$	20	20	13	16	12
$\frac{9}{16}"$	20	18	12	16	12
$\frac{5}{8}"$	20	18	11	14	11

GENERAL DATA
MODEL T120—BONNEVILLE
LUBRICATION SYSTEM

OIL PUMP

Body material	Brass
Bore diameter: Feed	·40625/·40675 in.
Scavenge	·4877/·4872 in.
Plunger diameter: Feed	·40620/·40623 in.
Scavenge	·4872/·4869 in.
Valve spring length	½ in.
Ball diameter	7/32 in.
Aluminium crosshead width	·497/·498 in.
Working clearance in plunger heads	·0015/·0045 in.

OIL PRESSURE RELEASE VALVE

Piston diameter	·5605/·5610 in.
Working clearance	·001/·002 in.
Pressure release operates	60 lb./sq. in. (4·22 kg./sq. cm)
Spring length	1 17/32 ins.
Load at 1 3/16 in.	12/12½ lbs.
Rate	37 lb./ins.

OIL PRESSURE

Normal running	65/80 lb./sq. in.
Idling	20/25 lb./sq. in.

ENGINE

BASIC DETAILS

Bore and stroke	71 × 82 mm.
Bore and stroke	2·795 × 3·228 in.
Cubic capacity	649 c.c. (40 cu. in.)
Compression ratio	9:1
Power output (B.H.P. @ R.P.M.)	47 @ 6,700

CRANKSHAFT

Crankshaft Type	Forged two throw crank with bolt-on flywheel. Located by the timing side main bearing
Main bearing (drive side) size and type	2 1/16 × 1 1/8 × 13/16 in. Single lipped roller bearing
Main bearing, (timing side) size and type	2 13/16 × 1 1/8 × 13/16 in. Ball Journal
Main bearing journal dia.	1·1247/1·1250 in.
Main bearing housing dia.	2·8095/2·8110 in.
Big end journal dia.	1·6235/1·6240 in.
Min. regrind dia.	1·6035/1·6040 in.
Crankshaft end float	·003/·017 in.

CONNECTING RODS

Length (centres)	6·499/6·501 in.
Big end bearings—type	Steel backed white metal
Bearing side clearance	·012/·016 in.
Bearing diametral clearance	·0005/·0020 in.

GUDGEON PIN

Material	High tensile steel
Fit in small end bush	·0005/·0012 in. clearance
Diameter	·6882/·6885 in.
Length	2·151/2·156 in.

SMALL END BUSH

Material	Phosphor bronze
Outer dia.	·8140/·8145 in.
Length	1·030/1·031 in.
Finished bore dia.	·6890/·6894 in.

GENERAL DATA

T120 Bonneville
TR6 Trophy

Also: USA variations T120R, TR6R, TR6C

Note:—Throughout this Section, read **All** Models as for T120 Bonneville, unless otherwise detailed under the particular Model

As the existing threaded parts on all Triumph motorcycles are gradually modified to a Unified thread, it becomes a matter of necessity to know the threads you are dealing with.

THREADS PER INCH

Size	Cycle Engineers Institute (C.E.I.)	UNIFIED Unified Fine (UNF)	UNIFIED Unified Coarse (UNC)	WHITWORTH British Standard Fine (BSF)	WHITWORTH British Standard Whitworth (Coarse) (BSW)
$\frac{1}{4}''$	26	28	20	26	20
$\frac{5}{16}''$	26	24	18	22	18
$\frac{3}{8}''$	26	24	16	20	16
$\frac{7}{16}''$	26	20	14	18	14
$\frac{1}{2}''$	20	20	13	16	12
$\frac{9}{16}''$	20	18	12	16	12
$\frac{5}{8}''$	20	18	11	14	11

GENERAL DATA
MODEL T120—BONNEVILLE
LUBRICATION SYSTEM

OIL PUMP
- Body material ... Brass
- Bore diameter: Feed ... ·40675/·40625 in.
- Scavenge ... ·4877/·4872 in.
- Plunger diameter: Feed ... ·40615/·40585 in.
- Scavenge ... ·4872/·4869 in.
- Valve spring length ... $\frac{1}{2}$ in.
- Ball diameter ... $\frac{7}{32}$ in.
- Aluminium crosshead width ... ·497/·498 in.
- Working clearance in plunger heads ... ·0015/·0045 in.

OIL PRESSURE RELEASE VALVE
- Piston diameter ... ·5605/·5610 in.
- Working clearance ... ·001/·002 in.
- Pressure release operates ... 60 lb./sq. in. (4·22 kg./sq. cm)
- Spring length ... $1\frac{17}{32}$ ins.
- Load at $1\frac{3}{16}$ in. ... 12/12½ lbs.
- Rate ... 37 lb./ins.

OIL PRESSURE
- Normal running ... 65/80 lb./sq. in.
- Idling ... 20/25 lb./sq. in.

OIL PRESSURE SWITCH
- Operating pressure ... 7/11 lb./sq. in.

ENGINE

BASIC DETAILS
- Bore and stroke ... 71 × 82 mm.
- Bore and stroke ... 2·795 × 3·228 in.
- Cubic capacity ... 649 c.c. (40 cu. in.)
- Compression ratio ... 9:1
- Power output (B.H.P. @ R.P.M.) ... 47 @ 6,700

CRANKSHAFT
- Crankshaft Type ... Forged two throw crank with bolt-on flywheel. Located by the timing side main bearing
- Main bearing (drive side) size and type ... $2\frac{3}{16} \times 1\frac{1}{8} \times 1\frac{3}{16}$ in. Single lipped roller bearing
- Main bearing, (timing side) size and type ... $2\frac{13}{16} \times 1\frac{1}{8} \times \frac{13}{16}$ in. Ball Journal
- Main bearing journal dia. ... 1·1247/1·1250 in.
- Main bearing housing dia. ... 2·8095/2·8110 in.
- Big end journal dia. ... 1·6235/1·6240 in.
- Min. regrind dia. ... 1·6035/1·6040 in.
- Crankshaft end float ... ·003/·017 in.
- Balance factor ... 85% (using 689 gramme weights)

CONNECTING RODS
- Length (centres) ... 6·499/6·501 in.
- Big end bearings—type ... Steel backed white metal
- Bearing side clearance ... ·012/·016 in.
- Bearing diametral clearance ... ·0005/·0020 in.

GUDGEON PIN
- Material ... High tensile steel
- Fit in small end bush ... ·0005/·0012 in. clearance
- Diameter ... ·6882/·6885 in.
- Length ... 2·151/2·156 in.

SMALL END BUSH
- Material ... Phosphor bronze
- Outer dia. ... ·8140/·8145 in.
- Length ... 1·030/1·031 in.
- Finished bore dia. ... ·6890/·6894 in.

GENERAL DATA

T120 BONNEVILLE—(cont)

CYLINDER BLOCK
Material	Cast iron
Bore size	2·7948/2·7953 in.
Maximum oversize	2·8348/2·8353 in.
Tappet guide block housing diameter	·9990/·9985 in.

CYLINDER HEAD
Material	D.T.D. 424 Aluminium
Inlet port size	$1\frac{3}{16}$ in. dia. tapering to $1\frac{1}{8}$ in.
Exhaust port size	$1\frac{3}{8}$ in. dia.
Valve seatings:	
Type	Cast-in
Material	Cast iron

VALVES
Stem diameter: Inlet	·3095/·3100 in.
Exhaust	·3090/·3095 in.
Head diameter: Inlet	1·592/1·596 in.
Exhaust	1·434/1·440 in.
Exhaust valve material	21/4NS

VALVE GUIDES
Material	Aluminium—Bronze
Bore diameter (Inlet and exhaust)	·3127/·3137 in.
Outside diameter (Inlet and exhaust)	·5005/·5010 in.
Length: Inlet	$1\frac{31}{32}$ in.
Exhaust	$2\frac{11}{64}$ in.

VALVE SPRINGS (RED SPOT INNER) (GREEN SPOT OUTER)

	Outer	Inner
Free length	$1\frac{1}{2}$ in.	$1\frac{17}{32}$ in.
Total number of coils	$5\frac{1}{2}$	$7\frac{1}{4}$

	Inlet	Exhaust
Total fitted load:		
Valve open	143 lbs.	155 lbs.
Valve closed	75 lbs.	87 lbs.
Fitted length (valve closed):		
Inner	$1\frac{3}{16}$ in.	$1\frac{1}{8}$ in.
Outer	$1\frac{7}{32}$ in.	$1\frac{5}{32}$ in.

VALVE TIMING

Set all tappet clearances @ ·020 in. (·5 mm.) for checking
- Inlet opens 34° before top centre
- Inlet closes 55° after bottom centre
- Exhaust opens 55° before bottom centre
- Exhaust closes 34° after top centre

ROCKERS
Material	High tensile steel forging
Bore diameter	·5002/·5012 in.
Rocker spindle diameter	·4990/·4995 in.
Tappet clearance (cold): Inlet	·002 in. (·05 mm.)
Exhaust	·004 in. (·10 mm.)

CAMSHAFTS
Journal diameter: Left	·8100/·8105 in.
Right	·8730/·8735 in.
Diametral clearance: Left	·0010/·0025 in.
Right	·0005/·0020 in.
End float	·013/·020 in.
Cam lift: Inlet and exhaust	·314 in.
Base circle diameter	·812 in.

TAPPETS
Material	High tensile steel body—Stellite tip
Tip radius	1·125 in.
Tappet diameter	·3110/·3115 in.
Clearance in guide block	·0005/·0015 in.

Exhaust tappet has flat, $\frac{3}{32}$ in. tall, 1·884 in./1·881 in. below top of tappet, flat is ·032 in. deep, and oil hole is ·047 in. diameter

T120 BONNEVILLE—(cont)

TAPPET GUIDE BLOCK
Diameter of bores	·3120/·3125 in.
Outside diameter	1·0000/·9995 in.
Interference fit in cylinder block	·0005/·0015 in.

CAMSHAFT BEARING BUSHES
Material	High density sintered bronze
Bore diameter (fitted): Left	·8125/·8135 in.
Right	·874/·875 in.
Outside diameter: Left	1·0010/1·0015 in.
Right	1·126/1·127 in.
Length: Left inlet	1·104/1·114 in.
Left exhaust	·932/·942 in.
Right inlet and exhaust	1·010/1·020 in.
Interference fit in crankcase: Left	·001/·002 in.
Right	·0010/·0025 in.

TIMING GEARS
Inlet and exhaust camshaft pinions:	
No. of teeth	50
Interference fit on camshaft	·000/·001 in.
Intermediate timing gear:	
No. of teeth	47
Bore diameter	·5618/·5625 in.
Intermediate timing gear bush:	
Material	Phosphor bronze
Outside diameter	·5635/·5640 in.
Bore diameter	·4990/·4995 in.
Length	·6775/·6825 in.
Working clearance on spindle	·0005/·0015 in.
Intermediate wheel spindle:	
Diameter	·4980/·4985 in.
Interference fit in crankcase	·0005/·0015 in.
Crankshaft pinion:	
No. of teeth	25
Fit on crankshaft	+·0003/−·0005 in.

IGNITION TIMING
Crankshaft position (B.T.D.C.)	
Static timing	14°
Fully advanced	38°
Piston position (B.T.D.C.)	
Static timing	·060 in. (1·5 mm.)
Fully advanced	·415 in. (10·4 mm.)
Advance range:	
Contact breaker	12°
Crankshaft	24°

CONTACT BREAKER
Gap setting	·014–·016 in. (·35–·40 mm.)
Fully advanced at	2,000 r.p.m.

SPARKING PLUG
Type	Champion N3
Gap setting	·025 in. (·635 mm.)
Thread size	14 mm. × ¾ in. reach

GENERAL DATA

T120 BONNEVILLE—(cont)

PISTONS

Material	Aluminium Alloy—diecasting
Clearance: Top of skirt	·0106/·0085 in.
Bottom of skirt	·0061/·0046 in.
Gudgeon pin hole dia.	·6882/·6886 in

PISTON RINGS

Material	Cast iron
Compression rings (tapered):	
Width	·0615/·0625 in.
Thickness	·092/·100 in.
Fitted gap	·010/·014 in.
Clearance in groove	·001/·003 in.
Oil control ring:	
Width	·092/·100 in.
Thickness	·124/·125 in.
Fitted gap	·010/·014 in.
Clearance in groove	·0005/·0025 in.

FUEL SYSTEM

Twin Carburetters

	Concentric float	Monobloc
Amal type	R930/9 and L930/10	389/203
Main jet size	220	206
Pilot jet size	—	25
Needle jet size	·106	·106
Needle type	STD	D
Needle position	2	3
Throttle valve:		
Type	$2\frac{1}{2}$	389/95
Return spring free length	$2\frac{1}{2}$ in.	$2\frac{1}{2}$ in.
Carburetter nominal bore size	30 mm.	$1\frac{1}{8}$ in. dia.

Air cleaner type (where fitted) ... Filter cloth and metal gauze

TRANSMISSION

CLUTCH DETAILS

Type	Multiplate with integral shock absorber
No. of plates: Driving (bonded)	6
Driven (plain)	6
Pressure springs:	
Number	3
Free length	$1\frac{13}{16}$ in.
No. of working coils	$9\frac{1}{2}$
Spring rate	113 lbs./in.
Approximate fitted load	62 lbs.
Bearing rollers:	
Number	20
Diameter	·2495/·2500 in.
Length	·231/·236 in.
Clutch hub bearing diameter	1·3733/1·3743 in.
Clutch sprocket bore diameter	1·8745/1·8755 in.
Thrust washer thickness	·052/·054 in.
Engine sprocket teeth	29
Clutch sprocket teeth	58
Chain details	Duplex endless—$\frac{3}{8}$ in. pitch × 84 links

CLUTCH OPERATING MECHANISM

Conical spring:	
Number of working coils	2
Free length	$\frac{13}{16}$ in.
Diameter of balls	$\frac{3}{8}$ in.
Clutch operating rod:	
Diameter of rod	$\frac{7}{32}$ in.
Length of rod	11·822/11·812 in.

GEARBOX

T120 BONNEVILLE—(cont)

RATIOS

Internal ratios (Std.) 4th (Top) ... 1·00 : 1
                                 3rd ... 1·19 : 1
                                 2nd ... 1·69 : 1
                                 1st (Bottom) ... 2·44 : 1

	Solo	Sidecar
Overall ratios: 4th (Top)	4·84	5·41
3rd	5·76	6·44
2nd	8·17	9·15
1st (Bottom)	11·8	13·4
Engine R.P.M. @ 10 M.P.H. in 4th (Top) gear	648	725
Gearbox sprocket teeth	19	17

GEAR DETAILS

Mainshaft high gear:
    Bore diameter (bush fitted) ... ·8135/·8145 in.
    Working clearance on shaft ... ·0032/·0047 in.
    Bush length ... $2\frac{19}{32}$ in.
    Bush protrusion length ... $\frac{7}{16}$ in. None after DU66246

Layshaft low gear:
    Bore diameter (bush fitted) ... ·8135/·8145 in.
    Working clearance on shaft ... ·0025/·0045 in.

GEARBOX SHAFTS

Mainshaft:
    Left end diameter ... ·8098/·8103 in.
    Right end diameter ... ·7494/·7498 in.
    Length ... $\begin{cases} 10\frac{23}{32} \text{ in. (up to DU48143)} \\ 11\frac{13}{32} \text{ in. (DU48144 onwards)} \end{cases}$

Layshaft:
    Left end diameter ... ·6845/·6850 in.
    Right end diameter ... ·6845/·6850 in.
    Length ... $6\frac{21}{64}$ in.

Camplate plunger spring:
    Free length ... $2\frac{1}{2}$ in.
    No. of working coils ... 22
    Spring rate ... 5·6 lb./in.

BEARINGS

High gear bearing ... $1\frac{1}{4} \times 2\frac{1}{8} \times \frac{5}{8}$ in. Ball Journal
Mainshaft bearing ... $\frac{3}{4} \times 1\frac{7}{8} \times \frac{9}{16}$ in. Ball Journal
Layshaft bearing (left) ... $\frac{11}{16} \times \frac{7}{8} \times \frac{1}{2}$ in. Needle Roller
Layshaft bearing (right) ... $\frac{11}{16} \times \frac{7}{8} \times \frac{3}{4}$ in. Needle Roller

KICKSTART OPERATING MECHANISM

Bush bore diameter ... ·751/·752 in.
Spindle working clearance in bush ... ·003/·005 in.
Ratchet spring free length ... $\frac{1}{2}$ in.

GEARCHANGE MECHANISM

Plungers:
    Outer diameter ... ·4315/·4320 in.
    Working clearance in bore ... ·0005/·0015 in.
Plunger springs:
    No. of working coils ... 12
    Free length ... $1\frac{1}{4}$ in.
Inner bush bore diameter ... ·6245/·6255 in.
    Clearance on shaft ... ·0007/·0032 in.
Outer bush bore diameter ... ·7495/·7505 in.
    Clearance on shaft ... ·0005/·0025 in.
Quadrant return springs:
    No. of working coils ... $9\frac{1}{2}$
    Free length ... $1\frac{3}{4}$ ins.

GENERAL DATA

T120 BONNEVILLE—(cont)

FRAME AND ATTACHMENT DETAILS

HEAD RACES
No. of balls: Top ... 20
Bottom ... 20
Ball diameter ... $\frac{1}{4}$ in.

SWINGING FORK
Bush type ... Pre-sized, steel-backed—phosphor bronze
Bush bore diameter ... 1·4460/1·4470 in.
Sleeve diameter ... 1·4445/1·4450 in.
Distance between fork ends ... $7\frac{1}{2}$ in.

REAR SUSPENSION
Type ... Swinging fork controlled by combined coil spring/hydraulic damper units

Spring details:
Fitted length ... 8 in.
Free length ... $8\frac{3}{16}$ in.
Mean coil diameter ... $1\frac{3}{4}$ in.
Spring rate ... 145 lbs./in.
Colour code ... Blue/yellow
Load at fitted length ... 38 lb.

WHEELS, BRAKES AND TYRES

WHEELS
Rim size: Front and rear ... WM2-19 Front WM2-18 rear
Type: Front ... Spoke—single cross lacing
Rear ... Spoke—double cross lacing
Spoke details: Front: Left side ... 20 off 8/10 SWG butted $5\frac{5}{8}$ in. U.H. straight
Right side ... 10 off 8/10 SWG butted $4\frac{25}{32}$ in. U.H. 78° head
Right side ... 10 off 8/10 SWG butted $4\frac{7}{8}$ in. U.H. 100° head
Rear: Left side ... 20 off 8/10 SWG butted $7\frac{9}{16}$ in. U.H. 90° head
Right side ... 20 off 8/10 SWG butted $7\frac{7}{8}$ in. U.H. 90° head

WHEEL BEARINGS
Front and rear, dimensions and type ... 20 × 47 × 14 mm.—Ball Journal
Front and rear, spindle diameter (at bearing journals) ... ·7862/·7867 in.

STANDARD REAR WHEEL
Bolt size for detachable sprocket ... $\frac{1}{4}$ in. dia. × $1\frac{13}{16}$ in. U.H. × 26 C.E.I.
Number of bolts ... 8

Q.D. REAR WHEEL
Bearing type ... $\frac{3}{4} \times 1\frac{7}{8} \times \frac{9}{16}$ in. Ball Journal
Bearing sleeve: journal diameter ... ·7500/·7495 in.
Brake drum bearing ... $\frac{7}{8} \times 2 \times \frac{9}{16}$ in. Ball Journal
Bearing sleeve: journal diameter ... ·8745/·8740 in.
Bearing housing: internal diameter ... 1·9890/1·9980 in.

REAR WHEEL DRIVE
Gearbox sprocket ... See "Gearbox"
Rear wheel sprocket teeth ... 46
Chain details:
No. of links: Solo ... 104
Sidecar ... 103
Pitch ... $\frac{5}{8}$ in.
Width ... $\frac{3}{8}$ in.
Speedometer drive gearbox ratio ... 2:1
Speedometer cable length ... 65 ins.

T120 BONNEVILLE—(cont)

BRAKES

Type	Internal expanding twin leading shoes
Drum Diameter: Front	8 in. ⎫ ± .002 in.
Rear	7 in. ⎭
Lining thickness: Front	·183/·193 in.
Rear	·177/·187 in.
Lining area: Front	24·4 sq. in.
Rear	14·6 sq. in.
Pre-set length of adjustable cam lever rod	6½ in. between centres

TYRES

Size: Front	3·25 × 19 in.
Rear	3·50 × 18 in.
Tyre pressure: Front	24 lb./sq. in. (1·685 Kg/sq. cm.)
Rear	24 lb./sq. in. (1·685 kg/sq. cm.)

FRONT FORKS

TELESCOPIC FORK

Type	Telescopic—Shuttle valve damping	
Spring details:	Solo	Sidecar
Free length	9¾ in.	9¾ in.
No. working coils	12½	15½
Spring rate	26½ lb. in.	32½ lb. in.
Gauge	6 SWG	5 SWG
Colour code	Yellow/blue	Yellow/green

Damper sleeve	
Length	2⅛ in.
Internal diameter	1·387—1·393 in.
Material	Black polypropylene

Bush details:	Top bush	Bottom bush
Length	1 in.	·870/·875 in.
Outer diameter	1·498/1·499 in.	1·4935/1·4945 in.
Inner diameter	1·3065/1·3075 in.	1·2485/1·2495 in.

Stanchion diameter	1·3025/1·3030 in.
Working clearance in top bush	·0035/·0050 in.
Bleed holes	8 holes 3/32 in. dia.
Fork leg bore diameter	1·498/1·500 in.
Working clearance of bottom bush	·0035/·0065 in.
Shuttle valve:	
Outer diameter (large)	1·018/1·016 in.
Outer diameter (small)	0·875/0·874 in.

ELECTRICAL SYSTEM

ELECTRICAL EQUIPMENT

Battery type (12v.)	PUZ 5A
Rectifier type	2DS 506
Alternator type	RM.19
Horn type (12v.)	6H

Bulbs:	No.	Type
Headlight (L/H dip)	414	50/40 watts—pre-focus
Parking light	989	6 watts—MCC
Stop and tail light	380	6/21 watts—offset pin
Speedometer light	987	3 watts—MES
Ignition warning light	281	2 watts (BA 7S)
High beam indicator light	281	2 watts (BA 7S)

Zener diode type	ZD 715
Coil type (2 off)	MA12 (12v.) 2 off or later, 17M12 (12v.) 2 off
Contact breaker type	6CA
Fuse rating	35 amp.

T120 BONNEVILLE—(cont)

GENERAL

CAPACITIES

Fuel tank	4 gall. (4·8 U.S. galls., 18 litres)
Oil tank	6 pint (7¼ U.S. pints, 3 litres)
Gearbox	⅞ pint (500 c.c.)
Primary chaincase	⅝ pint (350 c.c.)
Telescopic fork legs	⅓ pint (200 c.c.)

BASIC DIMENSIONS

Wheel base	55 in. (140 cm.)
Overall length	84 in. (214 cm.)
Overall width	27½ in. (70 cm.)
Overall height	38 in. (97 cm.)
Ground clearance	5 in. (13 cm.)

WEIGHTS

Unladen weight	365 lb. (166 kgm.)
Engine unit (dry)	130 lb. (59 kgm.)

TORQUE WRENCH SETTINGS (DRY)

Flywheel bolts	33 lb. ft. (4·6 kg.m.)
Conn. rod bolts	28 lb. ft. (3·9 kg.m.)
Crankcase junction bolts	13 lb. ft. (1·8 kg.m.)
Crankcase junction studs	20 lb. ft. (2·8 kg.m.)
Cylinder block nuts	35 lb. ft. (4·8 kg.m.)
Cylinder head bolts (⅜ in. dia.)	18 lb. ft. (2·49 kg.m.)
Cylinder head bolt (5/16 in. dia.)	15 lb. ft. (2·1 kg.m.)
Rocker box nuts	5 lb. ft. (·7 kg.m.)
Rocker box bolts	5 lb. ft. (·7 kg.m.)
Rocker spindle domed nuts	22 lb. ft. (3·0 kg.m.)
Oil pump nuts	5 lb. ft. (·7 kg.m.)
Kickstart ratchet pinion nut	45 lb. ft. (6·3 kg.m.)
Clutch centre nut	50 lb. ft. (7 kg.m.)
Rotor fixing nut	30 lb. ft. (4·1 kg.m.)
Stator fixing nuts	20 lb. ft. (2·8 kg.m.)
Primary cover domed nuts	10 lb. ft. (1·4 kg.m.)
Headlamp pivot bolts	10 lb. ft. (1·4 kg.m.)
Headrace sleeve nut pinch bolt	15 lb. ft. (2·1 kg.m.)
Stanchion pinch bolts	25 lb. ft. (3·5 kg.m.)
Front wheel spindle cap bolts	25 lb. ft. (3·5 kg.m.)
Brake cam spindle nuts	20 lb. ft. (2·8 kg.m.)
Zener diode fixing nut	1.5 lb. ft. (·21 kg.m.)
Fork cap nut	80 lb. ft. (11·1 kg.m.)

N.B.—18 lb. ft. replaces earlier recommendation of 25 lb. ft. for ⅜ in. dia. cylinder head bolts for all unit construction 650 c.c models.

GENERAL DATA
MODEL TR6—TROPHY

FOR DATA NOT GIVEN HERE REFER TO GENERAL DATA—MODEL T120

ENGINE

BASIC DETAILS

Bore and stroke	71 × 82 mm.
Bore and stroke	2·795 × 3·228 in.
Cubic capacity	649 c.c. (40 cu. in.)
Compression ratio	9 : 1
Power output (B.H.P. @ R.P.M.)	43 @ 6,500

PISTONS

Material	Aluminium Alloy—Die Casting
Clearance: Top of skirt	·0106/·0085 in.
Bottom of skirt	·0061/·0046 in.
Gudgeon pin hole diameter	·6882/·6886 in.

VALVE TIMING

Set all tappet clearances @ ·020 in. (·50 mm.) for checking
- Inlet opens 34° before top centre
- Inlet closes 55° after bottom centre
- Exhaust opens 55° before bottom centre
- Exhaust closes 34° after top centre

FUEL SYSTEM

	Prior to DU59320	After DU59320
Single Carburetter		
Amal type	389/239	930/23
Main jet size	330	230
Pilot jet size	25	
Needle jet size	·106T	·107
Needle type	D	STD.
Needle position	1	2
Throttle valve:		
Type	389/4	3
Return spring free length	2½ in.	2½ in.
Carburetter nominal bore size	1¾ in.	30 mm.
Air cleaner type	Coarse felt	Filter cloth and metal gauze

WHEELS

FRONT WHEEL

Tyre size	3·25 × 19 in.

GENERAL DATA

FRAME AND ATTACHMENT DETAILS

REAR SUSPENSION

Spring details:	Solo	Sidecar
Fitted length	$8\frac{3}{8}$ in.	$8\frac{3}{8}$ in.
Free length	$8\frac{5}{8}$ in.	$8\frac{7}{8}$ in.
Mean coil diameter	$1\frac{3}{4}$ in.	$1\frac{3}{4}$ in.
Spring rate	100 lb./in.	150 lb./in
Colour code	Green/green	Blue/red
Load at fitted length	28 lb.	73 lb.

GENERAL

BASIC DIMENSIONS

Ground clearance ... 6 in. (15 cm.)

GD GENERAL DATA

U.S.A. ONLY

TR6R, TR6C, T120R, T120TT (T120TT ONLY UP TO DU.66245)
FOR DATA NOT GIVEN HERE REFER TO GENERAL DATA FOR MODELS T120 AND TR6

ENGINE

Compression ratio T120TT	11 : 1
Power output T120TT	54 @ 6,500

CYLINDER HEAD T120TT

Inlet port size	$1\frac{3}{16}$ dia. tapering to $1\frac{1}{8}$ in.
Exhaust port size	$1\frac{3}{8}$ in. dia.
Carburetter adaptors	$1\frac{3}{16}$ in. dia.

CARBURETTERS

	T120TT
Choke size	$1\frac{3}{16}$ in.
Type	389/95
Main jet size	330
Pilot jet size	25
Needle jet size	·106
Needle type	D
Needle position	2
Throttle valve	389/4

AIR CLEANER

T120R and T120TT	Coarse felt
TR6R and TR6C	Cloth

SPARKING PLUGS

T120TT	Champion N58R

TACHOMETER DRIVE (TR6R, T120R)

Type of tachometer gearbox	90° drive from L/H end of exhaust camshaft
Drive ratio	4:1
Cable length	28 in.
Tachometer head	RSM 3003/01

IGNITION TIMING (A.C. MAGNETO) TR6C AND T120TT (Up to DU66245)

Crankshaft position (B.T.D.C.)	
Static timing	29°
Fully advanced	39°
Piston position (B.T.D.C.)	
Static timing	$\frac{1}{4}$ in. (6·3 mm.)
Fully advanced	$\frac{7}{16}$ in. (11.5 mm)
Advance range:	
Contact breaker	5°
Crankshaft	10°

CONTACT BREAKER (A.C. MAGNETO) TR6C and T120TT (Up to DU66245)

Gap setting	·014/·016 in. (·35/·40 mm.)
Advance range	5°
Fully advanced at	2,000 R.P.M.

TRANSMISSION

REAR CHAIN

T120TT	103 links

GEARBOX SPROCKET

TR6R	19 teeth
TR6C	18 teeth
T120R	19 teeth
T120TT	17 teeth

GENERAL DATA

USA VARIATIONS—(cont)

FRAME

PETROL TANK

TR6R	3¼ galls. (4·117 U.S. galls.)
TR6C, T120R, T120TT, TR6R	2½ galls. (2·912 U.S. galls.)

SUSPENSION UNITS TR6C, TR6R, T120R, T120TT

Spring details:
Fitted length	8⅜ in.
Free length	8⅝ in.
Mean coil diameter	1¾ in.
Spring rate	100 lb/in.
Colour code	Green/Green
Load at fitted length	28 lb.

WHEELS

REAR WHEEL NON-Q.D.

Rim size	WM3-18
Tyre size	4·00 × 18 in.
Security bolt	WM3

FORKS

TR6C and T120TT only (Up to DU66245)

Oil restrictor assembly:
Rod diameter	·3115/·3125 in.
Cup outer diameter	·5845/·5855 in.
Body bore diameter	·590/·592 in.

N.B. With this hydraulic damping unit it is essential that SAE 20 oil only is used.

ELECTRICAL

TR6C and T120TT (Up to DU66245)

Alternator type		RM19E.T.
Horn, type		Clear hooter, A.C. 585, S.G.
Coil type		3 E.T.
Condensers (Capacitors)		54441582
Contact breaker type		Lucas 4CA
Lighting system:	No.	Type
Bulbs (6v.):		
Headlight	Lucas 166	24/24 watts—Pre Focus
Stop and tail light	Lucas 384	6/18 watts—Offset pin
Tail lamp type		L679
Kill button type		151.SA SS5 up to DU66245

HEADLAMP MCH 66

Light unit diameter	5¾ in.
Bulb, main	12 V. Lucas 464 type 40/27 watt, vert-dip prefocus
Bulb, pilot	12 V. Lucas 989 type 6 watt, M.C.C.

TAIL LAMP

Type	Type L679
Bulb	12 V. Lucas 380 21/6 watt, S.B.C. offset pin

COILS, TR6R, TR6C, T120R

Type	Siba 32,000,1 or Lucas 17M12

GENERAL DATA
ALTERNATIVE FITMENTS FOR SPORTS MODELS TR6 AND T120

ENGINE

PISTONS (11 : 1 C.R.)

Material	Aluminium Alloy—Die Casting
Clearance: Top of skirt	·0146/·0125 in.
Bottom of skirt	·0084/·0070 in.
Gudgeon pin hole diameter	·6882/·6886 in.

TAPPETS ("R" TYPE)

Material	High tensile steel—stellite tip
Tip radius	1·125 in.
Tappet diameter	·3105/·3115 in.
Clearance in guide block	·005/·0015 in.

GEARBOX

RATIOS

Internal ratios (Close): 4th (Top)	1·00 : 1
3rd	1·09 : 1
2nd	1·30 : 1
1st (Bottom)	1·695 : 1
Internal ratios (Wide): 4th (Top)	1·00 : 1
3rd	1·425 : 1
2nd	2·21 : 1
1st (Bottom)	2·915 : 1
Gearbox sprocket	15, 16, 17, 18, 19 or 20 teeth

GENERAL DATA

FRONT FORKS

TELESCOPIC FORK (Only applicable up to DU66245)

Oil restrictor assembly:
- Rod diameter ... ·3115/·3125 in.
- Cup outer diameter ... ·5845/·5855 in.
- Body bore diameter ... ·590/·592 in.

ELECTRICAL SYSTEM

IGNITION CAPACITOR
- Model ... 2MC
- Storage life ... At 20°C. (68°F.) shelf life 18 months
- At 40°C. (86°F.) shelf life 9 to 12 months

GENERAL

CAPACITIES

Fuel tank ... 2½ gall. (2·8 U.S. galls., 11 litres)

TACHOMETER

Type of tachometer gearbox ... 90° drive from L/H end of exhaust camshaft
- Drive ratio ... 4 : 1
- Cable length ... 28 in.
- Tachometer head ... RSM 3003/01

GD15

GENERAL DATA
MISCELLANEOUS INFORMATION PRIOR TO ENGINE NUMBER DU.66246

LUBRICATION SYSTEM

OIL PUMP (Before DU44394 all models)

Scavenge bore diameter	·4372/·4377 in.
Scavenge plunger diameter	·4369/·4372 in.

OIL PUMP (DU44394 to DU.66245)

Scavenge bore diameter	·4877/·4872 in.
Scavenge plunger diameter	·4872/·4869 in.
Feed bore diameter	·3748/·3753 in.
Feed plunger diameter	·3747/·3744 in.

OIL PRESSURE RELEASE VALVE (with indicator button prior to DU13375)

Indicator spring length (free)	$\frac{9}{32}$ in.
Release spring length (free)	$\frac{31}{32}$ in.

BASIC ENGINE DETAILS

	Compression ratio	Combustion chamber capacity	Power output (b.h.p. @ r.p.m.)
6T up to DU44393	7·5 : 1	50 c.c.	37 @ 6,700
TR6 up to DU44393	8·5 : 1	43·3 c.c.	40 @ 6,500
T120 up to DU24874	8·5 : 1	43·3 c.c.	46 @ 6,500

MAIN BEARING (All models up to DU24875)

Both ball journal size	$2\frac{13}{16} \times 1\frac{1}{8} \times \frac{13}{16}$ in. ball journal

CRANKSHAFT LOCATION

All models DU101 to DU13374	Located to timing side
All models DU13375 to DU24874	Located to drive side
All models DU24875 onwards	Located to timing side

FLYWHEEL (prior to DU24875)

Weight	$8\frac{1}{2}$ lbs.

PISTON CLEARANCES (Triumph pistons) before DU44394

	6T (DU101-DU5824)	6T (DU5825-DU44393)	TR6	T120	T120TT (11 : 1 CR)
Top of skirt	·0088/·0098 in.	·0046/·0057 in.	·0088/·0098 in.	·0093/·0103 in.	·0093/·0103 in.
Bottom of skirt	·0033/·0043 in.	·0016/·0027 in.	·0033/·0043 in.	·0038/·0048 in.	·0073/·0083 in.

VALVES

Sizes	6T & TR6 DU101-DU44393	T120 DU101-DU5824	T120 DU5824 onwards
Inlet	$1\frac{1}{2}$ in.	$1\frac{1}{2}$ in.	$1\frac{1}{2}$ in.
Exhaust	$1\frac{11}{32}$ in.	$1\frac{11}{32}$ in.	$1\frac{7}{16}$ in.

VALVE SPRINGS

6T DU101 onwards	Red spot
TR6 DU101 onwards	Red spot
T120 DU101 to DU24874	White spot
T120 DU24875 to DU44394	Red spot

GENERAL DATA

MISCELLANEOUS DATA PRIOR TO ENGINE No. DU.66246—(cont)

VALVE SPRINGS (RED SPOT)

	Outer	Inner
Free length	$1\frac{5}{8}$ in.	$1\frac{17}{32}$ in.
Total number of coils	$5\frac{1}{2}$	$7\frac{1}{4}$
Total fitted load valve open	125 lbs.	
Total fitted load valve closed	50 lbs.	

VALVE SPRINGS (WHITE SPOT)

	Outer	Inner
Free length	$2\frac{1}{32}$ in.	$1\frac{5}{8}$ in.
Total number of coils	$6\frac{1}{2}$	7
Total fitted load valve open	130 lbs.	
Total fitted load valve closed	77 lbs.	

VALVE TIMING

Set all tappets to 0·020 in. for checking

	6T (DU101 onwards)	TR6 (DU101-DU44393)	T120 (DU101-DU24874)	T120 (certain later machines series DU24874 and DU44393)
Inlet opens 25° before top centre		34°	34°	34°
Inlet closes 52° after bottom centre		55°	55°	55°
Exhaust opens 60° before bottom centre		48°	48°	55°
Exhaust closes 17° after bottom centre		27°	27°	34°

TAPPETS (T120 prior to DU24875)

Tip radius ... ·750 in.

CAMSHAFT

	6T	TR6	T120
Cam lift	·305 in.	·314 in. Inlet ·296 in. Exhaust	·314 in. Inlet ·296 in. Exhaust

(Certain later T120 between DU24875 and DU44393 have ·314 in. both Inlet and Exhaust)

IGNITION TIMING A.C. Magneto (E.T.) Ignition equipment

Crankshaft position (B.T.D.C.)
- Static timing ... 29°
- Fully advanced ... 39°

Piston position (B.T.D.C.)
- Static timing ... $\frac{1}{4}$ in. (6·3 mm.)
- Fully advanced ... $\frac{7}{16}$ in. (11·5 mm.)

Advance range:
- Contact breaker ... 5°
- Crankshaft ... 10°

IGNITION TIMING

	6T	TR6	T120
Static { Crankshaft position DU101-DU5824	7°	10°	10°
Static { Crankshaft position DU5825-onwards	11°	14°	15°

FULLY ADVANCED

	6T	TR6	T120
	35°	39°	39°
Static { Piston position DU101-DU5824	$\frac{1}{64}$ in.	$\frac{1}{32}$ in.	$\frac{1}{32}$ in.
Static { Piston position DU5825-onwards	$\frac{1}{32}$ in.	$\frac{1}{16}$ in.	$\frac{1}{16}$ in.
Advance range:			
Contact breaker } Up to DU5824	14°	14°	14°
Crankshaft } Up to DU5824	28°	28°	28°
Contact breaker } From DU5825	12°	12°	12°
Crankshaft } From DU5825	24°	24°	24°

CARBURETTER

	6T DU101 onwards	TR6 DU101-DU5824	TR6 DU5825-DU44393	T120 DU101-DU5824	T120 DU5825-DU66246
Type	376	376	389	376	389
Main jet	230	250	310	240	260
Needle jet	·106	·106	·106	·106	·106
Needle type	C	C	D	C	D
Needle position	3	3	1	2	3
Throttle valve	376/4	376/3½	389/3½	376/3½	389/3
Pilot jet	25	25	25	25	25
Bore	$1\frac{1}{16}$ in.	$1\frac{1}{16}$ in.	$1\frac{1}{8}$ in.	$1\frac{1}{16}$ in.	$1\frac{1}{8}$ in.

MISCELLANEOUS DATA PRIOR TO ENGINE No. DU.66246—(cont)

GEARBOX

Mainshaft length (prior to DU48144)	10 43/64 in.
Gearbox sprocket teeth number:	
6T up to DU44393	20 teeth solo, 18 teeth sidecar
T120 and TR6 DU101 onwards	19 teeth solo, 17 teeth sidecar
Speedometer gear ratio (prior to DU24875)	solo 1·50 : 1, sidecar 1·67 : 1

FRONT BRAKE (prior to DU24875)

Lining area	16·2 sq. in.

REAR CHAIN

All models before DU44394	103 links
USA T120TT only	102 links

WHEELS

Front wheel 6T and T120 DU101-DU44393	
Size	3·25 × 18
Spoke details: Left	20 off 8/10 SWG × 5 1/16 in. straight
Right	10 off 8/10 SWG × 4 5/16 in. 78° head
Right	10 off 8/10 SWG × 4 5/16 in. 100° head
Q.D. Rear wheel prior to DU24875 rim size	WM3 × 18

Q.D. REAR WHEEL (Before Eng. No. DU13375)

Bearing type	·75 × 1·8504 × ·566 in. Taper Roller
Bearing sleeve: journal diameter	·7500/·7495 in.
Brake drum bearing	7/8 × 2 × 9/16 in. Ball Journal
Bearing sleeve: journal diameter	·8745/·8740 in.
Bearing housing: internal diameter	1·9990/1·9980 in.

TYRES

Size: Front 6T and T120	3·25 × 18 in.
Rear TR6 only	4·00 × 18 in.
Tyre pressures: Front	20 lb./sq. in. (1·4 kg./sq. cm.)
Rear	18 lb./sq. in. (1·3 kg./sq. cm.)

6 VOLT MACHINES (Eng. No. DU.101-DU.5824)

Battery type	6 v.—MLZ9E or ML9E
Rectifier type	Lucas 2DS506
Alternator type	Lucas RM.19
Horn	8H (6v.)

Bulbs (6v.)

	No.	Type
Headlight	Lucas 373	30/24 watts, pre focus
Parking light	Lucas 988	6 watts—MCC
Stop and tail light	Lucas 384	6/18 watts, offset
Speedometer light	Smiths P52305	2 watts special

Coil type	Lucas MA6 (6v.)
Contact breaker type	Lucas 4CA (14°)

12 VOLT MACHINES (Eng. No. DU.5825 to DU.24874)

Battery type	MK9E, 6v.—2 in series
Rectifier type	Lucas 2DS506
Alternator type	Lucas RM.19
Horn	8H, 12v.

Bulbs

	No.	Type
Headlight	Lucas 414	50/40 watts, pre focus
Parking light	Lucas 222	4 watts—MCC
Stop and tail light	Lucas 380	6/21 watts, offset pin
Speedometer light	Lucas 987	2 watts MES

Zener diode type	ZD.715
Coil type	Lucas MA.12 (12v.) 2 off
Contact breaker type	Lucas 4CA (12°)
Fuse rating	25 amp.

GENERAL DATA

MISCELLANEOUS DATA PRIOR TO ENGINE No. DU.66246—(cont)

FRONT FORKS

Engine Numbers and Model

	DU101—DU5824			DU5825—DU13374		DU13375— TR6 & T120 up to DU66245	
STANCHIONS	6T	TR6	6T	6T	TR6 & T120	6T	
Part Number	H1123	H1299	H1595	H1695	H1649	H1890	H1889
Length	20⅞ in.	22 3/16 in.	20⅞ in.	22 in.	22 in.	22 in.	22 in.
One 3/16 in. Filler Hole	Yes	No	No	Yes	No	Yes	No
Damping Holes:— Level from Bottom—5⅜ in.	2 No. 42 holes	2 No. 42 holes	2 No. 42 holes	—	—	—	—
—4½ in.	—	—	—	2-3/16 in.	2-3/16 in.	—	—
—3 1/16 in.	4-3/16 in.	4-3/16 in.	4-3/16 in.	2-3/16 in.	2-3/16 in.	2-3/16 in.	2-3/16 in.
—2 5/16 in.	—	—	—	2-3/16 in.	2-3/16 in.	2-3/16 in.	2-3/16 in.
—1⅛ in.	2 No. 42	2 No. 42	2 No. 42	2 No. 42	2 No. 42	2 No. 42	2 No. 42

To use 6T type stanchion where appropriate for TR6 or T120, solder up the filler hole.

Note:—No. 42 hole is 0·0935 in.

DAMPER SLEEVE							
Length	4 5/16 in.	3 11/16 in.	4 5/16 in.	3⅛ in.	3⅛ in.	2⅛ in.	2⅛ in.

Internal Diameter ... ... 1·387/1·393 ins.

FRONT FORKS

TELESCOPIC FORK

Type	Telescopic—Oil Damping		
	Eng. No. DU.101 to DU.5824	Eng. No. DU.5825 onwards	Eng. No. DU.13375 to DU.66245
Spring details: Solo			
Free length	17 1/16 in.	8¾ in.	9¾ in.
No. of working coils	52	13	12½
Spring rate	32 lb./in.	30 lb./in.	26½ lb. in.
Colour code	Black/Green	Unpainted	Yellow/blue
Spring details: Sidecar			
Free length	18 5/16	8¾	9¾ in.
No. of working coils	58	15	15½
Spring rate	37 lb./in.	37 lb./in.	32½ lb. in.
Colour code	Red/white	Yellow/white	Yellow/green

Bush details: Material ... ... Sintered bronze

	Top bush	Bottom bush
Length	1 in.	·870/·875 in.
Outer diameter	1·498/1·499 in.	1·4935/1·4945 in.
Inner diameter	1·3065/1·3075 in.	1·2485/1·2495 in.
Stanchion diameter		1·3025/1·3030 in.
Working clearance in top bush		·0035/·0050 in.
Fork leg bore diameter		1·498/1·500 in.
Working clearance of bottom bush		·0035/·0065 in.

CAPACITIES

Fork legs: DU.101-DU.5824 ... ¼ pt. (150 cc.)
DU.5825-DU.66245 ... ⅓ pt. (190 cc.)
Oil tank: DU.101-DU.24874 ... 5 pt. (6 U.S. pints; 3 litres)

NOTES

SECTION A
LUBRICATION SYSTEM

	Section
ROUTINE MAINTENANCE	A1
TABLE OF RECOMMENDED LUBRICANTS	A2
ENGINE LUBRICATION SYSTEM	A3
CHANGING THE ENGINE OIL AND CLEANING THE OIL FILTERS	A4
OIL PRESSURE	A5
STRIPPING AND REASSEMBLING THE OIL PRESSURE RELEASE VALVE	A6
STRIPPING AND REASSEMBLING THE OIL PUMP	A7
REMOVING AND REPLACING THE OIL PIPE JUNCTION BLOCK	A8
REMOVING AND REPLACING THE ROCKER OIL FEED PIPE	A9
CONTACT BREAKER LUBRICATION	A10
GEARBOX LUBRICATION	A11
PRIMARY CHAINCASE LUBRICATION	A12
REAR CHAIN LUBRICATION AND MAINTENANCE	A13
GREASING THE STEERING HEAD BALL RACES	A14
WHEEL BEARING LUBRICATION	A15
TELESCOPIC FORK LUBRICATION	A16
LUBRICATION NIPPLES	A17
LUBRICATING THE CONTROL CABLES	A18
SPEEDOMETER CABLE LUBRICATION	A19
REAR BRAKE PEDAL SPINDLE LUBRICATION	A20
CHECK PROCEDURE FOR WET SUMPING	A21

LUBRICATION SYSTEM

SECTION A1
ROUTINE MAINTENANCE

	Section
Every 250 miles (400 Kms.)	
Check level in oil tank	A4
Check level in primary chaincase	A12
Check chain oiler adjustment	A13
Every 1,000 miles (1,600 Kms.)	
Change oil in primary chaincase	A12
Lubricate control cables	A18
Grease swinging fork pivot	A17
Remove rear chain for cleaning and greasing	A13
Every 1,500 miles (2,400 Kms.)	
Change engine oil	A4
Every 2,000 miles	
Lubricate the contact breaker	A10
Every 3,000 miles (4,800 Kms.)	
Check gearbox oil level	A11
Check front forks for external oil leakage	A16
Grease brake pedal spindle	A20
Every 6,000 miles (9,600 Kms.)	
Change oil in gearbox	A11
Change oil in front forks	A16
Every 12,000 miles (19,200 Kms.)	
Grease wheel bearings	A14
Grease steering head bearings	A15

LUBRICATION SYSTEM

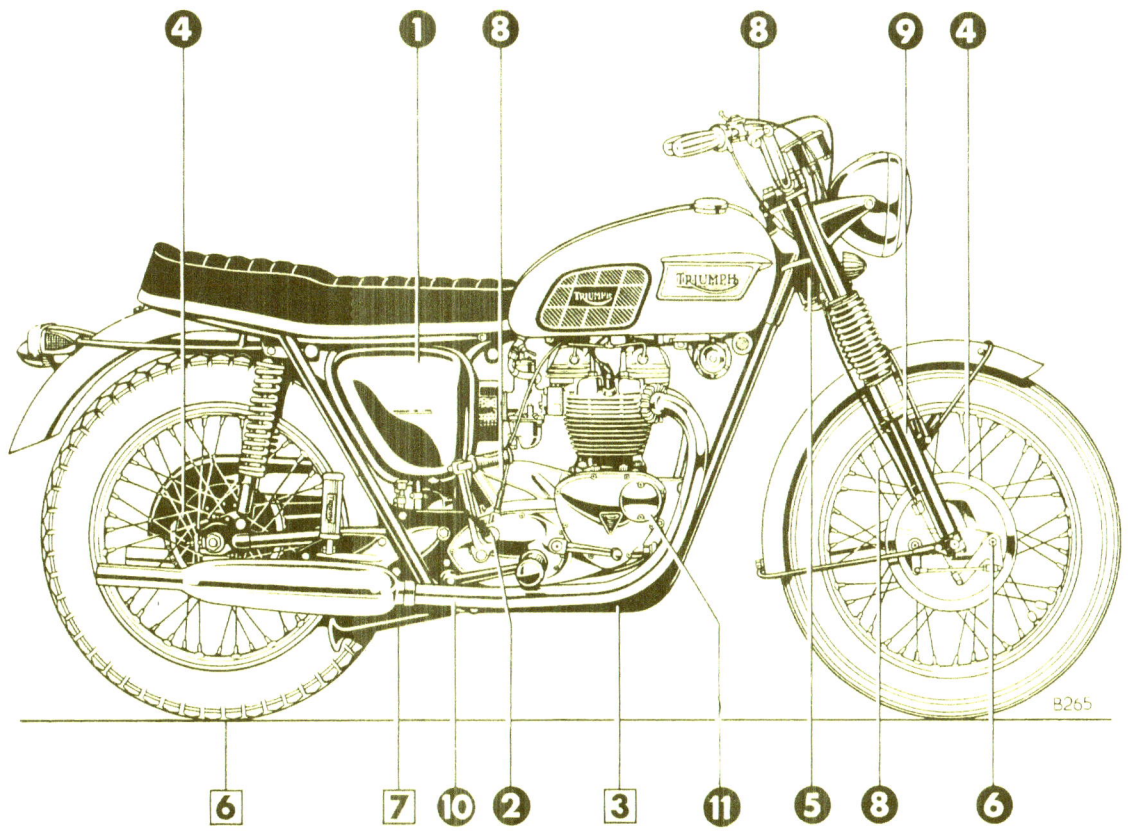

Fig. A1. LUBRICATION CHART
Numbers in circles refer to right side of machine
Numbers in squares refer to left side of machine

GUIDE TO LUBRICATION POINTS

Illustration No.	Description	SAE Oil grade
1	Engine oil tank	20 or 50
2	Gearbox	50
3	Primary chaincase	20
4	Wheel hubs	Grease
5	Steering head	Grease
6	Brake cam spindle	Grease
7	Brake pedal spindle	Grease
8	Exposed cables	20
9	Telescopic fork	20 or 30
10	Swinging fork pivot	Grease
11	Contact breaker cam	Grease
—	All brake rod joints and pins	20

SECTION A2
RECOMMENDED LUBRICANTS

UNITED KINGDOM

UNIT	MOBIL	B.P.	CASTROL	ESSO	SHELL	REGENT
Engine—Summer —Winter	Mobiloil A Mobiloil Arctic	Energol SAE 30 Energol SAE 20W	Castrol XL Castrolite	Esso Extra Motor Oil 20W/30	Shell X-100 30 Shell X-100 20W	Havoline SAE 30 Havoline SAE 20W
Gearbox	Mobilube GX90	BP Gear Oil 90EP	Castrol Hypoy 90EP	Esso Gear Oil GP90/140	Shell Spirax 90EP	Multigear EP90
Primary Chaincase	Mobiloil Arctic	Energol SAE 20	Castrolite	Esso Extra Motor Oil 20W/30	Shell X-100 20W	Havoline SAE 20W
Telescopic Fork	Mobiloil Arctic	Energol SAE 20W	Castrolite	Esso Extra Motor Oil 20W/30	Shell X-100 20W	Havoline SAE 20W
Wheel Bearings Swinging Fork Steering Races	Mobilgrease M.P.	Energrease L2	Castrolease L.M.	Esso Multipurpose Grease H	Shell Retinax A	Marfak Multipurpose 2
Easing Rusted Parts	Mobil Spring Oil	Energol Penetrating Oil	Castrol Penetrating Oil	Esso Penetrating Oil	Shell Donax P	Graphited Penetrating Oil

OVERSEAS

UNIT	MOBIL	B.P.	CASTROL	ESSO	SHELL	TEXACO (or REGENT)
Engine—Above 90°F. 32°—90°F. Below 32°F.	Mobiloil AF Mobiloil A Mobiloil Arctic	Energol SAE 40 Energol SAE 30 Energol SAE 20W	Castrol XXL Castrol XL Castrolite	Esso Extra Motor Oil 20W/40 10W/30	Shell X-100 40 Shell X-100 30 Shell X-100 20W	Havoline 40 Havoline 30 Havoline 20-20W
Gearbox	Mobilube GX90	BP Gear Oil 90EP	Castrol Hypoy 90EP	Esso Gear Oil GP90/140	Shell Spirax 90EP	Multigear EP90
Primary Chaincase	Mobiloil Artic	Energol SAE 20W	Castrolite	Esso Extra Motor Oil 20W/40	Shell X-100 20W	Havoline 20-20W
Telescopic Fork	Mobiloil Arctic	Energol SAE 20W	Castrolite	Esso Extra Motor Oil 20W/40	Shell X-100 20W	Havoline 30 Havoline 20-20W
Wheel Bearings, Swinging Fork, Steering Races	Mobilgrease M.P.	Energrease L2	Castrolease L.M.	Esso Multipurpose Grease H	Shell Retinax A	Marfak All Purpose
Easing Rusted Parts	Mobil Spring Oil	Energol Penetrating Oil	Castrol Penetrating Oil	Esso Penetrating Oil	Shell Donax P	Graphited Penetrating Oil

LUBRICATION SYSTEM

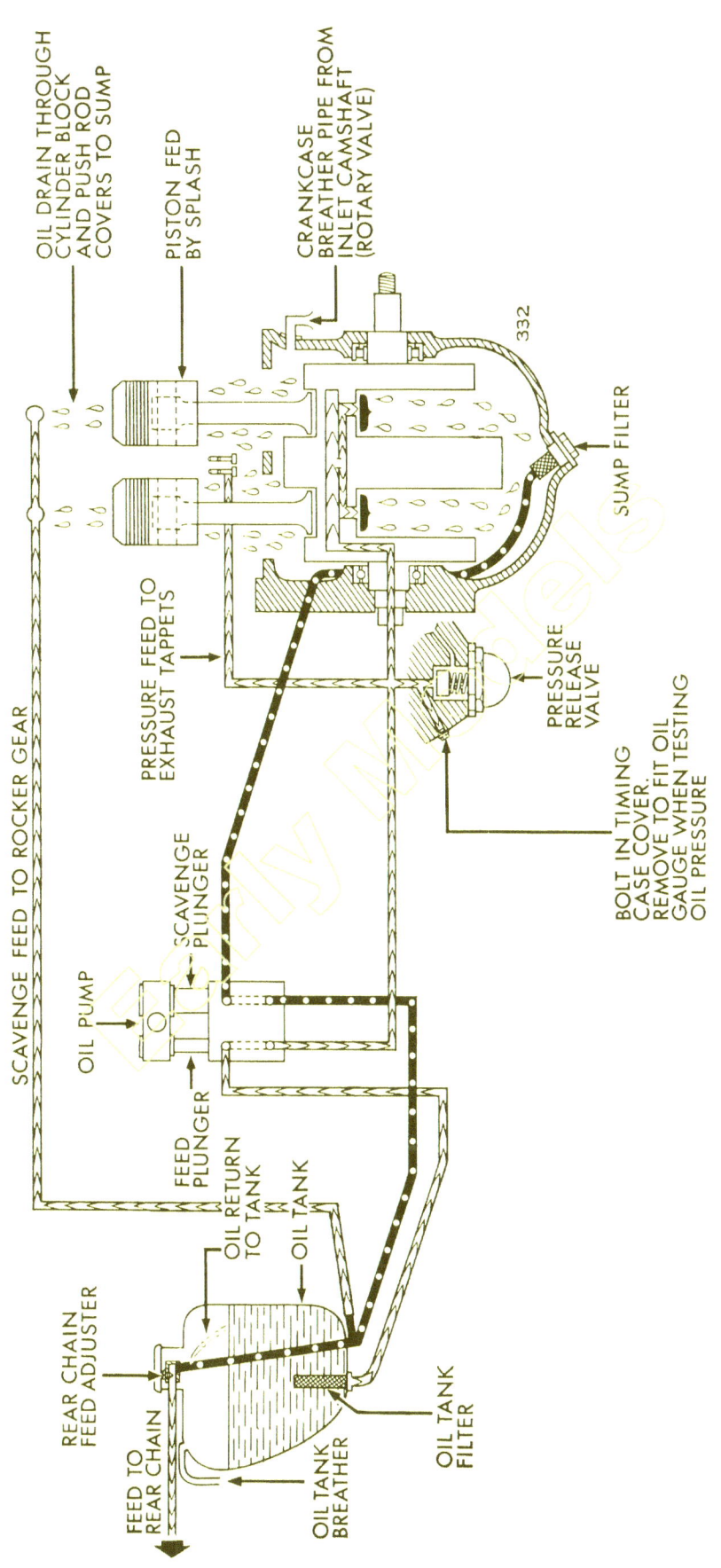

Fig. A2. Engine lubrication diagram

SECTION A3
ENGINE LUBRICATION SYSTEM

The engine lubrication system is of the dry sump type. The oil is fed by gravity from the oil tank to the oil pump; the oil, under pressure from the oil pump, is forced through drillings to the crankshaft big ends, where it escapes, and lubricates the cylinder walls, ball journal main bearings and the other internal engine parts.

The oil pressure between the oil pump and crankshaft is controlled by the oil pressure release valve. After lubricating the engine, oil falls to the sump where it is scavenged through the sump filter, and returned to the oil tank by the action of the oil pump scavenge plunger. The oil pump has been designed so that the scavenge plunger has a greater capacity than the feed plunger; thus ensuring that the sump does not become flooded.

Oil is fed to the valve operating mechanism by means of the rocker oil feed pipe which is connected to the scavenge return pipe just below the oil tank. After travelling through the rocker spindles, the oil is fed into the rocker boxes and also passes through drillings in the rocker arms onto the push rod end caps, after which it falls by gravity down the push rod cover tubes. The oil then passes through holes drilled in the tappet guide blocks and into the sump, where it is subsequently scavenged.

A positive oil feed is provided for the exhaust tappets. The lubricant is ported through drillways from the timing cover, (on earlier models a fine oil filter is incorporated with the timing cover plug and oil passes through this and the hollow metering dowel and pin) and on through the crankcase and cylinder block base flange to an annular groove machined in the tappet guide block. Two oil holes are provided in the groove to mate with the oil holes in the tappets which provide a channel for the lubricant to the tappet and camshaft working faces. See Fig. A4 and Fig. A5. Current models use tappets ground to provide a timing effect for the lubricant.

SECTION A4
CHANGING THE ENGINE OIL AND CLEANING THE OIL FILTERS

The oil in new and reconditioned engines should be changed at 250, 500 and 1,000 miles (400, 800 and 1,500 km.) intervals during the running-in period and thereafter as stated in Section A1.

It is advisable to drain the oil when the engine is warm as the oil will flow more readily. When changing the oil it is essential that the oil filters are thoroughly cleaned in paraffin (kerosene).

The hexagon-headed sump drain plug, which also houses the sump filter, is situated underneath the engine adjacent to the engine bottom mounting lug, as shown in Fig. A3, reference No. 4. Remove the plug and allow the oil to drain for approximately ten minutes. Clean the filter in paraffin (kerosene) and re-fit the plug but do not forget the joint washer.

The oil tank filter is screwed into the bottom of the oil tank, the oil feed pipe is connected to it by means of a union nut. Access to the union nut and oil tank filter on earlier machines fitted with rear enclosure panels is gained by removing the right panel which is undertaken by unscrewing the two domed nuts, a plain nut just below the rear of the fuel tank, and the two front panel junction screws. The right panel is then free to be removed.

Remove the oil tank filler cap, place a drip tray underneath the oil tank and remove the tank drain plug, where fitted, or alternatively unscrew the union nut and disconnect the oil feed pipe. Allow the oil to drain for approximately ten minutes. Unscrew the large hexagon-headed oil tank filter and thoroughly clean it in paraffin (kerosene).

It is advisable to flush out the oil tank with a flushing oil (obtainable from most garages), or, if this is not available, paraffin (kerosene) will do. However, if this is used ensure that all traces are removed from the inside of the oil tank prior to re-filling with oil. (For the correct grade of oil see Section A2).

When re-fitting the oil tank filter do not forget the fibre washer; and when connecting the oil feed pipe union nut, care should be taken to avoid over-tightening as this may result in failure of the union nut. Replace the drain plug where fitted.

NOTE: The level in the oil tank should be 1½ in. (4 cm.) below the filler cap. Further addition of oil will cause excessive venting through the oil tank breather pipe due to lack of air space.

LUBRICATION SYSTEM

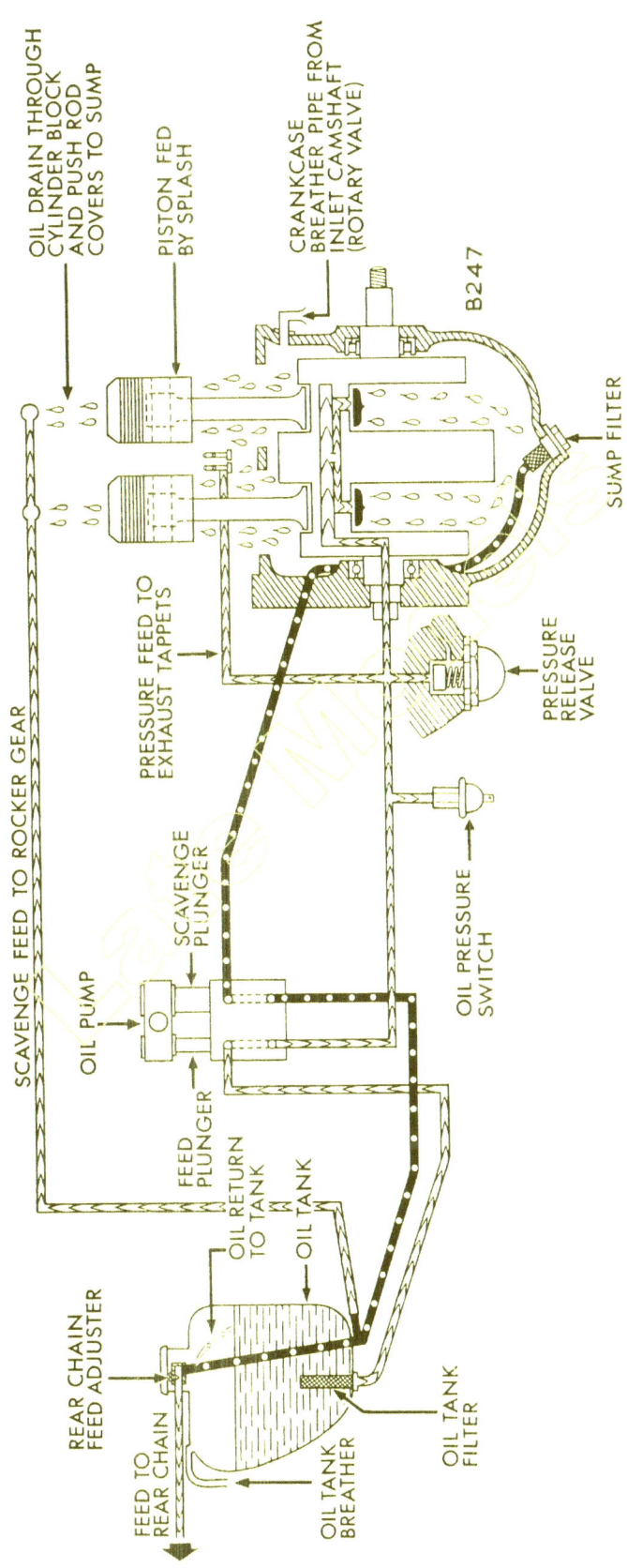

Fig. A2. Engine lubrication diagram

SECTION A3
ENGINE LUBRICATION SYSTEM

The engine lubrication system is of the dry sump type. The oil is fed by gravity from the oil tank to the oil pump; the oil, under pressure from the oil pump, is forced through drillings to the crankshaft big ends, where it escapes, and lubricates the cylinder walls, ball journal main bearings and the other internal engine parts.

The oil pressure between the oil pump and crankshaft is controlled by the oil pressure release valve. After lubricating the engine, oil falls to the sump where it is scavenged through the sump filter, and returned to the oil tank by the action of the oil pump scavenge plunger. The oil pump has been designed so that the scavenge plunger has a greater capacity than the feed plunger; thus ensuring that the sump does not become flooded.

Oil is fed to the valve operating mechanism by means of the rocker oil feed pipe which is connected to the scavenge return pipe just below the oil tank. After travelling through the rocker spindles, the oil is fed into the rocker boxes and also passes through drillings in the rocker arms onto the push rod end caps, after which it falls by gravity down the push rod cover tubes. The oil then passes through holes drilled in the tappet guide blocks and into the sump, where it is subsequently scavenged.

A positive oil feed is provided for the exhaust tappets. The lubricant is ported through drillways from the timing cover, and on through the crankcase and cylinder block base flange to an annular groove machined in the tappet guide block. Two oil holes are provided in the groove to mate with the oil holes in the tappets which provide a channel for the lubricant to the tappet and camshaft working faces. See Fig. A4 and Fig. A5. Current models use tappets ground to provide a timing effect for the lubricant.

SECTION A4
CHANGING THE ENGINE OIL AND CLEANING THE OIL FILTERS

The oil in new and reconditioned engines should be changed at 250, 500 and 1,000 miles (400, 800 and 1,500 km.) intervals during the running-in period and thereafter as stated in Section A1.

It is advisable to drain the oil when the engine is warm as the oil will flow more readily. When changing the oil it is essential that the oil filters are thoroughly cleaned in paraffin (kerosene).

The hexagon-headed sump drain plug, which also houses the sump filter, is situated underneath the engine adjacent to the engine bottom mounting lug, as shown in Fig. A3, reference No. 4. Remove the plug and allow the oil to drain for approximately ten minutes. Clean the filter in paraffin (kerosene) and re-fit the plug but do not forget the joint washer.

The oil tank filter is screwed into the bottom of the oil tank, the oil feed pipe is connected to it by means of a union nut.

Remove the oil tank filler cap, place a drip tray underneath the oil tank and remove the tank drain plug, where fitted, or alternatively unscrew the union nut and disconnect the oil feed pipe. Allow the oil to drain for approximately ten minutes. Unscrew the large hexagon-headed oil tank filter and thoroughly clean it in paraffin (kerosene).

It is advisable to flush out the oil tank with a flushing oil (obtainable from most garages), or, if this is not available, paraffin (kerosene) will do. However, if this is used ensure that all traces are removed from the inside of the oil tank prior to re-filling with oil. (For the correct grade of oil see Section A2).

When re-fitting the oil tank filter do not forget the fibre washer; and when connecting the oil feed pipe union nut, care should be taken to avoid overtightening as this may result in failure of the union nut. Replace the drain plug.

NOTE: The level in the oil tank should be 1½ in. (4 cm.) below the filler cap. Further addition of oil will cause excessive venting through the oil tank breather pipe due to lack of air space.

LUBRICATION SYSTEM

A

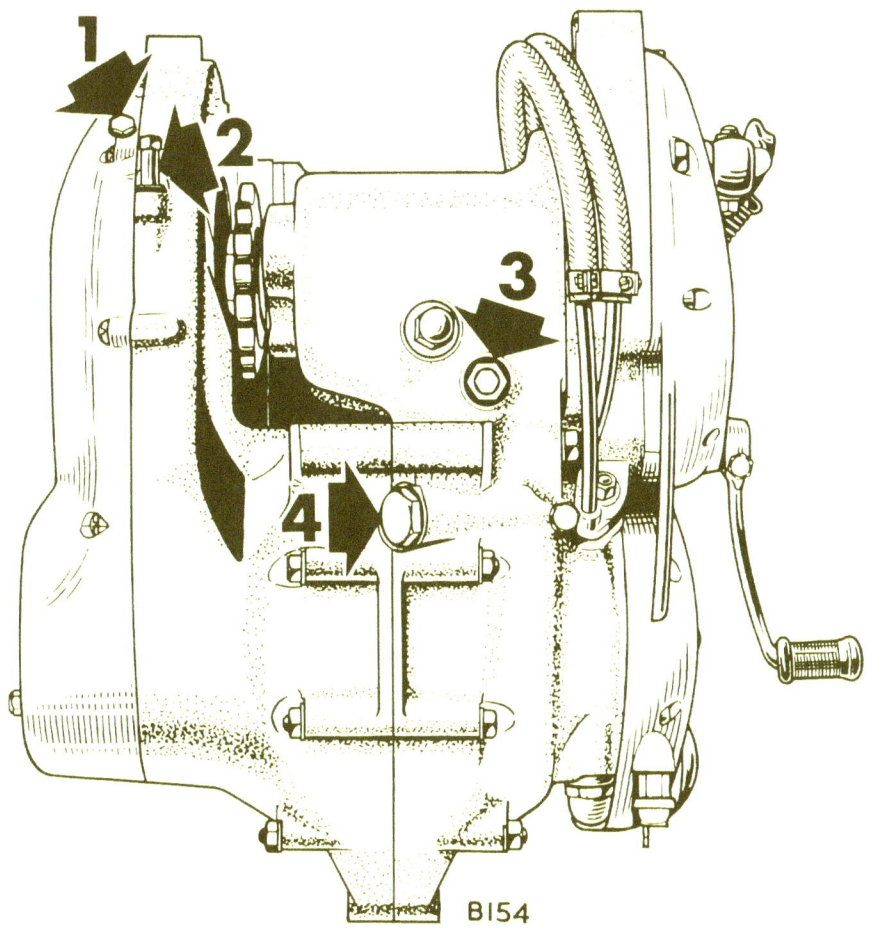

Fig. A3. Underside view of engine/gearbox unit

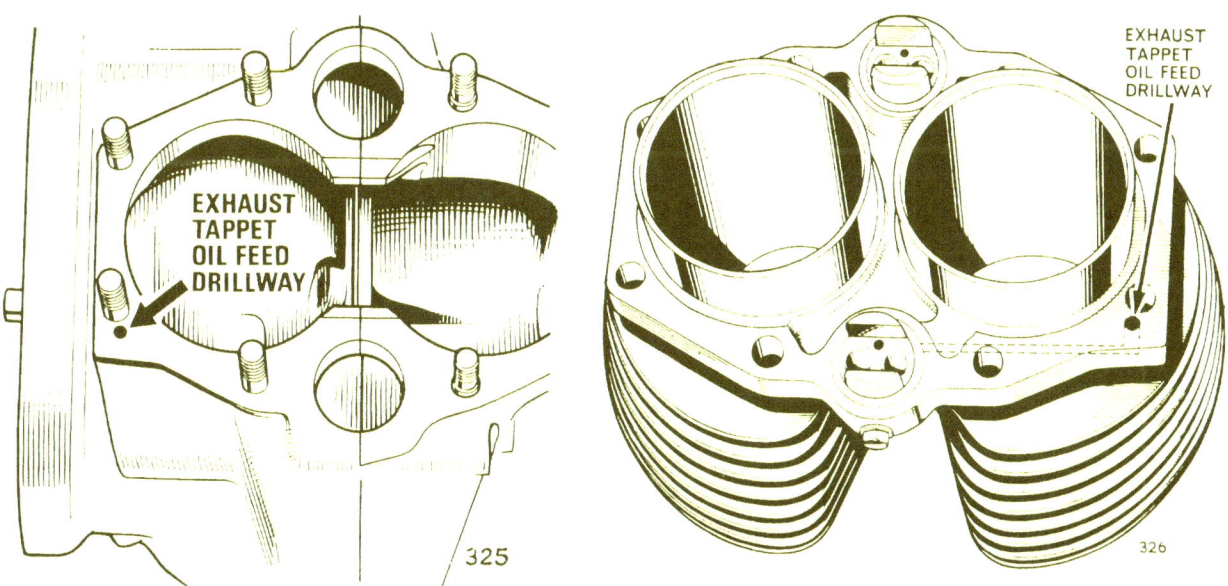

Fig. A4. Tappet oil feed drillway

Fig. A5. Tappet oil feed arrangement

A7

SECTION A5

OIL PRESSURE

The oil pressure is controlled by means of the release valve situated at the front of the engine at the right side adjacent to the timing cover.

When the engine is stationary there will be nil oil pressure. When the engine is started from cold pressure may be as high as 80 lb./sq. in. reducing when hot to a normal running figure of 65/80 lb./sq. in. At a fast idle when hot pressure should be 20/25 lb./sq. in.

Pressure can only be checked with an oil gauge connected to an adaptor replacing the oil pressure on the front of the timing cover.

If satisfactory readings are not obtained, check the following:—

(1) That the oil pressure release valve is clean and that the piston has the correct working clearance in the valve body (see "GENERAL DATA").

(2) That the oil tank level is not below minimum and that oil is being returned to the tank.

(3) That the sump filter and oil tank filter are clean and not blocked.

(4) That the oil pump is functioning properly and that there is a supply of oil to the pump. Refer to Sections A7 and A8 for checking the oil pump and oil pipes with junction block respectively.

(5) That the drillings in the timing cover are clean and that the drillings in the crankcase connecting the oil pipe junction block to the oil pump are clear.

(6) That the oil seal in the timing cover which fits over the crankshaft is not badly worn, thus resulting in the oil escaping to the sump.

(7) That the big ends are not badly worn. Should the big end bearings not have the correct working clearance, the oil will escape more readily, particularly when the oil is warm and is more fluid, thus giving a drop in pressure.

Extensive periods of slow running (such as in heavy traffic), or unnecessary use of the air control, can cause dilution in the oil tank, and an overall drop in lubricating pressure due to the lower viscosity of the diluted oil.

Most lubrication and oil pressure troubles can be avoided by regular attention to the recommended oil changes.

SECTION A6

STRIPPING AND REASSEMBLING THE OIL PRESSURE RELEASE VALVE

The oil pressure release valve is very reliable and should require no maintenance other than cleaning. It is situated at the front of the engine on the right side, adjacent to the timing cover.

Oil pressure is governed by the single spring situated within the release valve body. When the spring is removed it can be checked for compressive strength by measuring the length. Compare this figure with that given in "GENERAL DATA".

To remove the complete oil pressure release valve unit from the crankcase, unscrew the hexagonal nut adjacent to the crankcase surface. When removed the cap can then be unscrewed from the body thus releasing the piston which should be withdrawn.

Thoroughly clean all parts in paraffin (kerosene) and inspect for wear. The piston should be checked for possible scoring and the valve body filter for possible blockage or damage. To reassemble the release valve unit offer the piston into the valve body and screw on the valve cap with a new fibre washer. Similarly, when screwing the release valve unit into the crankcase, fit a new fibre washer between the release valve body and the crankcase. See Fig. A6.

LUBRICATION SYSTEM

1 Cap
2 Main spring
3 Piston
4 Fibre washer
5 Valve body
6 Fibre washer

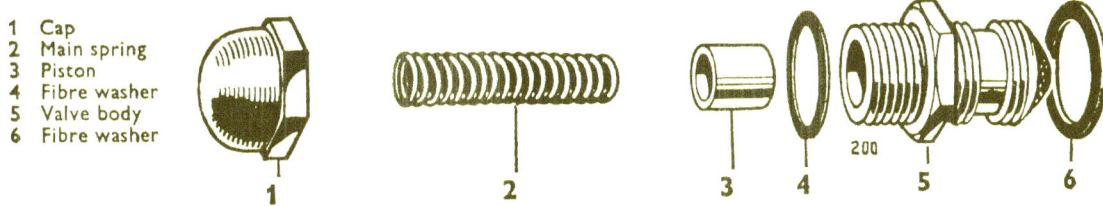

Fig. A6. Oil pressure release valve

Before engine number DU.13375 the two spring type pressure release valve was used, this being equipped with a pressure indicator button. See Fig. A7

To dismantle, remove the complete valve and cap as on later models. The main spring, auxiliary spring, rubber sleeve and indicator shaft can be removed from the valve cap by unscrewing the brass shaft nut.

The oil seal cover in the valve cap should be levered out and the seal replaced with a new one.

To reassemble the release valve unit, first press the rubber seal and retaining cup into the valve cap, place the sealing rubber on the button shaft (use a small amount of oil) and, using the button shaft as a guide, press the sealing rubber over the stub on the inside of the valve cap. Now replace the button shaft into its correct position and assemble the main spring and auxiliary spring, finally screwing on the brass shaft nut.

Reassembly should then be completed as for the later type.

1 Indicator shaft
2 Cup
3 Rubber 'O' ring
4 Valve cap
5 Rubber sleeve
6 Main spring
7 Auxiliary spring
8 Nut
9 Piston
10 Fibre washer
11 Valve body
12 Fibre washer

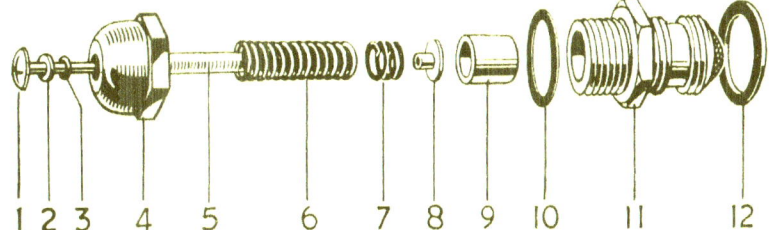

Fig. A7. Earlier oil pressure release valve

SECTION A7

STRIPPING AND REASSEMBLING THE OIL PUMP

The oil pump is situated inside the timing cover and is driven by an eccentric peg on the nut fitted to the end of the inlet camshaft. The only part likely to show wear after considerable mileage is the oil pump drive block slider, which should be replaced to maintain full oil pumping efficiency. The plungers and pump body being constantly immersed in oil, wear is negligible.

For removal of the timing cover see Section B32

The oil pump is held in its position by two conical nuts. When these are removed the oil pump can then be withdrawn from the mounting studs. The scavenge and feed plungers should be removed and the two square caps from the end of the oil pump unscrewed. This will release the springs and balls.

All parts should be thoroughly cleaned in paraffin (kerosene).

The plungers should be inspected for scoring, and for wear by measuring their diameters and comparing them with those given in "GENERAL DATA". The springs should be checked for compressive strength by measuring their lengths. Compare the actual lengths with those given in "GENERAL DATA".

LUBRICATION SYSTEM

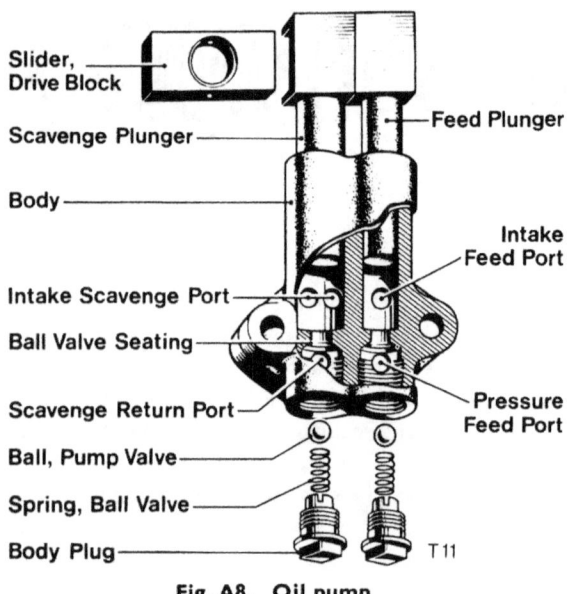

Fig. A8. Oil pump

When reassembling the oil pump all parts should be well lubricated and the oil pump finally checked for efficiency by the following means:—

Place a small amount of oil in both bores (approximately 1 c.c.) and press the plungers until oil is forced through both outlet ports (these are the two holes nearest the square caps (see Fig. A8). Place the thumb over the intake ports (the holes nearest the plunger tops) and withdraw the plungers slightly. If the oil level falls in either outlet port then the ball valve is not seating properly and the square caps should be removed and the cleaning process repeated. On machines fitted with brass-bodied oil pumps the ball valves can be tapped lightly, but sharply into their seating to ensure an efficient and adequate seal. Under no circumstances, however, should this operation be attempted on a pump body of cast iron material, where, if the ball seating is distorted, the body must be renewed.

The aluminium drive block slider which fits over the eccentric peg on the inlet camshaft nut should be checked for wear on both the bore and in the plunger cross-head.

When refitting the oil pump a new gasket should be used and always remember that the cones of the conical nut and washers fit into the countersunk holes in the oil pump body.

When replacing the timing cover care should be taken that the junction surfaces are cleaned prior to application of the fresh coat of jointing compound

SECTION A8

REMOVING AND REPLACING THE OIL PIPE JUNCTION BLOCK

Drain the oil from the gearbox by removing the oil drain plug situated underneath the gearbox as shown in Fig. A3, reference No. 3.

On earlier machines with rear enclosure panels, remove the right panel by unscrewing two domed nuts, a plain nut (just below the rear of the petrol tank) and two front panel junction screws.

Remove the right-hand exhaust pipe, removing the right footrest on earlier models, then remove the gearbox outer cover as shown in Section D1.

Place a drip tray underneath the engine and remove the drain plug where fitted, or, alternatively, remove the nut securing the oil pipe junction block to the crankcase and allow the oil tank to drain for approximately ten minutes.

Disconnect the rubber pipes from the oil tank, remove the junction block and thoroughly clean it in paraffin (kerosene).

Check the pipes for cuts and abrasions and that the rubber connections are a good tight fit on the junction block pipes. If there is any doubt about the reliability of the rubber connectors, they should be renewed.

Reassembly is the reversal of the above instructions but remember to fit a new gasket between the junction block and the crankcase.

LUBRICATION SYSTEM

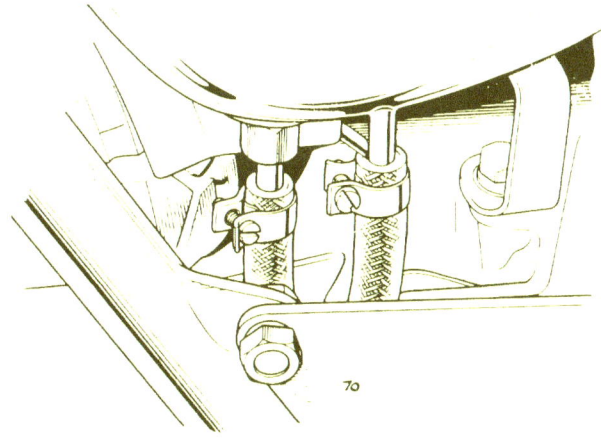

Fig. A9. Oil pipe securing clips

When replacing the rubber connection tubes, care must be exercised to prevent chafing the inside of the rubber connections. Failure to observe this may result in fragments of rubber entering the oil system and causing blockage.

Replace the screwed clips and firmly clamp them in position. If the machine is not fitted with these clips it may well be advisable to obtain them from a Triumph spares stockist and fit them. This can be done for a very small cost.

SECTION A9
REMOVING AND REPLACING THE ROCKER OIL FEED PIPE

To disconnect the rocker oil feed pipe for removal, the two domed nuts should be removed from the ends of the rocker spindle, and the banjos withdrawn.

On earlier machines with panels, it is necessary to remove the right panel by unscrewing two domed nuts, a plain nut (just below the rear of the fuel tank) and two front panel junction screws.

Disconnect the rocker oil feed pipe from the oil tank.

To free the rocker oil feed pipe from the frame it may be necessary to disconnect several frame clips from underneath the fuel tank. Care should be taken that the pipe is not bent excessively as this might ultimately result in a fracture. When removed, the rocker oil feed pipe should be thoroughly cleaned in paraffin (kerosene) and checked for blockage by sealing the first banjo with the thumb and first finger, whilst blowing through the other. Repeat this procedure for the other banjo.

When refitting the rocker oil feed pipe it is advisable to use new copper washers, but if the old ones are annealed they should give an effective oil seal. Annealing is achieved by heating to cherry red heat and quenching in water. Any scale that is formed on the washers should be removed prior to re-fitting them.

SECTION A10
CONTACT BREAKER LUBRICATION

The contact breaker is situated in the timing cover and it is imperative that no oil from the engine lubrication system gets into the contact breaker chamber. For this purpose there is an oil seal at the back of the contact breaker unit pressed into the timing cover. However slight lubrication of the cam and auto advance unit spindles is necessary. The cam is lubricated by means of an oil-soaked wick which should be fed with a few drops of oil (SAE 20 or SAE 30) every 5,000 miles (8,000 km.).

LUBRICATION SYSTEM

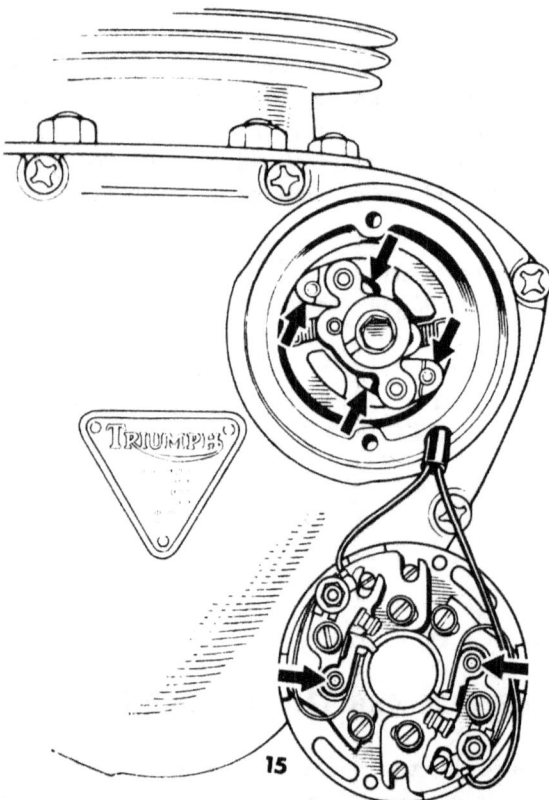

Fig. A10. Contact breaker mechanism lubrication points (6CA Contact breaker)

To lubricate the auto advance mechanism it is necessary to withdraw the mounting plate. Mark the C.B. plate and housing so that it can be subsequently replaced in exactly the same location, then unscrew the two hexagonal pillar bolts. When the mounting plate is removed, the mechanism should be lightly oiled (see arrows shown in Fig. A10) at the same interval that is given above for the cam wick.

Finally, replace the mounting plate and re-set the ignition timing. If the setting has been disturbed, the correct procedure for accurate ignition timing is given in Sections B32 and B33.

At each 6000 mile interval apply a light dab of grease to each side of the contact breaker cam to provide lubrication for the nylon heels of the contact breakers.

SECTION A11
GEARBOX LUBRICATION

The gearbox is lubricated by means of an oil bath. Oil is splash fed to all gearbox components including the enclosed gearchange and kickstarter mechanisms. The oil in the gearbox should be drained and the gearbox flushed out after the intial 500-mile (800 km.) running-in period. Thereafter, the oil should be changed as stated in Section A1.

The oil can be drained from the gearbox by means of the oil drain plug located underneath the gearbox (see Fig. A3, reference No. 3). It is best to drain the oil whilst the engine is warm as the oil will flow more readily.

The gearbox oil filler plug is situated on top of the gearbox adjacent to the clutch cable abutment. When replenishing the oil, the oil drain plug should be replaced omitting the smaller oil level plug which screws into it. Oil should be poured into the gearbox until it is seen to drip out through the oil level plug hole. (See Fig. A11). The correct level has then been obtained (see Section A2 for recommended oil).

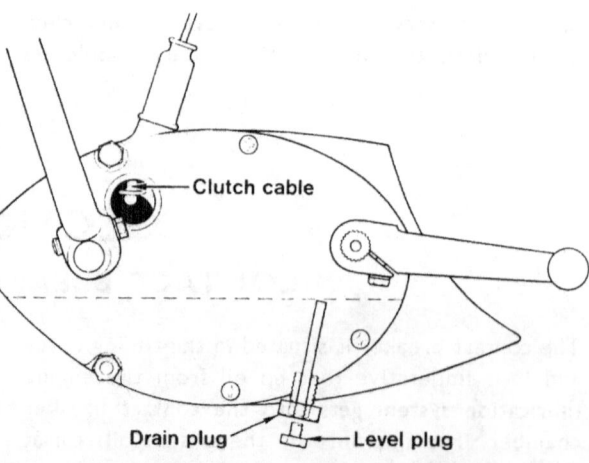

Fig. A11. Gearbox drain and level plugs

LUBRICATION SYSTEM

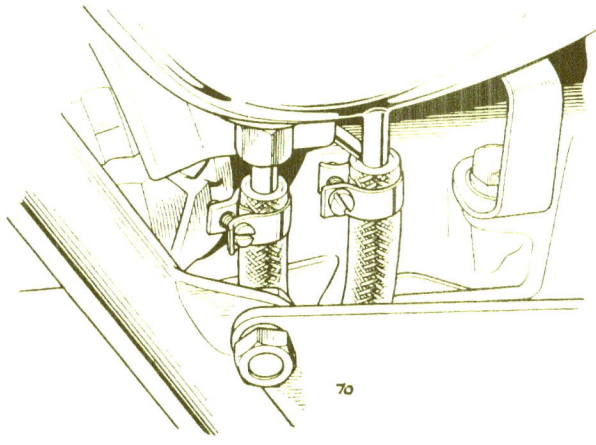

When replacing the rubber connection tubes, care must be exercised to prevent chafing the inside of the rubber connections. Failure to observe this may result in fragments of rubber entering the oil system and causing blockage.

It is important to replace the screwed clips and firmly clamp them in position.

Fig. A9. Oil pipe securing clips

SECTION A9

REMOVING AND REPLACING THE ROCKER OIL FEED PIPE

To disconnect the rocker oil feed pipe for removal, the two domed nuts should be removed from the ends of the rocker spindle, and the banjos withdrawn.

Disconnect the rocker oil feed pipe from the oil tank.

To free the rocker oil feed pipe from the frame it may be necessary to disconnect several frame clips from underneath the fuel tank. Care should be taken that the pipe is not bent excessively as this might ultimately result in a fracture. When removed, the rocker oil feed pipe should be thoroughly cleaned in paraffin (kerosene) and checked for blockage by sealing the first banjo with the thumb and first finger, whilst blowing through the other. Repeat this procedure for the other banjo.

When refitting the rocker oil feed pipe it is advisable to use new copper washers, but if the old ones are annealed they should give an effective oil seal. Annealing is achieved by heating to cherry red heat and quenching in water. Any scale that is formed on the washers should be removed prior to re-fitting them.

SECTION A10

CONTACT BREAKER LUBRICATION

The contact breaker is situated in the timing cover and it is imperative that no oil from the engine lubrication system gets into the contact breaker chamber. For this purpose there is an oil seal at the back of the contact breaker unit pressed into the timing cover. However slight lubrication of the auto advance unit spindles is necessary. The cam spindle is pre-lubricated with a preparation of molybdenum disulphide and an epoxy resin. Liquid lubricant must not be applied at this point since a glutinous paste would be formed which would seize the spindle and bearing.

LUBRICATION SYSTEM

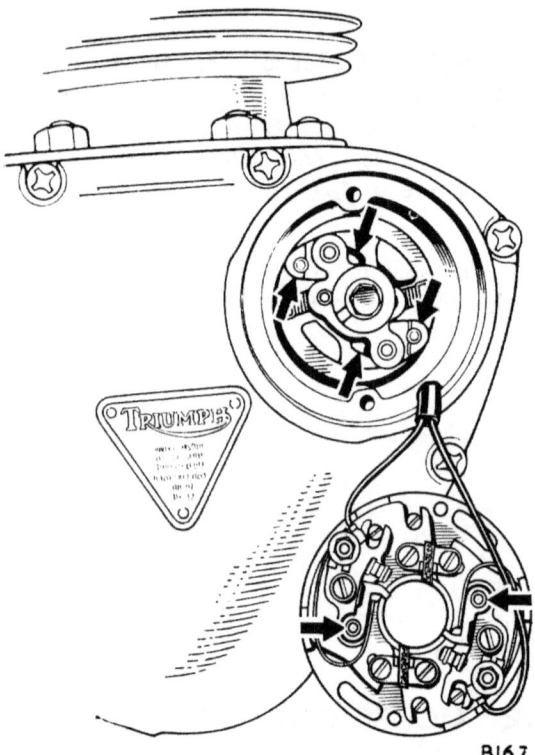

Fig. A10. Contact breaker mechanism lubrication points (6CA Contact breaker)

To lubricate the auto advance mechanism it is necessary to withdraw the mounting plate. Mark the C.B. plate and housing so that it can be subsequently replaced in exactly the same location, then unscrew the two hexagonal pillar bolts. When the mounting plate is removed, the mechanism should be lightly oiled (see arrows shown in Fig. A10) at the same interval that is given above for the cam wick. Do not allow more than one drop onto each pivot point, and wipe off any surplus.

Finally, replace the mounting plate and re-set the ignition timing. If the setting has been disturbed, the correct procedure for accurate ignition timing is given in Sections B29, B30 and B31.

The lubricating wicks adjacent to the contact breaker nylon heels are treated initially with Shell Retinax A grease and thereafter, 3 drops of clean engine oil should be added to the wicks at 1500 mile intervals.

SECTION A11
GEARBOX LUBRICATION

The gearbox is lubricated by means of an oil bath. Oil is splash fed to all gearbox components including the enclosed gearchange and kickstarter mechanisms. The oil in the gearbox should be drained and the gearbox flushed out after the intial 500-mile (800 km.) running-in period. Thereafter, the oil should be changed as stated in Section A1.

The oil can be drained from the gearbox by means of the oil drain plug located underneath the gearbox (see Fig. A3, reference No. 3). It is best to drain the oil whilst the engine is warm as the oil will flow more readily.

The gearbox oil filler plug is situated on the outer cover. When replenishing the oil, the oil drain plug should be replaced omitting the smaller oil level plug which screws into it. Oil should be poured into the gearbox until it is seen to drip out through the oil level plug hole. (See Fig. A11). The correct level has then been obtained (see Section A2 for recommended oil).

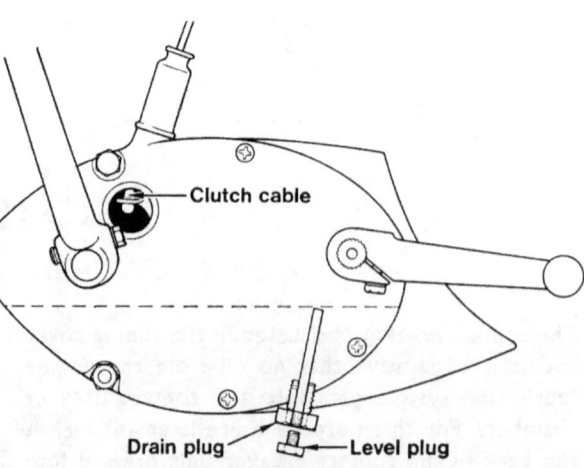

Fig. A11. Gearbox drain and level plugs

LUBRICATION SYSTEM

SECTION A12
PRIMARY CHAINCASE LUBRICATION

The primary chaincase is lubricated by means of an oil bath. To drain the oil, first remove the oil drain plug from the bottom of the chaincase adjacent to the left footrest. (See Fig. A3, reference No. 2). This plug also gives access to the chain tensioner. To remove the plug on the earlier models it may be necessary to loosen the left footrest. This can be done by slackening off the footrest mounting bolt and giving the footrest a sharp tap in a downwards direction to release it from its locking taper. When the plug is removed allow the oil to drain for approximately ten minutes and replace the plug, not forgetting the fibre washer. It is not necessary to disturb the rotor cover during oil changing.

So that the correct amount of oil can be put into the primary chaincase there is an oil level plug situated at the rear underside of the chaincase. (See Fig. A3, reference No. 1). Alternatively, the correct level can be achieved by using a measure of $\frac{5}{8}$ pint (350 c.c.) capacity.

Fresh oil can be put into the plug adjacent to the cylinder barrel base or alternatively through the clutch adjustment plug aperture which is in the centre of the outer cover.

The primary chain is lubricated by means of a collection chamber and oil feed pipe built into the primary chain housing. The oil feed pipe directs a continuous supply of oil at the point where the chain runs onto the engine sprocket. To check this for possible blockages it is necessary to remove the primary chaincase outer cover, and remove the front clip securing the oil feed pipe.

The oil ways can then be cleaned by a jet of compressed air from such as a cycle pump. When replacing the feed pipe clip ensure that the pipe is parallel to the top portion of the chain and firmly gripped by the clip.

The oil in the primary chaincase should be changed as stated in Section A1.

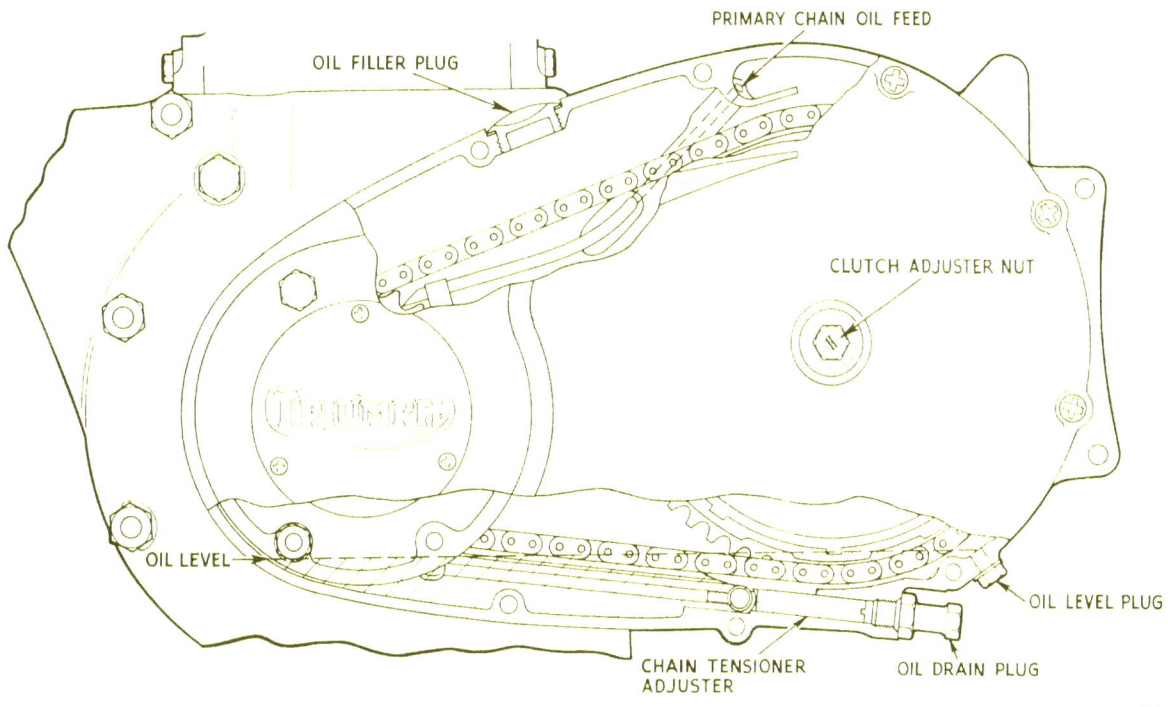

Fig. A12. Section through the primary chaincase

SECTION A13

REAR CHAIN LUBRICATION AND MAINTENANCE

The rear chain feed is taken from an oil junction block situated in the neck of the oil tank (see Fig. A13). The rate of flow of oil to the chain can be controlled by a threaded tapered screw provided in the oil junction block. The screw should be turned clockwise to reduce the flow and anti-clockwise to increase it. Earlier machines had firstly an oil feed through a set metering jet at the back of the primary chaincase and later the jet blanked off completely. These latter machines would require manual lubrication of the rear chain every 250 miles.

Disconnect the connecting link and remove the chain. If available, connect an old chain to the end of the chain being removed and draw it onto the gearbox sprocket until the chain to be cleaned is clear of the machine and can be disconnected.

Remove all deposits of road dust etc. by means of a wire brush. Clean thoroughly in paraffin or kerosene and allow to drain.

Inspect the chain for excessive wear of the rollers and pivot pins and check that the elongation does not exceed $1\frac{1}{2}\%$. To do this first scribe two marks on a flat table exactly $12\frac{1}{2}$ inches (31·75 cm.) apart, place the chain opposite the two marks. When the chain is compressed to its minimum free length the marks should coincide with two pivot pins 20 links apart. When the chain is stretched to its maximum free length, the extension should not exceed $\frac{1}{4}$ in. (6·25 mm.). If it is required to remove a faulty link, or shorten the chain, reference should be made to Section C11.

To lubricate the chain, immerse it into MELTED grease (melt over a low flame, or, more safely, over a pan of boiling water), and allow it to remain in the grease for approximately 15 minutes, moving the chain occasionally to ensure penetration of the grease into the chain bearings. Allow the grease to cool, remove the chain from the bath and wipe off the surplus grease.

The chain is now ready for refitting to the machine.

NOTE: The connecting link retaining clip must be fitted with the nose-end facing in the direction of motion of the chain.

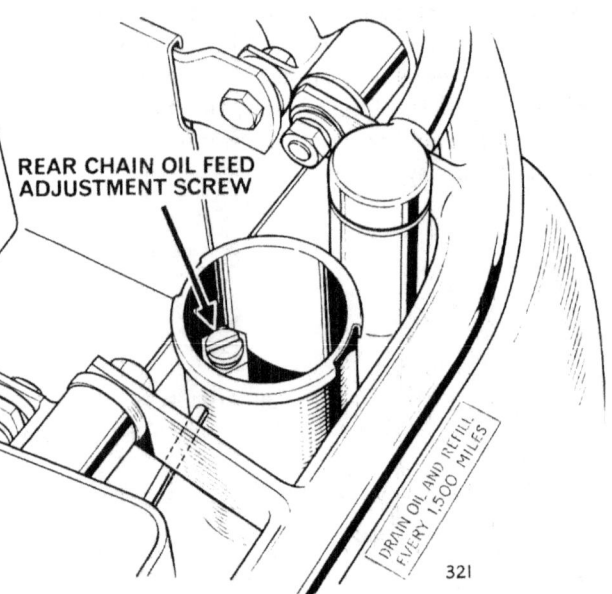

Fig. A13. Rear chain oil feed adjustment

SECTION A14

GREASING THE STEERING HEAD BALL RACES

The steering head races are packed with grease on assembly and require re-packing with the correct grade of grease at the interval stated in Section A1.

Removal and replacement of the ball bearings is comprehensively covered in the front fork section.

When the balls are removed they should be cleaned in paraffin (kerosene), also, the cups fitted to the frame head lug and the cones fitted to the middle lug stem should be cleaned thoroughly by means of a paraffin (kerosene) soaked rag, then inspected for wear, cracking or pocketing.

The fresh supply of grease should be utilised to hold the balls in position in the cups whilst the fork is assembled.

LUBRICATION SYSTEM

SECTION A15
WHEEL BEARING LUBRICATION

The wheel bearings are packed with grease on assembly but require re-packing with the correct grade of grease at the interval stated in Section A1.

The bearings on both the front wheel and rear wheel should be removed, cleaned in paraffin (kerosene) and assembled with the hubs well packed with the correct grade of grease. For details concerning the grade of grease to be used (which is the same for both wheels), see Section A2.

Removing and replacing the bearings for the front and rear wheels is comprehensively covered in Section F8.

SECTION A16
TELESCOPIC FORK LUBRICATION

The oil contained in the front fork has the dual purpose of lubricating the stanchion bearing bushes and also acting as the suspension damping medium. Therefore it is imperative that the fork legs have an equal amount of oil in them. On the current shuttle valve fork it is important that only SAE 20 oil is used for lubrication purposes.

Oil leakage at the junction between the stanchion and bottom fork leg is prevented by means of an oil seal. If there is excessive oil leakage at this junction it may be necessary to renew the oil seal (see Section G6), but before undertaking this work, the fork should be checked to ensure that there is the correct amount of oil in each of the fork legs.

The correct amounts are as follows:—
Engine No. DU.101–DU.5824—$\frac{1}{4}$ pint (150 c.c.)
Engine No. DU.5825 onwards—$\frac{1}{3}$ pint (200 c.c.)

In the case where an earlier model (i.e. DU.101–DU.5824) has been fitted with longer fork legs, to cater for the fitting of a sidecar, the correct amount of oil is $\frac{3}{8}$ pint (225 c.c.).

Particular attention should be given to the oil change period. The fork should be drained and refilled with the correct Summer or Winter grade of oil every Spring and Autumn if the mileage covered is less than the distance in Section A1.

To drain the oil from the fork legs remove the two small hexagonal drain plugs adjacent to the left and right ends of the front wheel spindle.

Oil can be expelled at a greater rate by compressing the fork two or three times.

To refill the fork legs on earlier machines incorporating "Nacelle" equipment first replace the drain plugs complete with fibre washers, then slacken the headlamp securing screw adjacent to the speedometer and withdraw the headlamp and rim assembly.

Remove the two small hexagonal filling plugs from the stanchions (these are located approximately 3 inches from the top lug and should be facing forward towards the headlamp aperture) and pump the advised amount of oil into each fork leg by means of a pressure can or gun. For the recommended grade of oil see Section A2.

When refitting the filler plugs do not forget the fibre washers.

If a pressure can or gun is not available the method recommended for filling the fork legs with oil is that of removing the cap nuts.

Access to the cap nuts can be gained by removing the nacelle top cover (if fitted) and handlebar as described in sections G1 and G3 respectively. Then, by means of spanner D220, the hexagonal cap nuts ($1\frac{1}{2}$ inches across flats) can be unscrewed and withdrawn. The correct amount of oil should then be poured into each fork leg.

To refill the fork legs on machines fitted with sports headlamp, the fork hexagonal cap nuts must be unscrewed and withdrawn, and the correct amount of oil poured into each fork leg. This will necessitate removal of the handlebar on machines with resiliently mounted handlebar equipment.

SECTION A17
LUBRICATION NIPPLES

Both the brake operating camshafts and the swinging fork pivot bearings should be lubricated by means of the lubrication nipples.

The brake camshafts have integral lubrication nipples. Care should be taken that the surface of the nipple is not damaged. Slight distortion may be removed with a fine grade file.

The front and rear wheel brake cam and spindle bearing surfaces should be sparingly lubricated with the correct grade of grease (Section A2). This can be done by giving the lubrication nipples on the ends of the camshafts one stroke each from a grease gun. However, if the grease does not penetrate, the brake cams should be removed and cleaned thoroughly in paraffin (kerosene). The cam bearing surfaces should then be greased on reassembly.

SWINGING FORK PIVOT

The greasing nipple is situated centrally underneath the swinging fork and should be given several strokes with a high pressure grease gun until grease is forced through each end of the pivot bearings or past the end cap 'O' ring seals on current machines.

If the grease does not penetrate then the pivot must be removed to ensure adequate lubrication.

Removal of the swinging fork is detailed in section E10. When the fork is removed the sleeves and distance tube should be withdrawn and all parts should be thoroughly cleaned out in paraffin (kerosene) and allowed to drain.

Reassembly is a reversal of the above instructions. The space surrounding the distance tube should be carefully packed with the correct grade of grease, and the sleeves should be well greased on their bearing surfaces.

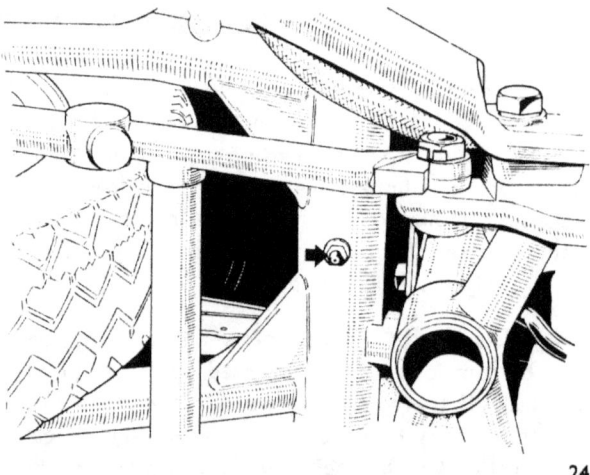

Fig. A14. Swinging fork pivot lubrication nipple

SECTION A18
LUBRICATING THE CONTROL CABLES

The control cables can be periodically lubricated at the exposed joints with a thin grade of oil (see Section A2).

A more thorough method of lubrication is that of feeding oil into one end of the cable by means of a reservoir. For this, the cable can be either disconnected at the handlebar end only, or completely removed.

The disconnected end of the cable should be threaded through a thin rubber stopper and the stopper pressed into a suitable narrow-necked can with a hole in its base. If the can is then inverted and the lubricating oil poured into it through the hole, the oil will trickle down between the outer and inner cables. It is best to leave the cable in this position overnight to ensure adequate lubrication.

LUBRICATION SYSTEM

SECTION A19
SPEEDOMETER CABLE LUBRICATION

The speedometer cable should be lubricated by means of grease (see Section A2 for correct grade).

It is not necessary to completely remove the cable, but only to disconnect it from the speedometer and withdraw the inner cable. To do this on nacelle models first remove the headlamp unit by slackening the securing screw adjacent to the speedometer on the nacelle. Unscrew the union nut at the base of the speedometer, withdraw the inner cable and clean it in paraffin (kerosene). Smear the surface with grease, except for 6 in. (15 cm.) nearest to the speedometer head.

The cable is now ready to be offered into the outer casing and excess grease wiped off. Care should be taken that both "squared" ends of the inner cables are located in their respective "square" drive housings before the union nut is tightened.

SECTION A20
BRAKE PEDAL SPINDLE LUBRICATION

The brake pedal spindle is bolted to the left rear engine mounting plate. The spindle should be covered with a fresh supply of grease occasionally otherwise corrosion and inefficient operation may result.

To gain access to the spindle, slacken off the rear brake rod adjustment, unscrew the brake pedal retaining nut and withdraw the pedal.

Remove any rust from the spindle with fine emery. Clean the bore of the pedal and smear the spindle with grease (see Section A2) prior to refitting.

Do not forget to replace the spring and plain washer between the retaining nut and brake pedal.

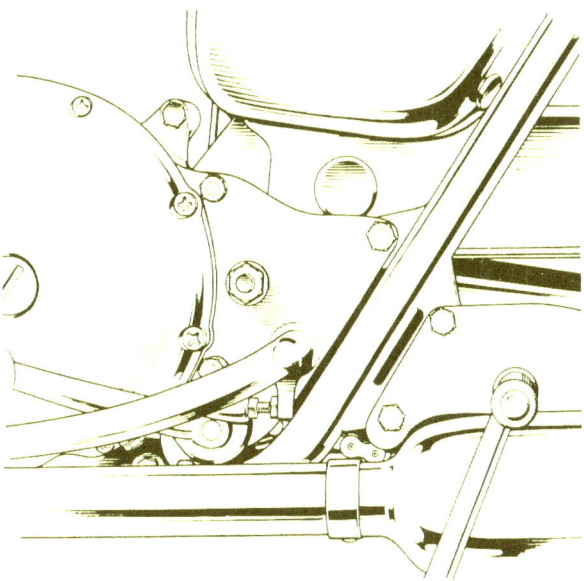

Fig. A15. Brake pedal spindle lubrication

SECTION A21

CHECK PROCEDURE FOR WET SUMPING

'Wet sumping' or a lack of scavenge is a condition which can occur due to a number of causes. The symptoms of this condition are:—
(1) Excessive oil emitting from crankcase breather tube and resulting high oil consumption.
(2) Smoking exhaust.

To verify that a wet-sumping condition exists, run the engine until it is thoroughly warm. Within five minutes after engine shutoff drain the sump. Measure the amount of oil that drains out. An amount of oil over 100 c.c. indicates a wet-sumping condition and corrective measures should be taken.

POSSIBLE CAUSES OF WET-SUMPING ARE

(1) Foreign material preventing ball valve from seating in the scavenge side of oil pump (most common cause).
(2) Poor check valve ball seat.
(3) Air leak in crankcase oil scavenge pipe.
(4) Air leak in oil pump to crankcase joint.
(5) Porous crankcase casting.
(6) Air leak at E4539 plug bottom of engine.
(7) Blockage in return oil pipe—could be caused by mis-aligned E3763 oil junction block gasket.
(8) Oil pressure release valve piston in full bypass position due to a stuck piston or broken or missing spring.
(9) Restriction in oil tank vent pipe.

SCAVENGE SUCTION TEST (for checking above causes numbers 1 to 6)

Obtain a vacuum gauge calibrated in inches of mercury. Attach a length of standard Triumph oil pipe to it and proceed as follows:
(1) Run engine until it is thoroughly warm.
(2) Remove the oil sump cap and screen.
(3) Connect hose from vacuum gauge to oil scavenge pipe.
(4) Run engine at a fast idle—gauge should read a vacuum of 18-26 inches of mercury.
(5) Stop engine and observe gauge. The needle should gradually—not immediately—drop to zero.

IF THE SCAVENGE SUCTION TEST IS SATISFACTORY

(1) Check oil pressure relief valve assembly and also check oil pressure.
(2) Check the return system from the pump to the oil tank and also the tank vent.

TO CHECK FOR A BLOCKED OR RESTRICTED OIL RETURN TO THE TANK

(1) On the oil tank using a hand brace or chuck and $\frac{7}{64}$" and $\frac{15}{64}$" drill bits, run the drill bits into the return tube and rocker feed tube (if fitted) at the bottom of the tank to see that both tubes are free from internal burrs and restrictions that can occur at their welded joints.
(2) After doing the above, blow out the return oil line and the return tube in the oil tank with compressed air.

IF THE ABOVE TEST IS NOT SATISFACTORY

(1) Remove oil pump—clean thoroughly and see that ball seats are concentric and free from pits or grooves. Re-assemble pump, tighten check valve caps securely and re-install pump with a new gasket.

To check for crankcase scavenge tube leakage or case porosity, fill a **good** "pumper" type oil can with light oil and squirt through a folded rag into pickup tube. Back pressure could prevent pumping oil out of the can in a few pumps. If the oil can still be pumped with no evidence of substantial back pressure, obviously there is a leak in the the crankcase tube or crankcase scavenge oil passageways.

To be sure that the oil can is satisfactory for this test, fill it with light oil and block the outlet tube. After one or two pumps the can should "liquid lock". If the can can stil be pumped, the pump mechanism is suffering from excessive blow-by and the can will not suffice for this test.

SECTION B

ENGINE

DESCRIPTION	Section
REMOVING AND REPLACING THE ENGINE UNIT	B1
REMOVING AND REPLACING THE ROCKER BOXES	B2
INSPECTING THE PUSH RODS	B3
STRIPPING AND REASSEMBLING THE ROCKER BOXES	B4
ADJUSTING THE VALVE ROCKER CLEARANCES	B5
REMOVING AND REPLACING THE AIR CLEANER	B6
CONCENTRIC CARBURETTER—DESCRIPTION	B7
REMOVING AND REPLACING THE CARBURETTER	B8
STRIPPING AND REASSEMBLING THE CARBURETTER	B9
INSPECTING THE CARBURETTER COMPONENTS	B10
CARBURETTER ADJUSTMENTS	B11
TWIN CARBURETTER ARRANGEMENT	B12
REMOVING AND REPLACING THE EXHAUST SYSTEM	B13
REMOVING AND REFITTING THE CYLINDER HEAD ASSEMBLY	B14
REMOVING AND REPLACING THE VALVES	B15
RENEWING THE VALVE GUIDES	B16
DECARBONISING	B17
RE-SEATING THE VALVES	B18
REMOVING AND REPLACING THE CYLINDER BLOCK AND TAPPETS	B19
INSPECTING THE TAPPETS AND GUIDE BLOCKS	B20
RENEWING THE TAPPET GUIDE BLOCKS	B21
REMOVING AND REFITTING THE PISTONS	B22
REMOVING AND REPLACING THE PISTON RINGS	B23
INSPECTING THE PISTONS AND CYLINDER BORES	B24
TABLE OF SUITABLE REBORE SIZES	B25
PISTON IDENTIFICATION	B26
RENEWING THE SMALL END BUSHES	B27
REMOVING AND REPLACING THE CONTACT BREAKER	B28
IGNITION TIMING—INITIAL PROCEDURE	B29
IGNITION TIMING WHERE A STROBOSCOPE IS NOT AVAILABLE	B30
IGNITION TIMING BY STROBOSCOPE	B31
REMOVING AND REPLACING THE TIMING COVER	B32
REMOVING AND REPLACING THE OIL PUMP	B33
EXTRACTING AND REFITTING THE VALVE TIMING PINIONS	B34
VALVE TIMING	B35
DISMANTLING AND REASSEMBLING THE CRANKCASE ASSEMBLY	B36
STRIPPING AND REASSEMBLING THE CRANKSHAFT ASSEMBLY	B37
REFITTING THE CONNECTING RODS	B38
INSPECTING THE CRANKCASE COMPONENTS	B39
RENEWING THE MAIN BEARINGS	B40
RENEWING THE CAMSHAFT BUSHES	B41
REMOVING AND REFITTING TACHOMETER DRIVE	B42

ENGINE

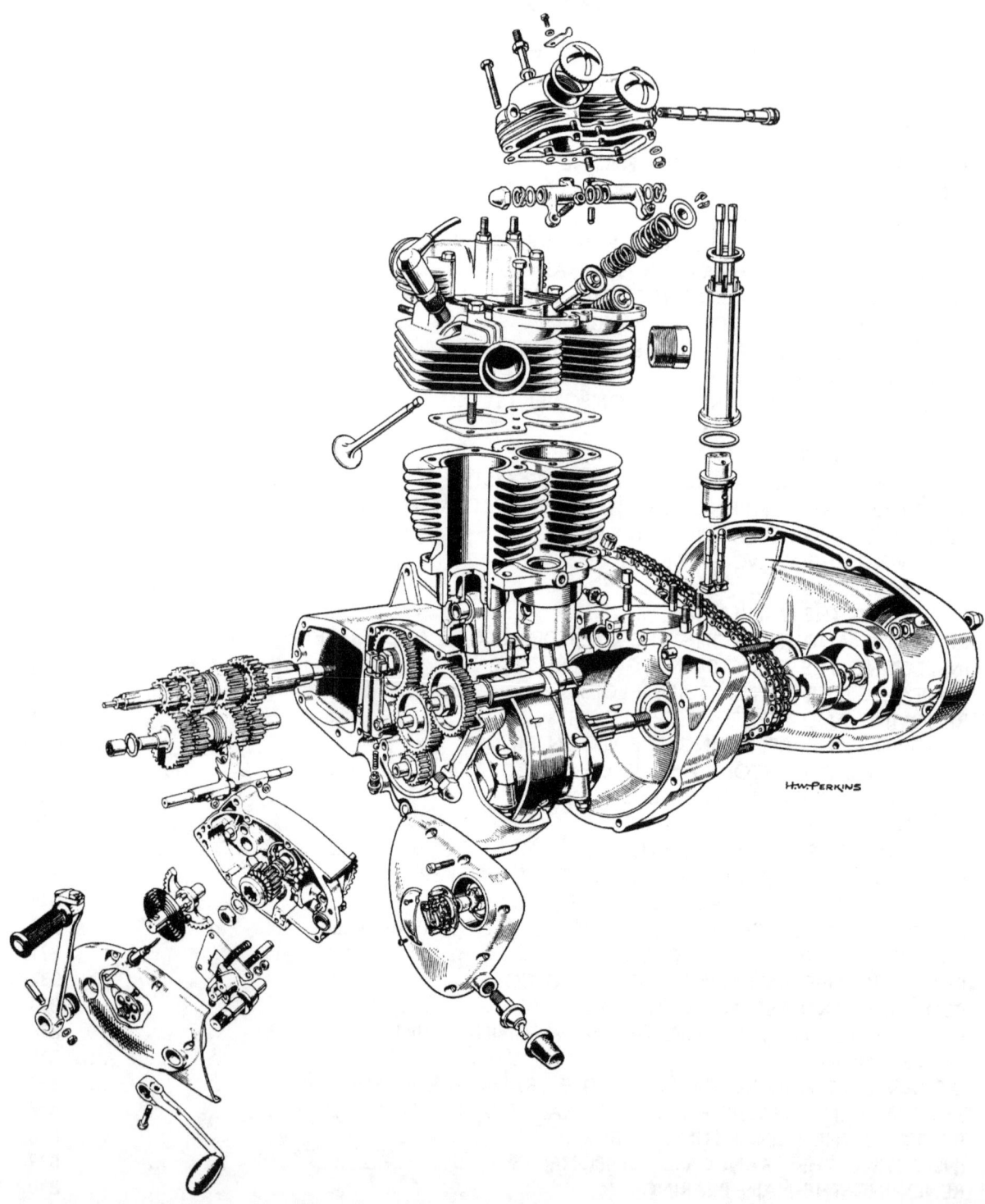

Fig. B1. Exploded view of 650 c.c. engine gearbox unit

ENGINE B

DESCRIPTION

The engine is of unit construction having two aluminium alloy mating crankcase halves, the gearbox housing being an integral part of the right half-crankcase and the primary chain case an integral part of the left half-crankcase.

The aluminium alloy cylinder head has cast in Austenitic valve seat inserts, and houses the overhead valves, which are operated by rocker arms housed in detachable alloy rocker boxes. Four aluminium alloy push rods operate the rocker arms, which are each fitted with adjusters, accessible when the rocker box inspection caps are removed.

The aluminium alloy die cast pistons each have two compression rings and one oil scraper ring. The connecting rods are of H Section in RR56 Hiduminium alloy, with detachable caps, and incorporate steel-backed renewable "shell" bearings. Each of the connecting rod caps is machined from a steel stamping and held in position by means of two high tensile steel bolts, which are tightened to a pre-determined extension figure to give the correct working clearance of the bearings on the crankshaft journals.

The inlet and exhaust camshafts operate in sintered bronze bushes which are housed transversely in the upper part of the crankcase. The inlet and exhaust camshafts are driven by a train of timing gears from the right end of the crankshaft. The inlet camshaft also operates the oil pump and rotary breather valve disc, whilst the exhaust camshaft drives the adjustable contact breaker, which is fitted with an automatic advance and retard unit, and the tachometer gearbox (when fitted).

The two-throw crankshaft has a detachable shrunk-on cast-iron flywheel which is held in position by three high tensile steel bolts, locked by the use of "TRIUMPH LOCTITE" sealant and tightened to a pre-determined torque figure.

The big end bearings are lubricated at pressure with oil which travels along drillings in the crankcase and crankshaft from the double plunger oil pump: oil pressure in the lubrication system is governed by means of the oil pressure release valve situated at the front of the engine, adjacent to the timing cover.

The cylinder barrel is made from a high-grade cast-iron and houses the press-fit tappet guide blocks.

Power from the engine is transmitted through the engine sprocket and primary chain to the shock absorbing clutch unit and four speed gearbox. Primary chain tension is governed by an adjustable rubber-pad chain tensioner which is immersed in the primary chain oil bath.

The electrical generator set consists of a rotor, which is fitted to the left end of the crankshaft, and an encapsulated six coil stator which is mounted on three pillar bolts inside the primary chain housing.

Carburation is by twin Amal carburetters with integral float chamber. The TR6 and earlier 6T have only one such instrument.

SECTION B1

REMOVING AND REPLACING THE ENGINE UNIT

Turn the fuel tap to the "OFF" position and disconnect the feed pipes. Cut the fuel tank bolt-securing wire, then unscrew three fuel tank mounting bolts. Raise the fuel tank at the rear to remove it. On earlier models with the nacelle type head lamp the two rear nacelle securing screws will have to be removed to gain sufficient clearance for tank removal.

Remove the fuse from the holder or on earlier models disconnect the leads from the battery terminals and remove the "Lucar" connectors from the left and right ignition coils. Remove the top and bottom coil mounting bolts and distance pieces. The ignition coils will then be free to be removed. **Care should be taken not to damage the light alloy casing of the ignition coils: indentations caused to the outer casing may ultimately result in ignition failure.**

Unscrew the four nuts securing the torque stays to the cylinder head and remove the front and rear torque stay mounting bolts and distance pieces, then remove the torque stays.

Disconnect the speedometer cable from underneath the speedometer and remove any necessary frame clips so that the cable is free. On models of the nacelle type the headlamp unit will have to be removed to gain access to the underside of the speedometer. To do this, slacken the screw in the headlamp rim, adjacent to the speedometer dial, then carefully lever off the headlamp unit.

Disconnect the tachometer cable (if fitted) by unscrewing the union nut at the right angled drive gearbox shown in Fig. B2.

On earlier machines that are fitted with rear enclosure panels, remove the two front panel junction screws and unscrew the two domed nuts from both the left and right panels. Finally, unscrew two nuts securing the panels just below the rear of the fuel tank, then remove both panels. Remove the distance piece from each of the engine plates and place them in safe keeping.

Unscrew the securing nuts and withdraw the carburetter. Note that there is a spring washer under each of the four nuts, on the twin carburetter models. On models fitted with one carburetter slacken the clamping screw and remove the air cleaner. Remove any necessary cable clips and place the carburetter(s) well clear of the engine in a safe position.

Unscrew the two domed nuts from the rocker spindles and disconnect the rocker oil feed pipe. Care should be taken not to bend the pipe excessively as this may ultimately result in the pipe fracturing.

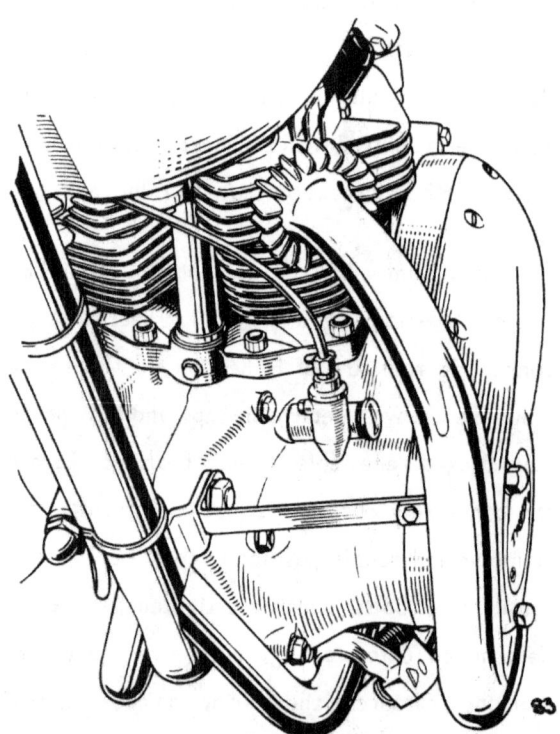

Fig. B2. Tachometer drive cable and adaptor

To drain the oil tank remove the drain plug from the base of the oil tank and allow the oil to drain for approximately 15 minutes. The oil feed pipe and return pipe should then be disconnected from the base of the oil tank. On earlier models the drain plug is absent, and in this case the oil tank should be drained by unscrewing the union nut and disconnecting the oil feed pipe. Where the oil pipe rubber connectors are secured by means of circular clips, the clips should be slackened prior to disconnecting the rubber connectors.

ENGINE   B

At this stage it is advisable to drain the oil from the gearbox and primary chaincase by removing the respective drain plugs. The sump should also be drained; this can be done by unscrewing the hexagon-headed filter drain plug situated underneath the engine adjacent to the bottom engine mounting lug. (See Fig. A3, reference No. 4).

Slacken off the clutch adjustment at the handlebar, withdraw the rubber seal from the clutch abutment at the gearbox and unscrew the abutment. Detach the slotted plug on the outer cover. Slip the bottom nipple of the clutch cable free of the operating arm. On earlier models there is no inspection cap on the outer cover. In such cases the cable lower nipple fits into a slotted barrel nipple revealed as the abutment is unscrewed.

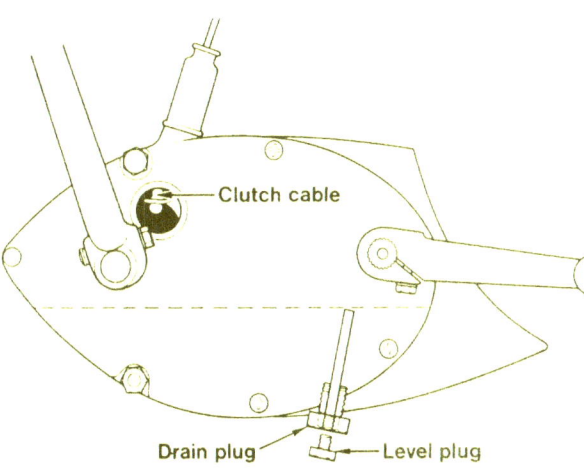

Fig. B3. Clutch cable adjustment and gearbox drain plug

Slacken the left and right finned clips and silencer clip bolts and remove the forward exhaust pipe nuts and bolts. Drive the exhaust pipes free with a hide hammer.

On earlier models where siamesed pipes are fitted, the pipe junction clip should also be slackened.

On earlier models, where the footrests are fitted direct onto the frame, underneath the engine, it will be necessary to remove them. To do this first remove the brake pedal and swing it clear. Unscrew the nuts from the two bolts securing the footrests, then give each footrest a sharp tap in a downward direction.

Remove the connecting link from the rear chain and withdraw the chain from mesh with the gearbox sprocket, then disconnect the 2 generator leads underneath the engine (3 snap connectors on earlier models or 5 in the case of a machine with A.C. ignition).

To avoid damage to the chainguard, when the engine is being removed, it should be moved rearwards several inches. This can be achieved by slackening the rear chainguard bolt and removing the front securing bolt. The guard should then be lifted upwards and rearwards until it is well clear.

Remove four bolts and a nut securing each of the left and right rear engine mounting plates and withdraw the plates. Remove a nut and washer from one end of each of the front and bottom engine mounting studs, the engine should now be loose in the frame.

Finally to gain clearance for removal of the engine unit from the LEFT, remove the following:—

(1) The two right-side rocker box-to-torque stay bolts.

(2) The two right-side screws securing the front and rear rocker cap retainer springs.

(3) The left side lower bolts securing the rear frame to the front frame.

If the front and lower engine mounting studs are now withdrawn the engine will be free to be removed. It is recommended that removing the engine should be aided by the use of a hoist or the help of a second operator, due to the engine weight, which is approximately 135 lbs.

Should difficulty be experienced in removing the engine, an easier removal can be facilitated by first detaching the rocker boxes. For details of this see Section B2.

Replacement is a reversal of the above instructions, but do not forget to refit the bolts in (1), (2) and (3) above when the engine is loosely positioned. When replacing the ignition coils, remember that the connector terminal end of each coil faces towards the rear of the machine. To ensure that the wiring harness is re-connected correctly refer to the appropriate wiring diagram in Section H19.

Do not forget to fit the distance pieces on the coil mounting bolts, torque stay mounting bolts, and, in particular, the lower engine mounting stud: also, attention is called to the distance pieces fitted to the bottom panel mounting studs on the left and right of the machine in the case of models fitted with the rear enclosure panels.

For the correct grade and quantity of lubricant for the engine, gearbox and chaincase, see Section A2.

SECTION B2

REMOVING AND REPLACING THE ROCKER BOXES

Disconnect the leads from the battery terminals and remove the fuel tank as detailed in Section E1.

Disconnect the high tension cables and wiring harness from the left and right ignition coils. Remove the top and bottom coil mounting bolts and distance pieces. The ignition coils will then be free to be removed. Care should be taken not to damage the light alloy casings of the ignition coils as indentations may ultimately result in ignition failure.

Unscrew the four nuts securing the torque stays to the rocker boxes and remove the front and rear torque stay mounting bolts and distance pieces. The torque stays should then be removed.

Unscrew the two domed nuts from the rocker spindles and disconnect the rocker oil feed pipe. Care should be taken not to bend the pipe excessively as this may ultimately result in a fracture.

Remove the rocker inspection caps.

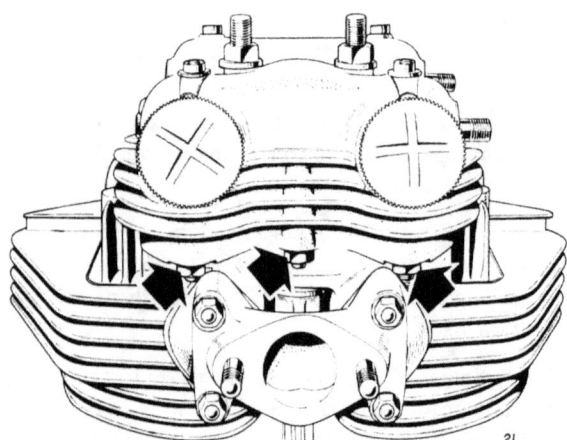

Fig. B4. Rocker box securing nuts

Unscrew three nuts from the studs fitted to the underside of the exhaust rocker box. Remove the outer exhaust rocker box securing bolts and unscrew the central cylinder head bolts. (Note that, at this stage the rocker box may rise slightly, due to a valve spring being compressed). The exhaust rocker box is now free to be removed. The procedure is the same for the inlet rocker box, but the two outer securing nuts indicated in Fig. B4 may not have sufficient clearance to be removed; if this is the case, they should be initially slackened and finally unscrewed at the last stage, prior to removal, when the rocker box can be lifted slightly.

Care should be taken to collect the six plain washers which are fitted (one beneath each of the underside securing nuts), as they sometimes adhere to the cylinder head flanges and may be subsequently lost.

After completion of the rocker box removal operation, the push rods should be withdrawn and stored in the order of their removal so that they can be replaced in their original positions.

The junction surfaces of the rocker boxes and cylinder head should be cleaned for reassembly, by means of a soft metal scraper.

Replacement is a reversal of the above instructions, but remember to fit new gaskets between the rocker boxes and cylinder head.

When replacing the push rods place a small amount of grease into the bottom cup of each of the push rods, then locate the push rods, one at a time, by means of feeling the engagement of the tappet ball end and the push rod cup, and then testing the resistance to lifting caused by suction between the dome of the tappet and push rod cup. When the push rods are correctly located, remove the sparking plugs and turn the engine over until the INLET push rods are level and at the bottom of their stroke. The inlet rocker box should then be assembled. Repeat this procedure for the exhaust rocker box.

Remember that the four central cylinder head through bolts should be fitted first and that the underside nuts are tightened last. Before finally clamping the rocker boxes in position, check that the valves are being operated by turning the engine over slowly.

Do not forget the distance pieces which fit over the engine torque stay mounting bolts and coil mounting bolts.

NOTE: It can be seen that the four double ended bolts also serve to retain the cylinder head and should be tightened first. The correct torque figures are given in GENERAL DATA, and sequence, in Fig B12.

Before fitting the rocker oil feed pipe the four copper washers which fit over the rocker spindle should be annealed by quenching in water from cherry red heat. Finally, remove any scale that may have formed. Annealing softens the copper thus giving it better sealing qualities.

ENGINE

SECTION B3
INSPECTING THE PUSHRODS

When the pushrods have been removed, examine them for worn, chipped or loose end-cups; also check that the push rod is true by rolling it slowly on a truly flat surface (such as a piece of plate glass).

Bent pushrods are found to be the cause of excessive mechanical noise and loss of power and should be straightened if possible, or, preferably, renewed.

SECTION B4
STRIPPING AND REASSEMBLING THE ROCKER BOXES

Removal of the rocker spindles from the rocker boxes is best achieved by driving out, using a soft metal drift. When the spindles are removed the rocker arms and washers can be withdrawn. All parts should be thoroughly cleaned in paraffin (kerosene) and the oil drillings in the spindles and rocker arms should be cleaned with a jet of compressed air.

Remove the oil seals from the rocker spindles and renew them.

If it is required to renew the rocker ball pins, the old ones should be removed by means of a suitable drift. New ones should then be pressed in with the drilled flat towards the rocker spindle.

To ensure an oil-tight seal between the rocker box and cylinder head, in cases where an oil leak cannot be cured by fitting new gaskets, the joint surface of the rocker box should be linished to remove any irregularities.

An effective linish can be achieved by first extracting the rocker box studs (two nuts locked together on the stud should facilitate an easy removal) then lightly rubbing the junction surface on a sheet of emery cloth mounted on a truly flat surface (such as a piece of plate glass).

Assembly of the rocker spindles into the rocker boxes is assisted by the use of the oil seal compressor D2221.

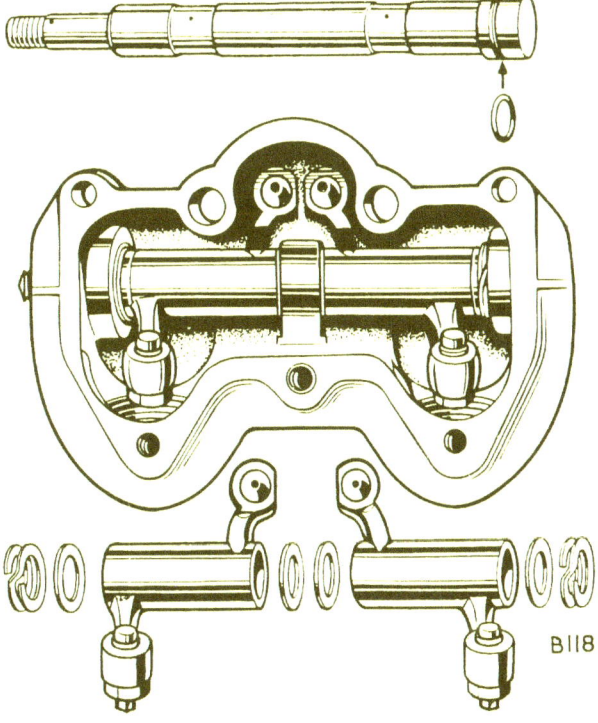

Fig. B5. Rocker box assembly

The following method of assembly incorporates the use of a home made alignment bar, which can be made from a $\frac{7}{16}$ in. dia. bolt x 6 in. long by grinding a taper at one end.

Before reassembly, note that, unlike earlier models, the four plain washers on each rocker spindle are all of the same size.

ENGINE

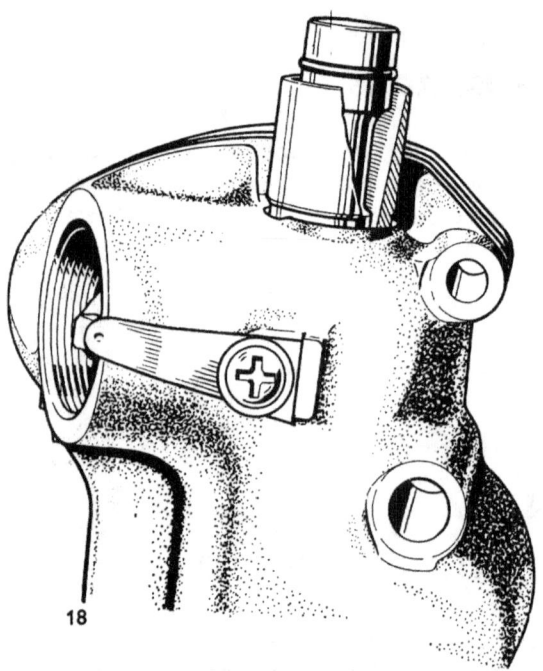

Fig. B6. Refitting the rocker spindle

Smear two plain washers with grease and place them one either side of the centre bearing boss. Place the left rocker arm in position, bringing it into line with the alignment tool and slide a plain washer and a spring washer (in the order shown in Fig. B5) into position. Carefully repeat this procedure for the other rocker arm and spring washer and slide the last plain washer into position. Finally bring each rocker arm in turn into line with the alignment bar.

Lubricate the spindle with oil and slide it (complete with oil seal) through the compressor (D2221) and as far as possible into the rocker box, finally tapping it home with a hammer and soft metal drift (see Fig. B6).

SECTION B5

ADJUSTING THE VALVE ROCKER CLEARANCES

The valve rocker clearance should be checked and adjusted if necessary every 3,000 miles (4,800 Km.). The correct clearance, for the type of camshaft employed, ensures that a high valve operating efficiency is maintained and that the valves attain their maximum useful lives. The correct clearances are given in "General Data".

NOTE: Adjustments should only be made when the engine is COLD.

Access to the rocker arm adjuster screws and locknuts is gained by removing the slotted inspection caps from the rocker boxes. Adjustment is aided by the toolkit spanners D370 ($\frac{3}{16}$ in. Whit, spanner) and D362 (tappet key).

First, remove the left and right sparking plugs to relieve compression, then slacken the four lock nuts securing the square-headed adjuster screws. Slowly turn the engine over until the left exhaust valve is fully open; the right tappet is then resting on the base-circle diameter of the cam-form opposite to the cam-lobe; the clearance for the right exhaust valve can then be set (see Fig. B7). Carefully turn the adjuster screw in the required direction until the correct feeler gauge just slides between the valve stem and the screw. Re-check the gap after the locknut has been tightened.

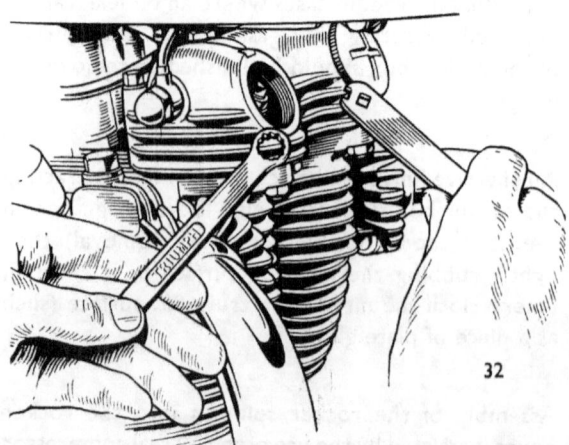

Fig. B7. Adjusting the valve rocker clearance

ENGINE

Repeat this procedure for the left exhaust valve and both of the inlet valves, ensuring that the clearances are in accordance with those given in "General Data".

An alternative way of setting the valve rocker clearance which is approximate but sufficient when carefully carried out, is that of using the pitch of the thread on the adjuster screw as a vernier scale.

The thread is $\frac{5}{16}$ in. x 26 C.E.I. hence the pitch is ·038 in. Therefore, $\frac{1}{4}$ turn of the adjuster screw represents ·010 in. approx.

If the adjuster screw is initially turned until it is finger tight on the valve stem, so that the rocker arm can only be moved sideways; then, by slackening the screw $\frac{1}{4}$ turn, a clearance of approximately ·010 in. will result. Similarly, slackening the screw $\frac{1}{8}$ turn will give a clearance of ·005 in.

SECTION B6
REMOVING AND REPLACING THE AIR CLEANER

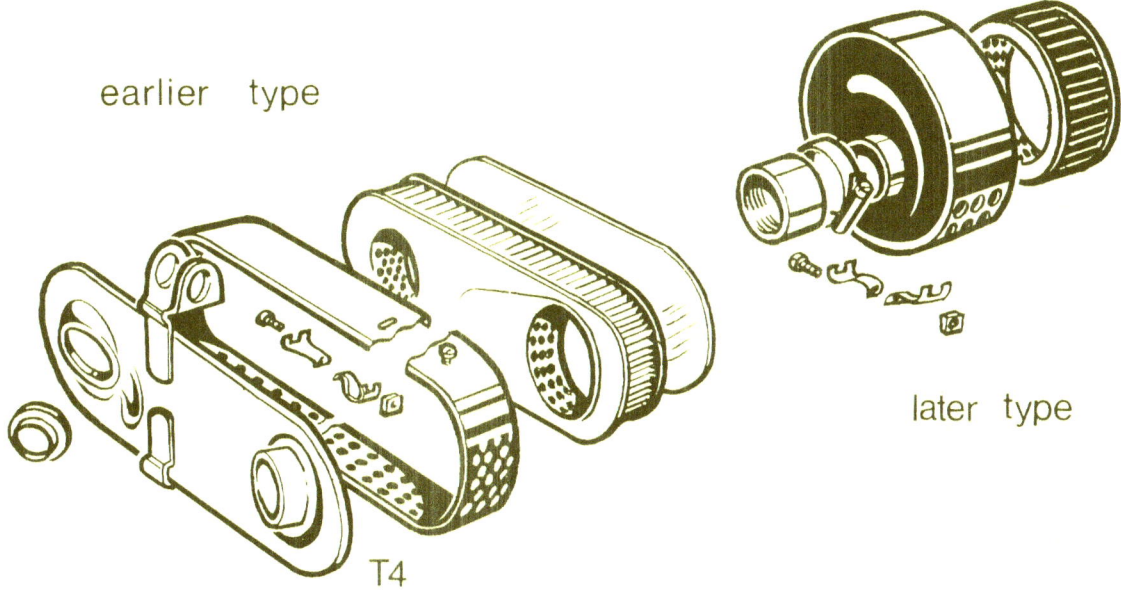

Fig. B8. Air cleaners

The T120 has separate air filters of a similar type to that used on the TR6. These have clip fittings or in the case of concentric carburetters are threaded directly on to the carburetter bodies. In the case of a TR6 the switch panel should be removed (Section E3). Then, when the central circular clip is slackened it should be possible to slide the air cleaner off the carburetter adaptor, and withdraw it. On earlier models with one carburetter where rear enclosure panels are fitted it will first be necessary to remove the right panel. This is done by unscrewing the two front panel junction screws, two domed nuts and a nut just below the rear of the fuel tank. If difficulty is encountered it is possible to remove the air cleaner by dismantling it. To do this remove the screwed clip which secures the outer perforated case, then remove the back plate, filter and finally, slide the front plate from over the carburetter adaptor.

Dry felt and coarse felt elements should be carefully rinsed in paraffin (kerosene) and allowed to drain thoroughly.

Under no circumstances should the filter be soaked with oil. Paper elements should be blown clean with a jet of compressed air.

Replacement is the reversal of the above instructions but do not forget to tighten the perforated case clip and the circular clip securing the air cleaner to the carburetter.

The earlier T120 model was fitted with a combined air cleaner for some markets, and the Spare Parts Catalogue lists the parts required. This type of air cleaner had a paper element which should be removed and cleaned with a jet of compressed air, or renewed, as necessary. **This paper element should not be washed or immersed in any liquid.**

SECTION B7

CARBURETTER—DESCRIPTION

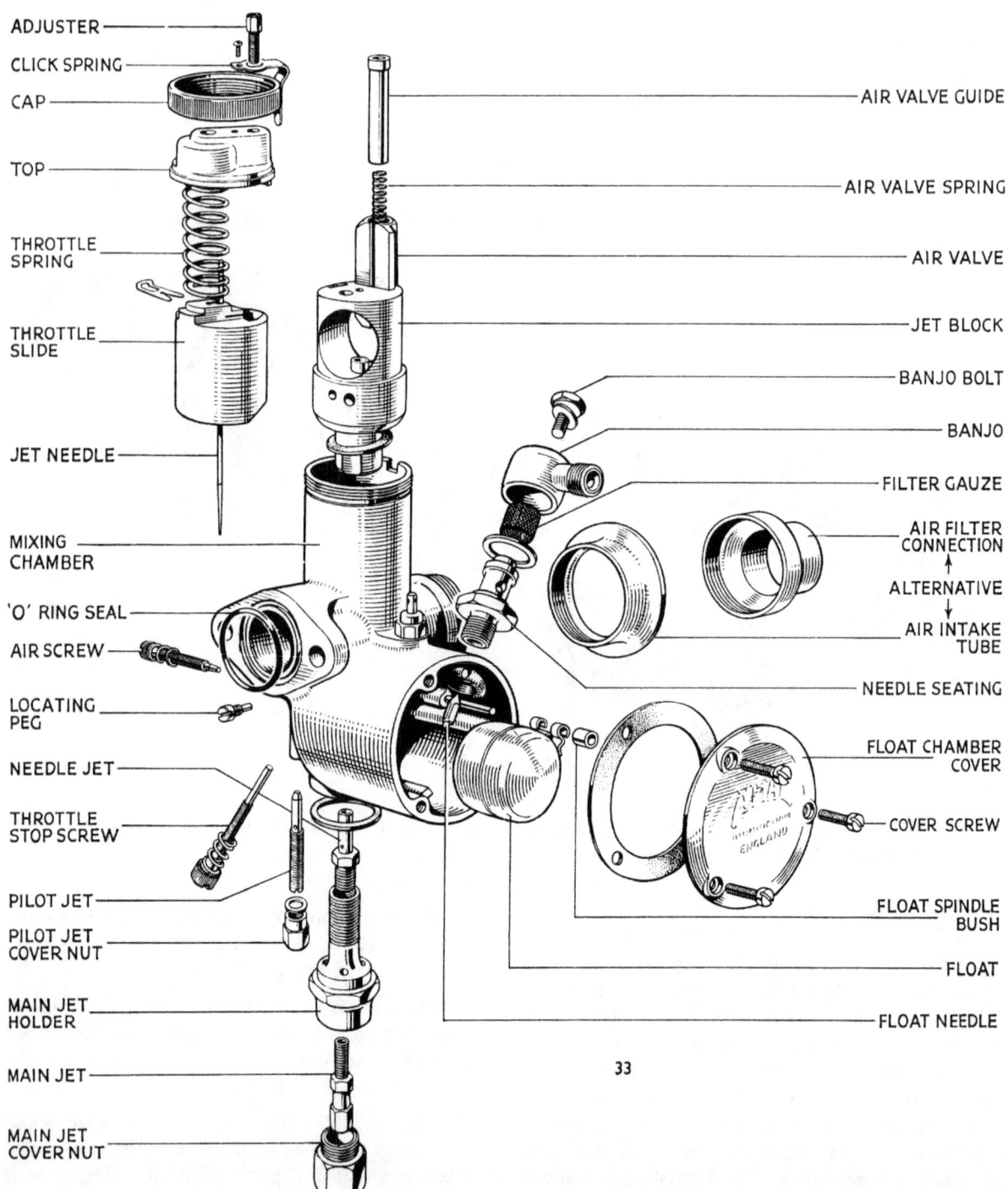

Fig. B9. Exploded view of carburetter

ENGINE

CONCENTRIC CARBURETTER TYPE 900
DESCRIPTION

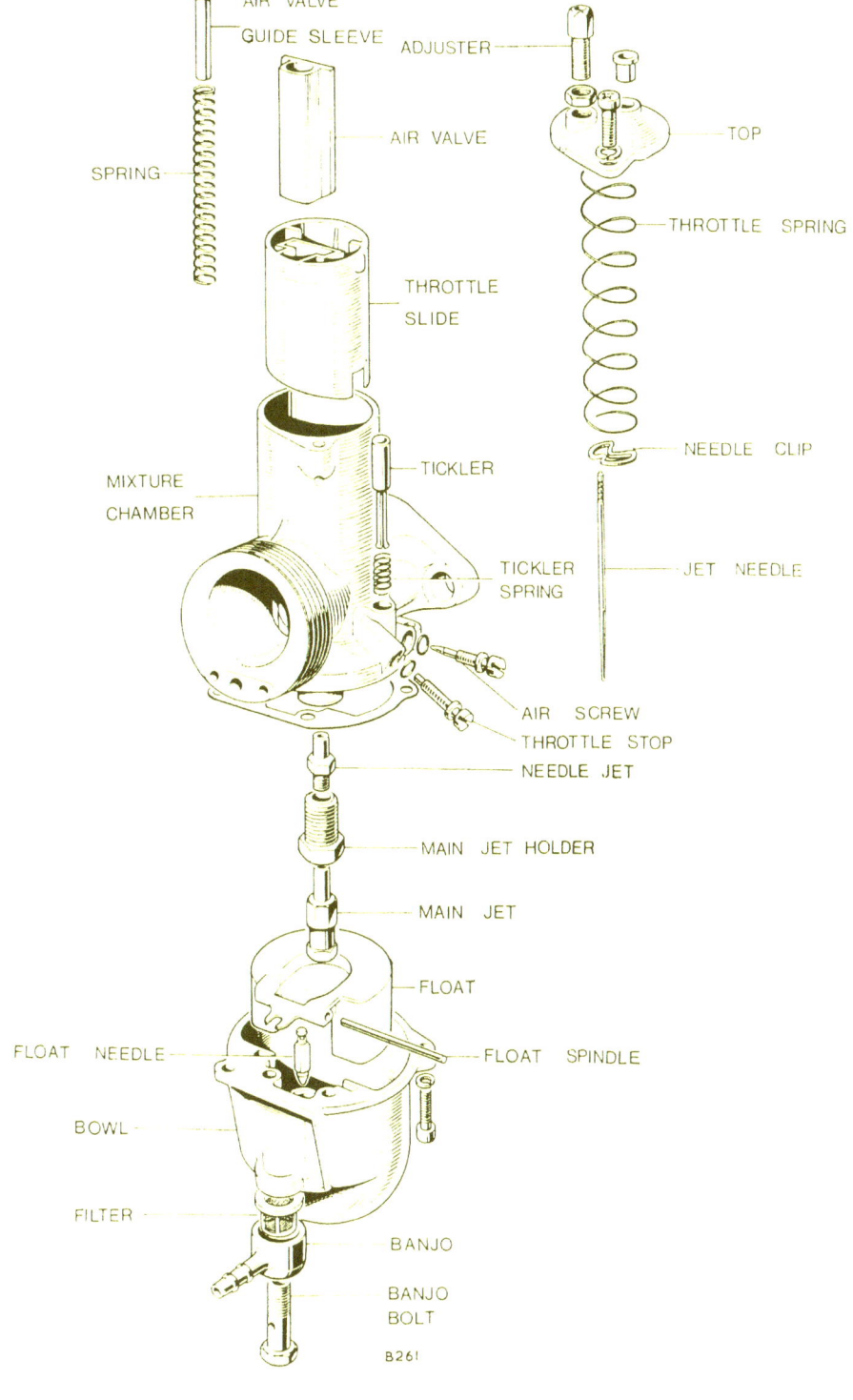

Fig. B9B Exploded view of carburetter

ENGINE

The T120 and TR6 are each fitted with Amal carburetters which are fully adjustable.
Briefly, they operate in the following way:
When the engine is idling, mixture is supplied from the sealed pilot jet system, then as the throttle slide is raised, via the pilot by-pass. With the throttle just opening the mixture is controlled by the tapered needle working in the needle jet and finally by the size of the main jet. The pilot system is supplied by a pilot jet, fitted into the carburetter body. The main jet does not feed direct into the mixing chamber but discharges through the needle jet into the primary air chamber and the fuel goes from there as a rich petrol-air mixture through the primary air choke into the main air choke.

This primary air choke has a compensating action in conjunction with bleed holes in the needle jet, which serves the double purpose of air-compensating the mixture from the needle jet, and allowing the fuel to provide a well, outside and around the needle jet, which is available for snap acceleration. The idling mixture is controlled by the pilot air screw which governs the amount of air that is allowed to mix with the fuel at tick-over speeds. The throttle stop screw is used to adjust the slide so that the throttle is kept open sufficiently to keep the engine running at a slow tick-over, when the twist-grip is closed.

SECTION B8

REMOVING AND REPLACING THE CARBURETTER

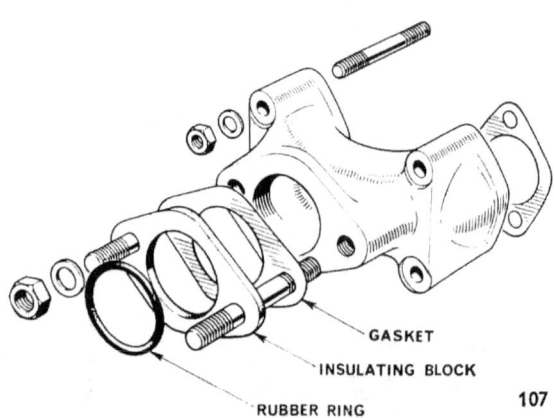

**Fig. B10A Manifold assembly
Single carburetter models**

Due to the carburetter top securing screws being inaccessible with the petrol tank fitted, it will be necessary to dismount the carburetter before removing the top for any reason.

First remove the air cleaner(s) as in Section B6. Ensure both taps are in the "off" position and disconnect the fuel pipes at the taps beneath the rear of the tank. Unscrew the two carburetter flange securing nuts (self-locking) then carefully withdraw the carburetter from over its mounting studs. In the case of twin carburetter models, lift off the cups and "O" rings shown in Fig. B10B The carburetters can then be lifted off the mounting studs.

To achieve this the carburetter should be tilted upwards so that it clears the frame. As the carburetter is lowered, the top can be removed by taking out the two Phillips headed screws. Unless the top, slides etc. are to be removed from the cables they can be wrapped carefully in a piece of cloth until the carburetter is to be refitted.

Machines prior to DU.66246 are fitted with a monobloc type of carburetter. The procedure for its removal is similar to above, except for the mixing chamber top. This item is secured by a screwed ring, and spring clip.

On single carburetter models the insulating block, paper washer and rubber "O" ring seal should be examined for damage which might impair their sealing qualities. If there is the slightest doubt about their serviceability, they should be renewed.

When replacing the carburetter, great care should be taken to ensure that the slide does not become damaged as it is lowered into the mixture chamber. The peg at the top right of the slide locates in a corresponding groove in the carburetter body. Care must be taken when replacing the slide as the needle must be located in the needle jet, before the slide can be positioned in the mixing chamber. When the slide has been assembled satisfactorily, refit the mixing chamber top, two screws and lock washers.

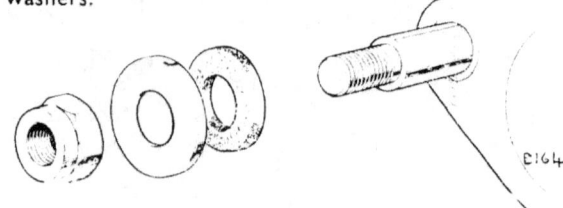

**Fig. B10B Manifold order of assembly
Twin carburetter models**

In the case of twin carburetter models, no insulating block and paper washer are used. On these models, fit the "O" ring seal and carburetter, followed by the small insulating "O" rings and cups (see Fig. B10B) over the locating studs. Care should be taken not to overtighten the two carburetter securing nuts.

ENGINE B

SECTION B9

STRIPPING AND REASSEMBLING THE CONCENTRIC CARBURETTER

When the carburetter is removed, disconnect the slide assembly from the throttle cable. To do this pull back the return spring and remove the needle and needle clip. With the spring still retracted, push the cable through the slide and when the nipple is clear, across the figure of eight slot. The slide and return spring can now be removed.

To remove the air valve, push the valve and spring along with air cable until the cable nipple protrudes sufficiently out of its counterbore to be pushed out of the slot. The cable and spring can now be pulled clear of the valve.

Unscrew the petrol pipe banjo connection and remove the banjo and nylon filter.

Unscrew two Phillips screws and remove the float bowl. The nylon float, spindle and triangular needle can now be withdrawn.

Unscrew the jet holder which will allow the main jet to be removed.

Unscrew the air adjusting screw and throttle stop screw.

Thoroughly clean all parts in petrol (gasoline) several times and dry with compressed air, or a hand pump, to remove any particles of dirt. Any external deposits are best removed with the use of a light wire brush.

Reassemble in the reverse order, referring to Fig. B9 for guidance.

When refitting the float and needle valve, make certain that the recess on the valve is properly located in the "U" shaped slot in the float. Replace the float bowl sealing washer, and if necessary the two rubber "O" rings fitted to the adjusting screws

STRIPPING AND REASSEMBLING THE MONOBLOC CARBURETTER

When the carburetter is removed, disconnect the slide assembly from the throttle cable. To do this, first remove the needle retaining spring clip, then compress the slide return spring, pushing the nipple of the throttle cable down through the slot until it is free.

Unscrew three slotted screws and withdraw the float chamber cover and remove the float spindle bush and float; then withdraw the triangular sectioned float needle.

Unscrew the banjo bolt which secures the fuel pipe banjo connector to the float needle seating block and withdraw the banjo, filter and junction washers. Unscrew the needle seating block. Unscrew the tickler body then withdraw the tickler and spring.

Unscrew the air screw and throttle stop screw, then the main jet cover nut from the bottom of the body.

Unscrew the main jet, main jet holder and needle jet. To release the jet block reinsert the main jet holder, until a few threads are engaged then tap it with a hide hammer. This will release the jet block upwards and through the carburetter body.

Unscrew the pilot jet cover, and unscrew the pilot jet. All that remains to be removed then is the hexagonal locating peg, the end of which can be seen protruding within the mixing chamber.

Thoroughly clean all parts in petrol (gasolene). Deposits on the carburetter body are best removed by a light grade wire brush. It is advisable to wash the parts several times each in a quantity of clean petrol, to avoid particles of dirt remaining. Allow the parts to drain, preferably using a jet of compressed air from such as a hand pump to ensure that oil holes and drillings are from from blockage.

ENGINE

Inspect the component parts for wear and check that the jets are in accordance with the recommended sizes given in GENERAL DATA.

Apart from one or two points that are mentioned below, reassembly is a reversal of the above instructions, referring to Fig. B9B for guidance.

Do not refit any fibre washer that looks unserviceable. It is advisable to purchase replacement washers before removing the carburetter.

When replacing the jet block, ensure that the fibre washer is in position; align the location flat in the jet block with the locating peg in the carburetter housing and drive the block home.

Finally, note that the float spindle bush fits on the outside end of the spindle, and that the float pressure pad is uppermost so that the float needle rests on it.

SECTION B10
INSPECTING THE CARBURETTER COMPONENTS
(CONCENTRIC AND MONOBLOC)

The only parts liable to show wear after considerable mileage are the throttle valve slide, mixing chamber and the air slide (if fitted).

(1) Inspect the throttle valve slide for excessive scoring to the front area and check the extent of wear on the rear slide face. If wear is apparent the slide should be renewed. In this case, be sure to replace the slide with the correct degree of cut-away (see "General Data").

(2) Examine the air valve for excessive wear and check that it is not actually worn through at any part. Check the fit of the air valve in the jet block. Ensure that the air valve spring is serviceable by inspecting the coils for wear.

(3) Inspect the throttle return spring for efficiency and check that it has not lost compressive strength by measuring its length and comparing it to the figure given in "General Data".

(4) Check the needle jet for wear or possible scoring and carefully examine the tapered end of the needle for similar signs. Check the correct needle is in use. The needle for petrol is marked above the top groove "000". The needle for alcohol is marked "Z".

(5) In the case of monobloc carburetters examine the float needle for efficiency by inserting it into the inverted float needle seating block, pouring a small amount of petrol (gasoline) into the aperture surrounding the needle and checking it for leakage.

(6) Check the float bowl joint surface for flatness and flatten if necessary on emery paper on a perfectly flat surface.

(7) Ensure that the float does not leak by shaking it to see if it contains any fuel. Do not attempt to repair a damaged float. A new one can be purchased for a small cost.

ENGINE   B

(8) Check the petrol filter, which fits into the petrol pipe banjo, for any possible damage to the mesh. Ensure that the filter has not parted from its supporting structure, thus enabling the petrol (gasolene) to by-pass it un-filtered.

(9) Concentric float carburetters have a pressed-in pilot jet which is not removable. If the jet becomes blocked the machine will be hard to start and will not run at low speeds. This can be cleared by blocking the low speed air passage at the bell end of the carburetter removing the pilot air screw and using a jet of air at this point.

SECTION B11
CARBURETTER ADJUSTMENTS

Throttle Stop Screw. This screw, which is situated on the right side of the carburetter (L.H. in case of current T120 left hand carburetter) sloping upwards and is fitted with a friction ring, should be set to open the throttle sufficiently to keep the engine running at a slow tick-over, when the twist-grip is closed. Monobloc instruments have locking springs rather than friction rings.

Pilot Air Screw. To set the idling mixture, this screw, which is situated on the right side, is also fitted with a friction ring or locking spring, and should be screwed in to enrich the tick-over mixture or outwards to weaken it. As a guide to its approximate required position, screw it in fully, then unscrew it approximately $2\frac{1}{2}$ turns.

The screw controls the suction on the pilot jet by metering the amount of air which mixes with the petrol.

Needle and Needle Jet. Carburation is governed by the cut-away and needle jet in varying degrees from when the throttle is just open to when it is approximately $\frac{3}{4}$ full throttle. The needle jet orifice is governed by the position of the needle. The needle position should not be altered from its specified setting without specialist advice.

Throttle Valve Cutaway. The amount of cut-away to the bottom of the throttle valve slide is indicated by a number marked on the slide, e.g. $930/3\frac{1}{2}$ means throttle type 930 with number $3\frac{1}{2}$ cutaway; a larger number such as 4 means that the throttle valve slide has a slightly larger cutaway and consequently gives a weaker mixture during the period of throttle opening through which a cutaway is effective, i.e. from just open to approximately $\frac{1}{4}$ throttle. Similarly, 3 indicates a slightly smaller cutaway and a slightly stronger mixture.

Jet Sizes. The recommended jet sizes are given in "General Data" and changing from these to any other size it is left entirely to the discretion of the rider. The main jet is operative from approximately $\frac{3}{4}$ to full throttle, this is when the needle jet orifice ceases to have any reduction effect on the petrol flow.

B ENGINE

SECTION B12
TWIN CARBURETTER ARRANGEMENT

DESCRIPTION

Twin carburetters are fitted to T120 and T120R machines. There is a balance pipe fitted between the inlet manifolds to improve tickover.

THROTTLE CABLE

On U.K. and General Export models a "one into two" throttle cable is used. The single throttle cable from the twistgrip enters a junction box where it is fitted into a slide. The twin shorter carburetter cables are fitted to the other side of the junction box slide. Both the slide and junction box being made of plastic require no maintenance. To remove the throttle cable the petrol tank must be lifted to release the cable to frame clip.

A similar cable arrangement is used for air slide operation.

SETTING TWIN CARBURETTERS

The twin carburetters fitted to the T120 and T120R may require synchronisation and a simple method is as follows: First adjust the cables from the junction box so that they have the minimum of free play.

Now start the motor and take off one plug lead and then adjust the pilot air screw and throttle stop screw in the OPPOSITE carburetter until the motor runs regularly. Replace the plug lead and repeat the process similarly for the other carburetter. With both plug leads replaced the tickover will be too fast and the stop screws should be lowered simultaneously until correct. It is most important the throttle slides lift simultaneously or the motor will run roughly, particularly when accelerating.

SECTION B13
REMOVING AND REPLACING THE EXHAUST SYSTEM

T120, T120R, TR6, TR6R

To remove the exhaust system slacken the exhaust pipe to silencer clamp bolts. Remove the self locking screws and cruciform headed screw from the front bracket.

Slacken the four clamp bolts at the front cross-over pipe and slide in the outer sleeves, tapping them with a rubber mallet if necessary. Slacken the finned cooling ring clamp bolts and drive the exhaust pipes clear of the exhaust adaptors.

Remove the silencer to exhaust pipe clips complete with bracing strap and remove the bolt, spring washer and nuts from back silencer hanger bracket. The silencers are now free to be removed.

To refit the exhaust system, first fit the silencers with the brackets inboard of the hangers. Loosely assemble the bolts, spring washers and nuts (the bolts from the inside). Loosely assemble the silencer forward clamp and bracing strap with the strap and nuts underneath. Offer the finned cooling rings over the exhaust pipes but do not tighten. Drive the exhaust pipes over the cylinder head stubs and into the silencers. Loosely assemble the front bottom exhaust stays to the exhaust pipes, the cruciform headed screws from the front and self locking nuts behind. Lift the cross-over pipe complete with sleeves into position. Slide the cross piece outer sleeves over the exhaust pipe "branches". Finally tighten all nuts and bolts securely.

ENGINE

TR6C MACHINES ONLY

To remove the exhaust system commence by removing the leg guard. This can be achieved by removing two screws and washers which screw into captive nuts. The leg guard retaining clips can now be withdrawn complete with the screws, and the leg guard removed.

It is advisable to remove the exhaust system in two sections, the first being the right and left exhaust pipes and brackets.

Slacken two bolts which secure the exhaust pipe rear stay, one bolt screws into each pipe, and remove one bolt and spring washers from the spacer at the top front engine mounting bolt on the left side rear engine plate. Slacken the finned cooling rings at the cylinder head, and slacken two exhaust pipe to "H" connector clips. Using a rubber mallet, drive the exhaust pipes forward off their stubs.

The second section to remove is the silencer assembly. This is simply a matter of removing one nut, spring washers and bolt from the upper mounting clips on the rear frame tube, and one nut, spring washer and bolt from the lower mounting point in the rear footrest mounting bracket. The assembly is now free to be removed.

If it is found necessary to dismantle the silencer assembly, reference should be made to Fig. B11 for guidance.

To replace the exhaust system, reposition the silencer assembly and replace the upper and lower retaining bolts, spring washers and nuts, noting that both bolts are fitted from the outside. It is not advisable to tighten these bolts at this stage. Ensure that the cooling rings are fitted to the cylinder head stubs, and replace both exhaust pipes, driving them into the silencers with a rubber mallet. Replace, but do not tighten the bolt and spring washers which secures the exhaust pipe bracket to the top front engine mounting bolt on the left side rear engine plate. Tighten the finned cooling rings, ensuring that both the rings and exhaust pipes are in contact with the cylinder head to avoid any gas leakage. Secure the clips which retain the exhaust pipes in the "H" connector at the silencers. Fully tighten all three exhaust pipe rear bracket bolts, and both the upper and lower silencer bracket bolts.

Finally refit the silencer leg guard. One screw, washer and clip should be fitted at the front of the leg guard, and screwed into the double curved bracket which is fitted from behind the exhaust pipes, and the rear screw, washer and clip should be attached to the fixed silencer bracket.

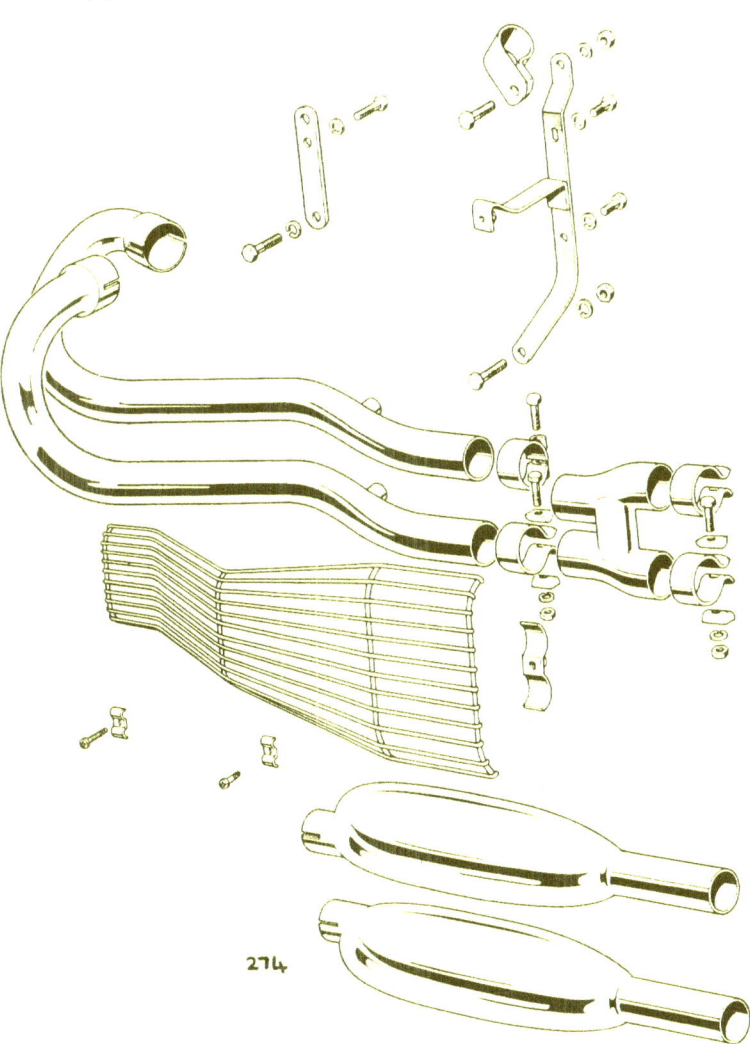

Fig. B11. Showing order of assembly of USA TR6C exhaust system

SECTION B14

REMOVING AND REFITTING THE CYLINDER HEAD ASSEMBLY

Proceed as detailed in Section B2 for removal of the rocker boxes and pushrods.

Remove the exhaust system as in Section B13.

Unscrew the left and right carburetter flange nuts and remove them complete with spring washers. Both carburetters should then be withdrawn from over the studs and placed well clear of the cylinder head. On models where one carburetter is fitted the manifold securing nuts should be unscrewed and the manifold withdrawn when the cylinder head is removed. Note that there is a plain washer under each of the four manifold securing nuts.

Unscrew the remaining five cylinder head bolts, a turn at a time, until the load has been released, and then remove the cylinder head, if necessary, sliding it forward to release the inlet manifold.

Remove the push rod cover tubes and note that it is essential to renew the rubber seals. Check for sharp edges on the corners of the top portion of the tappet guide blocks which could cut the new 'O' rings when reassembling. Use a file or emery cloth to smooth any such sharp edges.

The copper cylinder head gasket should be either renewed or reconditioned by annealing it to restore the sealing qualities of the copper. Annealing is achieved by heating the gasket to cherry-red heat and quenching it in water; finally, remove any scale that may have formed by means of a piece of fine grade emery cloth.

REFITTING THE CYLINDER HEAD

Ensure that the junction surfaces of the cylinder block, gasket and cylinder head are clean. Grease the gasket and place it in position (check that all 9 bolt holes are lined up), coat the tappet guide blocks with heavy grease and locate the push rod cover tubes (complete with top and bottom oil seals). Relieve any roughness at the push rod tube counterbores in the head.

Lower the cylinder head into position over the push rod cover tubes and fit the four outer cylinder head bolts finger tight, also, fit the central bolt finger tight.

Carefully rotate the crankshaft until both of the inlet push rods are at the bottom of their stroke, then lower the inlet rocker box into position, ensuring that the push rods are engaged correctly, then fit the two central cylinder head through bolts finger tight. Screw in the two outer inlet rocker box bolts and fit the three underside retaining nuts, with plain washers. Repeat this procedure for the exhaust rocker box.

Tighten the nine cylinder head bolts in the order given in Fig. B12 and to the torque settings given in "General Data". Finally tighten the remaining inlet and exhaust rocker box retaining nuts and bolts.

Reassembly then continues in the reverse order to the removal instructions. To obtain the correct valve rocker clearance settings, reference should be made to Section B5.

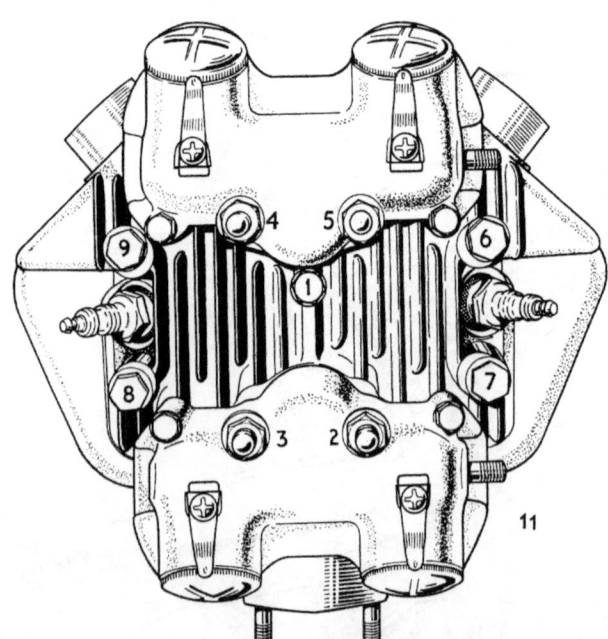

Fig. B12. Cylinder head bolt tightening sequence

SECTION B15
REMOVING AND REFITTING THE VALVES

Removal of the valves is facilitated by means of a "G" clamp type valve spring compressor. When the spring is compressed sufficiently, the split cotters can be removed with a narrow screwdriver, and the valve spring withdrawn when the compressor is released. As each valve is removed it should be marked so that it can be replaced in its original position.

NOTE: The inlet valves are marked "IN" and the exhaust valves "EX".

Fitting a new or reground valve necessitates seating by the grinding in process described in Section B18, but it does not necessitate recutting the cylinder head valve seat unless new valve guides have been fitted.

The valve springs should be inspected for fatigue and cracks, and checked for wear by comparing them with a new spring or the dimension given in "General Data".

All parts should be thoroughly cleaned in paraffin (kerosene) and allowed to drain before reassembling.

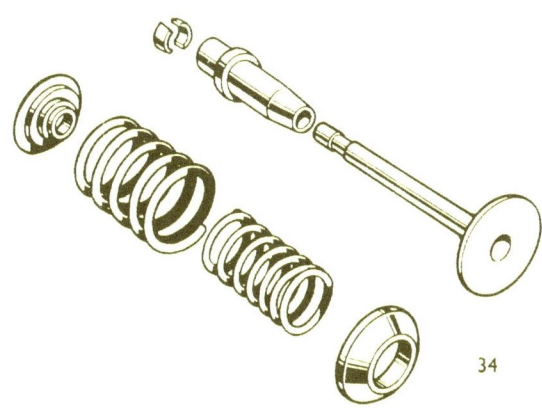

Fig. B13. Valve components

Assemble the inner and outer springs and top and bottom cups over the valve guide, then slide the valve into position lubricating the stem with a small amount of graphited oil.

Compress the springs and slide the two halves of the split cotter into the exposed groove in the valve stem.

SECTION B16
RENEWING THE VALVE GUIDES

The valve guides can be pressed or driven out using service tool 61-6013, with the cylinder head inverted on the bench. A suitable drift can be made by obtaining a 5 inch length of $\frac{1}{2}$ in. diameter mild steel bar (EN8) and machining one end to $\frac{5}{16}$ in. diameter for a length of 1 inch.

The same method may be employed to fit the new guide, although the use of a press is recommended. In either case lightly grease the valve guide to assist

assembly. Ensure that the guide is pressed in until the shoulder is flush with the cylinder head.

Bronze valve guides are fitted, the shorter ones being used in the inlet position.

Where new valve guides have been fitted it is necessary to re-cut the valve seats in the cylinder head and grind in the valves (see Section B18).

SECTION B17
DECARBONISING

It is not normally advisable to remove the carbon deposits from the combustion chamber and exhaust ports until symptoms indicate that decarbonising is necessary.

Such symptoms as falling off in power, loss of compression, noisy operation and difficult starting are all indications that decarbonising may be necessary.

When the cylinder head is removed unscrew the sparking plugs and clean them in paraffin (kerosene), or preferably have them grit-blasted and checked. Before fitting the plugs, check that the gap setting is correct (see "General Data").

If special decarbonising equipment is not available then a blunt aluminium scraper or a piece of lead solder flattened at one end, should be used to remove the carbon deposits. Do not use a screwdriver or a steel implement of any kind on an aluminium surface.

When removing the deposits from the piston crown, a ring of carbon should be left round the periphery of the pistons to maintain the seal. Also the carbon ring round the top of the cylinder bore should not be disturbed. To facilitate this an old piston ring should be placed on top of the piston, level with the top surface of the cylinder block.

Remove the valves as shown in Section B15 then remove the carbon deposits from the valve stems, combustion chamber and ports of the cylinder head. Remove all traces of carbon dust by means of a jet of compressed air or the vigorous use of a tyre pump, then thoroughly clean the cylinder head and valves in paraffin (kerosene). Finally, check the valves for pitting. If necessary, the valves can be ground-in as shown in Section B18.

SECTION B18
RE-SEATING THE VALVES

Where the valve guides have been renewed or the condition of a valve seat is doubtful, it is advisable to re-cut the cylinder head valve seat then grind in the valve, using a fine grade grinding-in paste.

It is important that the cylinder head valve seat and the valve guide bore should be concentric. For the purpose of re-cutting the valve seats the following service tools are available.

D1832   Valve seat cutter exhaust (45°)

D1833   Valve seat cutter inlet (45°)

D1834   Blending cutter (spherical form)

D1863   Arbor with pilot.

The valve seat cutting operation should be carried out with the greatest care, and only a minimum amount of metal should be removed.

ENGINE   B

After the seats have been re-cut, they should be blended to give an even seating of $\frac{3}{32}$ in. (2.4mm.).

Examine the face of the valve to see if it is pitted, scored or damaged. If necessary, the face can be reground, but excessive re-grinding is not advisable for this adversely affects the heat transference properties of the valve and will ultimately result in critical pocketing.

The stem of the valve should be inspected for wear or scuffing and if either is pronounced, the valve should be renewed.

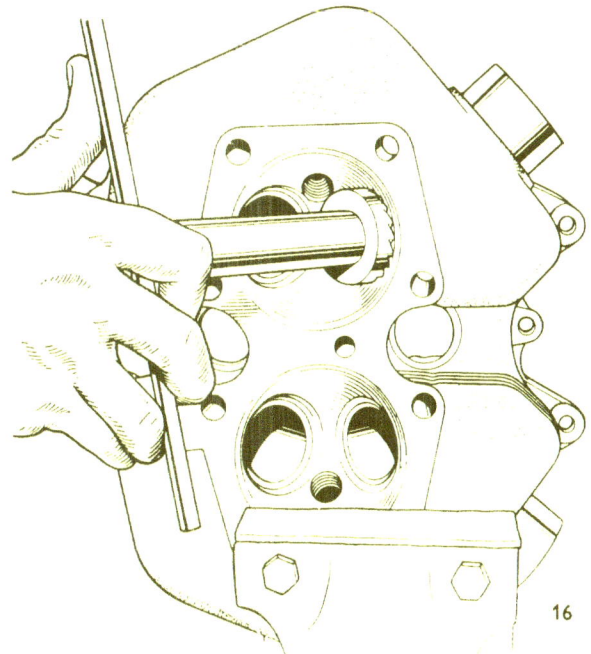

Fig. B14. Cutting a valve seat

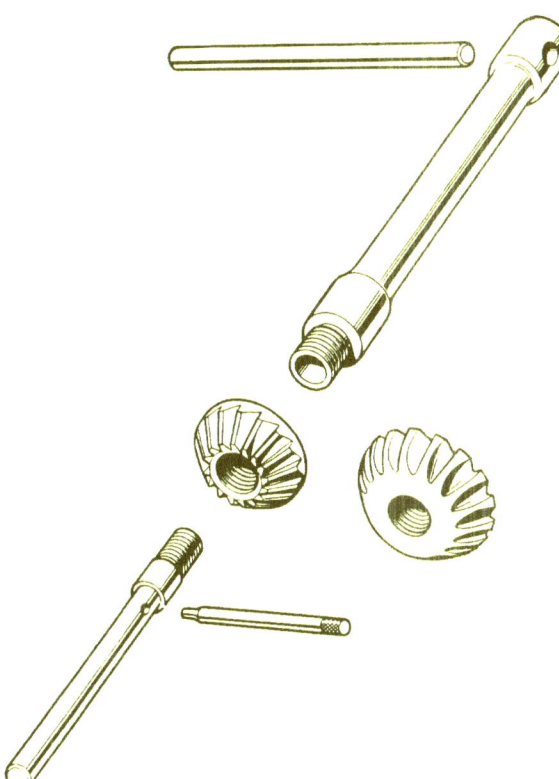

Fig. B15. Valve seating tools

To grind in the valve use a fine grade carborundum grinding paste. Place a small amount evenly on the valve seat and place the valve in its guide with a holding tool attached.

Use a semi-rotary motion, occasionally lifting the valve and turning it through 180°. Continue this process until a uniform seal results. Wash the parts in paraffin (kerosene) to remove the grinding paste. Apply a smear of "Engineer's" marking blue to the seat of the valve. Rotate the valve through one revolution and inspect both seats. Successful valve grinding will give an unbroken ring of blue on the valve seat.

Alternatively, assemble the springs and split cotters and pour a small amount of paraffin (kerosene) into the port. It should not penetrate the seating for at least 10 seconds if a good seal has been achieved.

Prior to reassembling the cylinder head, ensure that all traces of "Blue" or grinding paste are removed by thoroughly washing in paraffin (kerosene).

SECTION B19

REMOVING AND REPLACING THE CYLINDER BLOCK AND TAPPETS

Wedge a dis-used shock absorber rubber, or a suitable retainer between the inlet and exhaust tappets to prevent the tappets from falling through the tappet block into the crankcase when the cylinder block is removed. Turn the engine until the pistons are at T.D.C. then unscrew eight nuts from the base of the cylinder block and remove eight washers, carefully raise the block clear of the pistons. Raise the block sufficiently to insert non-fluffy rag into the crankcase mouth. It is also advisable at this stage to fit four rubber protectors (e.g. gear change lever rubbers) over four cylinder base studs (see Fig. B16) to avoid any damage to the alloy connecting rods. Remove the cylinder base gasket and ensure that the two locating dowels are in their correct position in the crankcase.

Remove the tappets from the cylinder block storing them in the order of their removal, and thoroughly clean all parts in paraffin (kerosene). It is important that the tappets are replaced in their original positions; failure to observe this may result in subsequent excessive tappet and cam wear.

If it has been decided to fit new piston rings then the bores must be lightly honed as described in Section B24.

Reassembly is a reversal of the above instructions, but care should be taken to ensure that the cylinder block is correctly located over the two dowels in the left half-crankcase.

The tappets should be well lubricated prior to wedging them in their original positions in the tappet guide blocks. To facilitate an easy assembly of the cylinder block over the pistons, two collars,

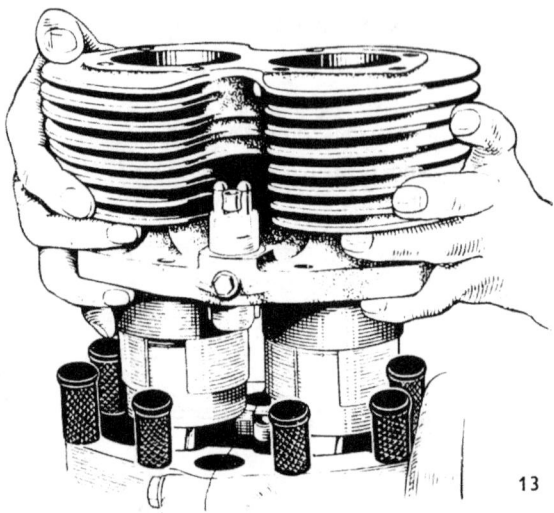

Fig. B16 Refitting the cylinder block

part number Z22, are required. The collars should be placed over the pistons to compress the piston rings, and withdrawn over the connecting rods when the pistons are sufficiently engaged in the block. Refit the eight cylinder base nuts. If desired, the latest 12 point base nuts and unified studs can be fitted as a set to existing crankcases.

NOTE: The smaller cylinder block retaining nuts should be fitted to the four central studs.

PRESSURE LUBRICATED EXHAUST TAPPETS

Lubricant is supplied under pressure direct to the exhaust tappet and camshaft working faces as described in section A3.

When replacing the cylinder block ensure that the cylinder base gasket is not fitted in such a way that the oil feed hole incorporated in the crankcase and cylinder block is obscured, so preventing lubricant from reaching the tappets.

If for any reason the tappet guide block is removed, it should be refitted as described in Section B19, but the oil feed holes should be checked to ensure that they are not blocked by foreign matter.

The correct method of assembly of the tappets is shown in Fig. B17. The machined cut away faces (C) should be facing the outside of the tappet guide block, i.e. the tappets must not be fitted with the cutaways facing one another, otherwise the oil holes (B) drilled in the annular groove of the tappet block (A) will not be able to supply lubricant to the tappets.

N.B. The inlet and exhaust tappets and tappet guide blocks must not be interchanged.

From engine number DU.24875, oil has been fed through drillways in the crankcase, timing cover,

ENGINE

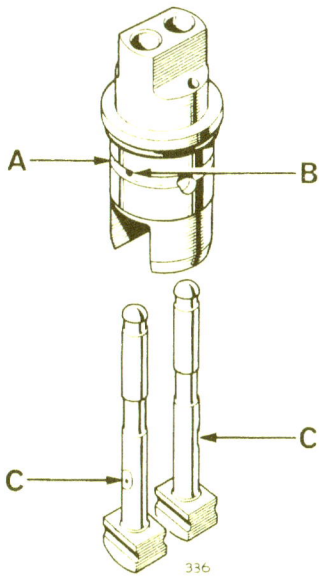

Fig. B17 Showing the correct method of assembly of the exhaust tappets

cylinder barrel and tappet block to the rubbing faces of the cam followers.

To prevent loss of oil pressure, several conditions and variations on the original theme have been employed.

Initially a metering plug was inserted into the crankcase at the front timing cover dowel and used in conjunction with cam followers with a flat of $\frac{9}{32}$ in. in length on the stem. Part No. E6490.

An alteration to this condition was made at engine number DU.44394, in as much that a floating pin was inserted into the metering screw, to combat blockage caused by particles in the lubrication system. Both metering jet and dowel can be obtained under Part Nos. E6800 and E6803 respectively, but these items must be used with cam followers, part No. E6490.

From engine number DU.63043 however, this assembly was removed, replaced with a plain dowel, part number T989 and cam followers used with a flat on the stem reduced in length to $\frac{3}{32}$ in., part No. E8801.

If the newer pattern cam follower is to be used in an engine previous to DU.63043, the metering plug must be removed from the crankcase. To facilitate this, simply screw in a timing cover screw and withdraw the assembly.

Do not remove the metering assembly if the old type cam followers, part number E6490, are to be used.

Do not attempt to use in the engine one of the old pattern cam followers in conjunction with one of the new type.

Engine No.	Type	Timing cover Dowel	Camfollower Exhaust	Camfollower Inlet	Tappet block
To Engine No. DU.24875	Non lubricated	Blind dowel None	E3059	E3059	E1477
From DU.24875 To DU.44394	Lubricated	Dowel E6348	E6329 6T/TR6 E6490 T120	E3059 6T/TR6 E3059R T120	E5861
From DU.44394 To DU.63043	Lubricated	Dowel and Pin E6803/6800	E6490 T120/TR6	E3059R	E5861
From DU.63043 To DU.66246	Lubricated	Dowel T989	E8801	E3059R	E5861

If conversion to the latest exhaust cam followers is desired on machines from engine number DU.24875 up to DU.63043, then the following procedure **must** be carried out.

Remove the E6348 metering jet in the manner prescribed above and replace with hollow dowel, part number T989. Replace exhaust cam followers with the equivalent shown in the scale below.

Exhaust cam followers		
E6329 6T/TR6	use	E8895 6T/TR6
E6490 T120	use	E8801 T120

SECTION B20
INSPECTING THE TAPPETS AND GUIDE BLOCKS

The base of the tappet is fitted with a "Stellite" tip. This material has good wear resisting qualities but the centre of the tip may show signs of slight indentation. If the width of the indentation exceeds $\frac{3}{32}$ in. then the tappet should be renewed.

It is not necessary to remove the tappet guide blocks for inspection purposes; the extent of wear can be estimated by rocking the tappet whilst it is in position in the guide block. It should be a sliding fit with little or no sideways movement, (see "General Data" for working clearances).

Excessive play between the tappets and guide block may cause undesirable mechanical noise.

SECTION B21
RENEWING THE TAPPET GUIDE BLOCKS

Place the cylinder block in an inverted position on the bench. Remove the locking screw and drift out the guide block using service tool 61-6008, as shown in Fig. B18.

"O" ring oil seals are fitted between the tappet blocks and cylinder block. The seals must be replaced whenever oil leakage is noted at this point or whenever the tappet blocks are removed and refitted. Under no circumstances must the tappet guide blocks be interchanged. The exhaust tappets are pressure lubricated through the exhaust tappet guide block and the oilways must therefore be cleaned out carefully before assembly.

To fit the new guide block, first grease the outer surface to assist assembly, then align the location hole in the guide block and cylinder block base, and drive in the guide block using 61-6008, until the shoulder is flush with the flange.

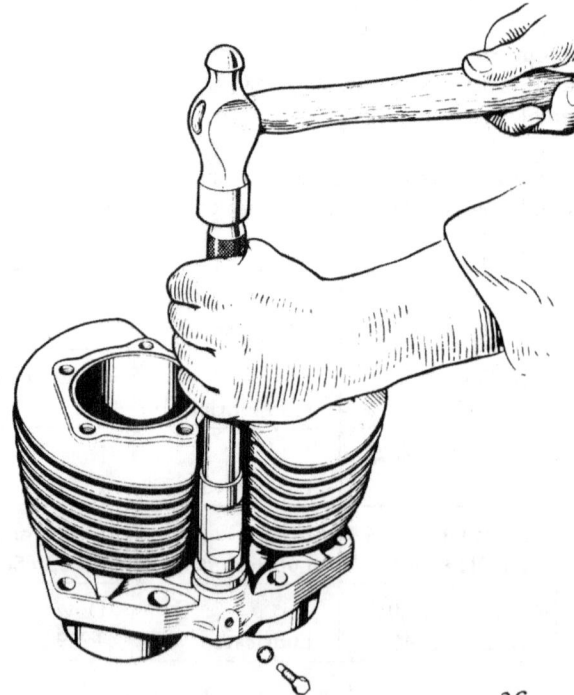

Fig. B18. Refitting a tappet guide block

SECTION B22

REMOVING AND REFITTING THE PISTONS

It is most important that the alloy connecting rods are not damaged by contact with the sharp crankcase edge. For this reason four gear lever rubbers should be placed over the four central cylinder base studs.

Removal of the pistons is facilitated by the use of a proprietary removal tool (see Fig. B19). Remove the inner and outer circlips and press out the gudgeon pin with the removal tool. The pistons are pistons are removed they should be suitably scribed inside so that they can be refitted in their original positions. When refitting the pistons, first place the inner circlip in position to act as a stop, then press the gudgeon pin into position using a service tool.

It is advisable to renew the four circlips; this can be done for negligible cost.

Fig. B19. Removing a piston

then free to be removed. Alternatively, the pistons may be removed by driving out the gudgeon pin with a suitable drift. However, this is not a recommended practice, and may result in a damaged piston or distorted connecting rod. **The need for care cannot be overstressed when using this method to remove the gudgeon pin.** When the

If there is no alternative to driving the gudgeon pin into position with a drift, the piston should be heated to 100°C (boiling-water temperature), to assist assembly.

Finally, check that all the gudgeon pin retainer circlips are in position, and are correctly fitted. This is extremely important.

SECTION B23

REMOVING AND REPLACING THE PISTON RINGS

There should be little difficulty in removing piston rings, if the following procedure is adopted. Lift one end of the top piston ring out of the groove and insert a thin steel strip between the ring and piston. Move the strip round the piston, at the same time lifting the raised part of the ring upwards with slight pressure. The piston rings should always be lifted off and replaced over the top of the piston.

If the piston rings are to be refitted the carbon deposits on the inside surface of the rings must be removed and the carbon deposits in the piston ring grooves must also be removed.

When fitting new piston rings, the bores must be lightly honed with a fine-grade emery cloth so that the new piston rings can become bedded down properly. The honing should be carried out with an oscillatory motion up and down the bore until an even "criss-cross" pattern is achieved. The recommended grade of emery for this purpose is 300. Thoroughly wash the bores in paraffin (kerosene) and check that all traces of abrasives are removed.

Pistons and rings are available in ·010, ·020, ·030 and ·040 inches. (·254, ·508, ·762 and 1·016 mm.) oversizes. When fitting new rings the gap must be checked in the lowest part of the cylinder bore. The ring must lie square to the bore for checking purposes, and to ensure this, place the piston crown onto the ring and ease it down the bore. Check the gap with feeler gauges.

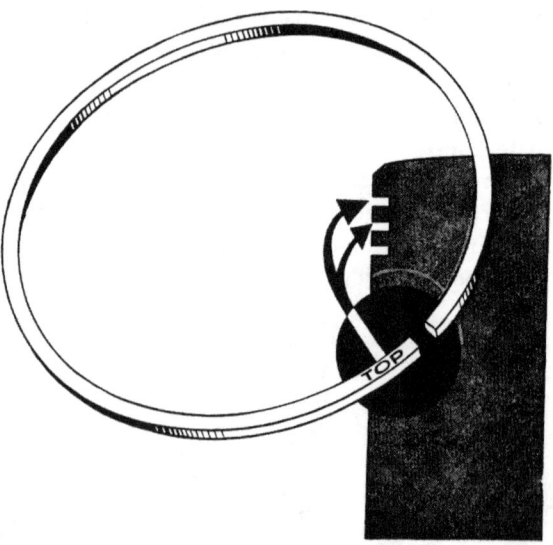

Fig. B20. Refitting a tapered piston ring

Piston rings, when new, should have the following gap clearances:

Compression ring gap: ·010" to ·014" (·25 to ·35 mm.)
Scraper ring gap: ·010" to ·014" (·25 to ·35 mm.)

Refitting the piston rings is straight forward, but check that the two compression rings are fitted the right way up.

The two taper compression rings are marked "TOP" to ensure correct assembly, and should be fitted with the "TOP" marking towards the cylinder head (see Fig. B20).

SECTION B24

INSPECTING THE PISTONS AND CYLINDER BORES

PISTONS

Check the thrust areas of the piston skirt for signs of seizure or scoring.
The piston skirt is of a special oval form and is designed to have limited working clearances within the bore. The clearances are given in "General Data".

Prior to inspection, ensure that both the cylinder bores and the pistons are clean and free from dirt, etc. Any deposits of burnt oil round the piston skirt can be removed by using a petrol (gasolene) soaked cloth.

ENGINE

NOTE: The top lands of the piston have working clearance varying from ·016 in. to ·020 in. and thus allows the top piston ring to be viewed from above, and the piston to be rocked slightly. However, this is not critical, it is the skirt clearances that are all-important.

CYLINDER BORES

The maximum wear occurs within the top half-inch of the bore, whilst the portion below the piston ring working area remains relatively unworn. Compare the diameters, measured at right angles to the gudgeon pin, to obtain an accurate estimate of the wear. A difference between these figures in excess of ·005 in. (·13 mm.) indicates that a rebore is necessary. Compare the figures obtained with those given below so that an accurate figure for the actual wear can be determined.

An approximate method for determining the wear in a cylinder bore is that of measuring the piston ring gap at various depths in the bore and comparing with the gap when the ring is at the bottom of the cylinder. The difference between the figures obtained, when divided by 3 (an approximation of π) equals the wear on the diameter. As above, if the difference exceeds ·005 (·13 mm.), this indicates that a rebore is necessary.

SECTION B25
TABLE OF SUITABLE RE-BORE SIZES

Piston marking in. (mm.)	Suitable bore sizes	
	in.	mm.
Standard:—	2·7948	70·993
	2·7953	71·006
Oversizes:—		
+·010 (·254 mm.)	2·8048	71·247
	2·8053	71·260
+·020 (·508 mm.)	2·8148	71·501
	2·8153	71·514
+·040 (1·016 mm.)	2·8348	72·009
	2·8353	72·022

SECTION B26
PISTON IDENTIFICATION

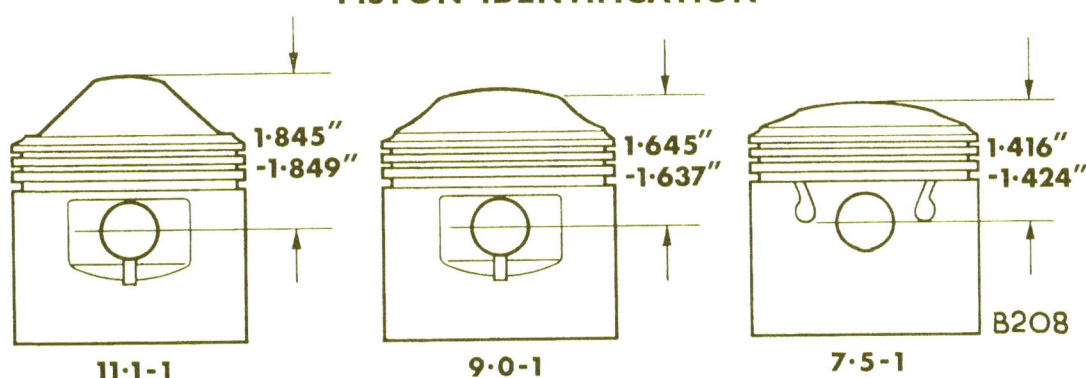

Fig. B21. Piston identification. All measurements taken from the gudgeon pin centre line to the highest point of the crown

SECTION B27
RENEWING THE SMALL END BUSHES

The small end bush wear, which normally is very slight, can be estimated when sliding the gudgeon pin through the bush. If it is in good condition the pin will be a sliding fit in the bush, with no play being in evidence.

Renewal of the small end bushes can be easily achieved by using the new bush to press out the old one. For this purpose a threaded bolt, about 4 in. long and a 1¼ in. long piece of tube with an inside diameter of ⅞ in. will be required.

Place a suitable washer and the new bush onto the bolt, then offer it into the old bush. Place the piece of tube and a suitable washer over the bolt and screw the nut on finger-tight. Centralise the bush and tube and align the oilway in the new bush with that in the connecting rod. When the nut is tightened the new bush will extract the old one.

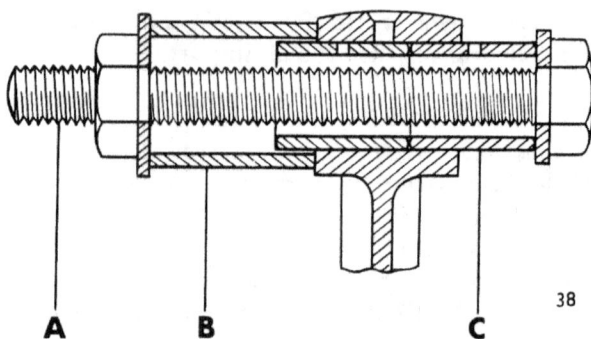

Fig. B22. Extracting a small end bush

Finally, ream the bore of the bush to the size given in "General Data", taking care not to allow any metallic particles to enter the crankcase. When reamering the bush, ensure that its bore is parallel with the big-end bore.

SECTION B28
REMOVING AND REPLACING THE CONTACT BREAKER

The contact breaker mechanism is housed in the timing cover on the right of the engine and is driven by the exhaust camshaft. It consists of two sets of points (one per cylinder), two auxilliary backplates with cam adjustment and a fully automatic centrifugal type advance and retard mechanism. The working parts are protected by a circular cover and gasket. The engine oil is prevented from entering the contact breaker cavity by means of an oil seal fitted to the inner wall of the timing cover. The complete contact breaker unit can be removed from the timing cover with the aid of service tool D782.

First, disconnect the leads from the battery terminals or remove the fuse from the holder adjacent to the battery, then remove the two screws and withdraw the outer cover and gasket. Remove the centre bolt and screw in service tool D782 until the cam unit is released from it's locking taper in the camshaft. Unscrew the tool and remove the cam unit.

To completely detach the contact breaker unit it will be necessary to disconnect the two leads from the ignition coils and remove the appropriate frame clips so that the leads can be withdrawn through the holes in the crankcase and timing cover.

It is advisable to make a note of the degree figure which is stamped on the back of the cam unit, as this indicates the advance range, which it is necessary to know for accurate static timing purposes.

Prior to replacing the cam unit it is advisable to add a small drop of lubricating oil to the pivot pins only, not the cam pivot. The cam unit slot should be located on the peg in the camshaft and the centre bolt screwed in and tightened.

IMPORTANT NOTE: "Run out" on the contact breaker cam or misalignment of the secondary backplate centre hole can result in contact between the cam and backplate. This can result in the auto advance remaining retarded or the spark retarding. To check for "run-out" check the point gap with the contact nylon heel aligned with the cam scribe mark for each set of points. Should there be a discrepancy greater then

ENGINE

0·003 in. tap the outer edge of the cam with a brass drift with the cam securing bolt tight. In cases of misalignment of the secondary backplate hole, check the cam clearance in different positions and elongate the hole only where the backplate rubs the cam.

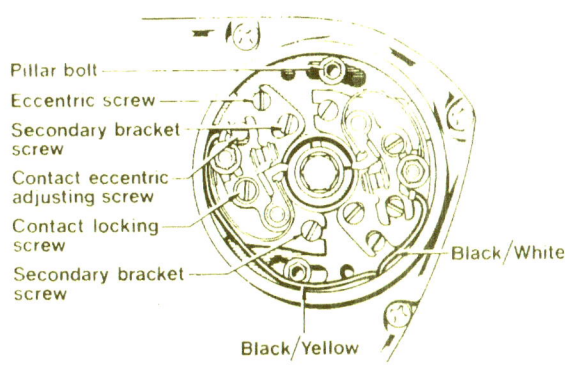

Fig. B23A Contact breaker 6CA

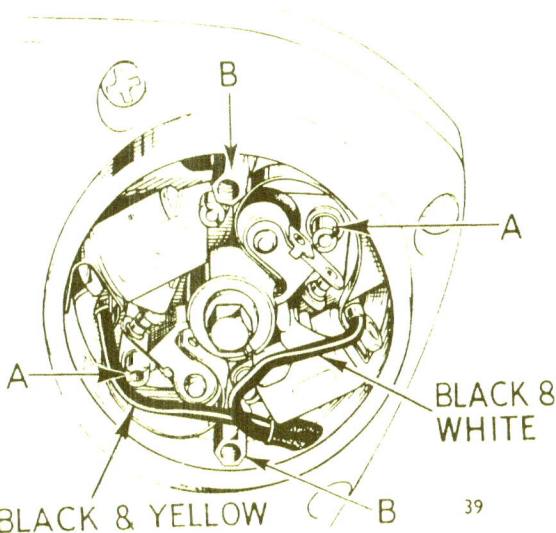

Fig. B23B Contact breaker 4CA

The base plate, on any other than very early machines with the 6CA contact breaker, should be assembled with the black/yellow leads rearmost. Certain early machines after DU.66246 had the black/white leads to the rear.

To adjust the contact breaker gaps, turn the motor with the starter pedal until the scribe mark on the cam aligns with the nylon heel of one set of points. Measure the point gap using a 0·015 in. feeler gauge. If outside the limits, slacken the contact adjusting screw, adjust the gap by turning the eccentric screw, and re-tighten the adjusting screw.

Revolve the motor until the second set of points is lined up with the scribe line, and adjust as before. and with the pillar bolts in the centres of the timing adjustment slots.

CONTACT BREAKER 4CA TYPE PRIOR TO DU.66246

The base plate should be re-positioned so that the set of points with the black/yellow lead is rearmost

To adjust contact breaker gaps slacken sleeve nuts 'A'. To rotate contact breaker base plate for setting ignition timing slacken pillar bolts 'B'.

For earlier models without the peg and slot arrangement in the cam unit and exhaust camshaft, the following procedure should be adopted to set the cam unit in its correct relative position in the camshaft:—

First set the base plate so that the pillar bolts are in the centres of their respective slots, then tighten the pillar bolts. Select 4th (top) gear and remove the left and right sparking plugs and all four rocker caps, then turn the engine over until the RIGHT piston is approximately $\frac{1}{32}$ in. (·9 mm) before top centre on its compression stroke (both valves closed). Turn the contact breaker cam unit until the REAR set of contact breaker points are just about to open and tighten the centre bolt. Note that the cam should be turned clockwise viewed from the right side of the machine.

Note:— When the correct setting is achieved, ensure that the contact breaker bolts are tight, then fit the cover and gasket.

SECTION B29

IGNITION TIMING — INITIAL PROCEDURE

INITIAL ASSEMBLY OF THE CONTACT BREAKER MECHANISM AND AUTO ADVANCE UNIT PRIOR TO FINAL TIMING THE ENGINE

(1) Remove both sparking plugs and all four rocker box caps. Set the engine at T.D.C. with both valves closed in the right hand cylinder.

(2) Assemble the auto advance unit into the exhaust camshaft, locating on the camshaft peg where it is fitted.

(3) Assemble the C.B. plate, taking care not to trap the C.B. leads, assembling the plate so that the C.B. points connected to the black/yellow leads are located at 7 o'clock. Loosely assemble the hexagon pillar bolts and flat washers.

(4) Lock the auto advance cam into the taper, using the central fixing bolt.

NOTE: When the degree disc is attached to the exhaust camshaft, the indicated setting and advance range will be half that of the engine, as the camshaft rotates at half engine speed.

ESTABLISHING TOP DEAD CENTRE POSITION

When setting the ignition timing on machines after engine no. DU.13375, the T.D.C. position can be quickly found using workshop tool D571/2. The blanking plug on top of the crankcase immediately behind the cylinder block is removed and the body of the tool is screwed into its place. Having removed both sparking plugs and engaged top gear, rotate the rear wheel forwards until the pistons are just coming up towards T.D.C. Then the plunger is inserted in the body of the tool and the rear wheel is rotated forwards slowly until the plunger locates itself in the centre flywheel. The T.D.C. position has now been established.

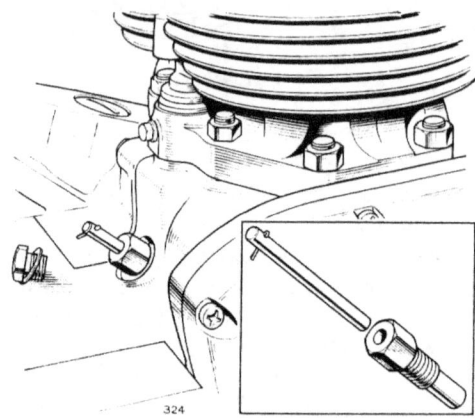

Fig. B24A Showing T.D.C. locating tool in use

IGNITION TIMING USING A STROBOSCOPIC LIGHT

After establishing T.D.C. as described in Section B29. fit the timing disc adaptor shaft and timing disc into the camshaft auto advance unit and set the pointer, fixed to a convenient bolt on the engine to rear T.D.C.

NOTE: When using a stroboscope powered by 6 or 12 volt batteries as an external power source, do not use the machine's own battery equipment. (A.C. pulses in the low tension machine wiring, can trigger the stroboscope, and give false readings).

(1) Connect the stroboscope to the right hand spark plug lead and start the engine. Read the strobo-light on the disc, revving the engine up until the auto advance range is fully achieved. Check against the correct specification and adjust the C.B. back plate on its slots until the correct advanced timing is accurately set.

(2) Repeat for L.H. plug and adjust the accuracy of the spark on the C.B. points adjustment.

NOTE: To advance the spark, open the points, approximately 0·001 in. for each engine degree required, and to retard, close the points setting similarly. Minor adjustments to the left cylinder C.B. points gap setting, to ensure accurate ignition timing are permissible.

(3) Check back on the stroboscopic reading and slow tickover for range of advance on both cylinders, for efficient action of the auto advance unit, remembering the most important final setting is at fully advanced, both cylinders. Timing the engine stroboscopically with a timing disc ensures that both plugs are firing at exactly similar angular crank rotation (i.e. piston movement), at fully advanced ignition, that is at full power, thereby ensuring the smoothest, most vibration free engine running condition and ensuring maximum engine power output.

It also eliminates variations encountered in differing auto advance ranges due to possible non-standard components, uneven wear, etc., etc.

ENGINE

SECTION B30

IGNITION TIMING WHERE A STROBOSCOPE IS NOT AVAILABLE PRIOR TO DU.66246

TO ESTABLISH THE ACCURATE STATIC IGNITION SETTING

(1) Check the General Data Section for the correct fully advanced ignition setting for the machine.

(2) Check the auto advance range stamped on rear of auto advance cam mechanism.

(3) Double the auto advance range and subtract the figure from the FULL ADVANCE setting for the machine. This is the correct STATIC SETTING for the engine.

(4) Use this figure for setting the position of the C.B. points opening, when assembling the contact breaker mechanism, using a degree plate or timing disc attached to the engine.

(5) Convert this figure in degrees to the equivalent piston movement B.T.C. if a timing stick is to be employed.

On machines where an engine camshaft peg is not fitted, rotate the auto advance mechanism until a position is reached where the rear set of C.B. points will just commence to open.

CONVERSION CHART–ENGINE DEGREES TO RELATIVE PISTON POSITION

Crankshaft position (B.T.D.C.)	Piston position (B.T.D.C.)	
Degrees	in.	mm.
7	·015	·38
8	·020	·51
9	·025	·64
10	·030	·76
11	·038	·96
12	·045	1·14
13	·054	1·30
14	·060	1·52
15	·068	1·73
16	·077	1·96
17	·087	2·20
18	·095	2·42
19	·108	2·75
20	·120	3·05
21	·135	3·45

EXAMPLE OF STATIC SETTING CALCULATION

T120 IGNITION TIMING = 39° B.T.C. Fully advanced.

C.B. range stamped on auto advance cam = 12°.
Twice 12° = 24°
Full advance 39° — 24° = 15° B.T.C. "STATIC SETTING".

POSITIONING THE TIMING DISC WHERE THERE IS NO PROVISION FOR THE T.D.C. PLUNGER (Earlier models)

(1) Fit the timing disc adaptor shaft and timing disc into the camshaft auto advance unit, and set the pointer, fixed to a convenient bolt on the engine, to read T.D.C.

Engage top gear, and use a timing stick with a suitable mark which aligns along the top of the cylinder head fins at about 1 in. of piston movement. (For greater accuracy, use a Dial Test Indicator through the spark plug hole). Rotate the engine either side of T.D.C. by rocking the rear wheel, to exactly the same measured point of movement on the stick (or D.T.I.), setting the pointer so that it reads an equal number of degrees either side of T.D.C. on the degree disc.

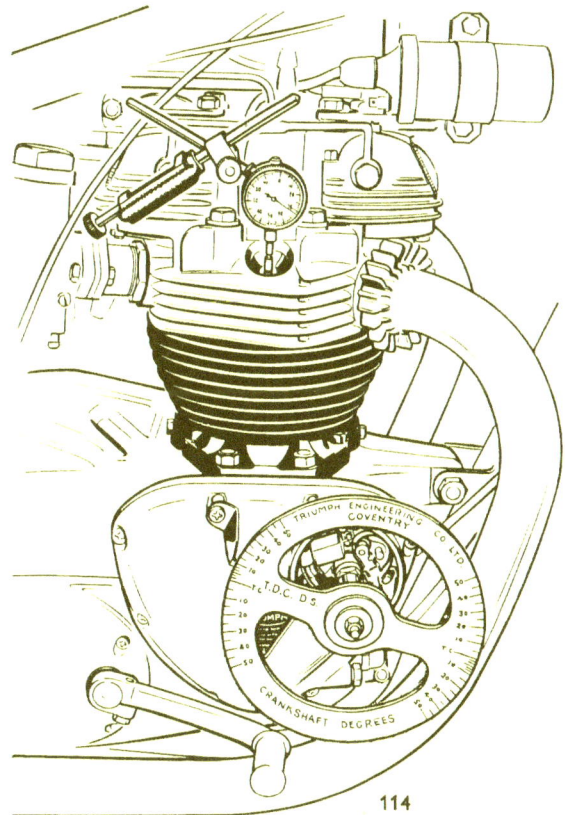

Fig. B24B Engine fitted with timing disc and dial indicator

STATIC IGNITION TIMING
(TO BE USED ONLY WHERE A STROBOSCOPE IS NOT AVAILABLE)
BEFORE DU.66246

(1) Rotate the engine so that the fibre heel of the C.B. points have just passed beyond the ramp of the auto advance cam, and just reached the full open position. Set the point gap 0·015 in.

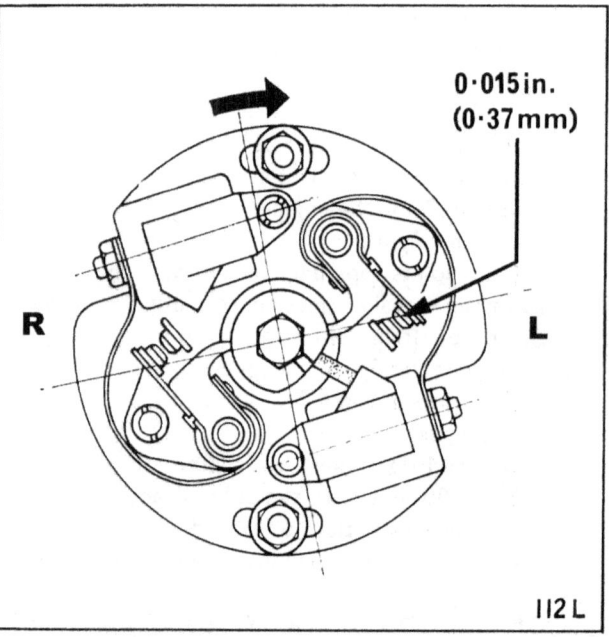

Fig. B24(b). Setting contact breaker point gap for the left cylinder (black/white) lead, illustrating the second position of the cam, where the points have just achieved the fully open position

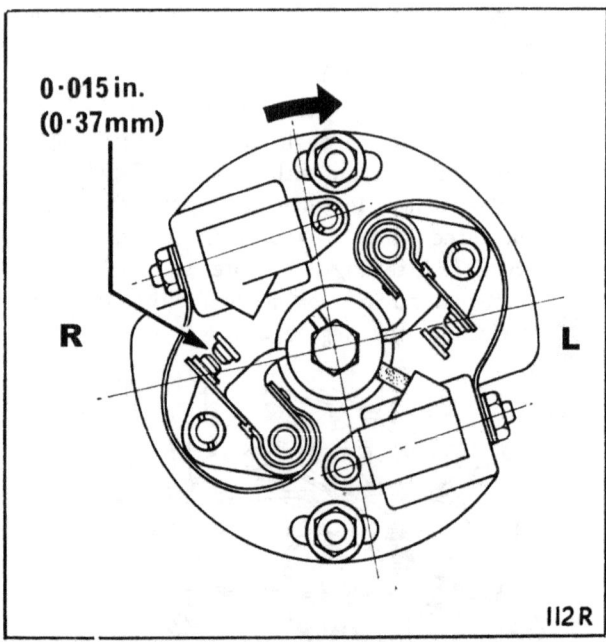

Fig. B24(a). Setting the contact breaker point gap for the right cylinder (black/yellow) lead, illustrating position of the cam where points are just fully open

(2) Rotate the engine "forwards" through 360° and set the second set of points in the corresponding position on the cam. Set these points at a gap of 0·015 in.

(3) ROTATE ENGINE AND ESTABLISH ACCURATE T.D.C. (See Section B34 prior to engine number DU.13375 and Section B33 after this number and prior to DU.66246.

If the machine is put in top gear, small increments in crank rotation and piston movement can be achieved by rotating the rear wheel slowly, and accurate piston T.D.C. established by "swinging" the engine either side of T.D.C. Mark the timing stick at T.D.C. Mark a second position on the timing stick ABOVE the T.D.C. mark appropriate to the specified timing for the machine, i.e. "piston movement before T.D.C.".

(4) Rotate the engine "backwards" beyond this mark and then slowly reverse the rotation "forwards" until the timing mark is set in line with the top of the cylinder head fins. If a timing disc is employed, rotate the engine forwards until the correct "static setting" is achieved in crankshaft degrees.

ENGINE

(5) Rotate the C.B. back plate on its slots until a position is reached where the points just open (check using a battery and light, or an 0·0015 in. feeler gauge. Alternatively, if a battery is fitted to the machine and the ignition switch turned to "IGN", the position where the points open can be identified by the ammeter needle giving a "flick" back to zero).

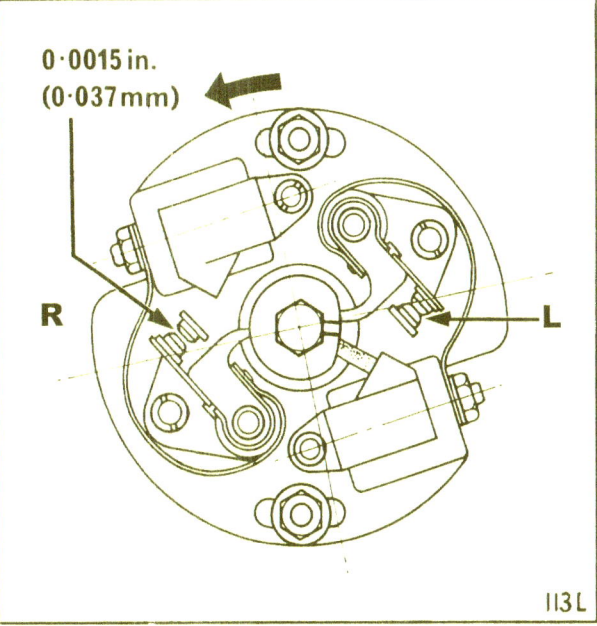

Fig. B24(b). Contact breaker points just opening on the left cylinder

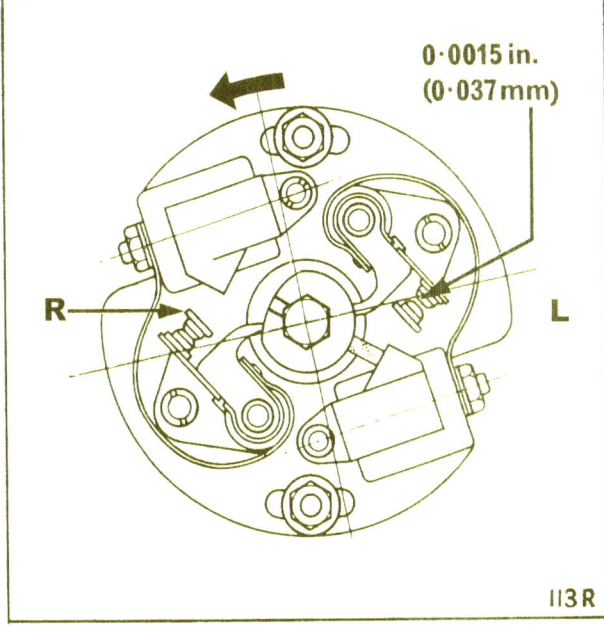

Fig. B24(a). Contact breaker points just opening on the right cylinder. With the engine set at the correct STATIC SETTING, the C.B. back plate assembly should be adjusted in the slots, to a position where the C.B. points just commence to open.

Rotate the engine through 360°. The other set of C.B. points should just have opened. If not, the accuracy of spark on the second set of C.B. points can be corrected by adjusting the points gap.

NOTE: To advance the spark, open the points, approximately 0·001 in. for each engine degree required, and to retard, close the points setting similarly. Minor adjustments to left cylinder C.B. points setting to ensure accurate ignition timing are permissible.

IGNITION TIMING—INITIAL PROCEDURE AFTER DU.66246

Initial assembly of the contact breaker mechanism and auto advance unit prior to final timing of the engine:—

(1) Remove both sparking plugs and all four rocker box caps. Set the engine at T.D.C. with both valves closed in the right hand cylinder.

(2) Assemble the auto advance unit into the exhaust camshaft, locating on the camshaft peg where it is fitted.

(3) Assemble the C.B. plate taking care not to trap the C.B. leads, assembling the plate so that the C.B. points are located at 7 o'clock.

Loosely assemble the hexagonal pillar bolts and flat washers.

(4) Lock the auto advance cam into the taper using the central fixing bolt. For static timing remove the bolt again, taking care not to release the taper of the cam. Temporarily fit another washer with a centre hole just large enough to fit over the cam bearing, thus allowing the washer to bear hard on the end of the cam. Rotate the cam carefully to its limit against the auto advance springs, holding in this position whilst the centre bolt is re-fitted and nipped up. The fully advanced position has then been located.

STATIC TIMING AT 38° BTDC
WHERE NO STROBOSCOPE IS AVAILABLE AFTER DU.66246

Rotate the engine until the nylon heel of the C.B. points aligns with the scribe marking on the cam. At this stage set both points gaps to 0·015 in.

Locate the crankshaft at 38° B.T.D.C. using the timing plunger tool D571 modified as shown below.

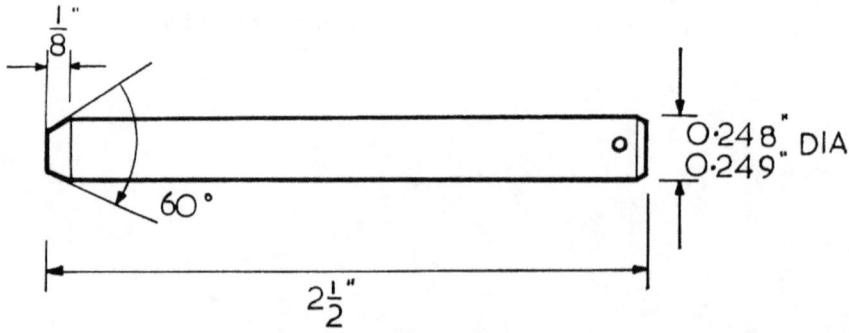

Fig. B25 Modified timing plunger

ENGINE B

There are three different conditions of flywheel and crankcase locating holes as shown in Fig. B26 below. Identify the condition relating to the particular machine being timed. It will be found easiest to start with the pistons at T.D.C. (checked through the sparking plug hole) and then, with both sparking plugs removed and second gear engaged, rotate the rear wheel backwards. As the crank is turned by this means, pressure on the timing plunger will locate it at 38° B.T.D.C. Remove the rocker caps to establish which cylinder is on the compression stroke (i.e. which cylinder has both valves closed). Note that the timing side cylinder is operated by the contact points with the black/yellow lead and the drive side with the black/white lead.

When it has been decided which cylinder is being timed, rotate the main contact breaker backplate on its slots until the particular contact points just open. This can be checked using a battery and light or by an 0·0015 in. feeler gauge between the points. Alternatively unless the battery has been removed or disconnected, turn the ignition switch "on" and the position where the points open can be identified by the ammeter needle giving a "flick" back to zero.

Attention should now be turned to the other cylinder. Remove the timing plunger, turn the engine forwards through 360° (1 revolution) and relocate the timing plunger. The second set of points should now be adjusted as above but the main backplate must not be disturbed. Adjust only on the secondary backplate. Finally secure all screws, lubricate both sides of the cam with Shell Retinax A grease, replace the cover plate and the sparking plugs, finally engaging neutral gear.

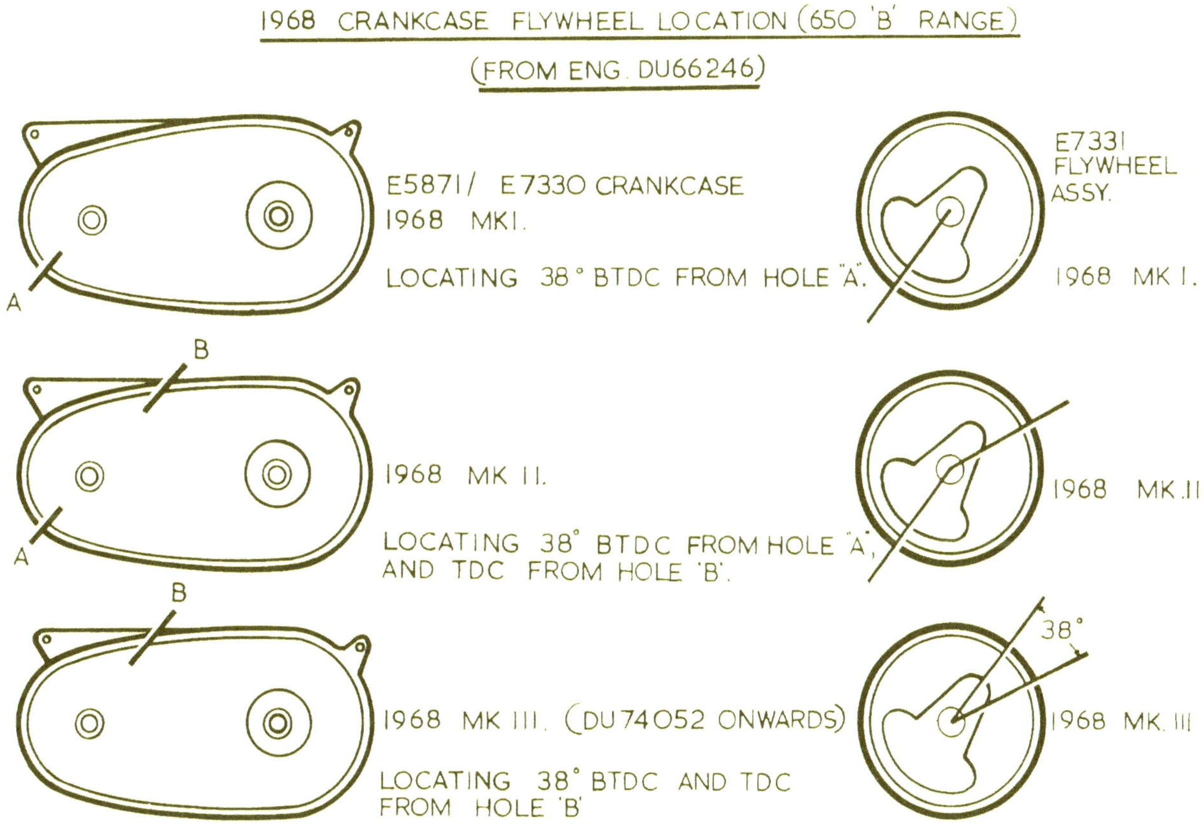

1968 CRANKCASE FLYWHEEL LOCATION (650 'B' RANGE)
(FROM ENG. DU66246)

E5871/ E7330 CRANKCASE
1968 MKI.
LOCATING 38° BTDC FROM HOLE "A".

E7331 FLYWHEEL ASSY.
1968 MK I.

1968 MK II.
LOCATING 38° BTDC FROM HOLE "A", AND TDC FROM HOLE 'B'.

1968 MK II

1968 MK III. (DU 74052 ONWARDS)
LOCATING 38° BTDC AND TDC FROM HOLE 'B'

1968 MK III

Fig. B26 Crankcase flywheel location

SECTION B31

IGNITION TIMING BY STROBOSCOPE AFTER ENGINE NUMBER DU.66245

Undertake the initial procedure as in Section B30

Remove the inspection plate secured by three screws) from the primary chaincase. As seen in Fig. B27A there is a marking on the outer face of the rotor which is to coincide with an ignition pointer on the primary chaincase to achieve the correct 38° ignition timing position.

On machines with the inspection plate on the primary cover but no provision for the timing pointer, a special timing plate D2014 is available and this is shown in Fig. B27B. Note that D2014 has two markings, the one 'B' only being used on 650 c.c. applications.

NOTE: When using a stroboscope powered by a 12 volt battery as on external power source, do not use the machines own battery equipment. (A.C. pulses in the low tension machine wiring can trigger the stroboscope and give false readings).

(1) Connect the stroboscope to the right hand spark plug lead and start the engine. Read the strobo-light on the rotor marking in relation to the timing pointer or timing plate marking with the engine running at 2,000 R.P.M. or more. Adjust the main backplate on its slots until the marks align whereupon the timing on the one cylinder is correct.

(2) Repeat for the L.H. plug and adjust the timing by slackening off the clamping screw on the auxilliary backplate and turning the eccentric screw (see Fig. B23A) until again the markings align. Timing is then correct. Refit the primary chaincase inspection plate.

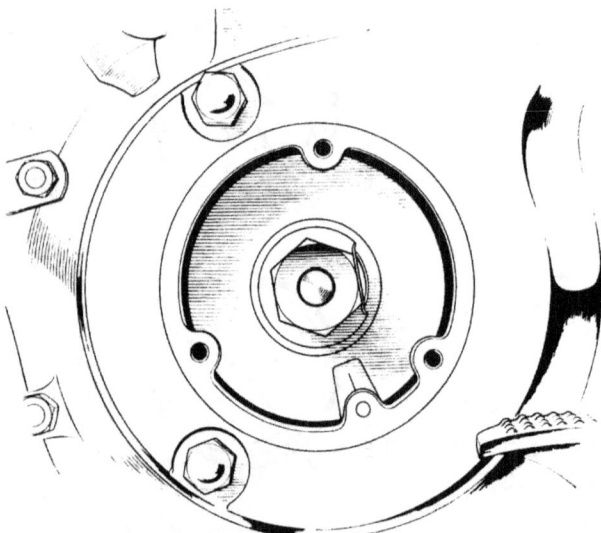

Fig. B27A Rotor marking

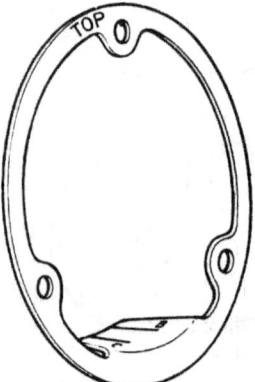

Fig. B27B Timing plate D2014

ENGINE

SECTION B32
REMOVING AND REPLACING THE TIMING COVER

Remove the contact breaker as described in Section B28.

Disconnect the oil switch lead at the spade terminal. Unscrew the eight recessed screws which serve to retain the timing cover and if necessary tap the cover on the front blanking plug with a hide mallet until the cover is free. When the cover is removed, the crankshaft and contact breaker oil seals should be inspected for wear and cracks and renewed if necessary. To remove the crankshaft oil seal, the retainer circlip must first be removed by means of long-nosed pliers or a narrow screwdriver.

Unscrew the hexagonal plug from the front edge of the cover and thoroughly clean all parts in paraffin (kerosene). Clean out the oil drillings with a jet of compressed air and replace the plug and copper washer.

The oil pressure switch in the front of the timing cover has a taper thread and requires no sealant on the threads, for competition use a blanking plug is available to take the place of the switch.

To replace the cover, first check that the oil seals are facing in the correct direction (see Fig. B28) and that the circlip is located correctly in its groove, then carefully clean the junction surfaces of the timing cover and crankcase and remove any traces of used jointing compound. Apply a fresh coat of a suitable proprietary jointing compound evenly over the timing cover junction surface. Screw the tapered adaptor pilot (service tool D486) into the exhaust camshaft and smear it with oil to assist assembly. Check that both the location dowels are in their correct positions, slide the cover into position and screw in the eight recessed screws.

Finally, replace the contact breaker assembly and reset the ignition timing as shown in Sections B29 to B31.

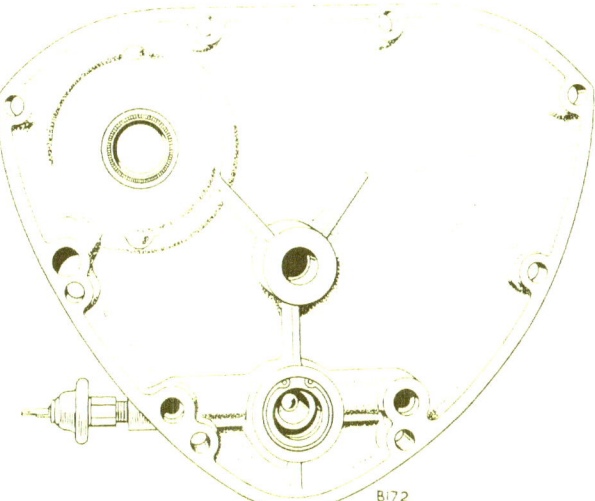

Fig. B28A Timing cover oil seal location

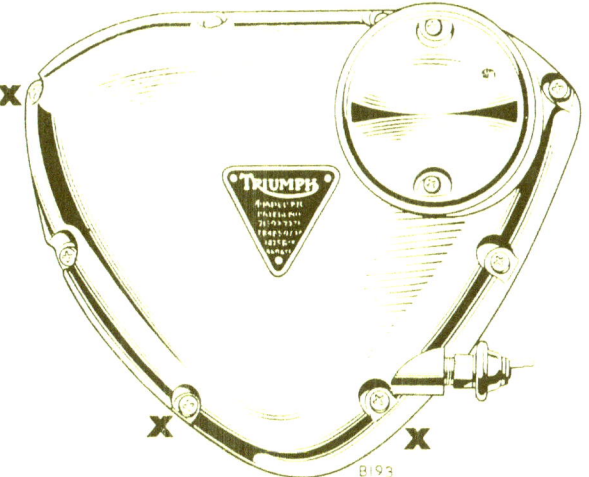

Fig. B28B Location of three long screws in timing cover

NOTE: The three longer screws should be fitted in the holes marked "X" in Fig. B28B

SECTION B33
REMOVING AND REPLACING THE OIL PUMP

To remove the oil pump, first remove the contact breaker mechanism, and the timing cover as described in Sections B28 and B32.

The oil pump is held in position by two conical nuts. When these are removed, the oil pump can be withdrawn from the mounting studs. The paper gasket should be renewed.

Full details concerning inspection, testing and rectification of the oil pump are given in Section A7.

When replacing the oil pump, care should be taken to ensure that the new gasket is fitted correctly and that the cones of the conical nuts and washers fit into the counter-sunk holes in the oil pump body.

SECTION B34
EXTRACTING AND REFITTING THE VALVE TIMING PINIONS

Before attempting to remove any of the valve timing gears it is necessary to release the load on the camshafts caused by compressed valve springs. This should be done by removing the rocker boxes as detailed in Section B2, or may be achieved by sufficiently slackening the valve clearance adjuster screws; however, this is not always advisable as it may result in a push rod becoming disengaged.

Remove the contact breaker as detailed in Section B28.

Remove the timing cover as described in Section B32 and the oil pump as shown in Section B33. Select 4th (top) gear, apply the rear brake and unscrew the nuts retaining the camshaft and crankshaft pinions, then withdraw the intermediate wheel.

NOTE: The camshaft pinion retainer nuts have LEFT-HAND threads. The crankshaft pinion retainer nut has a RIGHT-HAND thread.

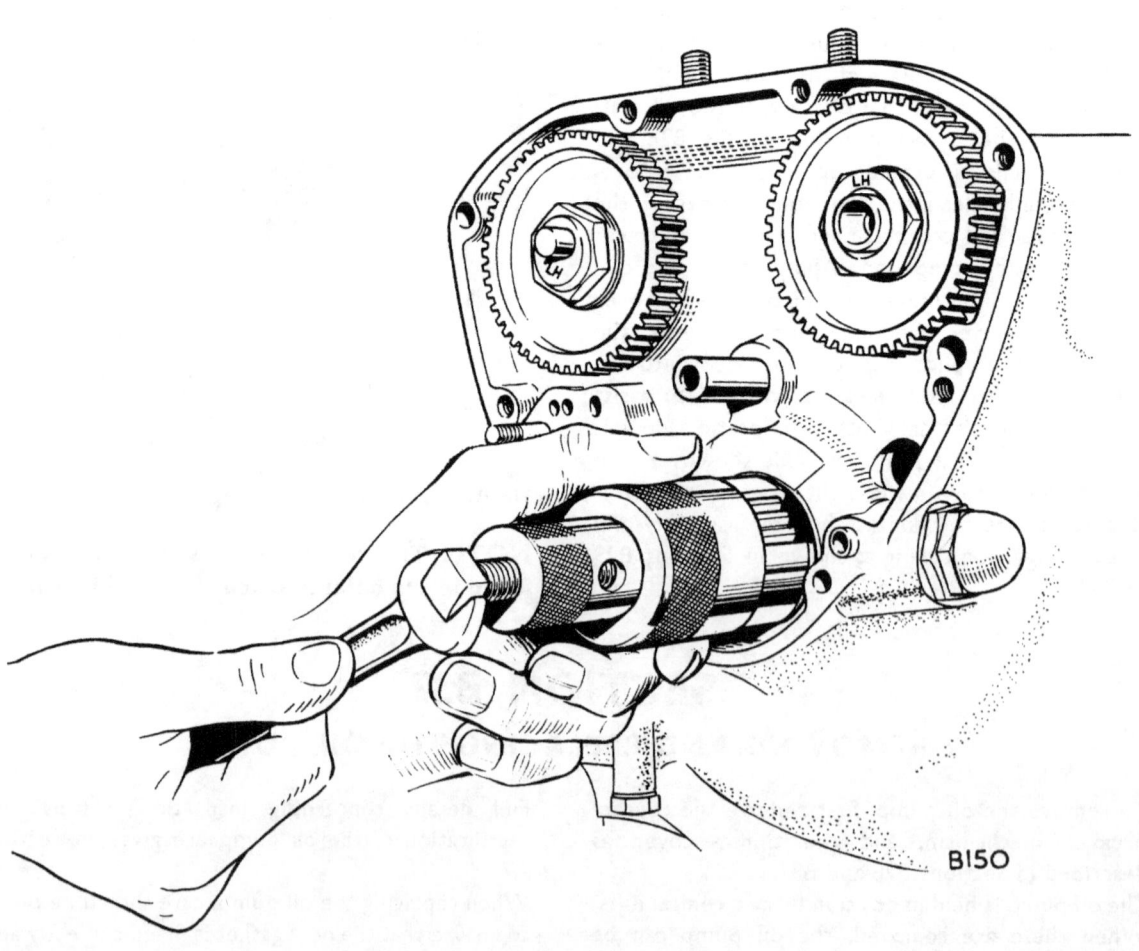

Fig. B29. Extracting the crankshaft pinion

ENGINE B

CRANKSHAFT PINION

Removal of the crankshaft pinion is facilitated by service tool 61-6019, which consists of a protective cap and three claw extractor body, complete with extractor bolt.

To extract the pinion, first press the protection cap over the end of the crankshaft, then place the extractor over the pinion, locate the three claws behind the pinion and screw down the body to secure them. Using a tommy bar and spanner the crankshaft pinion can then be extracted (see Fig. B31). When this is achieved, the key and (clamping washer if fitted) should be removed and placed in safe-keeping.

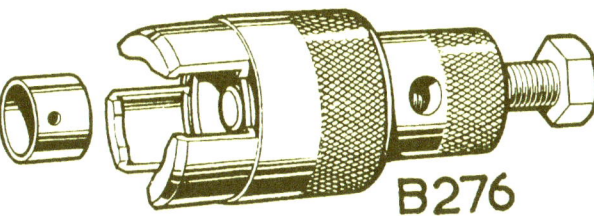

Fig. B30. Extractor tool 61-6019 showing protection cap which fits over crankshaft

Refitting the crankshaft pinion is aided by service tool Z79 which consists of a tubular drift and a guide, to ensure correct alignment.

When replacing the clamping washer ensure that the chamfered side is towards the crankshaft shoulder. Screw the guide onto the crankshaft. Smear the bore of the crankshaft pinion with grease to assist assembly and position it over the guide, so that the counter bore is outwards. Align the key and keyway and drive the pinion onto the crankshaft.

CAMSHAFT PINIONS

To facilitate extraction and replacement of both the inlet and exhaust camshaft pinions, the extractor and replacement adaptor should be used in conjunction with the service tool supplied under assembly number D2213.

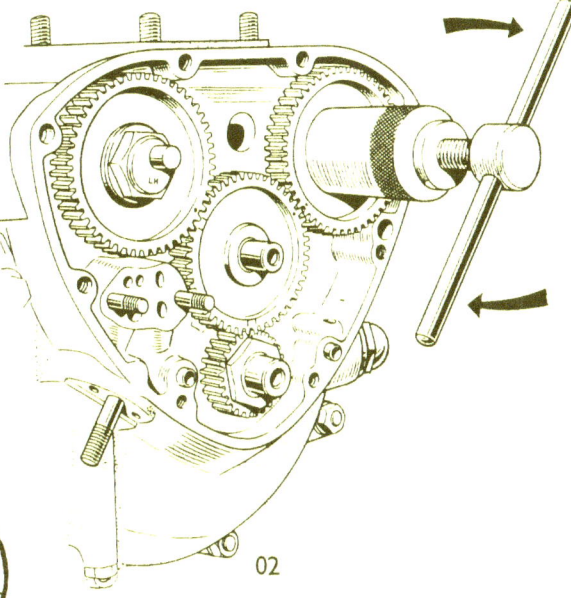

Fig. B31. Extracting camshaft pinion using D2213

To extract the pinion, first screw on the extractor body, then screw in the extractor bolt; the pinion will then be withdrawn from the camshaft (see Fig. B31).

In the case of the exhaust camshaft, the adaptor should be positioned on the end of the camshaft to avoid damage to the contact breaker location taper. The location keys in each of the camshafts are a tight fit, and may be left in position if it is not intended subsequently to remove the camshafts from the crankcase.

When replacing the pinions, first check that the keys are located correctly, then screw the adaptor into the assembler bolt and onto the camshaft.

The camshaft pinion should be lubricated to assist assembly, and the extractor body screwed onto it (remember that it is a left-hand thread). When this is done, slide the pinion and body over the replacer bolt, align the key and correct keyway and screw on the replacer nut and washer.

REFITTING THE INTERMEDIATE WHEEL

Turn the camshafts and crankshaft timing until the marks are towards the intermediate wheel spindle, then offer the wheel to the spindle with the timing marks aligned as shown in Fig. B33, for the particular model. Fourth gear should then be selected and the rear brake applied, so that the camshaft and crankshaft pinion retainer nuts can be tightened to the correct torque (see General Data). Reassembly then continues as a reversal of the above instructions.

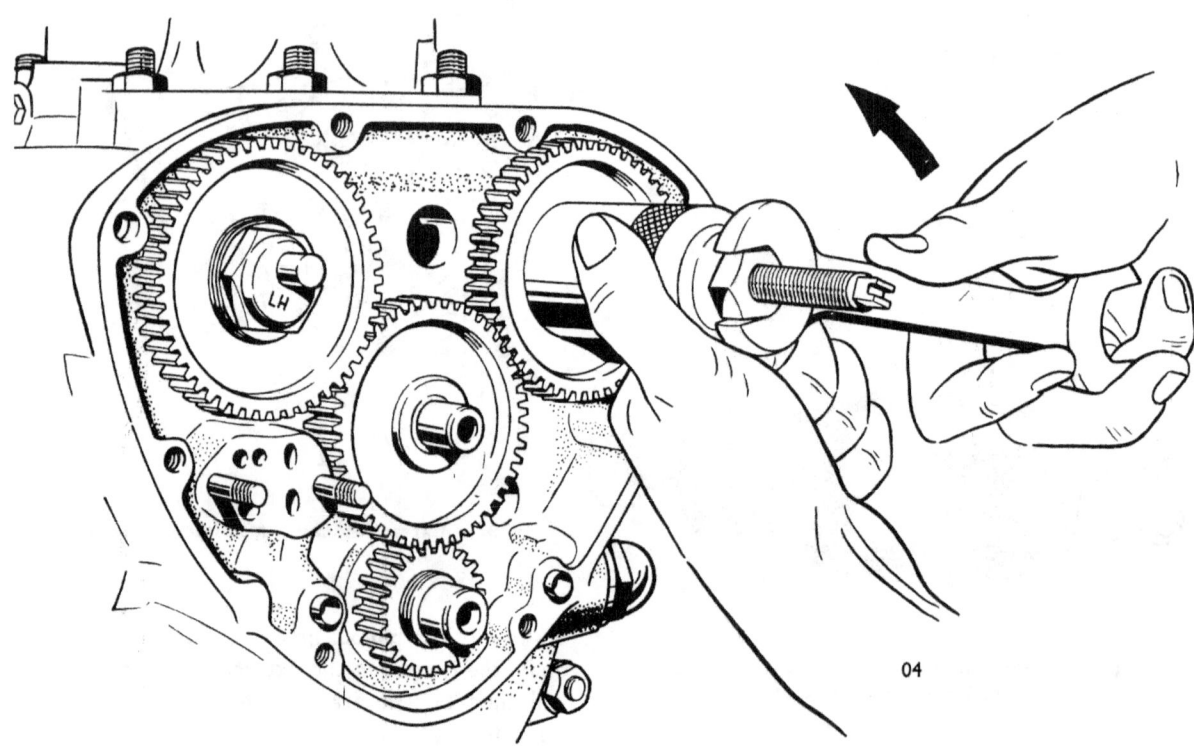

Fig. B32. Refitting the camshaft pinions

ENGINE

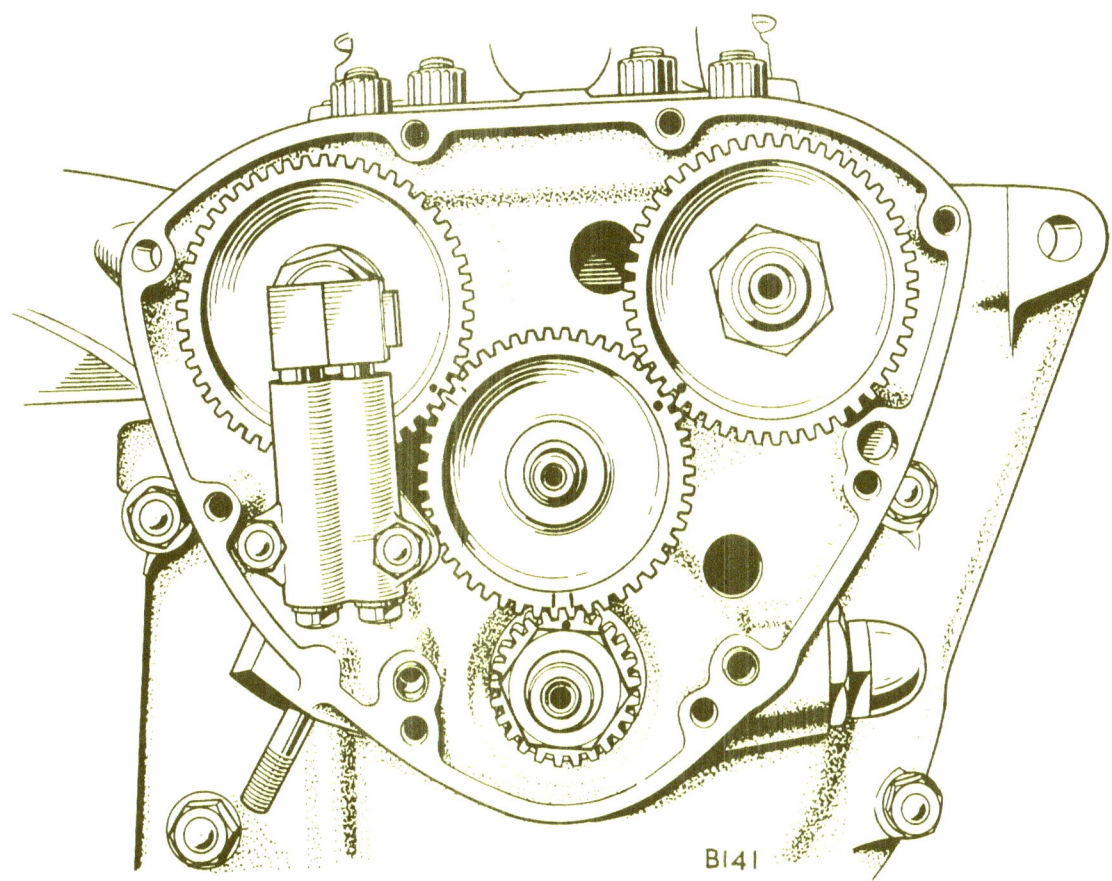

Fig. B33. Intermediate wheel location

(1) Exhaust camshaft pinion dot aligned with dot on intermediate wheel.

(2) Crankshaft pinion dot aligned with twin dashes on intermediate wheel.

(3) Inlet camshaft pinion. Dot aligned with:—(a) Long dash for T120 and TR6
    (b) Short dash for 6T.

SECTION B35
VALVE TIMING

The valve timing is sufficiently accurate for machines which are to be used under normal conditions, when the intermediate wheel is assembled in the position shown in Fig. B33, and the camshaft pinions are located by means of the keyway directly opposite the timing mark.

It should be noted that, due to the intermediate wheel having a prime number of teeth, the timing marks only coincide every 94th revolution, thus there is no cause for alarm if the timing marks will not readily re-align.

When checking the valve timing against the figures given in "General Data" for the particular model, it should be noted that these figures are relative to a valve rocker clearance of ·020 in. (·5 mm.) for checking only.

SECTION B36
DISMANTLING AND REASSEMBLING THE CRANKCASE ASSEMBLY

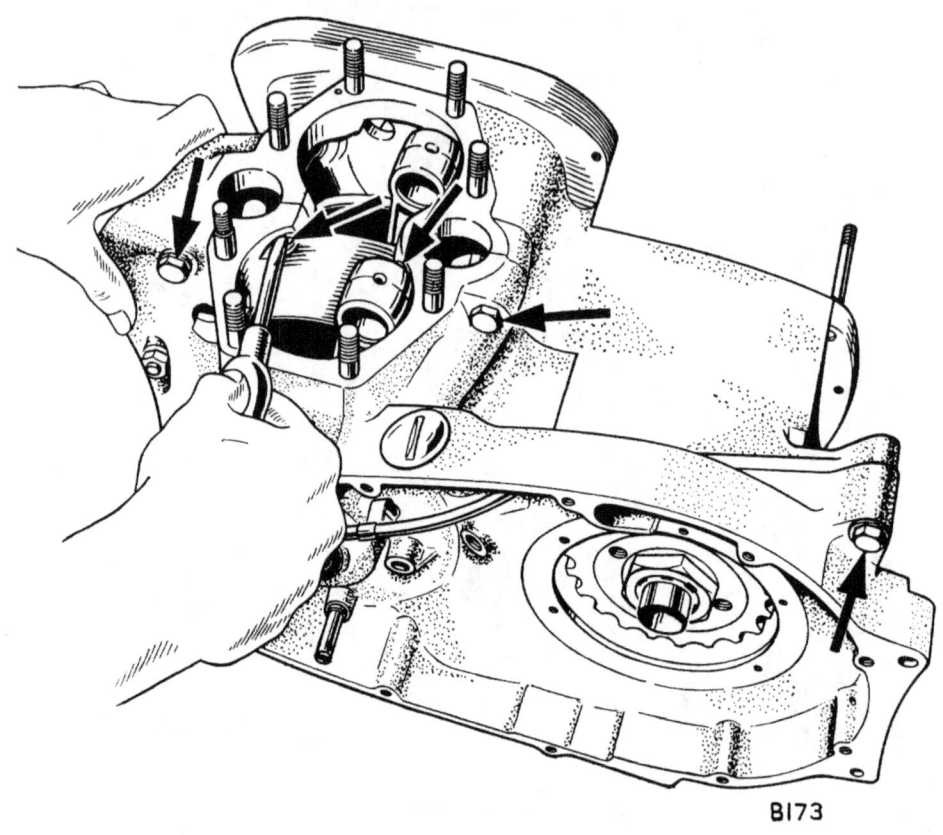

Fig. B34. Removing the crankcase junction screws

It is advisable to partially dismantle the engine unit whilst it is fixed to the motorcycle, then remove the remaining crankcase assembly and dismantle it on a work bench.

Proceed as described in Section B1 for removal of the engine unit, but leave the rear chain connected and the engine firmly mounted in the frame by means of the front and bottom engine mounting bolts. Remove the outer primary cover as shown underneath the engine (two snap connectors).

Unscrew three nuts securing the stator and withdraw it from over the mounting studs. Do not try to withdraw the leads at this stage.

Remove the pressure plate and clutch plates as detailed in Section C4. Select 4th gear and apply the rear brake, then unscrew the clutch hub securing nut and extract the clutch hub as shown in Section C9. When the primary chain has been threaded over the stator the sleeve nut should be unscrewed and the stator leads withdrawn.

Remove the gearbox outer cover and dismantle the gearbox (see Section D) then remove the rocker boxes, cylinder head, block and pistons as shown in Sections B2, B14, B19 and B22 respectively, then disconnect the control cable(s) and remove the carburetter(s).

ENGINE

Remove the contact breaker, timing cover complete with oil switch and oil pump (Sections B28, B32 and B33) then extract the crankshaft pinion. If it is required to inspect or change the camshafts or bushes, the camshaft pinions should also be extracted.

Remove the front and bottom engine mounting studs, disconnect the rear chain and remove the crankcase assembly.

Remove the crankcase filter and oilway blanking plug located at the bottom of the crankcase in line with the oil pump, and catch any oil that may be present in the crankcase.

Grip the crankcase firmly in a vice by means of the bottom mounting lug and unscrew the three bolts and the two screws shown in Fig. B34, then remove the remaining four studs and unscrew two nuts adjacent to the gearbox housing. The crankcase-halves may now be parted using extractor tool No. 61-6064. When the halves are apart, withdraw the crankshaft assembly and store it carefully, then remove the rotary breather valve from within the inlet camshaft bush in the left half-crankcase.

Thoroughly clean and degrease the crankcase paying particular attention to the oilways. DO NOT DAMAGE the scavenge pipe to crankcase joint.

REASSEMBLY

Prior to reassembly, the junction surfaces should be carefully scraped clean, giving special attention to the location spigot and dowels. Replace the oilway blanking plug located at the bottom of the R/H crankcase in line with the oil pump, and crankcase filter.

Mount the left half-crankcase on its side on two wooden blocks, or a bench with a hole in for crankshaft clearance, lubricate the main bearings and camshaft bushes. Place the rotary breather valve and spring into the camshaft bush, then assemble both camshafts ensuring that the slot in the end of the inlet camshaft engages the projection of the breather disc valve. Assemble the crankshaft into position ensuring that it is right home in the bearing by giving it a sharp blow with a hide mallet.

Note that the crankshaft is located to the timing side.

Apply a fresh coat of jointing compound to the junction surface of the left half-crankcase then lubricate the main bearings and camshaft bushes in both halves of the crankcase. Position the con-rods centrally and lower the right half-crankcase into position over the crankshaft. When the halves are mated, check the crankshaft and camshafts for freedom of rotation. The crankshaft should revolve freely whilst the camshafts should offer little or no resistance to rotation by hand.

Refit the crankcase securing bolts and studs, and tighten them until they are just "pinched-up". Check that the cylinder block junction surface of the crankcase is level.

If there is a slight step between the two halves, this should be corrected by tapping the front and rear of the crankcases as required, until a level surface is achieved. The crankcase securing bolts should then be tightened, a turn at a time, to the torque figures given in "General Data". The bolts arrowed in Fig. B34 should be tightened first, then the two inner screws, and so on.

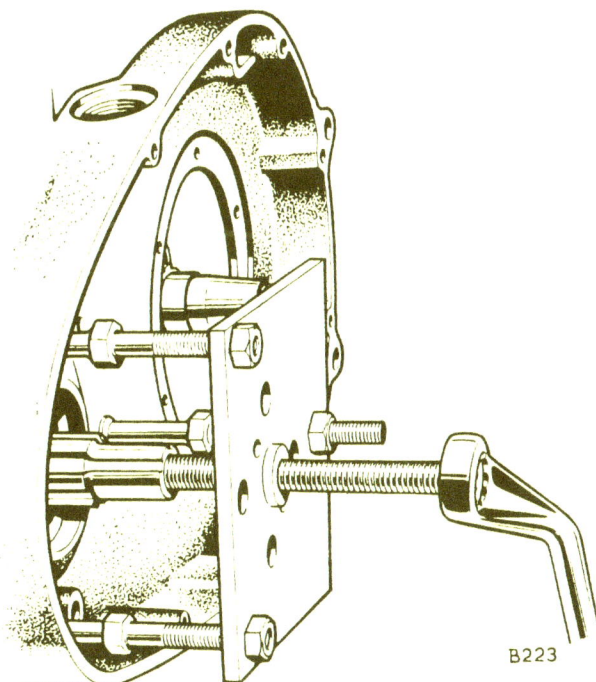

Fig. B35. Parting the crankcase halves using service tool 61-6046

Reassembly then continues as a reversal of the dismantling instructions. Prior to refitting the cylinder block, pour $\frac{1}{6}$ pint of oil into the crankcase.

SECTION B37
STRIPPING AND REASSEMBLING THE CRANKSHAFT ASSEMBLY

Grip the crankshaft conveniently in a suitable vice and place rag over any sharp edges to avoid the connecting rods becoming damaged. Mark the connecting rods, caps and crankshaft so that they can be replaced in their original positions.

NOTE: The connecting rod, cap and nut are centre punched on initial assembly so that the cap may be refitted correctly relative to the connecting rod.

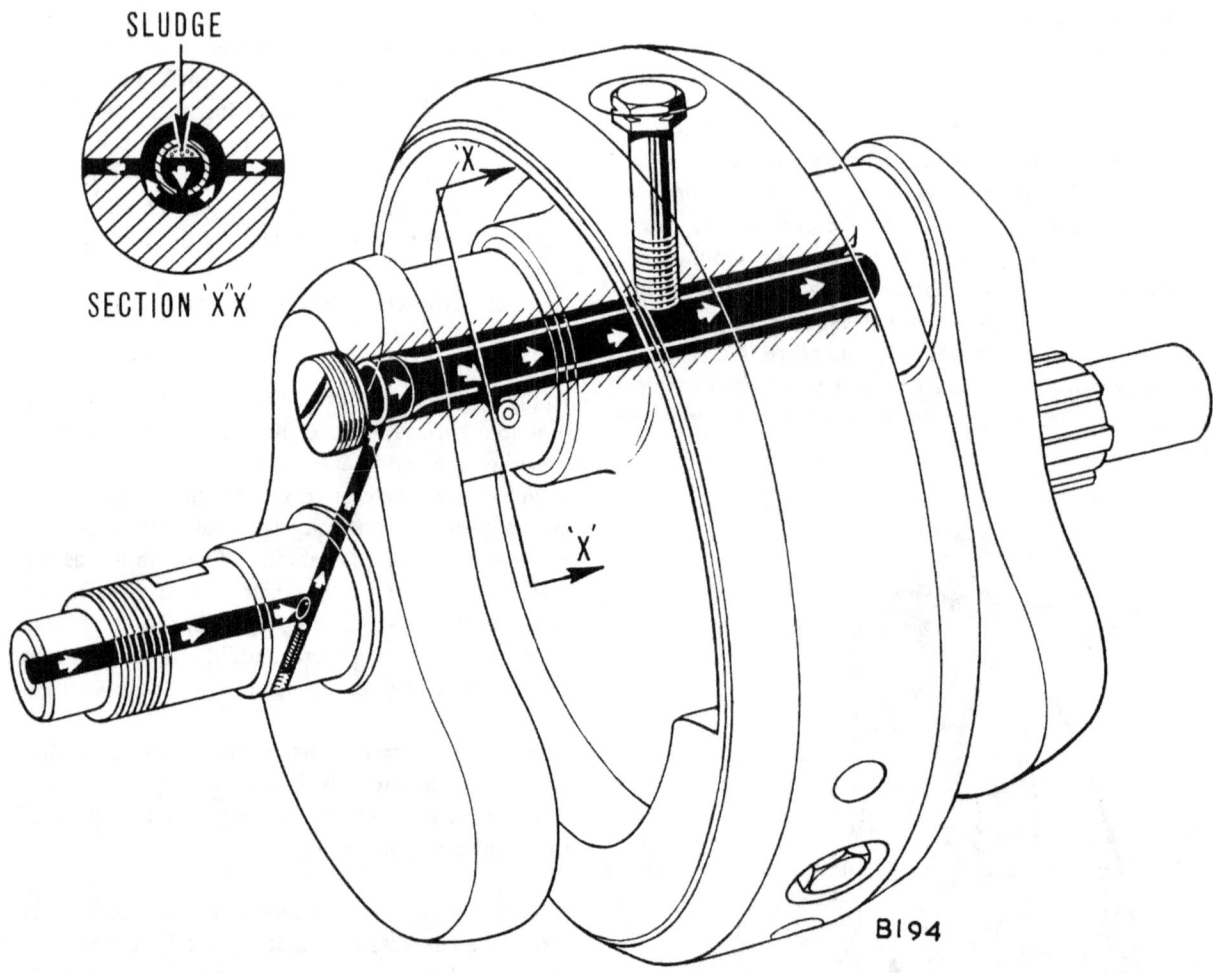

Fig. B36. Sectional view of crankshaft—showing oil tube

ENGINE

Unscrew the cap retainer nuts, a turn at a time to avoid distortion, then remove the caps and connecting rods. Refit the nuts to their respective bolts to ensure correct reassembly.

Using a large impact screwdriver, unscrew the oil tube retainer plug from the right end of the big-end journal. If difficulty is encountered, drill a $\frac{1}{8}$ in. dia. hole to $\frac{1}{8}$ in. depth in the crankshaft, to remove the centre punched indentation which locks the oil tube retainer plug in position.

Unscrew the flywheel bolt adjacent to the big-end journal, then withdraw the oil tube using a hooked rod located in the flywheel bolt location hole (see Fig. B36).

Thoroughly clean all parts in paraffin (kerosene) then clean the oil drillings using a jet of compressed air. Particular attention should be given to checking that each oil drilling is free from blockage.

To remove the flywheel, unscrew the remaining two bolts and press out the crankshaft, using a press which can give a load of up to 5 tons. (Ensure that there is a centre punch mark on the RIGHT side of the flywheel before removing; this enables the flywheel to be replaced in its original position).

Replacing the flywheel is best done when the oil tube is correctly located in position. Offer the oil tube into the crankshaft with the flywheel bolt holes in the tube and crankshaft aligned. Insert a flywheel bolt temporarily to locate the oil tube in position.

Tightly screw in the plug and centre punch the crankshaft opposite the slot so that the plug is locked in position.

To re-assemble the flywheel it should be heated to 100°C., then placed over the crankshaft (which should be cold) with the centre punch mark to the RIGHT. It will be necessary to turn the flywheel through 180° to get it over the crankshaft web. Turn it to its correct position relative to the crankshaft as soon as this is achieved, and align the bolt holes.

The flywheel bolts should be tightened to the torque figure given in "General Data" using a small amount of proprietary sealant such as "TRIUMPH LOCTITE" to obviate any possibility of the bolts working loose.

If a new or re-ground crankshaft or a new flywheel has been fitted, the assembly should be re-balanced,

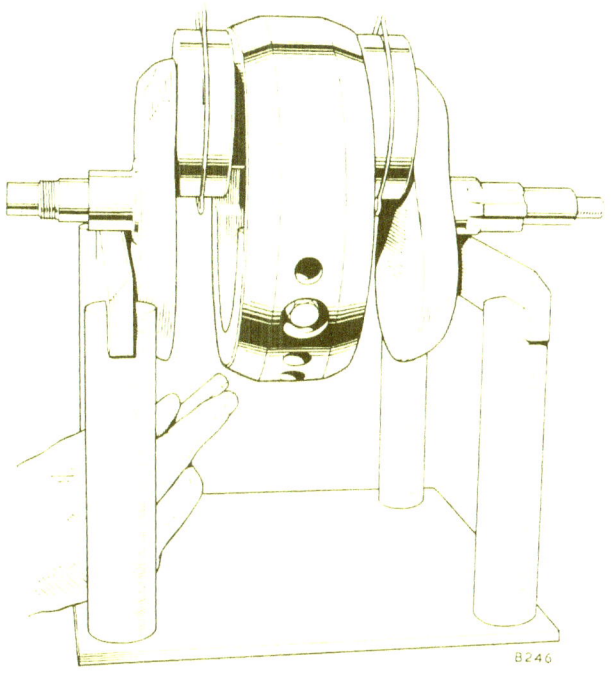

Fig. B37. Balancing the crankshaft

(to an 85% balance factor) using two service balance weights Z138 (689 gms. each) for both flywheel conditions. Place the assembly on true horizontal knife edges, resting it on the left and right main bearing diameters. Allow the assembly to come to rest, then mark the lowest point of the flywheel with chalk. Turn the assembly through 90° and if it returns to the same position drill a $\frac{3}{8}$ in. dia. hole centrally, adjacent to the chalk mark, to a depth of approximately $\frac{1}{2}$ in.

Repeat the balancing procedure again making a chalk mark as necessary, and drill further holes until the assembly will come to rest in any position when placed on the knife edges. The drilled holes should have a distance of approximately $\frac{3}{4}$ in. between centres.

Finally, thoroughly wash the assembly in paraffin (kerosene) and check that the oil-ways are free from blockage.

SECTION B38
REFITTING THE CONNECTING RODS

First, ensure that the connecting rod and cap and both the front and rear of the bearing shells are scrupulously clean, then offer the shells to the rod and cap and locate the shell tabs into their respective slots. Smear the bearing surfaces with oil and refit the rod and cap to their original journals, ensuring that the centre punch marks are aligned and that the tab location slots are adjacent (see Fig. B38).

Refit the bolts and screw on the nuts to the given torque figure.

On the very latest machines, centre punch marks are no longer used on the connecting rod nuts and on both these models and earlier ones with centre punch marks we now prefer the use of a torque wrench, to tightening to bolt extension as in previous instructions.

Finally, force oil through the drilling at the right end of the crankshaft with a pressure oil can until it is expelled from both big-end bearings, thus indicating that the oil passages are free from blockage and full of oil.

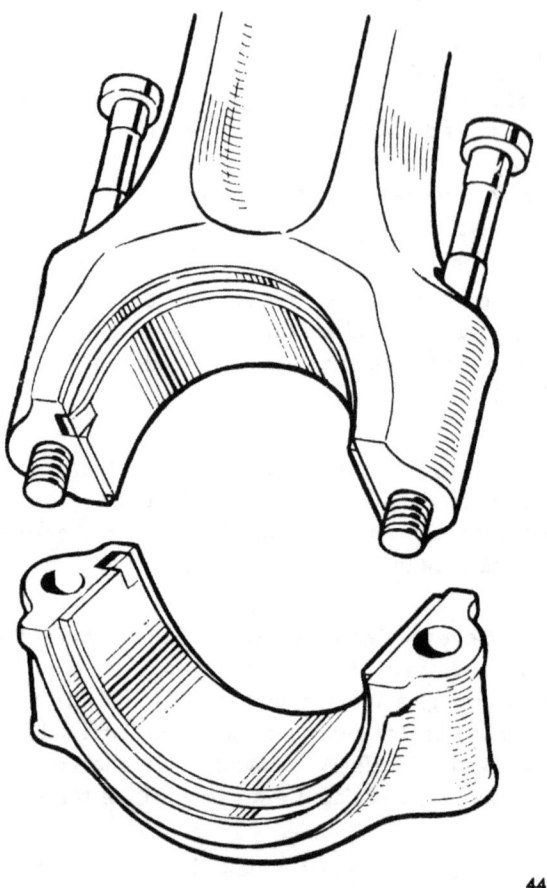

Fig. B38. Refitting the connecting rods

CRANKSHAFT LOCATION

Machines from DU.24875 onwards have the crankshaft located to the timing side as was the case between engine numbers DU.101-DU.13374. Machines between DU.13375 and DU.24874 had the crankshaft located to the drive side.

If such a machine was equipped with the roller drive side main bearing it would be necessary to fit also the timing pinion and clamping washer as shown in the No. 6 SPARE PARTS CATALOGUE.

ENGINE B

SECTION B39
INSPECTING THE CRANKCASE COMPONENTS

In preparation for inspection, thoroughly clean the crankcase-halves, main bearings, crankshaft and connecting rods, etc., in paraffin (kerosene) and allow them to drain. If there is an air pump accessible, then dry the components with a jet of compressed air and examine them as follows:—

(1) BIG-END BEARINGS

The extent of wear to the big-end journals can be determined by inspecting the bearing surfaces for scoring and by measuring the diameter of the journals. Light score marks can be reduced with smooth emery cloth but ensure that all parts are carefully washed after this operation.

Where a journal has been slightly scored the big-end shell bearings should be renewed. If the scoring and wear is extensive the big-end journals should be reground to a suitable size as given below.

NOTE: The replaceable white metal big-end bearings are pre-finished to give the correct diametral clearance. Under no circumstances should the bearings be scraped or the connecting rod and cap joint faces filed.

Shell bearing marking	Suitable crankshaft size	
	in.	mm.
Standard:—	1·6235	41·237
	1·6240	41·250
Undersize:—		
—·010	1·6135	40·983
	1·6140	40·996
—·020	1·6035	40·729
	1·6040	40·742

Service reground crankshafts are obtainable from a TRIUMPH dealer or in the U.K. from the TRIUMPH ENGINEERING CO. LTD., SERVICE DEPARTMENT.

(2) MAIN BEARINGS

Clean the bearings thoroughly in paraffin (kerosene), then dry them with a jet of compressed air. Test the bearing for roughness by spinning. Check the centre race for side-play and inspect the balls and tracks for any signs of indentation and pocketing. Examine the main bearing diameters on the crankshaft for wear. The bearings should be a tight push fit on the crankshaft and a press fit in the crankcase. A loose fitting bearing would tend to cause crankcase "rumble". The correct diameters of the main bearing journals are given in "General Data".

(3) CAMSHAFTS AND BUSHES

The camshaft bushes normally show very little sign of wear until a considerable mileage has been covered. A rough check on the wear can be made by inserting the camshaft into the bearing and feeling the up and down movement. An exact check can be made by measuring the camshaft with a micrometer and measuring the camshaft bushes with calipers. The working clearance figures are given in "General Data". Wear on the cam form will be mainly centred on the opening flank of the cam and on the lobe of the cam. Particular attention should be given to these areas when examining the cam form for grooving. In a case where there is severe grooving the camshaft and tappet followers should be renewed.

A method of estimating the extent of wear on the cam form is that of measuring the over-all height of the cam and the base-circle diameter. The difference is the cam lift. If all other aspects of the camshaft are satisfactory and the wear on the cam form does not exceed 0·010 in., then the camshaft may be used for further service.

(4) CRANKCASE FACES AND DOWELS

Ensure that the faces of the crankcases are not damaged in any way and that any dowels are in position, particularly the metering dowel on the timing cover face near the pressure release valve. The dowel is counter bored, incorporates a metering pin, and should be assembled with the larger bore outermost.

SECTION B40

RENEWING THE MAIN BEARINGS

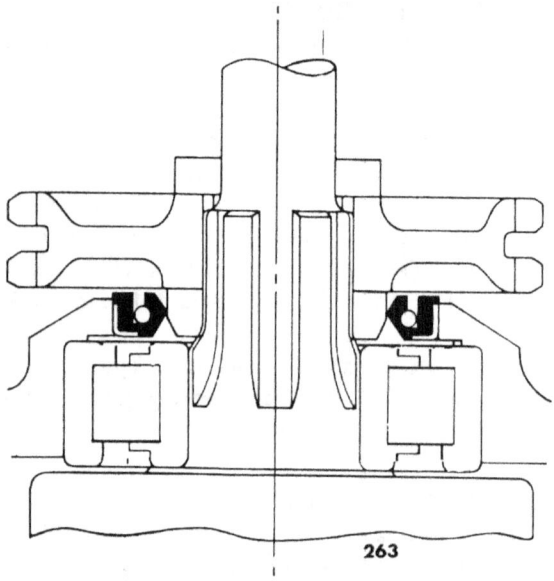

Fig. B39. Oil seal—left half-crankcase

The oil seal can be removed from the left half-crankcase by driving it outwards, in the opposite direction to the bearing after the bearing is removed. It is advisable to renew the oil seal, even if it does not appear badly worn.

To remove the timing side ball journal bearing heat the crankcases to approximately 100°C and drive the bearing inwards using service tool Z14. Alternatively, a suitable drift can be made from a piece of $1\frac{1}{4}$ in. diameter mild steel bar, about 6 in. long by turning it to $1\frac{1}{8}$ in. diameter for $\frac{1}{2}$ in. at one end.

On the drive side roller bearing the inner portion will be withdrawn with the crankshaft. The outer spool however will still involve heating the crankcase and if it is very tight in the case will require the use of special tool Z162 which expands to grip the outer spool.

To assemble the new bearings first ensure that the main bearing housing is clean, then heat the crankcase to approximately 100°C. and drive in the bearing using a tubular drift onto the outer race. Ensure that the bearing enters its housing squarely. If possible, use a press. Suitable dimensions for the drift are $2\frac{3}{4}$ in. outside diameter x 6 in. long.

When the bearings are in position, press the oil seal into place in the left half-crankcase (see Fig. B39).

The roller drive side bearing could be fitted to advantage on earlier machines. The roller bearing will be a direct replacement prior to Engine No. DU.13375. If fitted to machines between Engine Nos. DU.13375 and DU.24874 the crankshaft pinion and clamp washer must be changed to locate the crankshaft from the R.H. main bearing. The necessary parts are listed in the No. 6 replacement Parts Catalogue.

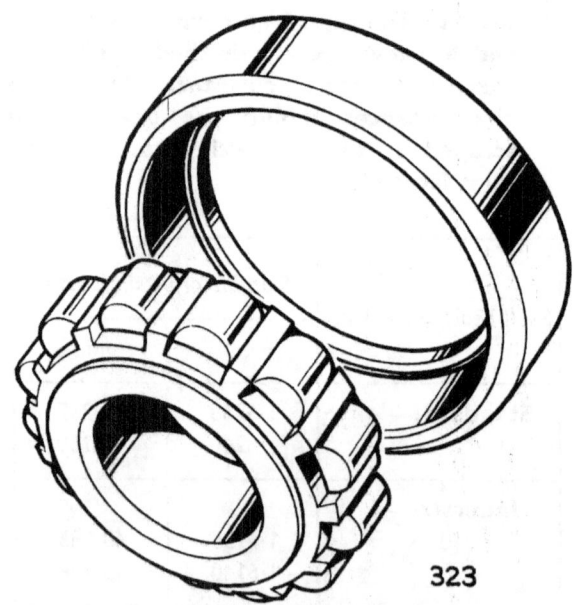

Fig. B40. Roller main bearing

ENGINE

SECTION B41
RENEWING CAMSHAFT BUSHES

To remove the camshaft bushes in the RIGHT half-crankcase heat the crankcase to 100°C. and drive the bush out from the outside, using a suitable drift. While the crankcase is still hot, drive in the new bush, ensuring that the oil feed hole in the bush and the crankcase drilling are aligned. A suitable drift for this purpose can be made from a 6 in. long piece of M.S. bar of $1\frac{1}{8}$ in. diameter, by machining a pilot on one end $\frac{7}{8}$ in. diameter x 1 in. long.

To remove the camshaft bush from the LEFT half-crankcase, a tap is necessary. An ideal size is $\frac{7}{8}$ in. diameter x 9 Whit. When a good thread has been cut in the old bush, heat the crankcase (100°C.) and screw in a suitable bolt. Grip the bolt in a vice and drive the crankcase with a hide mallet until the bush is removed. Do not attempt to lever the bush out of position with the bolt, or the case may be damaged. If the tap is used in place of the bolt, care must be taken not to give too hard a knock to the crankcase or the brittle tap may break.

Retained behind the inlet camshaft bush is the breather valve porting disc, which is located by means of a peg. When renewing the bush ensure that the disc is located correctly on the peg.

The sintered bronze camshaft bushes are machined to size before pressing in, therefore only the smallest amount of metal will need to be removed when they are renewed. See "General Data" for reaming sizes and working clearances.

When reaming is completed, the crankcase must be thoroughly washed in paraffin (kerosene) and allowed to drain. Preferably, use a jet of compressed air to ensure that all swarf is removed.

SECTION B42
REMOVING AND REPLACING THE TACHOMETER DRIVE

Where the optional tachometer is fitted, there is a right angled drive gearbox as shown in Fig. B41. It is not necessary to part the crankcases to remove the drive gearbox. When the large slotted end cap is removed and the engine turned over quickly the drive gear should be ejected. If this is not so, the gear can be withdrawn with long-nosed pliers. The left-hand threaded centre bolt holding the drive gearbox to the crankcase will then be seen. A $\frac{3}{16}$ in. Whitworth thin box spanner is needed to release this and the box will then come away from the crankcase. The driven gear housing is secured by a locking pin and is a relatively tight fit. See Fig. B41.

It will be noted that a spade in the back of the tachometer gearbox slots into a 'thimble' which is permanently fitted into the end of the exhaust camshaft.

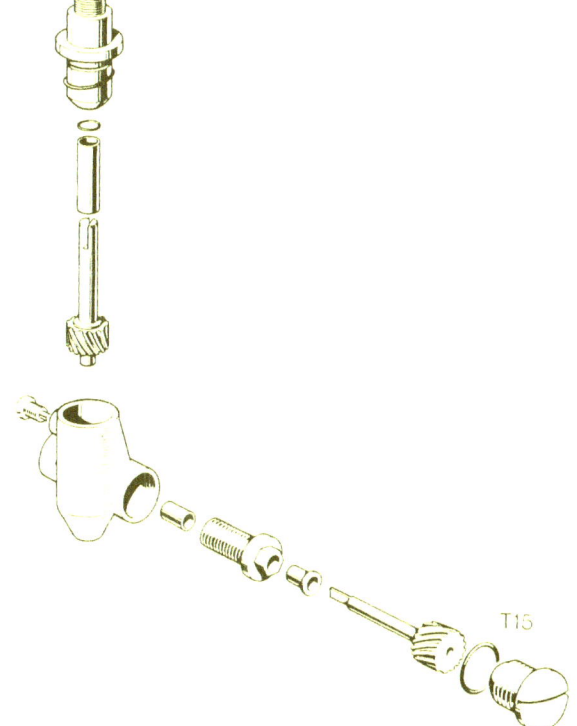

Fig. B41. Exploded view of tachometer gearbox.

ENGINE

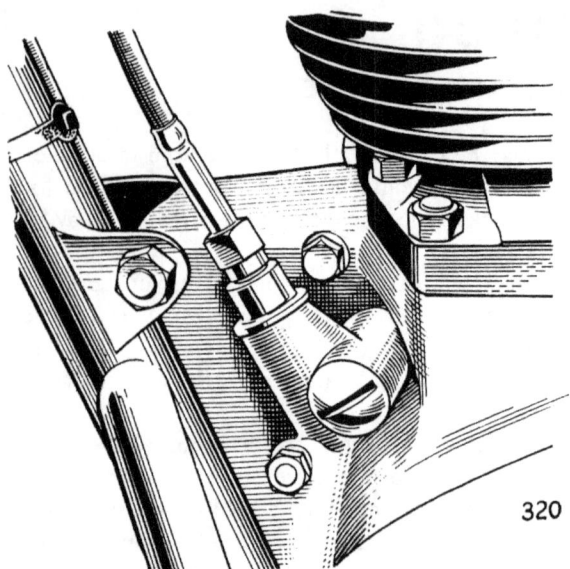

Fig. B46. Tachometer drive gearbox

The reassembly procedure for the drive gearbox is a reversal of the above.

Earlier machines had a simple spade and abutment which could if required be replaced by the right-angled drive used after engine number DU.24875. This would necessitate fitting also the later tachometer head and cable.

On U.S.A. market machines a "Stat-o-Seal" washer is used between the crankcase and tachometer gearbox. On such machines the seal should be renewed whenever the tachometer gearbox is removed and refitted.

If for any reason the tachometer drive thimble in the exhaust camshaft is displaced or damaged, this can be replaced with a special drive plug E7050 without dismantling the engine. To fit the plug, remove the tachometer drive gearbox or cable adaptor from the crankcase and using a $\frac{3}{8}$ in. diameter punch, drive the old thimble at least an inch back into the exhaust camshaft. If possible retrieve the broken off ears of the old thimble with a magnet. Thread the new drive plug through the tachometer drive hole in the crankcase and into the camshaft as far as possible. Finally make up a drift as below and drive the new plug into the camshaft until it is just flush with the end of the shaft. Take care that the drive plug is not driven too far in as the drive blade must engage adequately.

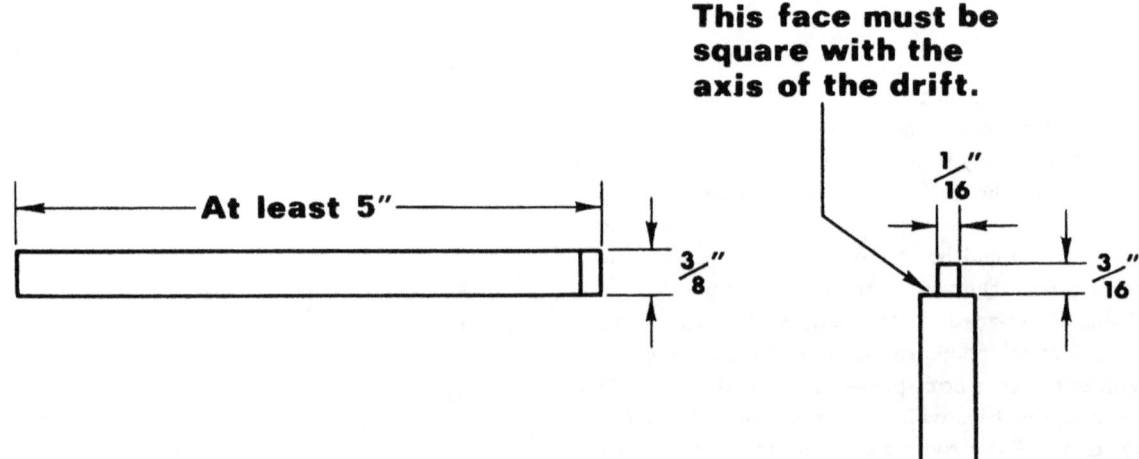

Fig. B51. Drive plug drift

SECTION C

TRANSMISSION

DESCRIPTION	Section
ADJUSTING THE CLUTCH OPERATING MECHANISM	C1
ADJUSTING THE PRIMARY CHAIN TENSION	C2
REMOVING AND REPLACING THE PRIMARY COVER	C3
REMOVING AND REFITTING THE CLUTCH PLATES	C4
INSPECTING THE CLUTCH PLATES AND SPRINGS	C5
ADJUSTING THE CLUTCH PRESSURE PLATE	C6
RENEWING SHOCK ABSORBER RUBBERS	C7
REMOVING AND REPLACING THE STATOR AND ROTOR	C8
REMOVING AND REPLACING THE CLUTCH AND ENGINE SPROCKETS	C9
INSPECTION OF THE TRANSMISSION COMPONENTS	C10
REAR CHAIN ALTERATIONS AND REPAIRS	C11

TRANSMISSION

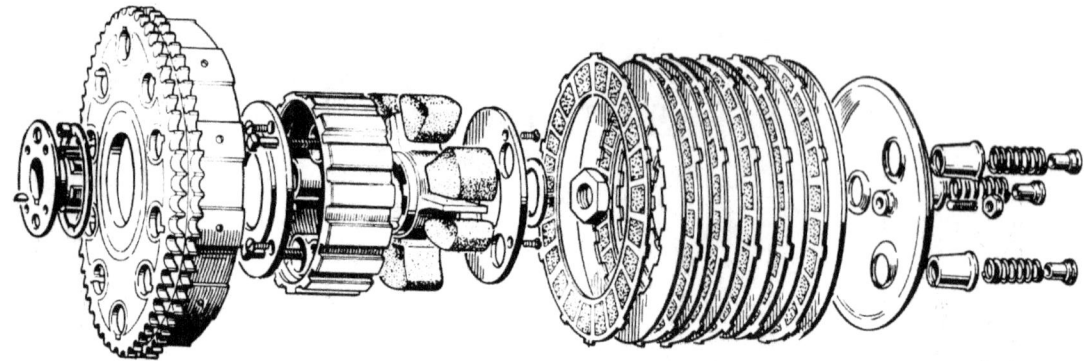

Fig. C1. General arrangement of clutch and shock absorber unit

DESCRIPTION

The clutch is of a multiplate type, using synthetic friction material on the bonded drive plates and incorporating a transmission shock absorber. The pressure on the clutch plates is maintained by three springs held in position by three slotted nuts.

The clutch is designed to operate in oil and it is essential that the oil level in the chaincase is maintained, otherwise the bonded segments of the driven clutch plates may burn and disintegrate under heavy loading. Always use the recommended grade of oil (see Section A2). If a heavier grade of oil is used the clutch plates will not readily separate when disengaged, which will cause a certain amount of difficulty when changing gear due to clutch drag.

The shock absorbing unit transmits the power from the clutch sprocket via the clutch plates to the gearbox mainshaft. Within the shock absorber unit the drive is transmitted through three large rubber pads to the three-armed spider which is splined to the clutch centre; this in turn is located to the gearbox mainshaft by means of a locking taper and key. In addition, there are three rubber rebound pads. The total effect of the rubber pads is to reduce the variations in engine torque at low speeds, providing an extremely smooth transmission of power to the gearbox.

SECTION C1
ADJUSTING THE CLUTCH OPERATING MECHANISM

The clutch, which is situated within the outer primary cover on the left of the machine, can be adjusted by means of the handlebar adjuster, pushrod adjuster and the pressure plate springs, the latter only being accessible for adjustment when the outer primary cover is removed. Section C4 fully describes adjusting the springs and pressure plate.

The clutch operating rod should have $\frac{1}{16}$ inches (1.5 mm.) clearance between the clutch operating mechanism and the pressure plate. To achieve this remove the inspection cap from the centre of the primary cover, then slacken the clutch cable handlebar adjustment right off.

Unscrew the hexagonal lock nut and screw in the slotted adjuster screw in the centre of the pressure plate until the pressure plate just begins to lift. Unscrew the adjuster one full turn and secure it in that position by re-tightening the lock-nut.

The clutch operating cable should then be re-adjusted, by means of the handlebar adjuster, until there is approximately $\frac{1}{8}$ inches (3 mm.) free movement in the cable.

TRANSMISSION

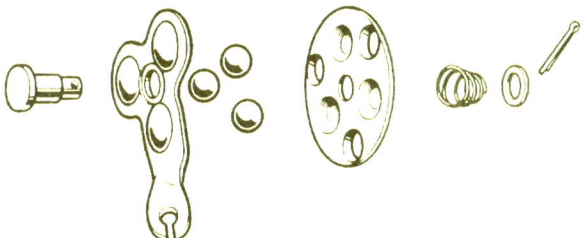

Fig. C2. Exploded view of clutch operating mechanism DU.66246 onwards

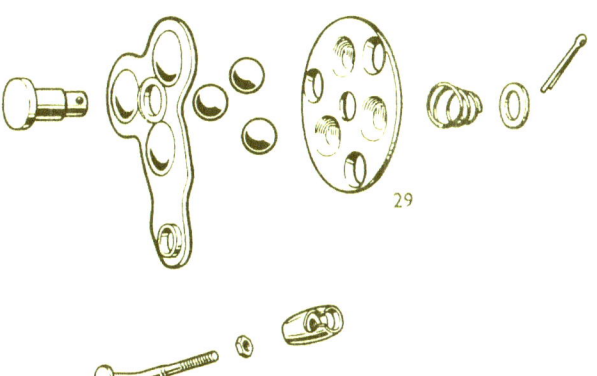

Fig. C3. Exploded view of clutch operating mechanism up to DU.66246

If the clutch is dragging and normal adjustment of the operating rod and operating cable produces no improvement, it will be necessary to remove the outer primary cover and check the pressure plate for true running as shown in Section C6.

Maladjustment of the clutch operating mechanism can be symptomised by a loud "click" when operating the clutch lever or on machines prior to DU.66246, the clutch cable becoming disconnected at the connector where the cable nipple joins the clutch mechanism operating spoke. In the former case adjustment of the clutch operating mechanism, as detailed above, will eliminate the noise. On earlier machines in the case where the clutch cable becomes disconnected at the gearbox, the clutch cable nipple and the spoke connector should be examined and renewed if necessary. This trouble may recur unless the adjustment procedure, as given above, is carefully followed. Full details of removal of the clutch operating mechanism are given in Section D6.

To maintain a smooth and easy clutch operation, particular attention should be given to the recommended primary chaincase oil change periods (see Section A1) and clutch cable lubrication (see Section A18).

SECTION C2

ADJUSTING THE PRIMARY CHAIN TENSION

The primary chain is of the Duplex type and is non-adjustable as the centres of the engine mainshaft and gearbox mainshaft are fixed. Provision for take-up of wear in the primary chain is made by means of a rubber faced tension slipper blade below the lower run of the chain. The free movement in the chain can be felt with the finger after removing the top inspection plug adjacent to the cylinder block, with the engine stopped, of course.

The correct chain adjustment is $\frac{3}{8}$ in. (9.5 mm.) free movement. To adjust the chain tension first place a drip tray underneath the chaincase and unscrew the hexagonal pillar bolt adjacent to the centre stand left hand lug. On some earlier models it may be necessary to loosen the left footrest to give sufficient clearance. To do this unscrew the footrest securing nut and tap the footrest in a downward direction to release it from its locking taper.

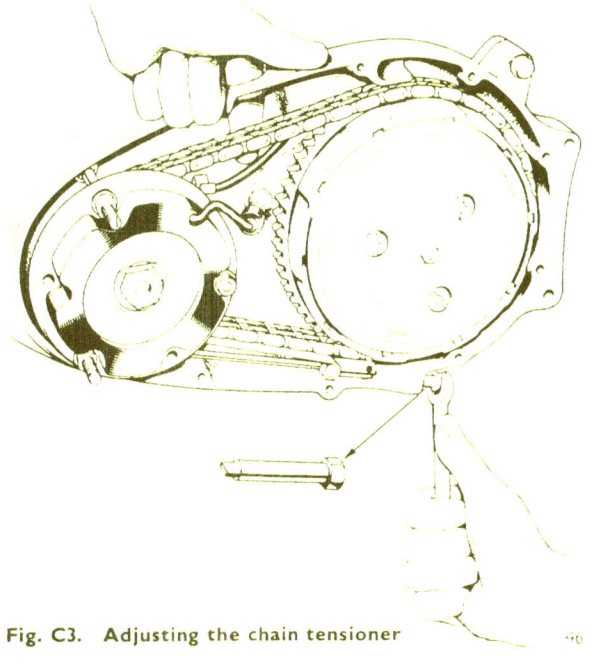

Fig. C3. Adjusting the chain tensioner

C

TRANSMISSION

Insert the short hexagon headed screwdriver D496 (supplied in the toolkit) and adjust the tension as required.

When adjustment is completed, check that the chaincase contains the recommended amount of oil (see Section A2).

SECTION C3
REMOVING AND REPLACING THE PRIMARY COVER

On machines fitted with twin exhaust pipes slacken the left finned clip bolt, left silencer clip bolt and remove the nut and bolt securing the left exhaust pipe bracket forward of the engine. Remove the exhaust pipe by tapping in a forward direction with a rubber or hide mallet.

Slacken off the adjustment at the rear brake operating rod until the brake pedal is clear of the primary cover.

Unscrew the left footrest securing nut and withdraw the footrest. On earlier machines where the footrest is bolted to the frame underneath the engine, the footrest should be tapped sharply in a downward direction to release it from its locking taper.

Place a drip tray underneath the primary cover and remove the hexagonal pillar bolt adjacent to the centre stand lug and allow the oil to drain from the chaincase. It is not necessary to disturb the rotor cover plate (on current models).

Remove the two domed nuts and copper washers and unscrew eight recess screws from the periphery of the primary cover. Withdraw the cover and paper gasket.

Refitting the cover is the reversal of the above instructions but fit a new paper gasket. Fitting the gasket can be aided by smearing the crankcase joint surface with grease. It is not advisable to use a jointing compound for this application.

Finally, replace the drain plug and fibre washer and pour in the recommended quantity of oil. (See Section A2).

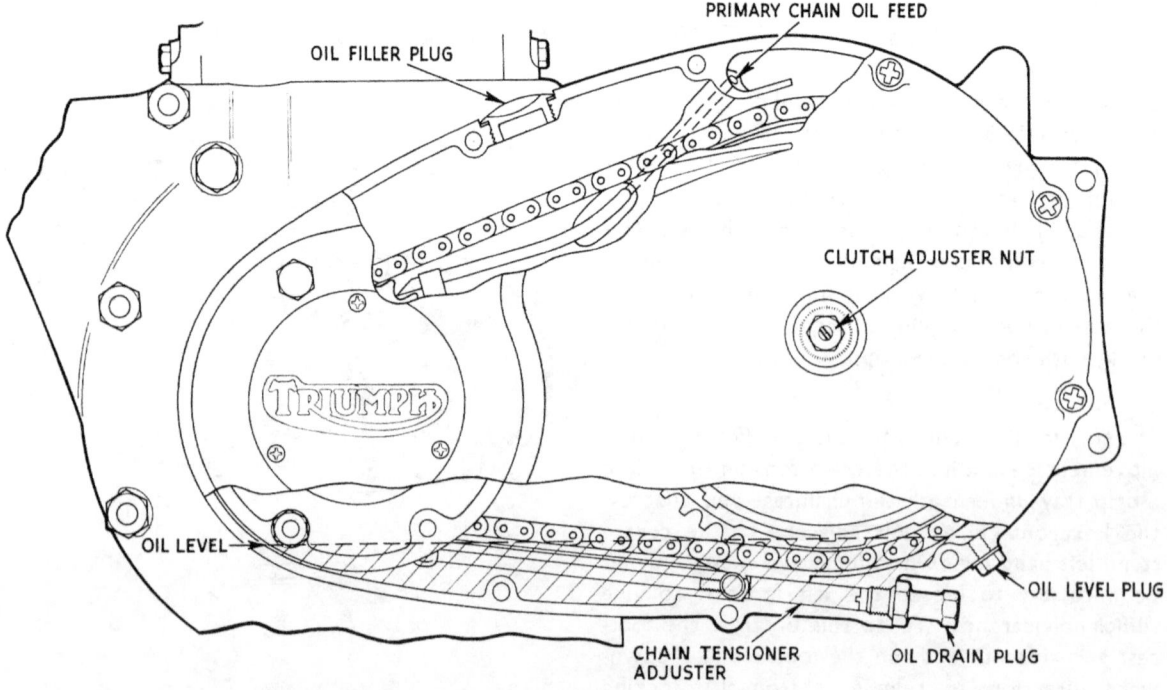

Fig. C4. Section through primary chaincase

SECTION C4
REMOVING AND REFITTING THE CLUTCH PLATES

Remove the outer primary cover as described in Section C3.

The three pressure plate springs are locked in position by means of location "pips" in the cups and on the drive adjuster nuts. To facilitate removal of the slotted adjuster nuts, insert a knife blade under the head of the nut whilst the nut is unscrewed (using a screwdriver of the type shown in Fig. C5). Withdraw the springs, cup and pressure plate assembly. Removal of the clutch plates is facilitated by means of two narrow hooked tools which can be made from a piece of $\frac{1}{32}$ in. dia. wire by bending to form a hook at one end. Thoroughly clean all parts in paraffin (kerosene) and inspect the clutch springs and plates for excessive wear (see section C5). When replacing the clutch plates remember that the bottom position is occupied by a bonded plate.

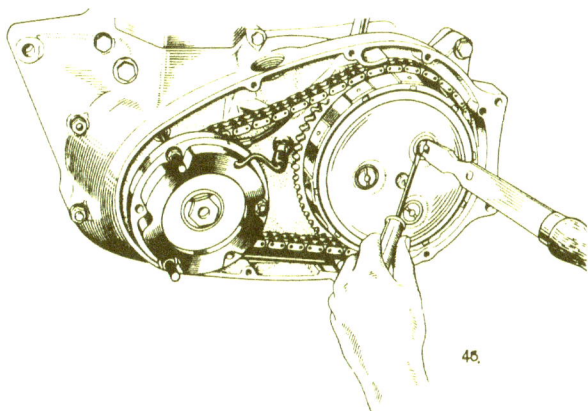

Fig. C5. Unscrewing the clutch spring nuts

Ensure that the cups are located correctly and assemble the springs and nuts, then adjust the pressure plate for true running as described below. Reassembly then continues as the reversal of the above instructions.

SECTION C5
INSPECTING THE CLUTCH PLATES AND SPRINGS

The bonded friction plates should be examined for excessive wear to the driving tags and the overall thickness of the clutch plates should be measured to determine the wear to the friction faces. If the reduction in thickness is more than ·030 in. (·75 mm.) when checked against a new plate the plate should be renewed. Check the fit of the driving tags in the clutch housing. The clearance should not be excessive.

Check the plain steel driven plates for flatness by placing the plates horizontally on a perfectly flat surface such as a thick piece of plate glass.

Original finish on the driven plates is a phosphoric acid etched surface and hence the plates need not be polished. Check the fit of the plate on the shock absorber housing. The radial clearance should not be excessive.

Inspect the clutch springs for compressive strength by measuring the length of the spring and comparing it with the dimensions given in "General Data". If a spring has shortened more than 0·1 in. (2·5 mm.) the complete set should be renewed. It is not advisable to renew just one or two springs as this may ultimately result in the pressure plate running unevenly.

SECTION C6
ADJUSTING THE CLUTCH PRESSURE PLATE

When the pressure plate is refitted or requires adjustment, the following procedure should be observed. With neutral selected, sit astride the machine, disengage the clutch, then depress the kickstart-pedal and observe the rotation of the pressure plate; it should revolve true relative to the clutch housing. If it does not do so, the three slotted nuts must be initially adjusted so the ends of the clutch pins are flush with the heads of the nuts. The nut is prevented from unscrewing by a "pip" on the underside and to unscrew a nut, a narrow screwdriver should be used to hold the spring away from the "pip" of the nut as shown in Fig. C5.

When the nuts are flush with the ends of the pins depress the kickstart again and mark the "high-spot" with chalk, then screw in the nearest nut(s) about half a turn and try again. Repeat this procedure until the plate rotates evenly without "wobbling".

SECTION C7
RENEWING SHOCK ABSORBER RUBBERS

When the primary cover and clutch plates are removed, access is gained to the shock absorber unit, which consists of a housing, paddle or spider, inner and outer cover plates and shock absorbing rubbers.

To remove the rubbers for inspection or renewal, first unscrew the three screws which serve to retain the shock absorber cover plate and lever the plate free, using a suitable small lever.

The shock absorber rubbers can be prised out of position, using a sharp pointed tool, commencing by levering out the smaller rebound rubbers first.

When the three small rebound rubbers are removed the large drive rubbers will be free to be withdrawn.

If the rubbers show no signs of punctures or cracking, etc., they can be refitted, but remember that a slight puncture in the rubber can ultimately result in the rubber disintegrating.

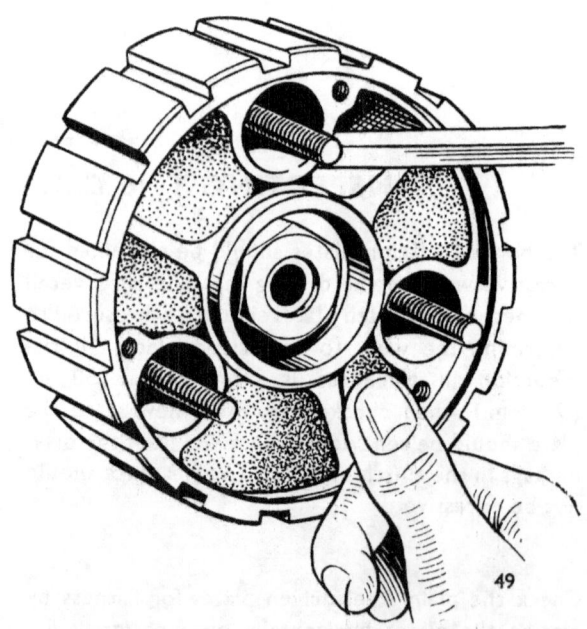

Fig. C6. Replacing the shock absorber rubbers

TRANSMISSION

To replace the shock absorber drive and rebound rubbers, first install all three of the larger drive rubbers in position as shown in Fig. C6. Follow through by inserting and replacing the smaller rebound rubbers. It may prove necessary to lever the shock absorber spider arms using a small tommy bar or similar to facilitate assembly, but this operation can be accomplished 'in situ' on the machine without the need for special tools or equipment, or necessity for removing the complete unit from the machine.

Although the rubbers are of an oil resistant type, it is not advisable to use oil or grease as an aid to reassembly as this may shorten the working life of the rubber.

Ensure that the three shock absorber outer cover screws are tight. Use a screwdriver that engages the complete length of the screw slot. Apply Triumph "LOCTITE" to the screw threads before final assembly.

SECTION C8
REMOVING AND REPLACING THE STATOR AND ROTOR

First disconnect the stator leads from underneath the engine (two snap connectors or three on earlier models) then, with the primary cover removed, unscrew the three stator retaining nuts and withdraw the stator from over the mounting studs and withdraw the lead from the sleeve nut. If any difficulty is encountered, unscrew the sleeve nut and the lead can then be withdrawn easily. To remove the rotor unbend the tab washer and unscrew the mainshaft nut using a box spanner and mallet, or, alternatively, select 4th (top) gear and apply the rear brake, then unscrew the nut.

Check the rotor carefully for signs of cracking or fatigue failure.

When replacing the rotor ensure that the key is located correctly, then tighten the nut to the torque figure given in "General Data".

When refitting the stator, ensure that the side of the stator with the leads connecting the coils together is outermost, then tighten the retaining nuts to the torque figure given in General Data Section. Insert the lead into the sleeve nut and connect the three wires to those of the same colour code underneath the engine. Check that the position of the lead is such that it cannot foul the chain.

Finally, rotate the crankshaft and ensure that the rotor does not foul the stator. It should be possible to insert a feeler gauge of 0·008 in. (0·2 mm.) thickness between each of the stator pole pieces and the rotor.

Fig. C7. Showing stator location on crankcase

SECTION C9

REMOVING AND REPLACING THE CLUTCH AND ENGINE SPROCKETS

Remove the primary cover as shown in Section C3, then remove the pressure plate and clutch plates, as shown in Section C4. Insert the locking plate Z13 into the clutch housing and remove the stator and rotor as described in Section C8. Remove the rotor key and distance piece and slacken off the chain tensioner. Unscrew the clutch hub self locking securing nut then remove the cupped washer. (Machines before DU.48145 have a plain nut and tab washer).

As the primary chain is of the endless type, the clutch and engine sprockets have to be extracted simultaneously using extractor D622/3 and extractor tool Z151 as shown in Figs. C8 and C9 (machines before DU.48145 use clutch extractor DA50/1).

engine sprocket extractor, No. Z151, and screw in the centre bolt and extract the engine sprocket.

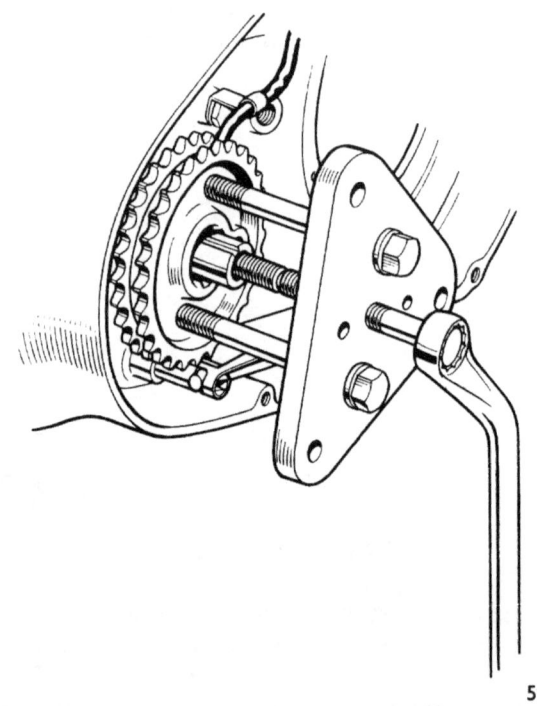

Fig. C9. Extracting the engine sprocket, using service tool Z151

Fig. C8. Extracting the clutch centre, using extractor D662/3 and locking plate Z13

Screw the body of the clutch extractor into the clutch hub until the maximum depth of thread is engaged, then tighten the centre bolt until the hub is released. When this is achieved, assemble the

Press out the hub from the shock absorber to release the sprocket, thrust washer, rollers and threaded pins.

Finally, remove the key from the gearbox mainshaft and check that the oil seal in the primary chain inner cover is a good fit over the high gear. To renew this oil seal the circular cover should be removed. When replacing the cover, use a new paper gasket and ensure that the oil seal is pressed in with the lip relative to the cover as shown in Fig. C10.

Note that on current models the actual 'nose' of the high gear has been extended and the cover and centre seal increased in diameter to suit. Seals, covers and high gears are only interchangeable as a set.

TRANSMISSION

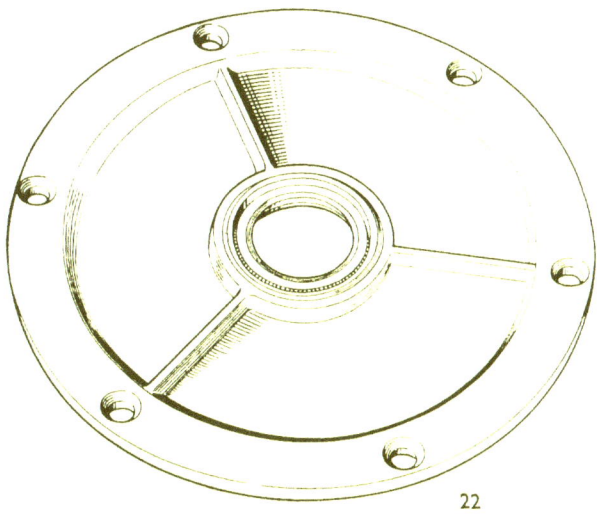

Fig. C10. Oil seal in gearbox sprocket detachable cover

Thoroughly clean all parts in paraffin (kerosene) and inspect them for wear or fatigue as shown in Section C10.

Grease the clutch hub and fit the thrust washer and 20 of the correct rollers.

Do not use $\frac{1}{4}$ in. $\times$ $\frac{1}{4}$ in. bright ended rollers.

Place the sprocket in position and press on the shock absorber complete with the three threaded pins. If the splines are loose use Triumph "LOCTITE".

When replacing the primary chain and sprockets, ensure that the taper ground boss of the engine sprocket is towards the crankshaft main bearing and the oil seal. With the gearbox mainshaft key carefully in position, locate the clutch hub onto the mainshaft taper and tap it slightly to lock it onto the taper.

Place the primary chain over the engine sprocket and drive the sprocket onto the crankshaft.

Offer the clutch locking tool Z13 into the clutch plate housing and then refit the cup washer, tab washer and clutch securing nut.

NOTE: The cup washer fits with the cup side out and the tab washer fits with the long tab located in the hole in the bore of the shock absorber spider.

On machines after DU.48144 the cupped washer, tab washer and nut are replaced by a modified cupped washer and self locking nut.

Engage fourth gear, apply the rear brake and tighten the clutch securing nut to the torque figure given in "General Data".

Do not forget to fit the distance piece between the engine sprocket and rotor and remember to refit the rectangular section rotor locating key. Re-assembly then continues as a reversal of the above instructions. Finally, replenish the chaincase with the recommended grade of oil (see Section A2).

Note.—Alternatively, the clutch sprocket may be removed by prising out the twenty roller bearings and allowing the sprocket to move both outwards and forwards until it can be unmeshed from the primary chain. This alternative only applies if the shock absorber assembly can readily be detached from the hub to allow access to the rollers.

SECTION C10
INSPECTION OF THE TRANSMISSION COMPONENTS

(1) Inspect the primary chain for excessive wear of the rollers and pivot pins and check that the elongation does not exceed $1\frac{1}{2}\%$. To do this first scribe two marks on a flat surface exactly 12 in. (30·5 cm.) apart, then after degreasing or washing the chain in paraffin (kerosene), place the chain opposite the two marks. When the chain is compressed to its minimum free length the marks should coincide with the centres of two pivot pins 32 links apart. When the chain is stretched to its maximum free length the extension should not exceed $\frac{1}{4}$ in. (6·25 mm.).

Inspect the condition of the sprocket teeth for signs of hooking and pitting.

A very good method of indicating whether the chain is badly worn or not is to wrap it round the clutch sprocket and attempt to lift the chain from its seating at various points round the sprocket. Little or no lift indicates that both the sprocket and chain are in good condition.

(2) Check the fit between the shock absorber spider and the clutch hub splines. The spider should be a push fit onto the clutch hub and there should not be any radial movement.

Similarly check the fit of the engine sprocket splines onto the crankshaft. Again, there should not be any radial movement.

If either the spider or the engine sprocket are tight fitting on the clutch hub and crankshaft respectively, there is no cause for concern as such a fit is to the best advantage.

(3) Check the clutch hub roller bearing diameter, the rollers themselves and the bearing of the clutch sprocket for excessive wear and pitting etc. Measure the rollers, clutch hub and clutch sprocket bearing diameters and compare them with the dimensions given in "General Data".

If the diameters of the rollers are below the bottom limit, they should be renewed. When purchasing new rollers ensure that they are in accordance with the dimensions given in "General Data". In particular, check that the length is correct.

(4) Check that the shock absorber spider is a good working fit in the inner and outer retaining plates and that the arms of the spider have not caused excessive score marks on the inner faces of the retaining plates. A good idea is to check the working clearance by assembling the shock absorber unit without the rubbers.

(5) Inspect the clutch operating rod for bending, by rolling it on a flat surface such as a piece of plate glass. Check that the length of the rod is within the limits given in "General Data". This component should not be replaced with anything other than a genuine Triumph spare part. The ends of the rod are specially heat treated to give maximum wear resistance.

TRANSMISSION

SECTION C11
REAR CHAIN ALTERATIONS AND REPAIRS

If the chains have been correctly serviced, very few repairs will be necessary. Should the occasion arise to repair, lengthen or shorten a chain, a rivet extractor, as shown in Fig. C13, and a few spare parts will cover all requirements.

To SHORTEN a chain containing an EVEN NUMBER OF PITCHES remove the dark parts shown in (1) and replace by cranked double link and single connecting link (2).

To SHORTEN a chain containing an ODD NUMBER OF PITCHES remove the dark parts shown in (3) and replace by a single connecting link and inner link as (4).

To REPAIR a chain with a broken roller or inside link, remove the dark parts in (5) and replace by two single connecting links and one inner link as (6).

Fig. C12. Rear chain alterations

RIVET EXTRACTOR (PART NUMBER 167)

The rivet extractor can be used on all motorcycle chains up to ¾ in. pitch, whether the chains are on or off the wheels.

When using the extractor:—

(1) Turn screw anti-clockwise to permit the punch end to clear the chain rivet.

(2) Open the jaws by pressing down the lever (see below).

(3) Pass jaws over chain and release the lever. Jaws should rest on a chain roller free of chain link plates (see below).

(4) Turn screw clockwise until punch contacts and pushes out rivet end through chain outer link plate. Unscrew punch, withdraw extractor and repeat complete operation on the adjacent rivet in the same chain outer link plate. The outer plate is then free and the two rivets can be withdrawn from opposite sides with the opposite plate in position. Do not use the removed part again.

When the alterations are finished the chain should be lubricated as shown in Section A13.

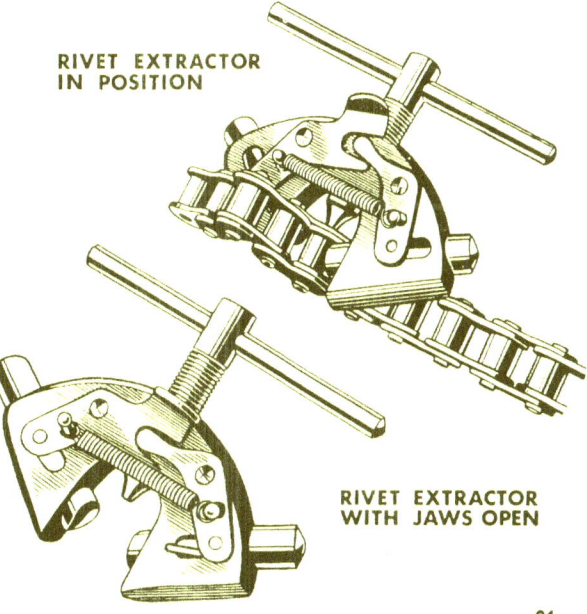

RIVET EXTRACTOR IN POSITION

RIVET EXTRACTOR WITH JAWS OPEN

Fig. C13. Chain link rivet extractor, part number 167

NOTES

SECTION D

GEARBOX

DESCRIPTION	Section
REMOVING AND REPLACING THE OUTER COVER ASSEMBLY	D1
DISMANTLING AND REASSEMBLING THE KICKSTART MECHANISM	D2
DISMANTLING AND REASSEMBLING THE GEARCHANGE MECHANISM	D3
INSPECTING THE GEARCHANGE AND KICKSTART COMPONENTS	D4
RENEWING KICKSTART AND GEARCHANGE SPINDLE BUSHES	D5
CLUTCH OPERATING MECHANISM	D6
DISMANTLING THE GEARBOX	D7
INSPECTION OF THE GEARBOX COMPONENTS	D8
RENEWING MAINSHAFT AND LAYSHAFT BEARINGS	D9
REASSEMBLING THE GEARBOX	D10
CHANGING THE GEARBOX SPROCKET	D11
SPEEDOMETER DRIVE GEAR COMBINATIONS (BEFORE DU.24875)	D12
GEARBOX SPROCKET AND MAINSHAFT HIGH GEAR	D13
SPEEDOMETER DRIVE GEARS	D14

GEARBOX

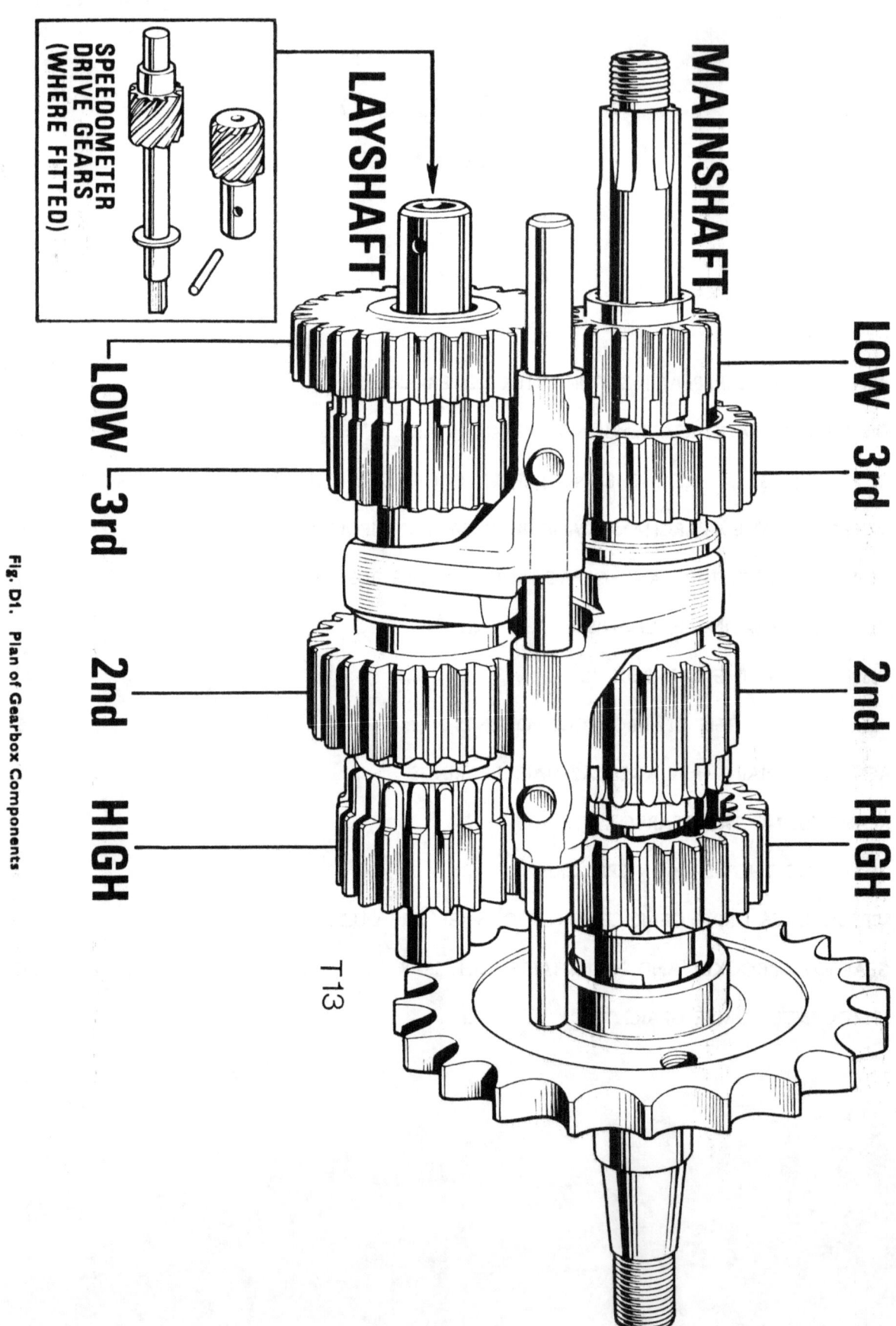

Fig. D1. Plan of Gearbox Components

GEARBOX

DESCRIPTION

The Triumph unit construction twin cylinder models are all fitted with a four-speed gearbox which is an integral part of the right half crankcase. The gearbox inner and outer covers are made of aluminium alloy D.T.D. 424 which gives the utmost rigidity and strength. Gears are manufactured from high quality nickel steel and subsequently case hardened and are designed to withstand heavy loading.

The mainshaft is supported by heavy duty ball races at each end, and the layshaft by special needle roller bearings which are pressed into the casing and inner cover. Keyed to the left end of the gearbox mainshaft is the multi-plate clutch, which runs in oil and is operated by a thrust rod which fits through the centre of the gearbox mainshaft.

The speedometer drive, which is enclosed in the inner cover is taken from the layshaft by means of spiral drive gears.

The clutch operating mechanism, kickstarter quadrant and the gearchange quadrant are all housed in the gearbox outer cover.

To meet special demands for certain sporting events there are available alternative close ratio and wide ratio gears which enables the gearbox to be suitably converted for road racing and trials riding respectively. For details of the parts required for such a changeover, consult the appropriate TRIUMPH Replacement Parts Catalogue.

SECTION D1

REMOVING AND REPLACING THE GEARBOX OUTER COVER ASSEMBLY

Slacken the right exhaust pipe finned clip bolt, silencer clip bolt and remove the exhaust pipe bracket nut and bolt and drive the R.H. exhaust pipe free with a hide mallet. Unscrew the right footrest securing nut and withdraw the footrest. In addition, on earlier machines with rear panels, remove two domed nuts, two front panel junction screws and the top nut securing the right panel. The panel is then free to be removed.

Slacken off the clutch cable adjustment and slip out the cable nipple at the handlebar control. Slide the rubber cover up away from the abutment for the cable at the gearbox end and unscrew the abutment.

Remove the large slotted plug from the gearbox outer cover and access will be gained to the clutch operating arm. It is only necessary then to release the cable nipple from the arm with the finger. On earlier models there is no plug on the outer cover. To release the cable after slackening at the handlebar end it is only necessary to remove the slotted adaptor, then to unscrew and lift the cable abutment. The slotted nipple seen in Section C1 will be revealed and the cable nipple detached from this.

Place a drip tray underneath the gearbox and unscrew the gearbox filler plug and drain plug.

Engage 4th (top) gear. This will allow several otherwise difficult nuts to be unscrewed by subsequently applying the rear brake when required.

Unscrew the top and bottom hexagonal nut and the recess screws from the periphery of the gearbox cover. Depress the kickstart lever slightly and tap the cover until it is free.

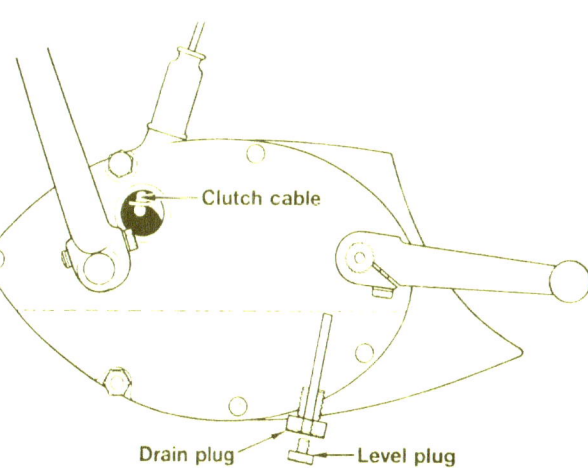

Fig. D2. Showing gearbox oil level and oil drain plugs

When the cover is removed, the gear-change mechanism, kickstart mechanism and clutch operating mechanism will be accessible. The gearchange pedal should be carefully raised then depressed, to control the release of the plungers and springs from the gearchange quadrant.

D GEARBOX

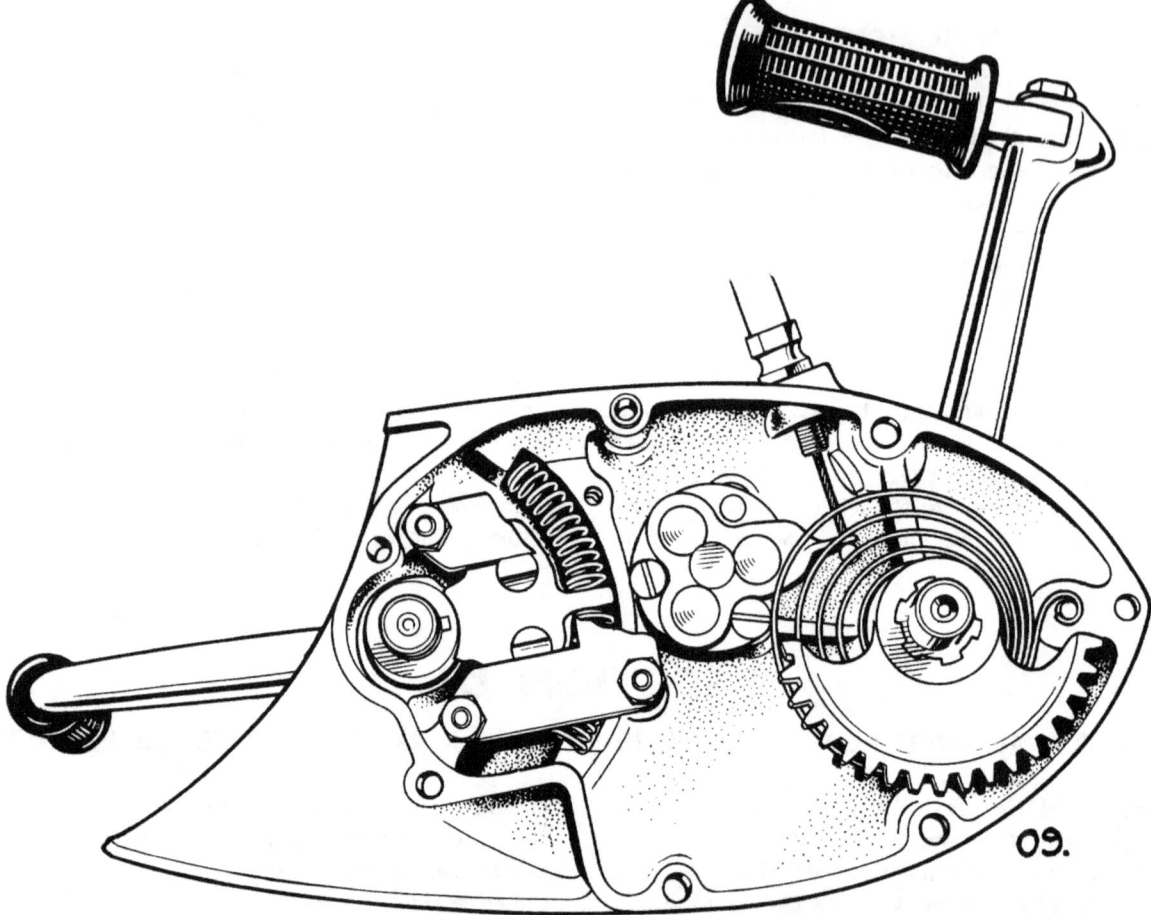

Fig. D3. Gearbox outer cover, showing gearchange mechanism, clutch operating mechanism and kick-start quadrant

Prior to refitting the outer cover ensure that the junction surface is clean and free from any deposits of old jointing compound, then thoroughly clean it in paraffin (kerosene). Apply a fresh coat of jointing compound to the junction surface and ensure that the two location dowels are in position.

Turn the kickstart pedal until it is half way down its operational stroke and offer the cover to the gearbox. Check that the kickstart pedal returns to its normal fully-returned position. Reassembly then continues as a reversal of the above instructions. Finally, refill the gearbox to the correct level with the recommended grade of oil (see Section A2).

SECTION D2
DISMANTLING AND REASSEMBLING THE KICKSTART MECHANISM

Slacken the kickstarter crank cotter pin nut about two or three turns and release the cotter pin from its locking taper by using a hammer and a soft metal drift. Slide the pedal off the shaft and withdraw the quadrant and spring assembly. Apply the rear brake, bend back the tab on the lock washer and unscrew the kickstart ratchet pinion securing nut from the gearbox mainshaft. Withdraw the pinion, ratchet, spring and sleeve, then thoroughly clean all parts in paraffin (kerosene) and inspect them for wear etc., as shown in Section D4.

If the kickstarter quadrant is to be renewed the spindle should be driven out using a hammer or press and the gear quadrant pressed onto the spindle so that the kickstart crank location flat is positioned correctly relative to the quadrant (see Fig. D4).

GEARBOX

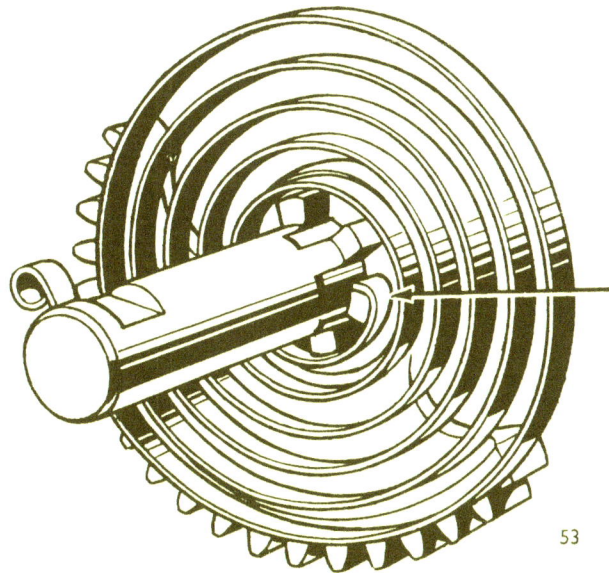

Fig. D4. Kickstart quadrant and spring. Arrow indicates correct spring location

To reassemble the mechanism, first refit the thin walled steel sleeve, spring, pinion and ratchet to the gearbox mainshaft and assemble the tab washer, then screw on the retaining nut to the torque figure given in "General Data". **Do not overtighten the retaining nut as this may result in failure of the thin walled inner steel sleeve.**

Fit the return spring to the kickstart quadrant as shown in Fig. D4. Offer the spindle into the kickstart bush and locate the return spring onto the anchor peg at the rear of the cover. Fit the oil seal over the spindle and assemble the kickstart crank, locking it into position with the cotter pin from the rear. Refit the outer cover as shown in Section D1. Do not forget to refit the oil seal. Refill the gearbox with the correct grade of lubricant (Section A2).

SECTION D3

DISMANTLING AND REASSEMBLING THE GEARCHANGE MECHANISM

Slacken off the gear change pedal locking bolt and withdraw the pedal from the serrated shaft. A little leverage between the pedal and the cover may be necessary. For this, choose a suitable tool to avoid damage to the cover.

Remove the four nuts and locking washers securing the guide plate. Withdraw the guide plate, plunger quadrant and curved return springs. Thoroughly clean the parts in paraffin (kerosene) and inspect them for wear etc., as shown in Section D4.

To reassemble the mechanism, first fit a **new** rubber "O" ring to the spindle and offer it to the outer cover bush using a smear of oil to assist assembly, then refit the two quadrant return springs and ensure that they locate correctly over the step in the cover. To facilitate assembly of the springs, first fit the gearchange pedal and clamp it in position, thus enabling the quadrant to be turned and the springs to be compressed (see Fig. D3).

Refit the retainer plate, not forgetting the locking washers which fit one under each of the four nuts. Finally, refit the springs and plungers, taking care that they are not suddenly ejected from their seats during assembly.

SECTION D4

INSPECTING THE GEARCHANGE AND KICKSTART COMPONENTS

GEARCHANGE:
(1) Inspect the gearchange plungers for wear and ensure that they are a clearance fit in the quadrant. Check the plunger springs by comparing their lengths with the figures given in "General Data".
(2) Examine the plunger guide plate for wear and grooving on the taper guide surfaces. Renew the plate if grooving has occurred.
(3) Inspect the footchange pedal return springs for fatigue and if they show signs of corrosion due to condensation, they should be renewed.
(4) Examine the gearchange quadrant bush for wear and possible ovality by inserting the quadrant into the bush and feeling the amount of play.

D   GEARBOX

(5) Check the tips of the plungers and the teeth of the camplate operating quadrant for chipping and wear. To remove the camplate quadrant, first remove the inner cover as shown in Section D7, then remove the two split pins and withdraw the spindle.

KICKSTART:

(1) Examine the kickstart quadrant for chipped or broken teeth or looseness on the spindle and the kickstart return spring for fatigue cracks and signs of wear, particularly at the centre where it engages on the splines of the spindle.

(2) Examine the kickstart spindle bush for wear. If the required measuring instruments are not available, use the spindle as a gauge and feel the amount of play.

(3) Examine the kickstart ratchet mechanism for wear, giving particular attention to the ratchet teeth ensuring that they have not become chipped or rounded. Check that the thin walled steel bush is a clearance fit in the kickstart pinion and that the spring is not badly worn.

(4) Finally, check that the kickstart stop peg is firmly pressed into the inner cover and is not distorted.

SECTION D5
RENEWING KICKSTART AND GEARCHANGE SPINDLE BUSHES

If it is found necessary to renew the kickstart spindle bush this should be done by completely stripping the outer cover of its assembly parts and heating it to 100°C., then driving the bush out using a suitable shouldered drift. Press in the new bush while the cover is still hot.

Adopt a similar procedure for renewal of the outer cover gearchange spindle bush. The inner cover bush does not usually wear much, even after great mileage has been covered. However, if it is required to renew the bush, the inner cover should be removed (Section D7) and the camplate operating quadrant disconnected.

Using a suitable tap (e.g. ¾ in. dia. x 10 Whit.) cut a thread in the bush to a depth of ¾ in.; heat the cover to 100°C., then reinsert the tap, or, preferably, a suitable bolt. Grip the bolt (or tap) firmly in a vice, then drive the cover away using a hide mallet until the bush is free.

A press or suitably shouldered drift is required to drive in the new bush, which should be done whilst the cover is still hot.

SECTION D6
CLUTCH OPERATING MECHANISM

The clutch operating mechanism, which is situated in the gearbox outer cover, consists of two spring loaded plates held apart by three balls, which are seated in conical indentations in the plates.

Wear in this mechanism is negligible, even after excessive mileage has been covered, so long as the gearbox oil level is maintained at the recommended level. The mechanism is removed as a unit by unscrewing two slotted screws and is then easily dismantled. The parts are arranged as shown in Fig. D5, which should be referred to when reassembling the mechanism.

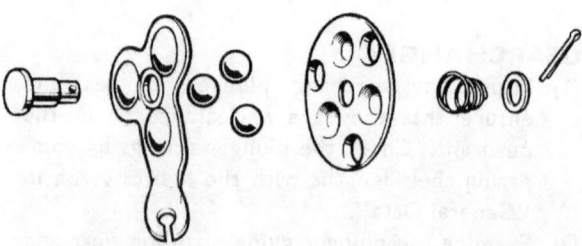

Fig. D5. Exploded view of clutch operating mechanism

SECTION D7
DISMANTLING THE GEARBOX

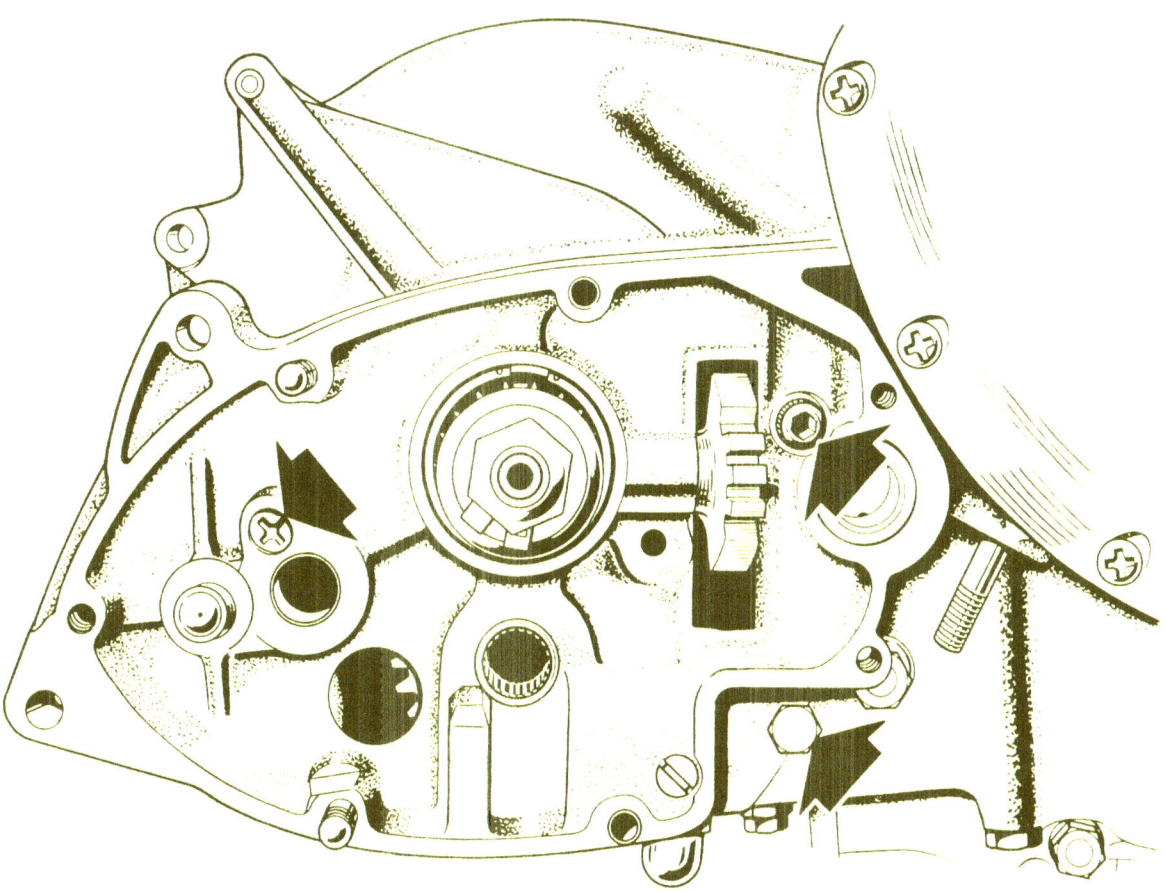

Fig. D6. Gearbox inner cover retaining screws

Remove the gearbox outer cover as shown in Section D1, leaving the gearbox with 4th (top) gear selected.

Remove the two short bolts, two long bolts and a centre nut which serves to retain the rear right engine mounting plate, then withdraw the plate.

Bend back the tags on the lock washer and unscrew the kickstart pinion ratchet retainer nut from the end of the gearbox mainshaft. This should be easily achieved with 4th (top) gear selected and the rear brake applied.

On machines prior to D.24875 the speedometer cable union nut must be undone and the cable withdrawn from the speedometer drive shaft at the front of the inner cover.

Remove the outer primary cover and dismantle the transmission as shown in Section C, not forgetting, finally, to remove the key from the gearbox mainshaft.

Unscrew the large domed nut from underneath the gearbox and withdraw the camplate indexing plunger and spring. The gearbox inner cover is retained by a socket screw, a Phillips recessed screw and a hexagonal bolt (see Fig. D6). When these are removed the cover can be released by tapping it outwards with a hide mallet. The gearbox mainshaft can be withdrawn easily after the selector fork spindle has been removed. The layshaft and remaining gears can then be withdrawn. Remove the camplate and spindle assembly, then remove the two brass thrust washers which locate over the needle roller bearings.

The mainshaft high gear, in which the gearbox mainshaft runs, is locked through the main bearing and gearbox sprocket. The oil is prevented from leaving the gearbox through the main bearing by an oil seal which runs on a ground boss on the gearbox sprocket. To remove the mainshaft high gear

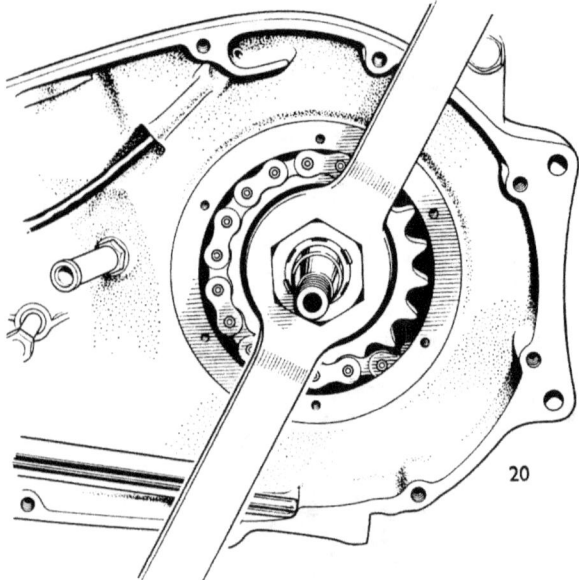

Fig. D7. Removing the gearbox sprocket nut with rear brake applied

and renew the oil seal it will be necessary to remove the sprocket. This can be done by removing the circular plate from the primary inner cover at the rear of the clutch, tapping back the bent over portion of the locking plate and unscrewing the large hexagonal gearbox sprocket nut (1·66 in. across flats). To facilitate removal of the nut, spanner number Z63 is available.

When the nut is removed, drive the high gear through into the gearbox using a hammer with a soft metal drift.

To remove the sprocket, disconnect the rear chain and remove it from around the sprocket, which can then be easily withdrawn through the aperture.

Check the oil seal for cracking and wear. If there has been any signs of excessive oil leakage, renew it.

SECTION D8
INSPECTION OF THE GEARBOX COMPONENTS

Thoroughly clean all parts in paraffin (kerosene) and check them for wear and fatigue, as follows:—

(1) Inspect the gearbox housing and inner cover for signs of cracking and damage to the joint faces. Check that the location dowels are in position correctly in the gearbox and inner cover (2 dowels each). In preparation for reassembly, clean the junction surfaces of the gearbox, inner cover and outer cover of any old deposits of jointing compound.

(2) Examine both the mainshaft and layshaft for signs of fatigue, damaged threads and badly worn splines. Check the extent of wear to the bearing diameters of both shafts by comparing them with the figures given in "General Data". Examine the shafts carefully for signs of seizure. Excessive friction resistance and seizure will be indicated by local colouring on the shaft.

(3) Check the layshaft needle roller bearing by inserting the layshaft and feeling the amount of play.

(4) Inspect the gearbox mainshaft ball bearing races for roughness due to pitting or indentation of the ball tracks. An estimate can be made of ball wear by feeling the amount of side play of the centre track. It should not be possible to detect any movement by hand if the bearing is in good condition. The mainshaft should be a hand press fit in the inner cover bearing. Similarly the mainshaft high gear should be a good hand press fit in the opposite bearing.

(5) Examine the gears thoroughly, for chipped, fractured or worn teeth. Check the internal splines and bushes. Make sure that the splines are free on their respective shafts with no tendency to bind, and the bushes in the mainshaft high gear and layshaft low gear are not loose or excessively worn. Again, reference should be made to the dimensions given in "General Data".

(6) Check that the selector fork rod is not grooved and that it is a good fit in the gearbox casing and the inner cover. Inspect the selector fork running faces for wear. This will only have occurred if the gearbox is being continually

GEARBOX

used with a badly worn mainshaft bearing. The camplate rollers which fit on the selector fork are of case hardened steel and consequently wear should be negligible.

(7) The gear selector camplate should be inspected for signs of wear in the roller tracks. Excessive wear will occur if the mainshaft main bearing has worn badly. Check the fit of the camplate spindle in its housing. Examine the camplate gear wheel for excessive wear. Difficulty will be encountered in gear selection, causing subsequent damage to the gears, if this gear is badly worn.

(8) Ensure that the camplate plunger works freely in the housing and that the moving parts are free from corrosion. To check if the spring has become inefficient, measure its length and compare it with "General Data".

(9) Examine the mainshaft high gear bush for wear by inserting the mainshaft into it and feeling the amount of play. It is advisable to take micrometer readings of the mainshaft and compare them with caliper readings of the bush. If the clearance is excessively greater than the figure given in "General Data" the bush should be renewed as shown in Section D9.

SECTION D9
RENEWING MAINSHAFT AND LAYSHAFT BEARINGS

MAINSHAFT
The mainshaft ball bearings are a press fit into their respective housings and are retained by spring circlips to prevent sideways movement due to end thrust. To remove the right bearing, first lever out the circlip, then heat the cover to approximately 100°C. and drive out the bearing using a suitably shouldered drift. The new bearing should be pressed or drifted in whilst the cover is still hot using a suitable tubular drift onto the outer race ($2\frac{1}{2}$ in. outside diameter x 6 in. long). Do not forget to refit the circlip.

To remove the high gear bearing on the left of the machine, first lever out the large oil seal (which must be renewed), then remove the retainer circlip. Carefully heat the casing locally to approximately 100°C. then drive out the bearing from the inside by means of service tool Z15 or a suitably shouldered drift. Whilst the casing is still hot, drive in the new bearing, using a suitable tubular drift onto the outer race, then refit the circlip and press in the new oil seal.

MAINSHAFT HIGH GEAR BUSH
If it is required to renew this bush, this can be done by pressing out the bush using a suitable drift, which can be made from a 5 in. x $\frac{7}{8}$ in. diameter piece of bar by machining a $\frac{13}{16}$ in. dia. x $\frac{3}{4}$ in. long pilot at one end. The bush must be pressed out by inserting the drift at the teeth end of the gear. The new bush must be pressed in with the oil groove in the bore of the bush at the teeth end.

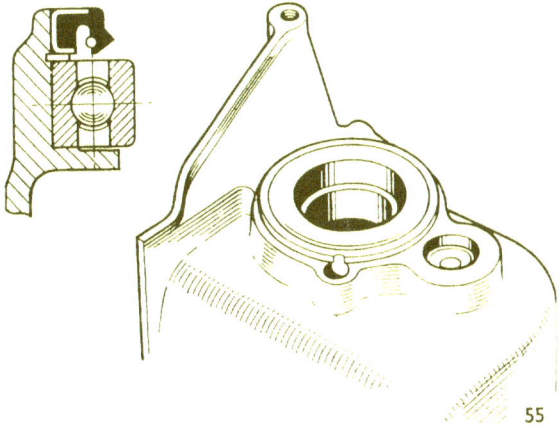

Fig. D8. Section through gearbox mainshaft oil seal

Finally, ream the bush to size using service tool reamer Z46. The pressed-in bore size is given in "General Data".

LAYSHAFT
The right needle roller bearing should be removed by heating the cover to approximately 100°C. then pressing or drifting out the bearing using a tool similar to that shown in Fig. D9 overleaf.

On earlier models with the speedometer driven from the layshaft, before it is possible to drift out the bearing it is necessary to remove the slotted screw which locates the speedometer driven shaft then to drive out the shaft complete with bush by means of a soft metal drift.

D9

GEARBOX

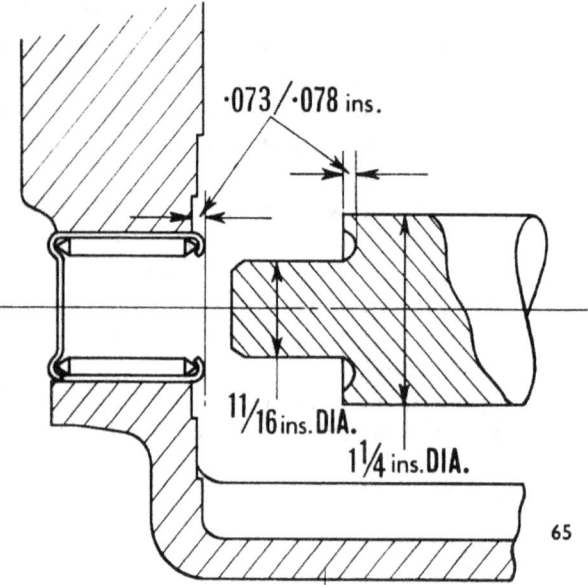

Fig. D9. Sketch of needle roller and drift

The new bearing should be pressed in, plain end first, whilst the cover is still hot, from the inside of the cover, until ·073/·078 in. of the bearing protrudes above the cover face (see Fig. D9).

The left needle roller bearing is of the closed-end type and is accessible from the left, through the sprocket cover plate aperture. The casing should be heated to approximately 100°C. and the bearing driven through into the gearbox using a soft metal drift, taking care not to damage the bore into which the bearing fits. The new bearing must be carefully pressed in whilst the casing is hot, until ·073/·078 in. protrudes above the spot face surface inside the gearbox. Do not use excessive force or the needle roller outer case may become damaged, resulting in the rollers seizing, or breaking up.

Finally, the outer portion of the bore into which the bearing fits, should be sealed with a suitable proprietary sealant.

SECTION D10
REASSEMBLING THE GEARBOX

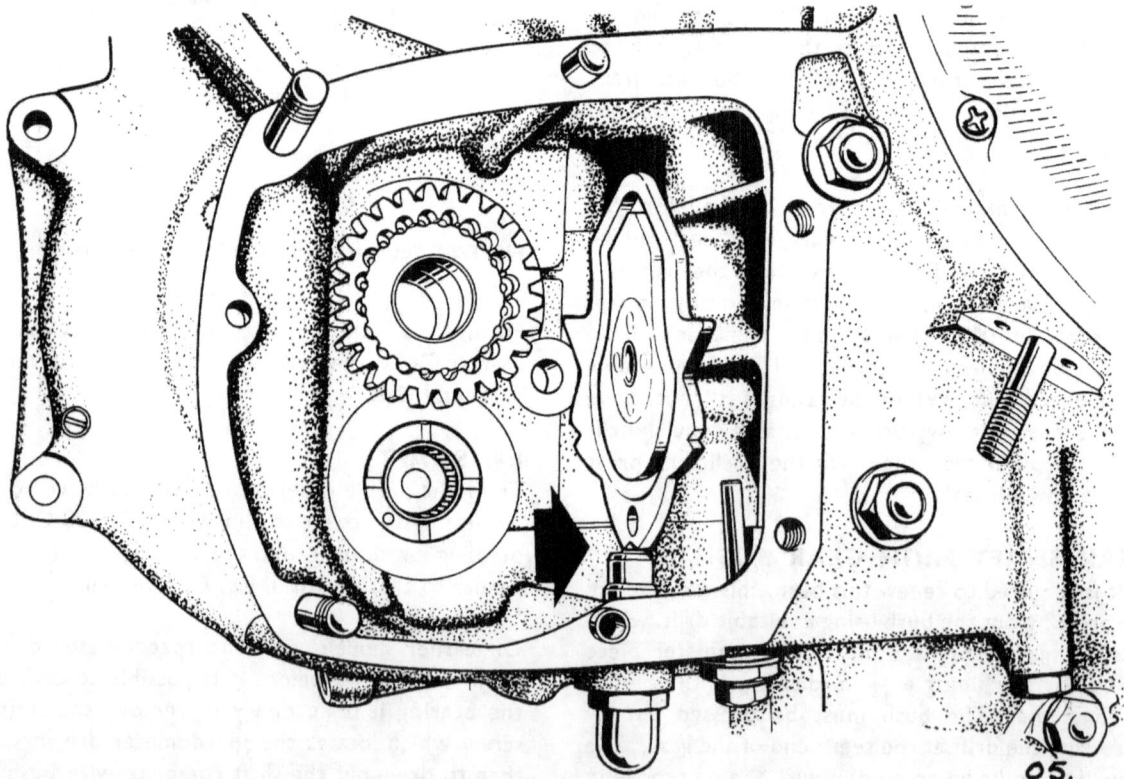

Fig. D10. Reassembling the gearbox. Arrow indicates camplate in notch between 2nd and 3rd gear position

GEARBOX

Drive the new oil seal up to the main bearing with the lip and spring towards the bearing. Press the high gear into the bearing. Lubricate the ground tapered boss of the sprocket with oil and slide it onto the high gear. Screw on the securing nut finger tight.

Re-mesh the rear chain with the sprockets and replace the connecting link. Apply the rear brake and tighten the sprocket securing nut as tight as possible using service tool Z63. (See Fig. D7.)

Smear the extended nose of the high gear (or on earlier models smear the bronze bush protruding from the mainshaft high gear) with oil and replace the circular cover plate using a new paper gasket.

Lubricate the camplate spindle and offer it into the spindle housing within the gearbox. Assemble the camplate plunger and spring into the domed plunger retaining nut and screw it into position underneath

Place the camplate rollers onto the selector forks and hold them in position with grease. Position the selector forks in their respective grooves in the gears as shown in Fig. D11. (The fork with the smaller radius is for the mainshaft cluster). The assembly is now ready to be offered into the gearbox housing. As the mainshaft and layshaft are being located in their respective bearings, the gears should be slid into position and aligned so that the selector fork rollers locate in the roller tracks in the camplate

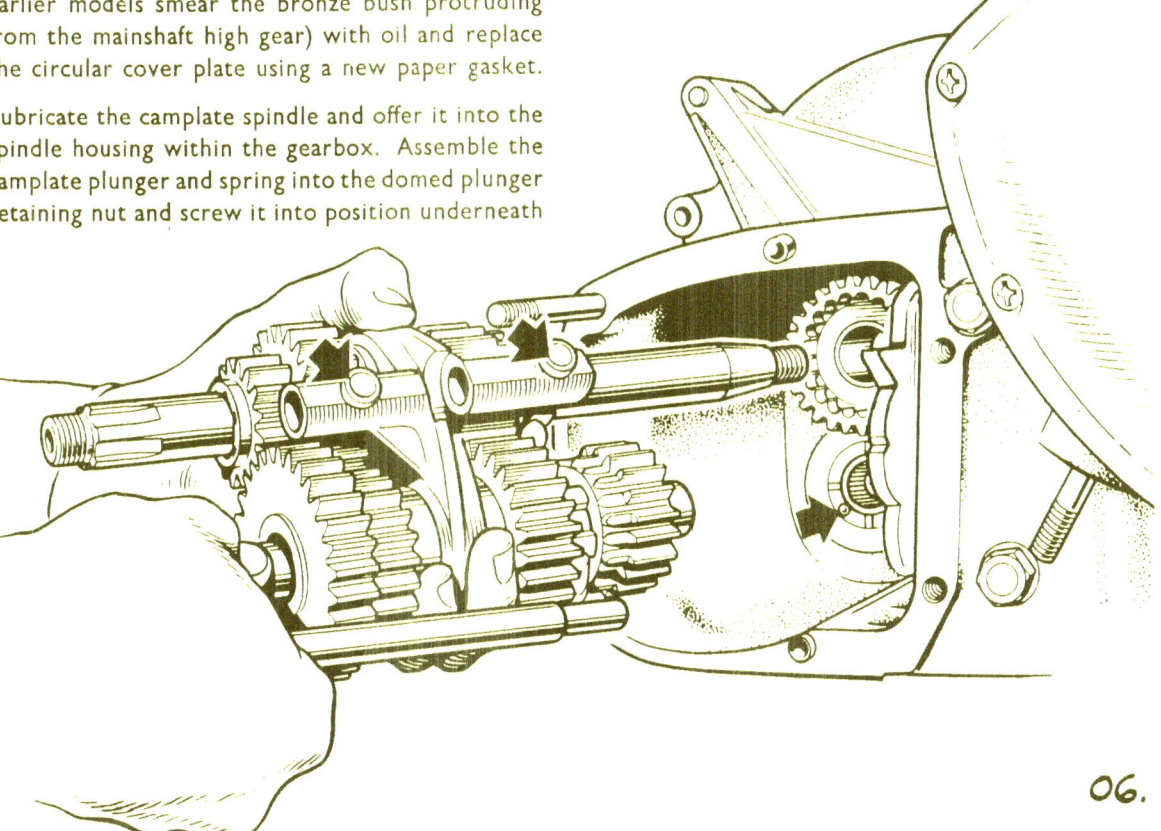

Fig. D11. Reassembling the gearbox components. Arrows indicate camplate rollers in position and thrust washer correctly located

the gearbox, but do not forget the fibre washer. Set the camplate with the plunger located to the notch between second and third gear (see Fig. D10). Locate the bronze thrust washer over the inner needle roller bearing. The thrust washer can be held in position by smearing its rear surface with grease. Note that the grooved surface of the thrust washer is towards the layshaft. (See Fig. D11).

Lubricate the mainshaft and layshaft captive gears, then assemble the mainshaft and layshaft gear clusters as shown in Fig. D11.

and the bores for the selector forks are approximately aligned. Smear the selector fork spindle with oil and slide it through the selector forks, shoulder end first, until it is fully engaged in the gearbox housing. The mainshaft selector fork will be noted to be in the innermost position.

Check the camplate operating quadrant is moving freely in the inner cover and position the bronze layshaft thrust washer over the needle roller bearing in the inner cover. Again, use grease to hold the thrust washer in position during assembly.

GEARBOX

Fig. D12. Refitting the gearbox inner cover

Using a pressure oil can, lubricate all the moving parts in the gearbox, then apply a fresh coat of ointing compound to the gearbox junction surface.

Ensure that the two location dowels are in position and offer the inner cover assembly to the gearbox. When the cover is approximately $\frac{1}{4}$ in. (6 mm.) away from the gearbox junction face, position the camplate quadrant in the middle point of its travel and push the cover fully home. The middle tooth then aligns with the mainshaft centre line.

Screw in the socket screw, recessed screw and the bolt, then temporarily assemble the outer cover and gearchange lever and check that the gearchanging sequence is correct by simultaneously operating the gearchange pedal and turning the rear wheel. In the event of any problem of selection it must be assumed that the quadrant teeth are not engaged accurately with the camplate pinion. To rectify this, remove the inner cover again and check that the camplate has been set as shown in Fig. D10. Offer up the inner cover again ensuring that the middle tooth is on the mainshaft centre line. (See Fig. D12.)

When correct gearchanging is established, re-assemble the kickstart pinion and ratchet, replace the tab washer and screw on the securing nut to the torque figure given in "General Data". To facilitate this, the rear brake should be applied with fourth gear selected.

Refit the gearbox outer cover as shown in section D1 then reassemble the transmission, referring to section A2 for the correct quantities and grades of lubricant for the primary chaincase and gearbox.

GEARBOX

SECTION D11
CHANGING THE GEARBOX SPROCKET

To gain access to the gearbox sprocket, first remove the left footrest and exhaust pipe and then remove the outer primary cover as shown in Section C3.

Remove the pressure plate, clutch plates and withdraw the shock absorber unit and clutch sprocket as shown in Section C9. Remove the key from the gearbox mainshaft and unscrew the six screws which serve to retain the circular cover.

Apply the rear brake, then unscrew the gearbox sprocket securing nut using service tool number Z63. The rear chain may now be disconnected and the gearbox sprocket withdrawn through the aperture. Current models use "Hydroseal" on the splines and will need to be removed with extractor Z151.

Before fitting the new sprocket check that the gearbox oil seal is in good condition and that the rear chain is not excessively worn. Check the extension as shown in Section A13. If the old chain is to be retained for further use it should be thoroughly cleaned in paraffin and lubricated in a grease bath, lubricate the ground boss with oil, fit a new locking plate and slide the sprocket over the gearbox mainshaft and high gear. When the sprocket is located on the splines screw on the securing nut finger tight, then re-connect the chain. With the rear brake applied tighten the nut until it is as tight as possible and tap over the lockplate. When replacing the circular cover plate, use a new paper gasket. Ensure that the oil seal is correctly engaged over the protruding bronze bush. Re-assembly then continues as a reversal of the above instructions. On earlier machines, with the speedometer driven from the layshaft, if it is required to change the gearbox sprocket for one with a different number of teeth from that of standard, then it will also be necessary to change the speedometer drive gear and driven gear. For further details of this, see Section D12.

SECTION D12
SPEEDOMETER DRIVE GEAR COMBINATIONS BEFORE ENGINE NUMBER DU.24875

On earlier machines the speedometer drive is taken from the right-hand end of the gearbox layshaft. As any overall gear ratio change is achieved by changing the gearbox sprocket and rear wheel sprocket, correction has to be made to this speedometer drive ratio, to preserve the correct speedometer drive cable speed.

The chart below gives the part numbers of the speedometer drive gears required for a change-over from the standard fitted gearbox sprocket to the recommended sprocket for use when fitting a sidecar.

For special purposes it may be necessary to calculate the speedometer drive gear combination requirement. If this is the case, reference should be made to Technical Information Bulletin No. 11 which is available on request from the TRIUMPH ENGINEERING CO. LTD., SERVICE DEPARTMENT.

Model		Gearbox Sprocket	Gears Required:		Cable R.P. Mile	Var. %
			Drive	Driven		
6T	Std.	20	T1744 (10T)	T1745 (15T)	1590	—0·6
	S/Car	18	T1747 (9T)	T1748 (15T)	1600	Zero
TR6	Std.	19	T1744 (10T)	T1745 (15T)	1610	+0·6
	S/Car	17	T1747 (9T)	T1748 (15T)	1640	+2·5
T120	Std.	19	T1744 (10T)	T1745 (15T)	1670	+4·2
	S/Car	17	T1747 (9T)	T1748 (15T)	1695	+5·9

TABLE OF SPEEDOMETER DRIVE GEAR COMBINATIONS

Note: The above chart only applies if the gearbox ratios, the number of teeth on the rear sprocket and the rear tyre size are as specified in "General Data" for the particular model, and % variation is calculated on the standard 1600 drive cable revolutions per mile.

D | GEARBOX

SECTION D13
GEARBOX SPROCKET AND MAINSHAFT HIGH GEAR

The splines on the gearbox sprocket and the mainshaft high gear were altered on all models from DU.5825 onwards. The old and new conditions are not interchangeable, and should either of the items require replacing ensure that the correct part number for the particular machine is obtained from the appropriate Replacement Parts Catalogue.

On current models, the nose of the high gear is extended to cover the long high gear bush. This new high gear necessitates a gearbox sprocket cover plate with a larger centre hole and oil seals. These parts can only be fitted as a set to earlier machines from DU.5825 where required.

SECTION D14
SPEEDOMETER DRIVE GEARS

From engine number DU.24875 the speedometer drive gears were deleted, as the speedometer drive is now taken from the rear wheel. This avoids having to change the drive gears when altering the gearbox final drive sprocket to vary the overall gear ratio.

SECTION E

FRAME AND ATTACHMENT DETAILS

	Section
REMOVING AND REFITTING THE FUEL TANK	E1
REMOVING AND REPLACING THE REAR PANELS (6T)	E2
REMOVING AND REPLACING THE SWITCH PANEL (TR6 AND T120)	E3
REMOVING AND REPLACING THE OIL TANK	E4
REMOVING AND REPLACING THE BATTERY CARRIER ASSEMBLY	E5
REMOVING AND REPLACING THE REAR MUDGUARD	E6
ADJUSTING THE REAR SUSPENSION	E7
REMOVING AND REFITTING THE REAR SUSPENSION UNITS	E8
STRIPPING AND REASSEMBLING THE SUSPENSION UNITS	E9
REMOVING AND REFITTING THE SWINGING FORK	E10
RENEWING THE SWINGING FORK BUSHES	E11
REMOVING AND REPLACING THE REAR FRAME	E12
FRAME ALIGNMENT	E13
FAIRING ATTACHMENT LUGS AND STEERING LOCK	E14
FITTING REPLACEMENT SEAT COVERS	E15
REPAIRS	E16
PAINTWORK REFINISHING	E17

FRAME

VERY IMPORTANT

PLEASE NOTE THAT U.N.F. (UNIFIED) THREADS ARE BEING INTRODUCED PROGRESSIVELY THROUGH THE FRAME GROUP. IT IS MOST IMPORTANT WHEN REPLACING NUTS, BOLTS AND THREADED PARTS THAT THE THREAD IS RECHECKED.

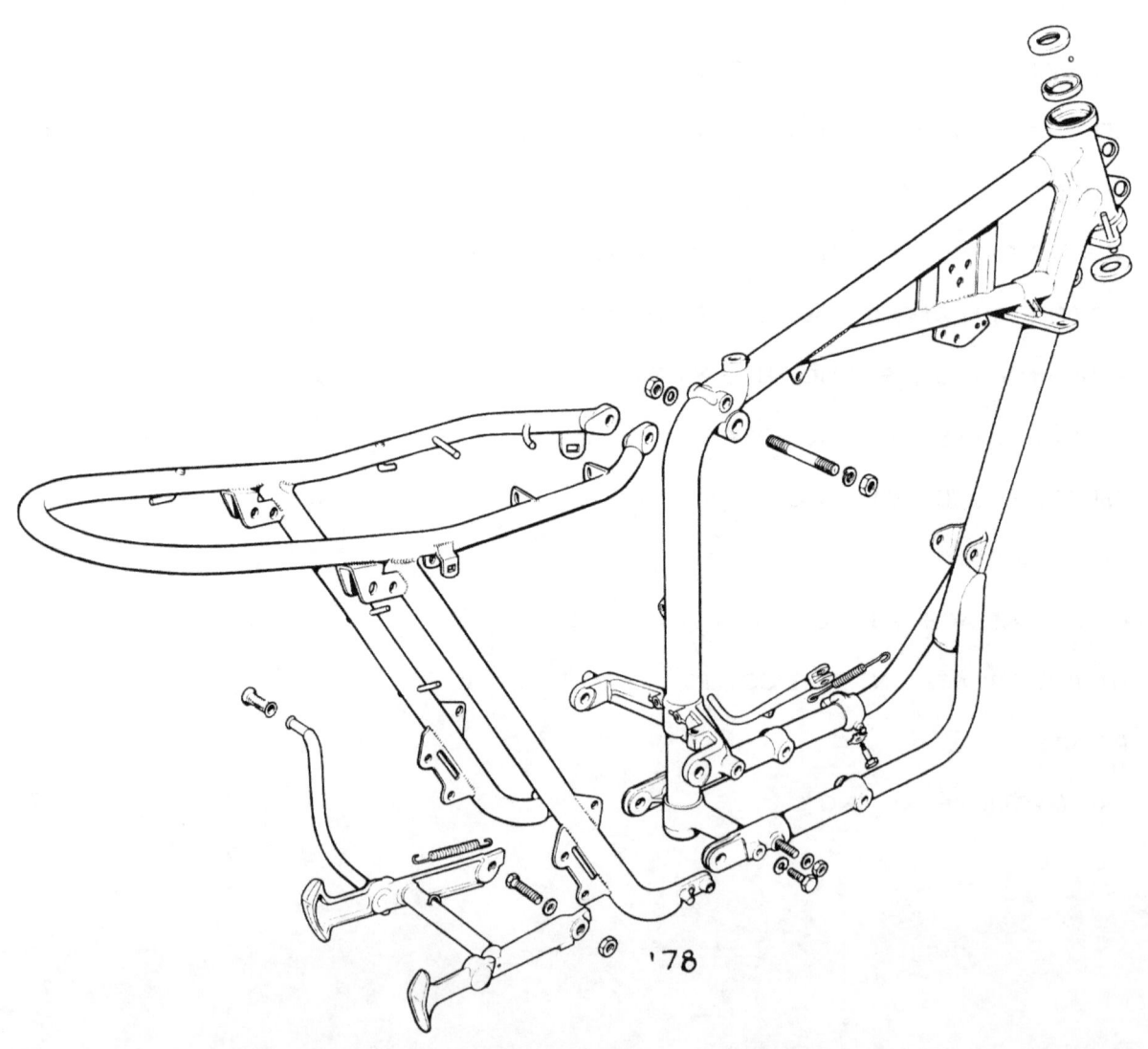

Fig. E1. General arrangement of front and rear frame assembly

SECTION E1
REMOVING AND REPLACING THE FUEL TANK

Turn both fuel taps to the "off" position then unscrew the union and disconnect the feed pipes at the taps. Raise the twinseat then unscrew the rear fuel tank securing bolt.

U.S.A. UP TO DU.66244
U.K. AND GENERAL EXPORT UP TO DU.77670

Detach the locking wire from the front tank bolts and unscrew them. The tank is then free to be removed. On earlier machines fitted with the nacelle type headlamp unit the tank may foul the underside of the nacelle cover, in this case the two two rear nacelle securing screws should be removed to give sufficient clearance.

Replacing the tank is the reversal of the above instructions, but do not forget to fit the mounting rubbers on the front and rear tank securing bolts. Do not over-tighten the feed pipe union nuts as this may result in failure of this part with subsequent fuel leakage. Finally, rethread the locking wire through the heads of the two front securing bolts to prevent them unscrewing.

U.S.A. FROM DU.66245

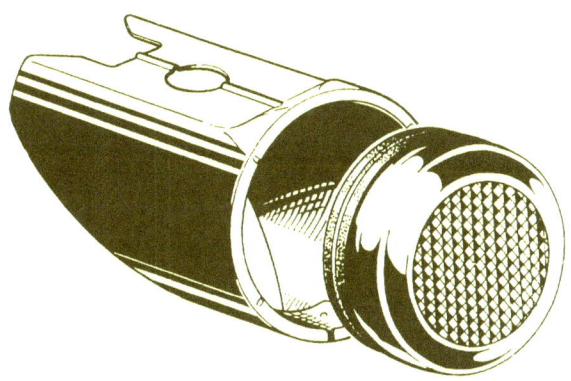

Fig. E2. Front reflectors (U.S.A.)

Reflectors are fitted below the front of the gas tank, secured by the front tank mounting bolts. (See Fig. E2).

To remove the petrol tank securing bolts, the locking wire must be removed. The easiest method is by cutting it with a pair of wire cutters. A box or "T" spanner can be used to unscrew the bolts, or alternatively the reflector lens may be removed to allow access with an open-ended spanner. The chrome plated rim should first be removed by pulling off a locating groove in the plastic retainer. Gently prise the reflector lens away from its retainer by inserting a blunt screwdriver between the lens and the plastic lip. Remove the retainer by again easing a blunt screwdriver between the plastic and the steel lip of the bracket.

Proceed then as for previous machines. Refit the reflectors in a similar manner.

ALL MARKETS FROM DU.77670

The petrol tank is secured at the two front mounting points by studs and "Cleveloc" (self locking) nuts. No locking wire is required on this arrangement.

Dismantling and reassembly procedure is as described above.

SECTION E2
REMOVING AND REPLACING THE PANELS (6T)
EARLIER 6T ONLY

Removal of the left and right rear enclosure panels is achieved by unscrewing two domed nuts, a plain nut (just below the rear of the fuel tank) from each panel and two front panel junction screws. The panels are then free to be removed.

When replacing them, it is important that the distance pieces which fit over each of the engine mounting plate centre studs are in position otherwise the panel will become distorted when the domed nuts are tightened.

SECTION E3

REMOVING AND REPLACING THE SWITCH PANEL

To remove the current side panel which also serves as the tool compartment, merely unscrew the plastic knob at the top left-hand corner of the panel and pull the panel with rubbers forwards and outwards off the two securing pins on the rear sub frame. On reassembly ensure that the plastic washer is fitted to the securing screw.

Remove the rear chain oil feed pipe from the oil tank neck and pull it through the rubber grommet in the switch panel. Disconnect the wires from the stop lamp switch after removing the battery retaining strap and battery from the machine.

(**NOTE:** The brake lamp switch wires are fitted with snap connectors and are a push fit into the switch. Pull the wires horizontally to remove). Carefully thread the wires through the rubber grommet in the switch panel.

Remove the two nuts and washers securing the top panel mounting brackets to the battery carrier and the nut retaining the bottom mounting bracket

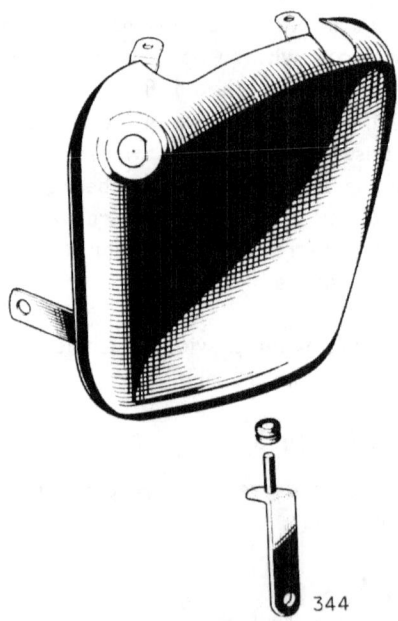

Fig. E3. Switch panel fixing arrangement (earlier models)

to the rear engine plate. Pull the bracket away from the engine plate and down from the rubber bush in the switch panel. The front bracket of the panel can then be released from the frame by unfastening the nut and bolt. At this stage it is necessary to remove lighting switch harness socket, pulling the socket away from the switch body. Disconnect the three Lucar connectors from the ignition switch and lift the panel clear.

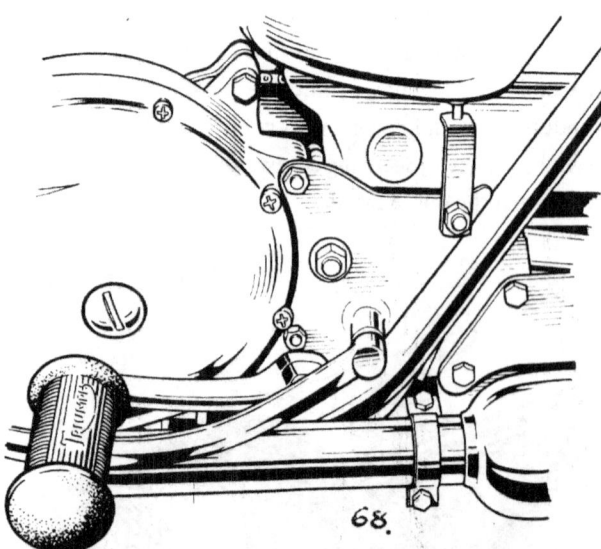

Fig. E4. Switch panel lower fixing bracket (earlier models)

The switch panel on earlier models is secured by a three point fixing. Removal is the same as on later types except that the bottom bracket is welded to the panel. On these earlier machines the switches should be removed by unscrewing the centre recessed screw, withdrawing the knob, and unscrewing the switch retaining nut. The rubber cover should be prised off the ignition switch before the central nut is unscrewed.

The replacement of the panel is the reversal of the above instructions.

When replacing the panel, ensure that the sockets are fully engaged. The pins in the sockets are so arranged that they cannot be re-connected wrongly. On models where the lower fixing pillar is fitted check that the mating rubber grommet is correctly replaced in the panel (see Fig. E4).

SECTION E4

REMOVING AND REPLACING THE OIL TANK

Remove the oil tank drain plug and filler cap and drain the oil into a suitable container. (On machines with rear decorative panels, first remove the right panel). If a tool tray is fitted, remove it at this stage by taking out two nuts and bolts. Disconnect the engine oil feed pipe securing clip, unscrew the return pipe union nut and oil tank filter. Remove the oil pipe feeding the rear chain located on the oil tank filler neck and disconnect the rocker feed pipe below the tank. Remove the battery carrier as described in Section E5. Remove the bolt holding the bottom bracket to the frame and remove the bracket completely from the oil tank bottom grommet. Take off the nuts from the oil tank mounting pegs in the rubbers, preventing the pegs from turning with a screwdriver if necessary. This will release the red earth (ground) leads at the front one and twin seat check strap at the rear one. Push the slotted pegs back through the rubber sleeves noting that the front peg has a spring washer. Lift the oil tank and push the top inwards to enable the froth tower to clear the frame brackets. Lastly, pull the lower part of the tank outwards and drop the tank clear of the frame.

Unscrew the large hexagon-headed oil tank filter body from beneath the oil tank and thoroughly clean it in paraffin (kerosene). On earlier machines unscrew the bottom mounting bolt and remove the oil tank. This is best achieved by allowing the bottom bracket to be lowered into the space behind the gearbox, then tilting the top of the oil tank outwards so that it can be lifted clear. After removal, clean very thoroughly both the oil tank filter and oil tank in paraffin (kerosene).

Reassembly is the reversal of the above instructions but remember to fit the bottom mounting rubber and also to connect the seat check wire to the rear top mounting bolt. When connecting the oil feed pipe union nut take care to avoid over-tightening as this may result in failure of the union nut. When connecting the oil lines ensure that chafing of the rubber connections does not occur. Failure to observe this may result in rubber fragments entering the oil system and subsequently causing blockage. The clips should be tightened carefully. If oil leakage is experienced from one of these junctions on earlier models, it is advisable to purchase and fit new clips. Refit the oil filler cap after adding the required quantity.

Fig. E5. Showing two 6 volt batteries in position in the battery carrier (earlier condition)

SECTION E5
REMOVING AND REPLACING THE BATTERY CARRIER

Lift the twinseat, disconnect the negative (−) and positive (+) battery leads. Release the battery retaining rubber strap by easing the front buckle off the carrier front sleeve nut. Lift the battery complete with breather pipe clear of the machine. Note for refitting that the breather pipe is intended to pass down under the machine, rearward of the swinging arm lug. Remove the nut holding the earth lead and rectifier to the battery carrier. Slacken the single nuts on both the front and rear cross straps and the carrier can then be lifted clear. (If the carrier pressing is very tight on the cross straps it may require some effort to lift it clear).

The cross straps can be removed at this stage if required by removing the nuts and bolts at the right side and sliding the straps complete with rubbers off the frame pegs.

On earlier models remove the battery retainer and bolts, lift the battery clear and the carrier can then be lifted sufficiently to unfasten the bolts securing the heat sink for the Zener Diode. The carrier can then be removed.

If it is desired to remove the rubber mounted battery carrier cross members, this is achieved merely by removing the nuts and bolts at the right hand end and disengaging the cross members at the other end.

Refitting is a reversal of the foregoing. This procedure applies for the single 12 volt battery, for two 6 volt batteries in series and the single 6 volt condition.

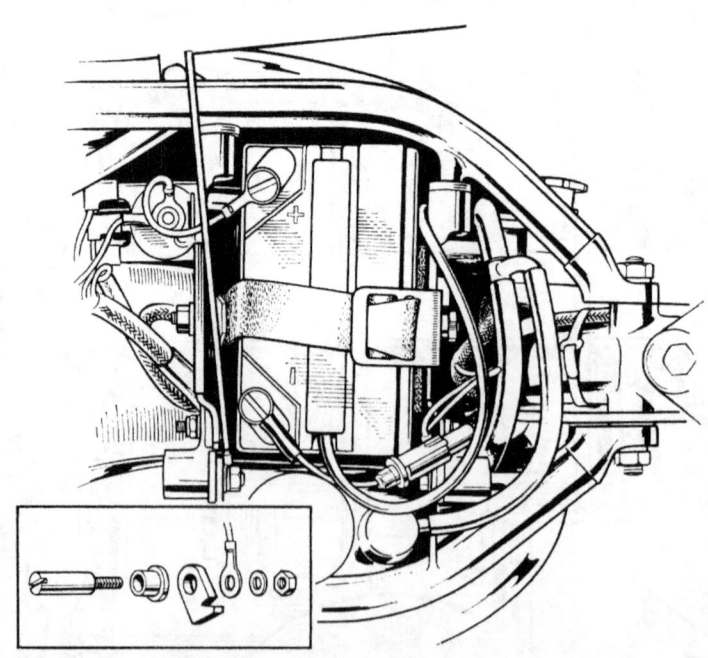

Fig. E6. Oil tank mounting bolt assembly. (12 volt single battery)

FRAME

SECTION E6
REMOVING AND REPLACING THE REAR MUDGUARD

Remove the split link and disconnect the rear chain from the rear wheel sprocket. Unscrew the rear brake rod adjuster nut and remove the nut securing the torque stay to the anchor plate. Unscrew the wheel spindle nuts and withdraw the wheel.

Slacken the rear number plate securing bolts and bottom nut, together with the bottom breather pipe clip on current models. Remove the two bolts securing the top clip and reinforcing strip below the mudguard. Disconnect the rear light at the two snap connectors (behind the number plate on late models or by the battery on earlier ones). Remove the number plate complete with tail lamp. On early 6T models remove the left and right valances and panels. Remove the nut, bolt and large plain washer securing the front of the mudguard to the pivot lug bracket.

Remove the two bolts securing the mudguard to the bridge, noting that the large washer fits below the mudguard and the small washer (and breather pipe clip on left side) on top.

Remove the last bolt holding the wiring protector in situ. On current models, for convenience disconnect the tail lamp lead at the double snap connector by the mudguard top bridge. Lower the mudguard, taking care not to scratch this on the lifting handle. Replacement is a reversal of the above instructions but ensure that the electrical connections are coupled correctly and when reconnecting the rear chain, check that the nose of the spring connection link is facing in the direction of rotation.

SECTION E7
ADJUSTING THE REAR SUSPENSION

The movement is controlled by Girling combined coil spring and hydraulic damper units. The hydraulic damping mechanism is completely sealed but the static loading of the spring is adjustable.

There is a three position cam ring below the chromium plated dust cover and a "C" spanner is provided in the toolkit. To increase the static loading of the spring place the machine on the stand so that there is least load on the spring and use the "C" spanner to turn the cam; both units must be on the same notch whichever may be chosen.

The table opposite shows the spring rates and colour codes for the purposes designated.

	Rate lb./in.	Fitted Length (ins.)	Colour Code
Standard T120, TR6 Earlier 6T	145	8·0	Blue/ Yellow
T120TT T120R TR6C TR6R	100	8·4	Green/ Green

The standard lowest position is for solo riding, the second position is for heavier solo riders or when luggage is carried on the rear of the machine and the third or highest position is for use when a pillion passenger is being carried.

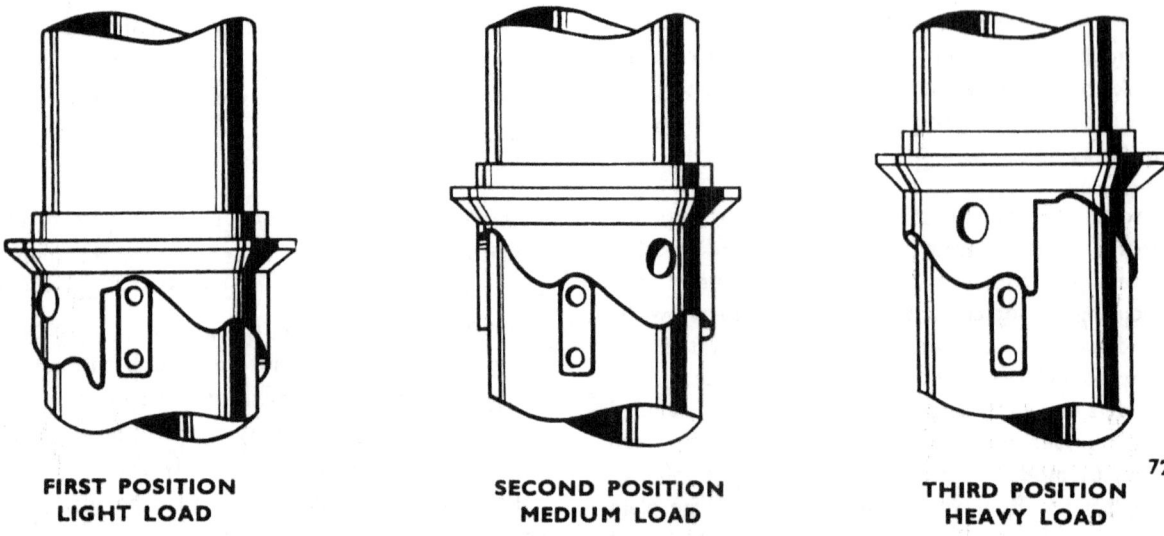

**FIRST POSITION
LIGHT LOAD**

**SECOND POSITION
MEDIUM LOAD**

**THIRD POSITION
HEAVY LOAD**

Fig. E7. Adjusting the rear suspension units

SECTION E8

REMOVING AND REFITTING THE REAR SUSPENSION UNITS

Removal of the suspension units is achieved by removing the top and bottom fixing bolts whilst the machine is suitably mounted so that the rear wheel is off the ground.

The top suspension fixing bolts are fitted with their heads towards the outside of the machine so that it is possible to remove the suspension units without dismantling the rear mudguard assembly etc. These bolts also serve to retain the lifting handles. The lower fixing bolts can also be removed without disturbing the chainguard.

On earlier 6T machines with panels the top fixing bolts are fitted from the inside and the rear wheel and mudguard require removing so that the pivot bolts can be withdrawn and the suspension units removed.

When refitting the units, ensure that the bridge bracket fits in-between the lifting handle and the frame prior to inserting the pivot bolts. It may be necessary to use an alignment bar to assist in bringing the holes into line.

FRAME

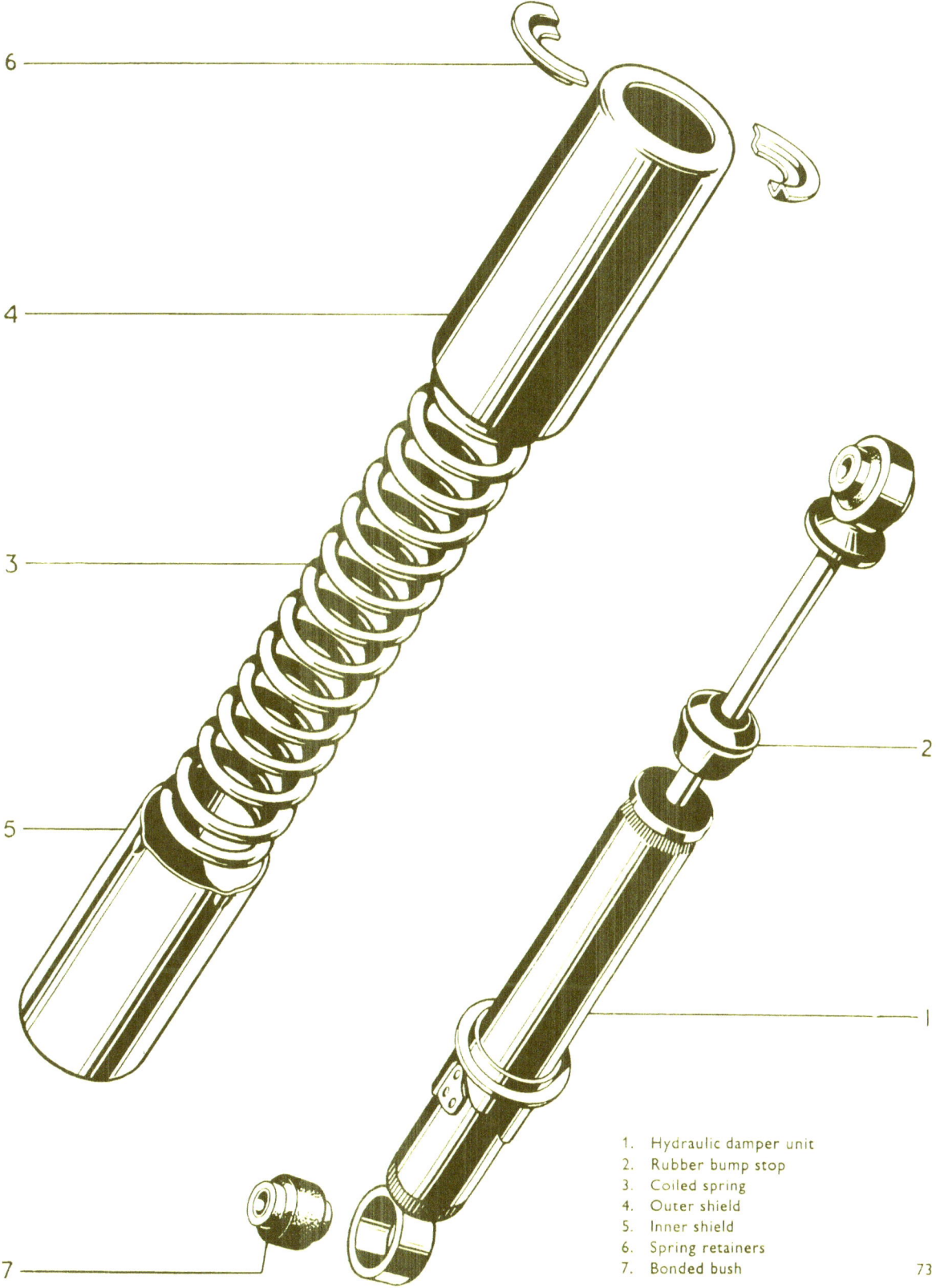

1. Hydraulic damper unit
2. Rubber bump stop
3. Coiled spring
4. Outer shield
5. Inner shield
6. Spring retainers
7. Bonded bush

Fig. E8. Exploded view of the rear suspension unit

SECTION E9
STRIPPING AND REASSEMBLING THE SUSPENSION UNITS

The suspension unit consists of a sealed hydraulic damper unit, outer coiled spring and dirt shields. The static loading on the spring is adjustable and should be set according to the type of conditions under which the machine is to be used (see Section E7).

To dismantle the suspension unit and remove the spring, it is required to compress the spring whilst the two semi-circular spring retainer plates are removed. To do this first turn the cam until it is in the "LIGHT-LOAD" position, then carefully grip the bottom lug in a vice. Take firm hold of the outer dirt shield and pull it until the spring is sufficiently compressed to allow the spring retainers to be removed.

The damper unit should be checked for leakage, bending of the plunger rod and damping action. Check the bonded pivot bushes for wear and ensure that the sleeve is not loose in the rubber bush.

The bushes can be easily renewed by driving out the old one and pressing in the new one using a smear of soapy water to assist assembly.

Squeaking coming from a suspension unit will probably be due to the spring rubbing on the bottom shield. To overcome this, smear some high-melting point grease on the inside of the shield. Under no circumstances should the plunger rod be lubricated.

Note.—For information concerning suspension units or spare parts, the local Girling agent should be consulted.

Reassembly is a reversal of dismantling. Check that the cam is in the light load position before compressing the spring.

SECTION E10
REMOVING AND REFITTING THE SWINGING FORK

Disconnect the chain and remove the front anchor stay securing bolt, then unscrew the brake operating rod adjuster nut. Slacken the wheel spindle nuts and withdraw the rear wheel.

On earlier machines where rear enclosure panels are fitted these must be removed. To do this unscrew two domed nuts, two front panel junction screws and a nut just below the rear of the petrol tank. The panels are then free to be removed.

Remove two long and two short bolts which serve to retain each of the left and right rear engine mounting plates and withdraw the plates. There is also a nut fitted centrally to the plates except on earlier models with rear enclosure panels.

Slacken off the rear chainguard bolt and remove the front chainguard securing bolt. Disconnect the leads from the stop lamp switch and remove the chainguard.

Remove the two bolts which secure the suspension units to the swinging fork.

On machines where the swinging fork pivot spindle nut is on the right of the machine the oil scavenge pipe should be disconnected from the oil tank to give spanner clearance for removing the pivot spindle. On earlier models the spindle was fitted from the left of the machine. To remove the spindle, first unscrew the locking nut, then unscrew the spindle until it is free to be withdrawn. The swinging fork can then be removed and the end plates, outer sleeves and distance tube withdrawn.

Note that some earlier swinging arm bolts have brazed-on heads. On later machines a 'one-piece' bolt S620 is used and this could be fitted to advantage in direct replacement of earlier bolts, since the 2 T.P.I. thread difference will be advantageous in a 'worn frame' condition.

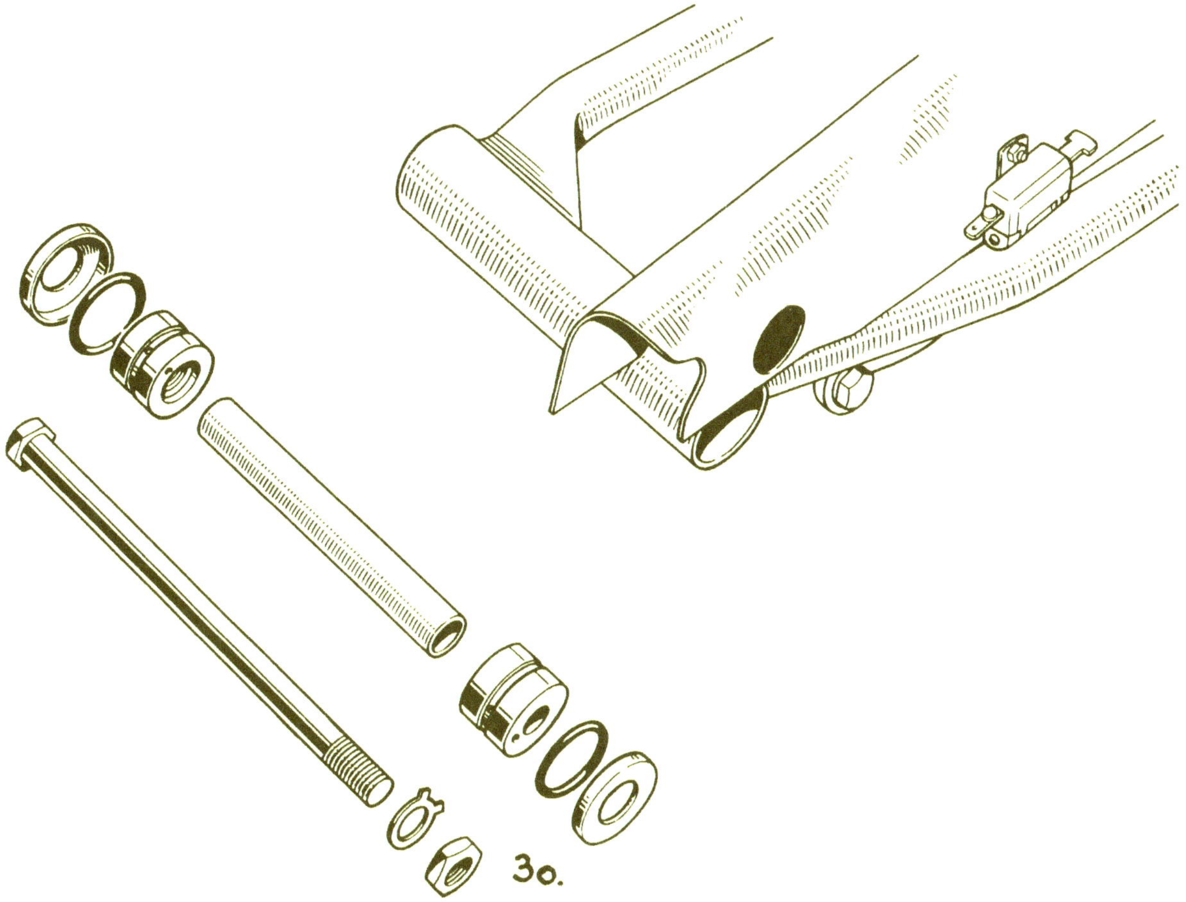

FRAME

Fig. E9. Exploded view of swinging fork assembly

All parts should be thoroughly cleaned in paraffin (kerosene) and inspected for wear giving particular attention to the fit of the two outer sleeves in the swinging fork bushes. The working clearance between sleeve and bush should not be excessive. If excessive wear is in evidence, the bushes will require renewing, for details of this see Section E11. The parts should be reassembled in the order shown in Fig. E9 with the addition of a sufficient quantity of the recommended grade of grease to fill the space surrounding the distance tube. Also, the sleeves and bushes should be well greased. The 'O' rings should be inserted into the lipped end plates and pushed over the ends of the swinging fork cross tube whilst the swinging fork is offered to the pivot lug and the swinging arm bolt inserted. The bolt should be tightened till the fork can just be moved upwards and downwards with little effort. The lock nut and tab washer should then be fitted and the nut tightened. Reassembly then continues as the reversal of the above instructions. To remove side play where the bushes are sound it is necessary only to take out the distance sleeve and file one end to reduce the overall length. A thicker end plate F7675 is available to maintain the correct distance between the frame lugs, only on earlier models. Should the swinging arm bolt be renewed, ensure the thread is the same in the frame and on the bolt.

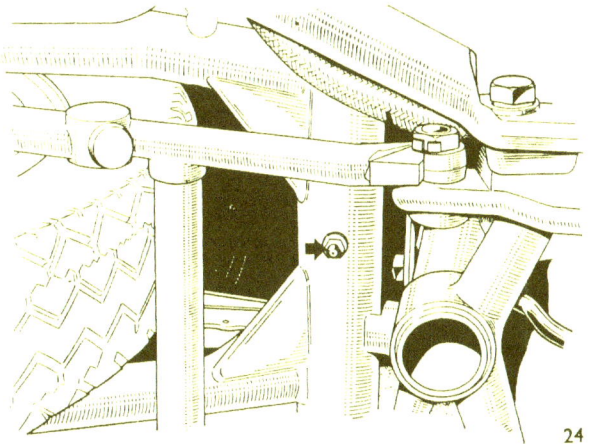

Fig. E10. Swinging fork lubrication nipple

SECTION E11
RENEWING THE SWINGING FORK BUSHES

If the swinging fork bushes require renewing they should be removed by means of a suitable soft metal drift inserted in the tubular housing at an angle and located onto the far side bush. By dexterous use of a hammer and a drift moving it round the edge of the bush a little at a time the bush should be easily removed with no resultant damage to the bore of the housing (see Fig. E11).

New bushes are of the steel backed pre-sized type and when carefully pressed in, using a smear of grease to assist assembly, they will give the correct diametral working clearance. If a press is not available the bush can be fitted by using a suitably turned drift and hammer. Ensure that the bush enters squarely and that no burr is set up due to misalignment. Bore sizes and working clearances are given in "General Data".

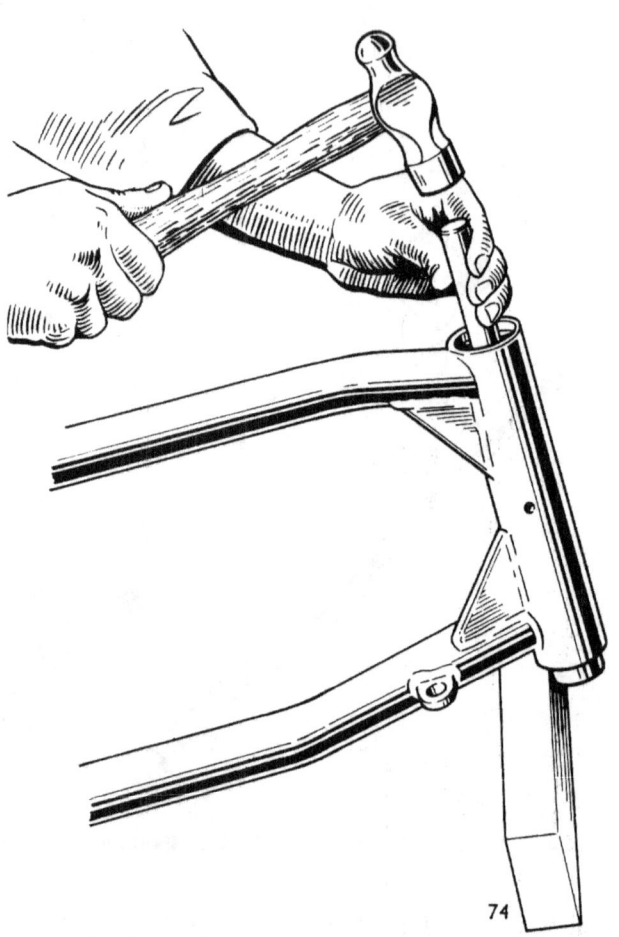

Fig. E11. Removing a swinging fork bearing bush

SECTION E12
REMOVING AND REPLACING THE REAR FRAME

Disconnect the leads from the battery terminals and remove the battery. Unscrew the four bolts which serve to secure the twinseat hinges, then disconnect the check wire and remove the twinseat. Remove the side or switch panel (TR6 and T120) or panels 6T, oil tank, and rear mudguard as described in Section E2 to E6 inclusive.

Slacken the finned clip bolts, silencer clip bolts and two nuts which serve to secure the exhaust pipes underneath the engine, then remove the exhaust pipes by tapping them in a forward direction with a hide or rubber mallet. Remove the left and right silencers, then remove two short bolts, two long bolts and a central nut which serve to retain each of the left and right rear engine mounting plates. Remove the plates complete with footrests.

On earlier models where the footrests are secured underneath the engine they should be removed by slackening their securing bolts and giving each footrest a sharp tap in a downward direction to release it from its locking taper.

Remove all frame clips which connect the wiring harness to the rear frame portion and unscrew the bottom left and right bolts which serve to secure the rear frame to the front frame, then remove the top securing stud. The rear frame is now free to be removed, this is best achieved by lifting it vertically upwards over the swinging fork.

Replacement is the reversal of the above instructions, but refer to the relevant wiring diagram in Section H17 when reconnecting the electrical units and wiring harness.

SECTION E13
FRAME ALIGNMENT

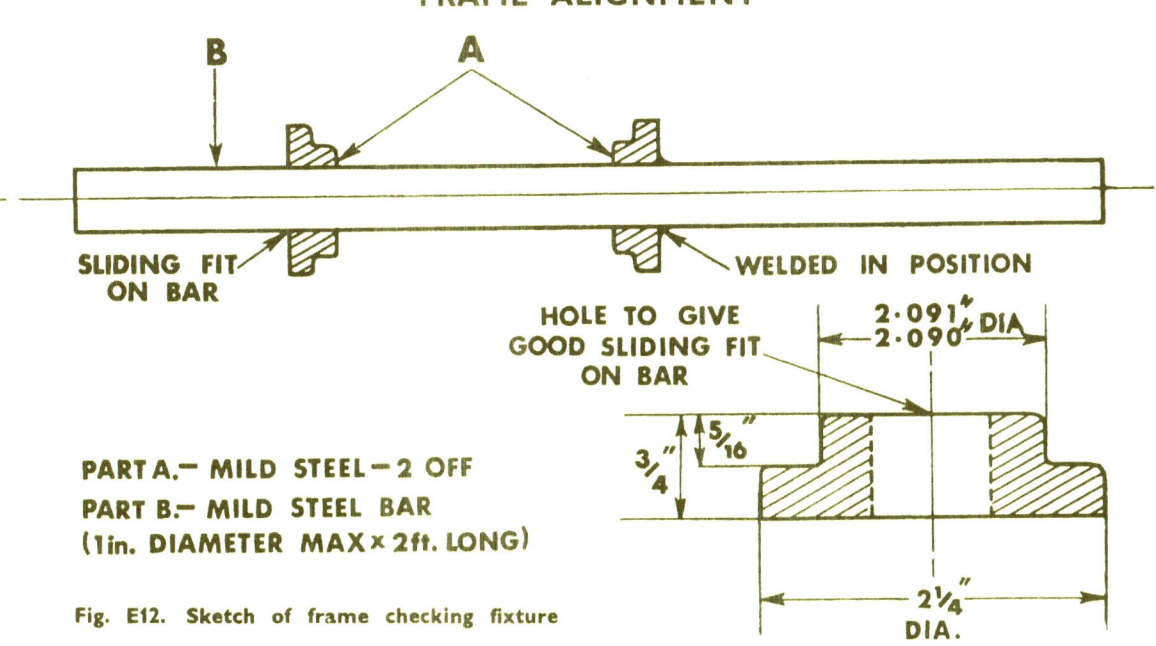

Fig. E12. Sketch of frame checking fixture

If the machine has been damaged in an accident the frame portions must be checked for correct alignment. In the following paragraph details are given of alignment checking for all parts of the frame (excepting the telescopic fork which is dealt with in Section G).

Basic requirements for alignment checking are a engineer's checking table (surface area approximately 3 feet × 5 feet), adjustable height gauge (Vernier type preferable) two suitable "V" blocks, several adjustable height pillars, a set-square and a suitable jig as shown in the sketch (Fig. E12).

FRONT FRAME

It is essential that after setting, or checking the front frame lug centre line is in a plane perpendicular to the plane of the swinging fork pivot lug centre line. It is also essential, that the remaining tubes and lugs are in their relative positions within the stated limits of accuracy.

The method of checking the front frame is that of securely fitting an adaptor spindle of the type shown in Fig. E12 to the head lug. It is then required to support the spindle and head lug on a plane parallel to, and approx. 6 ins. (15 cm.) from, the checking table surface. For this purpose two "V" blocks, packing pieces and two suitable "G" clamps will be required. At the other end of the frame (swinging fork and rear frame removed) an adjustable pillar should be placed under the down tube adjacent to the swinging fork pivot lug (see Fig. E13). The height of the pillar can be determined by measuring the diameter of the tube which is to rest on it, halving the diameter and then subtracting it from the dimension between the head lug centre line and table surface.

The frame centre line should now lie parallel to the checking table surface if the frame alignment is correct.

To verify this take height readings on the front down tube, top tube and rear down tube. See Figs. E13 and E14. Permissible maximum variation is $\frac{1}{32}$ in. (0·75 mm.).

Fit the swinging fork pivot spindle with the two outer sleeves and distance tube attached and check the pivot lug for squareness using a set square at the two location points as shown in Figs. E13 and F14.

Then, using a set square, check that the bottom tubes are aligned by bringing the set square to bear on them at the front and rear.

Using a steel rule or suitable instrument measure the hole centres and compare the figures obtained with those given in Figs. E15 and E16.

FRAME

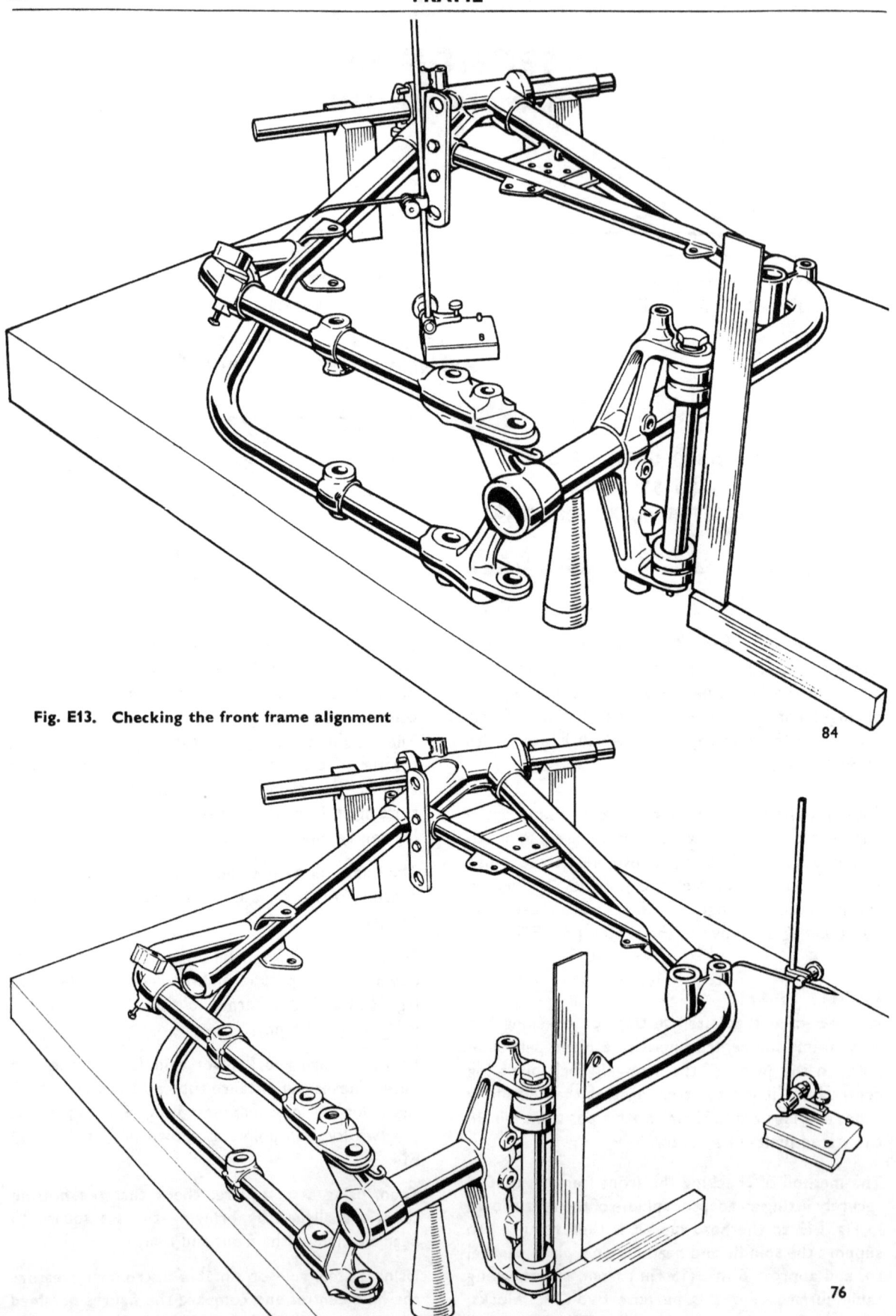

Fig. E13. Checking the front frame alignment

Fig. E14. Checking the front frame alignment

FRAME   E

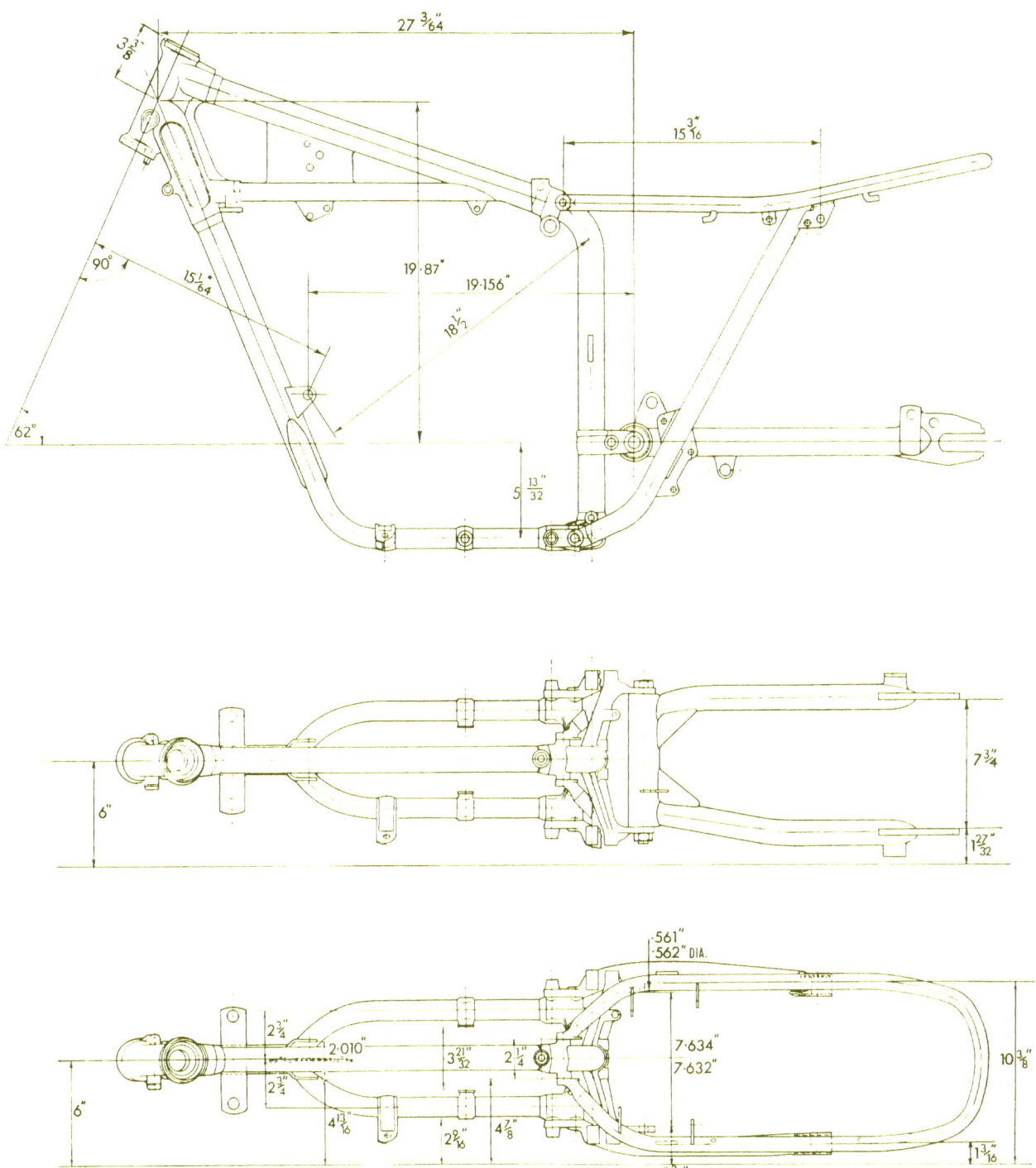

Fig. E15. Basic dimensions of the frame assembly

REAR FRAME

The rear frame basically serves to mount the rear suspension units and twinseat etc., and it is only alignment between the top suspension unit support brackets with those on the swinging fork that is of most importance. The best means of checking rear frame alignment is that of fitting it to the front frame and taking readings as indicated in the following paragraph.

FRAME ASSEMBLY

Securely bolt the rear frame to the front frame and fit the swinging fork so that it can just be rotated by slight hand pressure. Mount the complete assembly horizontally on the checking table as described above, then take height readings at the swinging fork ends and top and bottom suspension unit mounting brackets, referring to Figs. E15 and E16 for dimensions. These brackets should not

FRAME

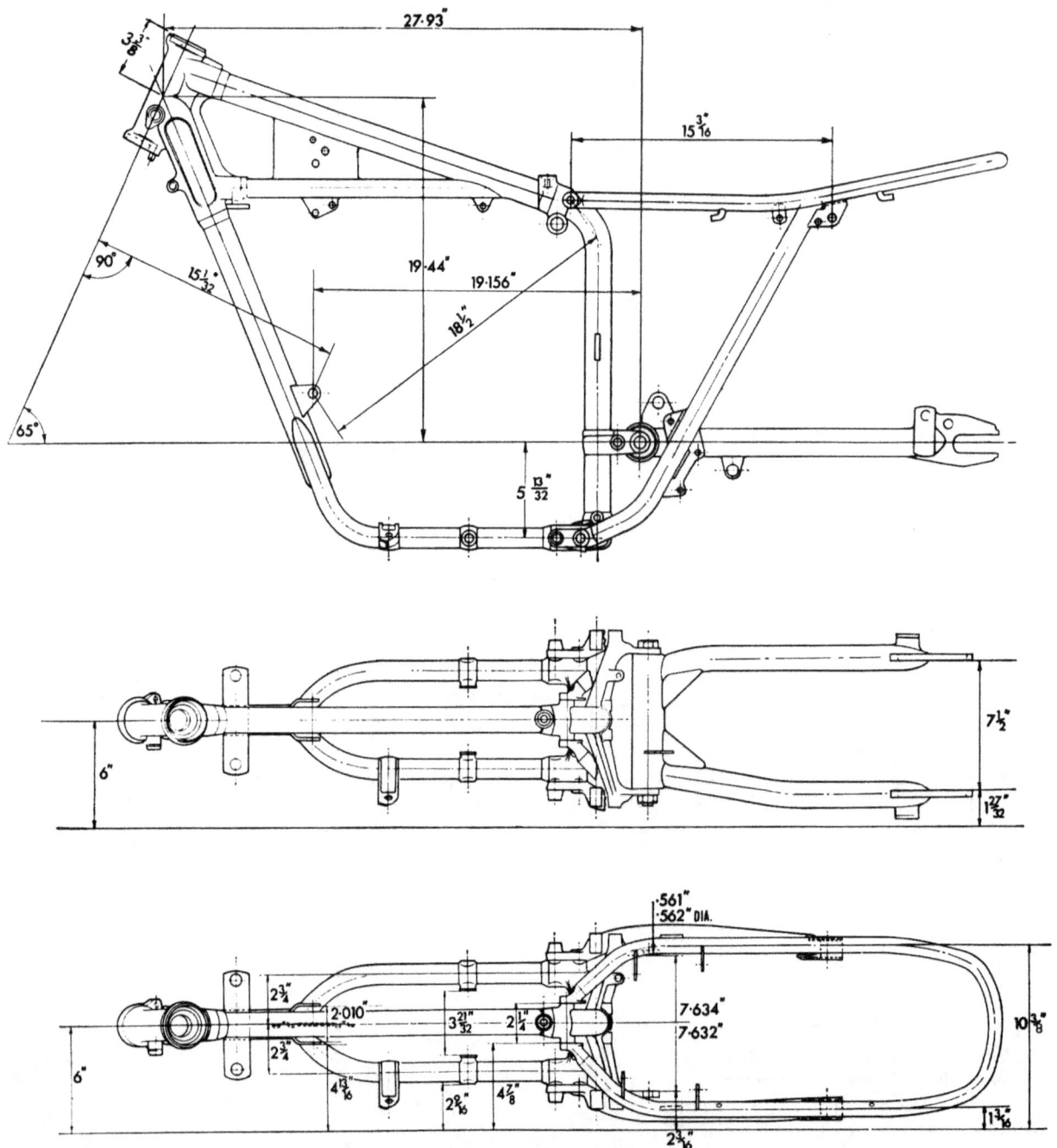

Fig. E16. Basic dimensions of earlier frame assembly (before engine number DU.24875)

Before engine number DU.24875 the basic frame measurements were different. See Fig. E16. Where an earlier machine requires a replacement front frame for any reason, e.g. accident, the later frame will be supplied. This front section is directly interchangeable with the earlier frames, and no additional parts will be required to fit it.

FRAME

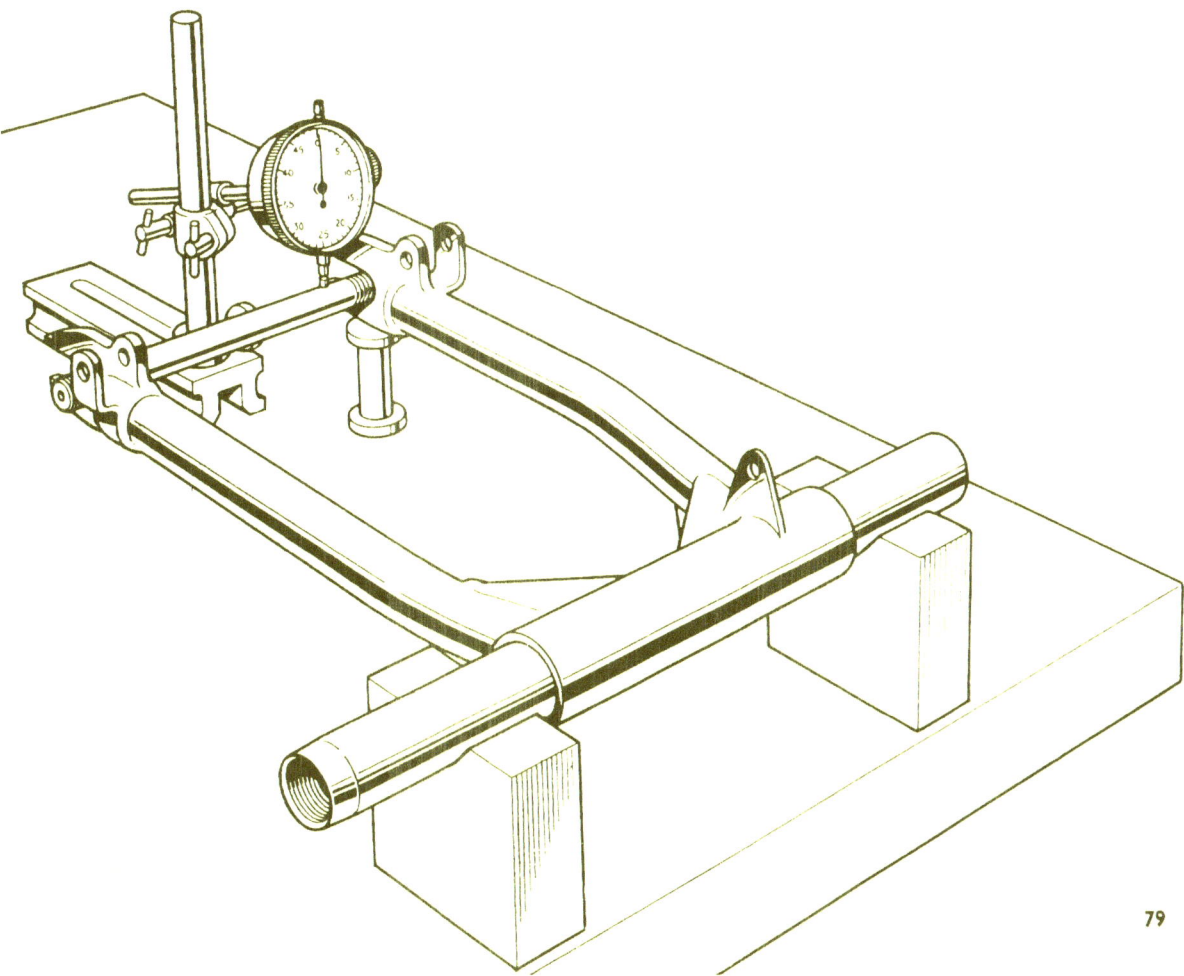

Fig. E17. Checking the swinging fork

be more than $\frac{1}{16}$ in. (1·5 mm.), out of line otherwise the suspension units will be working under excessive stress.

If, when frame alignment is completed, the amount of discrepancy is excessive and rectification is needed, then it is advisable to return the damaged part to the Service Department of Triumph Engineering Company. However, in the case of the swinging fork where the misalignment is not more than $\frac{1}{4}$ in. (6 mm.), measured at the tips of the fork ends, it may be possible to rectify this by the following means.

SWINGING FORK

It is required to check that the centre line of the pivot spindle is in the same plane as the centre line of the rear spindle. To do this, first place a tube or bar of suitable diameter into the swinging fork bearing bushes, then mount the swinging fork on two "V" blocks, one either side, and clamp it lightly to the edge of the checking table. Fit the rear wheel spindle into the fork end slots or, alternatively, use a straight bar of similar diameter, then support a fork end so that the swinging fork is approximately horizontal. Height readings should then be taken at both ends of the wheel spindle to establish any mis-alignment. (Fig. E17).

Next, check that the distance between the fork ends is as given in "General Data".

It is now necessary to lever the fork ends in the correcting direction until the wheel spindle can be inserted and found to be parallel with the pivot bush centre line. To do this, a bar of 4 ft. length by $1\frac{1}{4}$ ins. diameter is required. It is now that great care is required. Insert the bar at the end of the swinging fork adjacent to the suspension unit mounting brackets so that it is over the "high" fork leg and under the "low" fork leg. Exert gentle pressure at the end of the bar then insert the spindle and re-check the alignment. Repeat this procedure using increased loads until the spindle height readings shows that the swinging arm is now mis-aligned in the opposite sense. A small leverage now applied from the other side will bring the wheel back to parallel.

Note: Apply the leverage bar as near as possible to the suspension unit brackets, otherwise the tubes may become damaged. DO NOT USE THE FORK ENDS.

SECTION E14
FAIRING ATTACHMENT LUGS AND STEERING LOCK

From engine number DU.24875 fairing attachment lugs are incorporated in the steering head assembly to simplify the fitting of fairings. These are shown in Figs. E1 and E18.

An extension of the steering head lug accommodates the peg of the steering lock fitted to the fork crown. See Fig. E19.

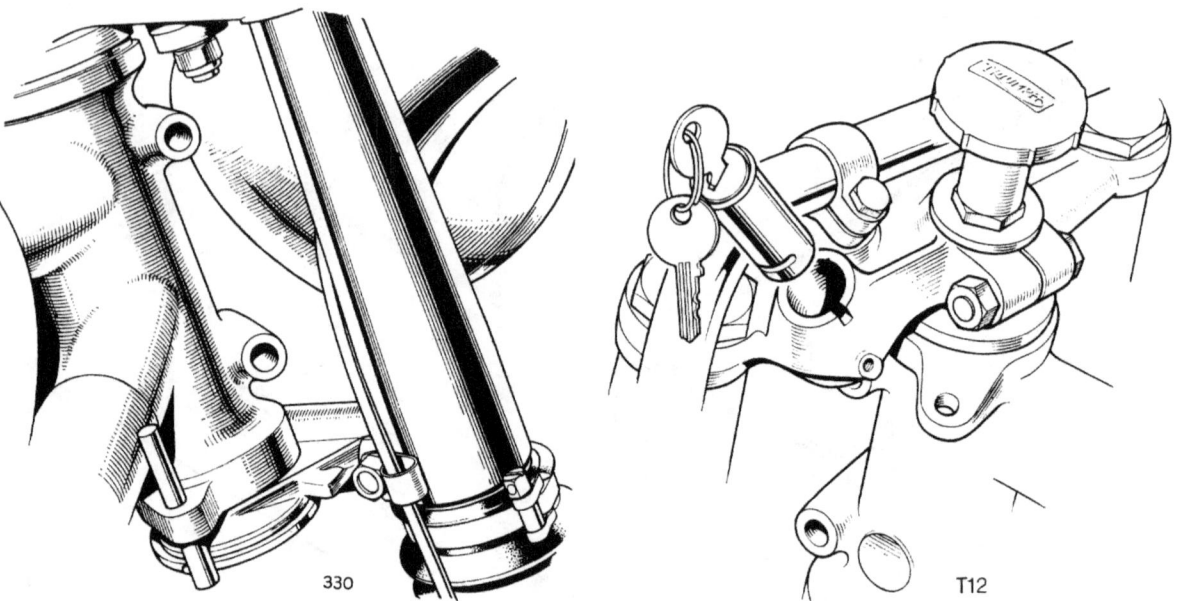

Fig. E18. Fairing attachment lugs **Fig. E19. Steering lock**

SECTION E15
FITTING REPLACEMENT SEAT COVERS

'Quiltop' twinseats have a cover retained by sprags which are part of the seat pan.

When fitting a replacement seat cover it is **very important** to first soak the complete cover assembly in hot water in order to soften the plastic so that it can easily be stretched into place. After soaking the cover in hot water, wring out the excess water and you will find that the cover can very easily be stretched into place to give a neat fit without any wrinkles. This job is very difficult if you do not follow this suggested method.

Ideally the seat should be allowed to dry out in a warm place before being put back into service.

SECTION E16

REPAIRS

Repairs covered in this section are simple operations requiring only a minimum of special tools. The type of repairs possible with these tools are those such as small dents to mudguards, panels etc., caused by flying stones or slight grooves which have not affected a large area or torn the metal. The tools required are shown below in Fig. E20.

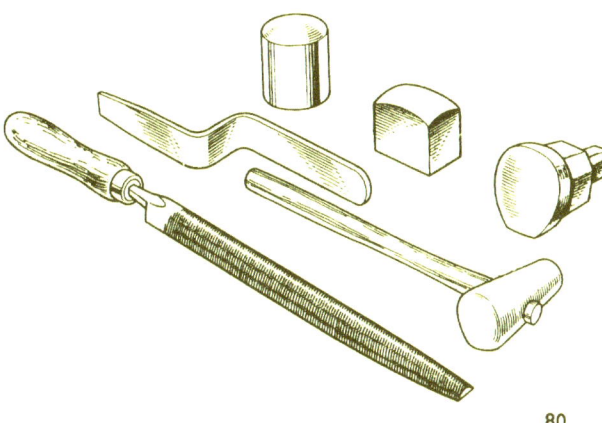

Fig. E20. Tools used for panel repairs

REMOVAL OF DENTS

To remove small dents a spoon and suitably shaped dolly block are required. A suitable spoon can be made from a file by removing the teeth and polishing the surface then cranking it as shown in Fig. E20.

Place the dolly block underneath the panel then hammer the dent(s) carefully with the spoon until something like the original contour is achieved. Lightly file the surface to show any high spots there may be and use the dolly and spoon to remove them.

Note.—Do not file more than is necessary to show up the high spots. Care should be taken to keep filing to a minimum otherwise serious thinning of the metal will occur.

Where denting has occured without resultant damage to the paint-work the dent(s) may be removed whilst the paintwork is preserved by careful use of a polished spoon and dolly block. Dents which are comparatively larger may be removed whilst the paintwork is preserved by placing a "sandbag" against the outer surface and hammering the inside of the panel with a suitably shaped wooden mallet. A "sandbag" can be made from a piece of 18 in. square leather by folding it and packing it tightly with sand. Finally, finish off using a suitable dolly block and polished spoon as required.

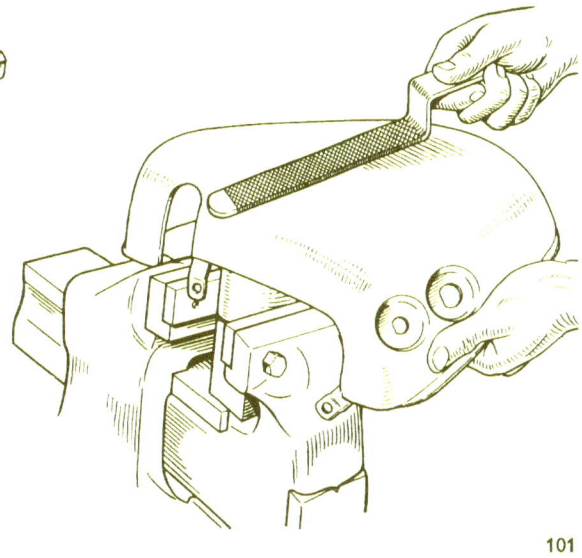

Fig. E21. Removing a dent with dolly block and spoon

Note.—It is not advisable to use a hammer as hammer-blows tend to stretch the surrounding metal, giving rise to further complications. Also, unless the aim is true, damage of a more serious nature may result.

Where a fuel tank has become damaged the repair work should only be entrusted to a competent panel beater, or preferably, return the tank to the Service Department—Triumph Engineering Company Ltd.

SECTION E17

PAINTWORK REFINISHING

PAINT STRIPPING

Except in cases where a "touch-up" is to be attempted, it is strongly recommended that the old finish is completely stripped and the refinish is carried out from the bare metal. A suitable paint stripper can be obtained from most paint stores and accessory dealers.

The stripper should be applied with a brush and allowed approximately 10 minutes to react. A suitable scraper should be used to remove the old finish, then the surface cleaned with water using a piece of wire wool. Ensure that all traces of paint stripper are removed. If possible, blow out crevices with compressed air.

It is advisable to strip a small area at a time to avoid the stripper drying and also to enable easier neutralizing of the stripper.

Finally, the surface should be rubbed with a grade 270 or 280 emery cloth to give a satisfactory finish then washed off with white spirits or a suitable cleaner solvent.

PRIMING

A thin coat of cellulose primer must be sprayed onto the surface prior to application of an undercoat or stopper. Undercoat and stopper will not adhere satisfactorily to bare metal. It is advisable to thin the primer by adding 1 part cellulose thinners to 1 part primer. Ensure that the primer is dry before advancing further.

APPLYING STOPPER

Imperfections and slight dents in the surface may be filled with stopper, but rubbing down with "wet and dry" should not be attempted until the undercoat or surfacer has been applied.

Apply the stopper with a glazing knife in thin layers, allowing approximately 20 minutes for drying between each layer. After the last layer, allow the stopper about 6 hours (or over-night if possible) to dry. Heavy layers or insufficient drying time will result in risk of surface cracking.

UNDERCOAT (SURFACER)

Most cellulose undercoats also called surfacers, will suffice for a base for TRIUMPH finishes. About two or three coats are required and should be sprayed on in a thinned condition using 1 part cellulose thinners to 1 part undercoat. Allow approximately 20 minutes between each coat.

If stopper has been applied the final layer of undercoat should be sprayed on after smoothing the surface with "wet and dry" abrasive as shown below.

WET AND DRY SANDING

After application of the undercoat, the surface should be rubbed down with 270 or 280 grade abrasive paper used wet. An ideal method is to have a rubber block approximately 3in. ×2in. ×1in. around which to wrap the emery paper. However, this is only recommendable for flat surfaces; where rapid change of sections occur, a thin felt pad is more useful.

The abrasive paper should be allowed to soak in cold water for at least 15 minutes before use. A useful tip is to smear the abrasive surface of the paper with soap prior to rubbing down. This will prevent clogging and should at least treble the useful life of the paper if it is washed thoroughly after each rub-down.

When the surface is smooth enough, wash it thoroughly with water and dry off with a clean sponge.

If smoother surface than this is required it can be given another layer of undercoat and then the rubbing down procedure repeated using 320 or 400 grade of paper depending upon conditions.

FINISHING

Before spraying on the finishing coats the surface must be quite smooth, **dry** and clean. It is important that conditions are right when finish spraying is to be carried out otherwise complications may occur. Best conditions for outdoor spraying are those on a dry sunny day without wind. Moisture in the atmosphere is detrimental to paint spraying.

FRAME E

The first coat should be thinned in the ratio of 50% cellulose thinners to 50% lacquer. Subsequent coats should have a higher proportion of thinners as shown below.

	Cellulose Thinners	Lacquer
1st Coat	50%	50%
2nd Coat	60%	40%
3rd Coat	70%	30%
4th Coat	80%	20%

Between each coat the surface may be flatted by hand with 320 or 400 abrasive paper as required.

Allow at least 10 minutes between each coat and after the final coat leave overnight or 24 hours if possible. For most purposes the 2nd coat of finishing is more than adequate.

POLISHING

The final colour coat must be completely dry before cutting and polishing. Using a clean rag rub down with brass polish or fine cutting paste and burnish to a high gloss using a clean mop before applying a suitable wax polish for protection and shine.

Note.—TRIUMPH supply only the finishing lacquers. These are available in $\frac{1}{4}$ pint tins and aerosol sprays or, for workshop use, 1 gallon tins.

FLAMBOYANT FINISHES

To regain the original depth of colour or shade, when applying flamboyant finishes, they must be applied onto the correct base colour e.g.

Finish	(Ser. Ref.)	**Base Colour**	(Ser. Ref.)
Kingfisher blue	K	Silver	V
Hi-Fi red	HF	Gold	G
Regal purple	P	Silver	V
Burnished gold	BG	Gold	G
Pacific blue	PB	Silver	V
Flame	F	Gold	G
Burgundy	B	Gold	G

METALLIC FINISHES

Metallic finishes can be applied equally as well to either a white or brown primer, and no base colour is needed. These finishes are as follows:—

Finish	(Ser. Ref.)
Riviera blue	RB
Mist Green	MG

NOTES

SECTION F

WHEELS, BRAKES AND TYRES

DESCRIPTION	Section
REMOVING AND REFITTING THE FRONT WHEEL	F1
REMOVING AND REFITTING THE REAR WHEEL	F2
REMOVING AND REFITTING THE QUICKLY DETACHABLE (Q.D.) REAR WHEEL	F3
FRONT AND REAR WHEEL ALIGNMENT	F4
BRAKE ADJUSTMENTS	F5
STRIPPING AND REASSEMBLING THE BRAKES	F6
RENEWING BRAKE LININGS	F7
REMOVING AND REFITTING THE WHEEL BEARINGS	F8
WHEEL BUILDING	F9
WHEEL BALANCING	F10
REMOVING AND REPAIRING TYRES	F11
SECURITY BOLTS	F12
TYRE MAINTENANCE	F13
SIDECAR ALIGNMENT	F14

WHEELS, BRAKES AND TYRES

SECTION F1

REMOVING AND REFITTING THE FRONT WHEEL

Place the machine with the front wheel approximately six inches off the ground. First, unscrew the handlebar front brake adjuster then disconnect the cable at the actuating lever on the brake plate by removing the spring pin on current models or the split pin, washer, and pivot pin on earlier models. On twin leading shoe brakes, to release the cable from the anchor plate it is necessary to remove the split pin at the cable abutment. Unscrew the two wheel spindle cap bolts from the base of each fork leg and remove the wheel.

Refitting the wheel is the reversal of the above instructions but care should be taken to ensure that the anchor plate locates correctly over the peg on the inside of the right fork leg. Tighten the spindle cap bolts evenly a turn at a time. On twin leading shoe brakes the cable retaining split pin should be replaced.

SECTION F2

REMOVING AND REFITTING THE REAR WHEEL

First unscrew the rear brake adjuster, then disconnect the rear chain. Slacken the bolt at the rear of the chainguard so that the chainguard can be swung upwards. Remove the nut securing the rear brake torque stay to the anchor plate, then slacken the left and right wheel spindle securing nuts. The speedometer cable must be disconnected The rear wheel is now free to be removed.

To refit the rear wheel first ensure that the spindle nuts are sufficiently unscrewed then offer the wheel to the swinging fork. Locate the adjuster caps over the fork ends then lightly tighten the wheel spindle nuts. Place the chain around the rear wheel sprocket and connect up the brake anchor plate torque stay. Refitting the chain may necessitate slackening off both the left and right adjusters. It is now necessary to ensure that the front and rear wheels are aligned. This is shown in Section F4 below. Finally, lock up the two spindle nuts, ensure the torque stay securing nut is tight, and reconnect the speedometer cable.

SECTION F3

REMOVING AND REFITTING THE QUICKLY DETACHABLE REAR WHEEL

The Q.D. wheel is mounted on three bearings, two ball journal bearings being situated in the hub and one in the brake drum. The wheel is quickly detachable by the simple method of splining the hub into the brake drum thereby eliminating the necessity of removing the rear chain etc., when required to remove the wheel.

To remove the quickly detachable rear wheel first unscrew the wheel spindle from the right side of the machine and drop out the distance piece between the wheel and the fork end. Pull the wheel clear of the spline and the brake drum when the wheel can then be removed.

When replacing the wheel slight variations may be felt in the fit of the splines at various points. Select the tightest position and mark with a small spot of paint on the brake drum and corresponding spot on the hub to facilitate replacement on future occasions. In addition there is a rubber ring which is assembled over the splines on the wheel and is in compression when the spindle is tight. This ring seals the spline joint and prevents abrasive wear at the joint. If it is perished or damaged fit a new one.

Replacement of the wheel is a reversal of the above instructions and if the chain adjuster is not altered it will not be necessary to re-check the rear wheel alignment. However if this is necessary full details are given in Section F4 opposite.

WHEELS, BRAKES AND TYRES

SECTION F4
FRONT AND REAR WHEEL ALIGNMENT

When the rear wheel has been fitted into the frame it should be aligned correctly by using two straight edges or "battens", about 7 feet long. With the machine off the stand the battens should be placed along-side the wheel, one either side of the machine and each about four inches from the ground. When both are touching the rear tyre on both sides of the wheel the front wheel should be midway between and parallel to both battens. Turn the front wheel slightly until this can be seen. Any necessary adjustments must be made by first slackening the rear wheel spindle nuts, then turning the spindle adjuster nuts as required ensuring that rear chain adjustment is maintained. Refer to Fig. F1 for illustration of correct alignment. Note that the arrows indicate the adjustment required.

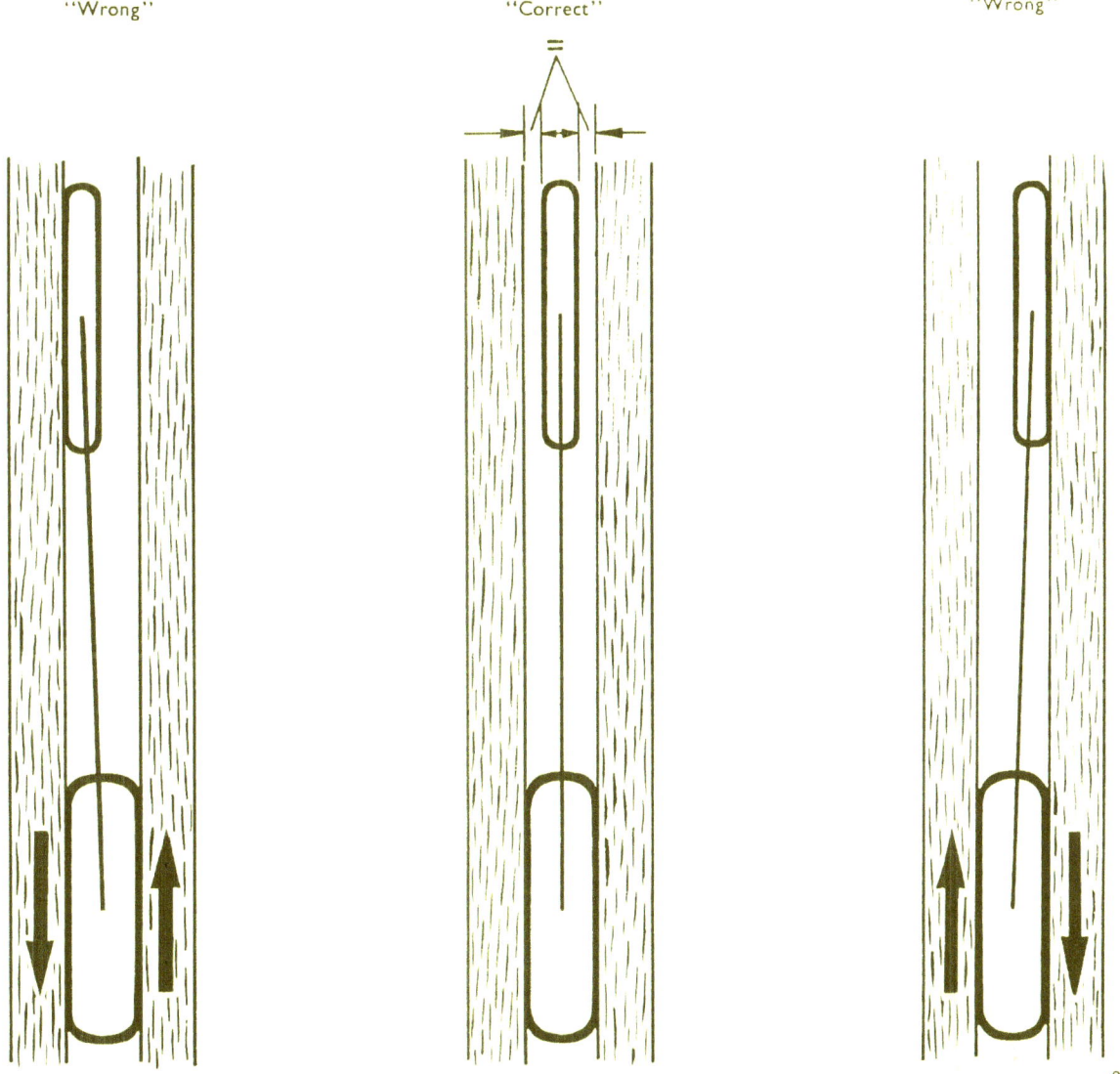

Fig. F1. Aligning the front and rear wheels

SECTION F5
BRAKE ADJUSTMENTS

BEFORE ENGINE NO. DU.66246

The front and rear brake shoes are semi-floating to allow them to self centralise on the fulcrum pin. In addition the front wheel brake shoe fulcrum pin is adjustable and is identified by a hexagonal nut just behind the fork bottom member on the anchor plate. To adjust, slacken the nut, apply full pressure to the front brake handlebar lever, and whilst holding this pressure, re-tighten the nut. This locks the fulcrum pin in the position which ensures the maximum area contact of the brake shoes within the brake drum.

AFTER DU.66246

The front brake being of the two leading shoe variety has the length of the lever adjusting rod pre set during assembly or reset after the brake shoes have been replaced (see Section F6). The shoes are however self centreing on the abutments and are equipped with steel end caps for this purpose. Cable adjustment is by means of the knurled adjuster at the handlebar lever. Turn the knurled nut anti-clockwise to take up the slack in the control cable. The correct adjustment is with not less then $\frac{1}{16}$ in. (1·5 mm.) and not more than $\frac{1}{8}$ in. (3 mm.) slack in the inner cable, at the handlebar lever.

Any wear on the brake shoe lining is indicated by the angular position of the brake operating lever when the brake is fully applied. Fig. F2 illustrates the limiting position before wear is obviously excessive. This applies to both front and rear brake operating levers. In this case the brake should be dismantled and worn parts renewed as shown in Section F6.

The adjustment of the front brake operating mechanism is by means of a knurled adjuster nut incorporated in the handlebar abutment. Turn the

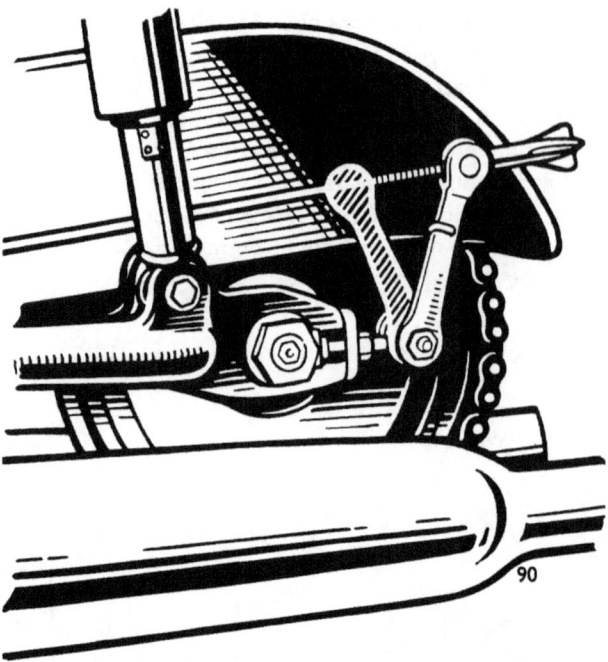

Fig. F2. Rear brake operating lever

nut anti-clockwise to take up the slack in the control cable. The correct adjustment is with not less than $\frac{1}{16}$ in. (1·5 mm.) and not more than $\frac{1}{8}$ in. (3 m.m.) slack in the inner cable at the handlebar lever.

The rear brake pedal is adjustable for position and any adjustment for the pedal position to suit the rider should be made before adjusting the free movement. From the static position before the brake is applied there should be about $\frac{1}{2}$ in. (1·2 c.m.) of free movement before the brake starts to operate. The actual adjustment is by means of a finger operated nut on the rear end of the brake operated rod. Turn the nut clockwise to reduce the clearance.

WHEELS, BRAKES AND TYRES

SECTION F6

STRIPPING AND REASSEMBLING THE BRAKES

FRONT BRAKE—TWO LEADING SHOE FROM DU.66246

Access to the front brake shoes is gained by removing the wheel (see Section F1). The brake plate is retained by a centre nut. This is recessed into the anchor plate and will require the use of a thin box spanner. The brake plate assembly will then lift away complete. Holding the brake plate with one hand lift up one shoe as in Fig. F3 until it is free. Disconnect one end of each brake return spring and lift away the second shoe. Remove the splitpin from the pivot pin at each end of the lever adjustment rod and lift the pivot pins clear. Remove the brake cam nuts and washers and remove the return spring from the front cam. Finally prise off the levers in turn and the brake cams are free to be removed from the back of the anchor plate.

To reassemble the brake shoes to the front anchor plate first grease the spindles lightly and refit both cams, wedge shape outboard on both. Refit the outside return spring to the front cam and then refit both brake cam levers (at a similar angle) and secure with the plain washers and nuts. Fit the abutment plates to the anchor plate, tag side towards the anchor plate.

Link the two shoes together with the return springs (the narrow end of the shoe abuts to the cam in each case). Both shoes fit with the radiused end to the pivot. Fit the first shoe to both the cam and abutment pad then stretch the springs by grasping the second shoe and fitting it as shown in Fig. F3.

The complete brake plate is now ready for fitting to the wheel. Replace the anchor plate over the wheel spindle and lock it home with the spindle nut, using spanner D1815.

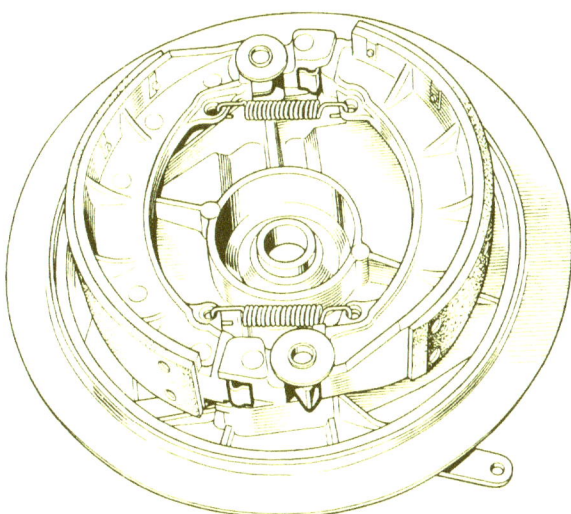

Fig. F4. 2LS brake assembled showing position of shoes

FRONT BRAKE BEFORE DU.66246 AND ALL REAR BRAKES

Access to the brake shoes (front or rear) is obtained by removing the wheel and unscrewing the central nut which retains the brake anchor plate. If the brake operating lever is then turned to relieve the pressure of the shoes against the drum, the complete brake plate assembly can be withdrawn from the spindle. Slowly release the lever and continue until the return spring can be removed, then take off the brake shoes by the method shown in Fig. F5. Remove the nut and washer securing the brake lever to the cam spindle and remove the lever. The cam spindle can then easily be withdrawn from the plate.

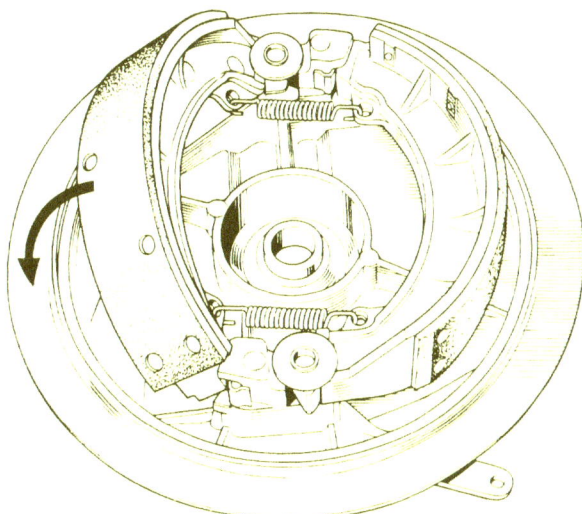

Fig. F3. Refitting shoe to 2LS brake

F WHEELS, BRAKES AND TYRES

INSPECTION PROCEDURE

(1) Examine the anchor plate for cracks or distortion, particularly in the brake cam housing.

(2) Clean out the grease in the brake cam spindle and remove any rust with a fine emery cloth.

(3) Inspect the return springs for signs of fatigue and distortion. Renew them if necessary.

(4) Examine the brake drum for scoring or ovality. In the case of the rear wheel if the drum requires skimming it should be removed from the wheel. Do not skim more than ·010 in. from the drum. If the diameter exceeds more than that given in "General Data" by more than ·010 in. the drum should be renewed.

In the case of the front wheel drum, scoring or signs of ovality can be removed by similar procedure but a large swing lathe of 18 in. diameter is required.

(5) Examine the brake shoes. The brake linings should be replaced immediately the rivets show signs of having worn level with the linings face, or the linings show signs of cracks or uneven wear. Replacement is described fully in Section F7. Also check that the brake shoes are not cracked or distorted in any way.

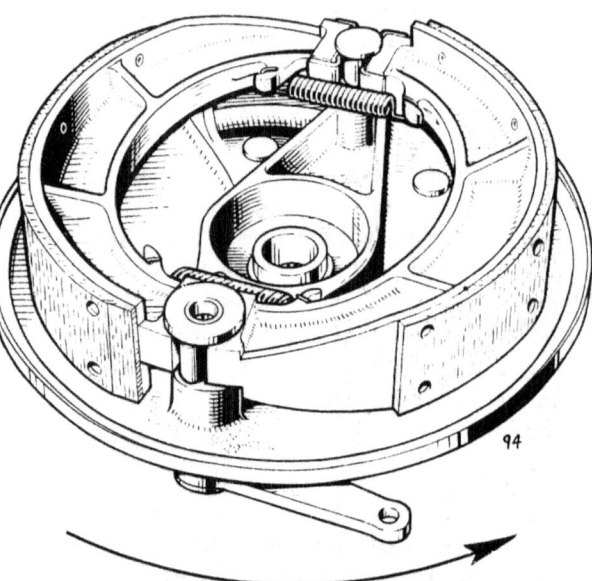

Fig. F6. Correct assembly of brake shoes onto front anchor plate. Arrow indicates direction of rotation

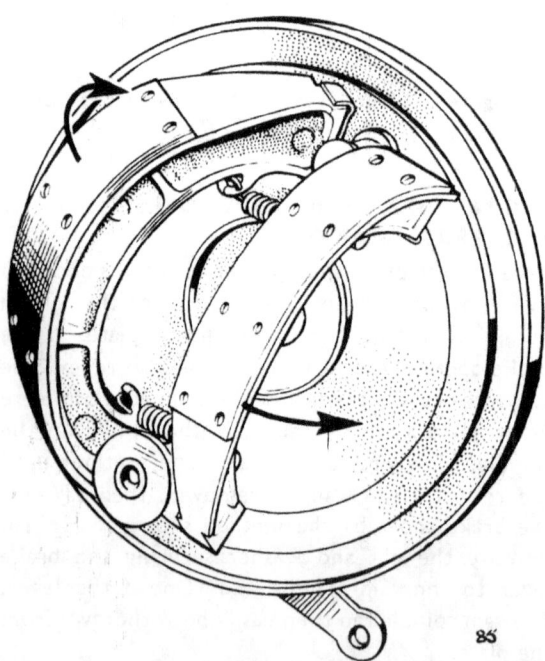

Fig. F5. Refitting brake shoes

To reassemble the brake shoes to the anchor plate first place the two brake shoes on the bench in their relative positions. Fit the return springs to the retaining hooks, hooked ends uppermost, then taking a shoe in each hand (see Fig. F5) and at the same time holding the springs in tension, position the shoes as shown over the cam and fulcrum pin and snap down into position by pressing on the outer edges of the shoes. Rotate the brake lever in an anti-clockwise direction and engage the return spring.

Note.—When replacing the brake shoes, note that the leading and trailing brake shoes are not interchangeable in either the front or rear brake and ensure that they are in their correct relative positions as shown in Fig. F6.

Reassembly then continues by placing the anchor plate over the wheel spindle and locking home with the spindle nut. Refer to Section F4 for final re-alignment of the wheels if this is found to be necessary.

WHEELS, BRAKES AND TYRES

SECTION F7
RENEWING THE BRAKE LININGS

The old linings can be removed by either drilling through the rivets with a suitable sized drill (No. 23 ·154 in. dia.) or chiselling the lining off at the same time shearing through the brass rivet. Drilling is of course preferred and is best undertaken from the inside of the shoe to remove the peened over portion of the rivet.

New linings are supplied ready drilled, counter bored and the correct shape. If no jig is available for riveting, a simple method of spreading the rivet is shown in Fig. F7.

Rivet the linings in the centre holes first, working towards each end: great care must be taken to ensure that the rivets are tight and that the linings do not lift between the rivets. After fitting, all sharp edges of the lining should be chamfered and the leading and trailing edges tapered off to the extent of $\frac{1}{8}$ in. deep × $\frac{1}{2}$ in. long.

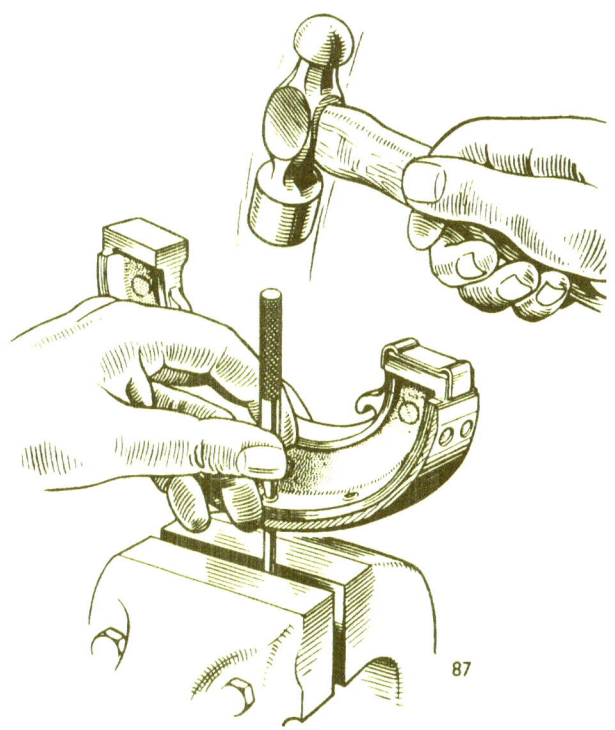

Fig. F7. Riveting lining onto brake shoe

SECTION F8
REMOVING AND REFITTING THE WHEEL BEARINGS

Access to the wheel bearings differs in front and rear wheels and therefore each wheel is dealt with separately in this section.

FRONT WHEEL
Remove the front wheel from the fork and withdraw the brake anchor plate from the brake drum. Unscrew the retainer ring (left hand thread) using service tool Z76.

The right bearing can be removed by using the spindle and driving through from the left hand side. Withdraw the backing ring and inner retaining disc. (note that current wheels use a single part replacing these two). To remove the left bearing, spring out the circlip and insert the spindle from the right side driving the bearing out complete with inner and outer grease retainer plates.

Fully clean all parts in paraffin (kerosene). Clean and dry the bearings thoroughly. Compressed air should be used for drying out the ball races. Test for end float and inspect the balls and races for any signs of pitting. If there is any doubt about their condition, the bearings should be renewed.

To refit the bearings, first insert the left inner grease retainer, bearing, and outer dust cap using a liberal amount of grease (see Section A2). Refit the spring circlip and insert the shouldered end of the wheel spindle from the right, using it as a drift to drive the bearing and grease retainer until they come up to the circlip. Re-insert the spindle the opposite way round and re-fit the right hand grease retainer disc and backing ring. Drive the right bearing into position well smeared with grease, then screw in the retainer ring (left hand thread) until tight.

Finally, tap the spindle from the left to bring the spindle shoulder up against the right bearing. Refer to Fig. F8 or F9 for correct layout. Reassembly then continues as the reversal of the above instructions.

F

WHEELS, BRAKES AND TYRES

Fig. F8. Latest wheel with twin leading shoe brake

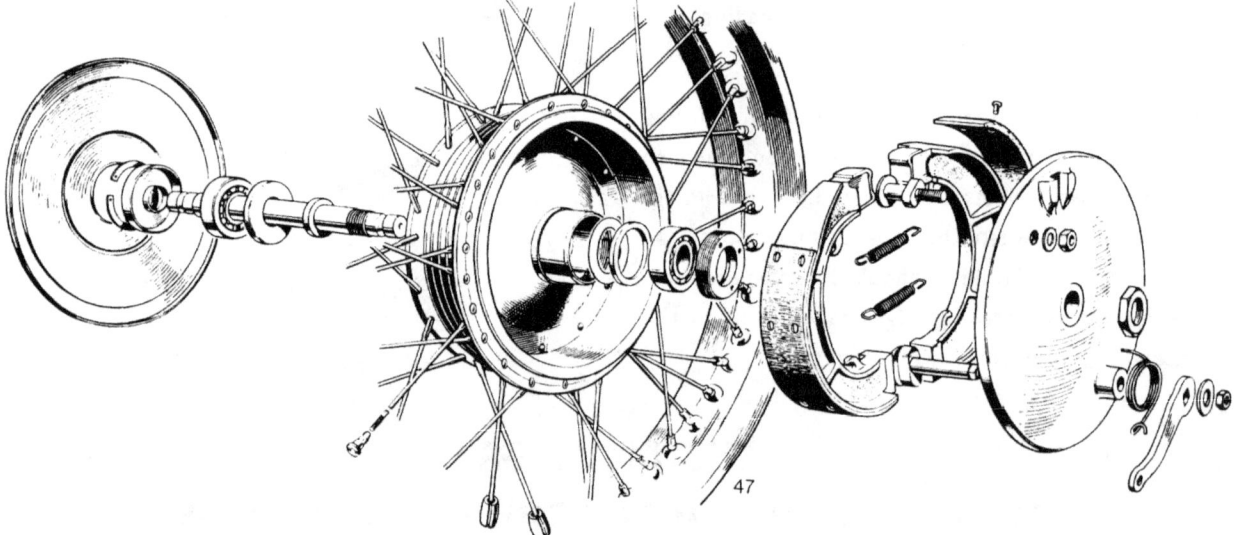

Fig. F9. Exploded view of front wheel bearing arrangement (before DU.66246)

REAR WHEEL (STANDARD)

Remove the rear wheel then unscrew the anchor plate retainer nut and withdraw the brake anchor plate assembly. Withdraw the wheel spindle then unscrew the slotted screw which serves to lock the bearing retainer ring. *The retainer ring can then be unscrewed using service tool Z76. So that the left bearing can be removed the central distance piece must be displaced to one side to allow a drift to be located on the inner ring of the left bearing. To do this, first insert a drift from the left and move the distance piece to one side so that the grease retainer shim collapses, as shown in Fig. F11. A soft metal drift should then be inserted from the right and the left bearing driven out. The speedometer drive adaptor must first be unscrewed from the hub before removing the right hand wheel bearing. When this is done, withdraw the backing ring, dam aged grease retainer and distance piece then drive out the right bearing and dust cap using a drift of approximately $1\frac{5}{8}$ in. diameter.

Fully clean all parts in paraffin (kerosene) and clean and dry the bearing thoroughly. Compressed air should be used for drying out if possible. Test the end float and inspect the ball races for any signs of indentation or pitting. If the condition of the bearing is in doubt it should be renewed.

The damaged grease retainer shim usually can be reclaimed for further service by carefully hammering it flat to restore its original shape.

To refit the bearings first drive in the right inner grease retainer disc, the bearing and then press on the outer dust cap ensuring that the bearing and both cavities are well filled with grease. From the left, insert the distance piece, grease retainer shim, backing ring and having packed the bearing with grease, press it in the hub and bring the distance piece into line with the spindle. Screw in the retainer ring and tighten it with service tool Z76

*IMPORTANT: RH side slotted nut is LH thread.

WHEELS, BRAKES AND TYRES

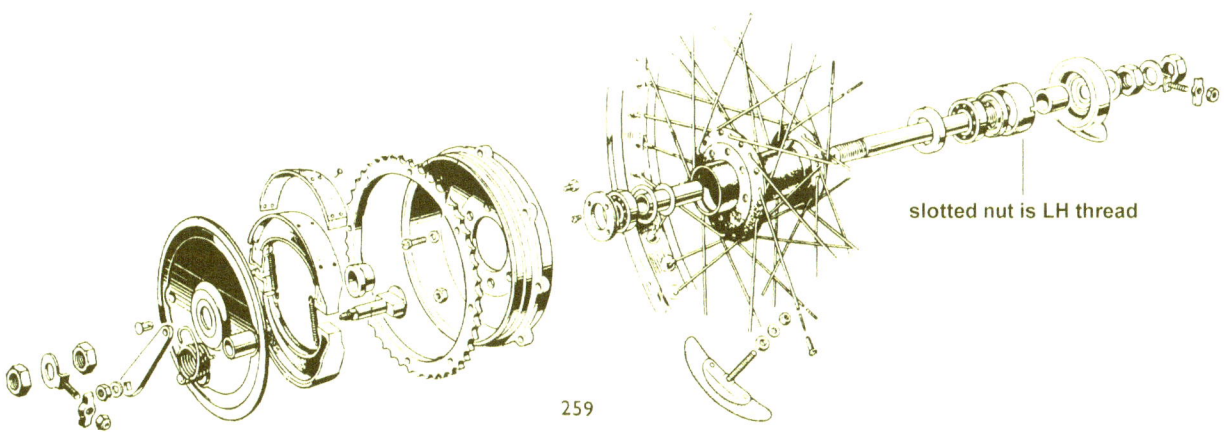

Fig. F10. Exploded view of the standard rear wheel

Finally, tighten the locking screw to ensure that the bearing retainer ring is locked in position. Reassembly then continues as a reversal to the above instructions, but do not forget to refit the outer distance piece before assembling the anchor plate and brake shoe assembly.

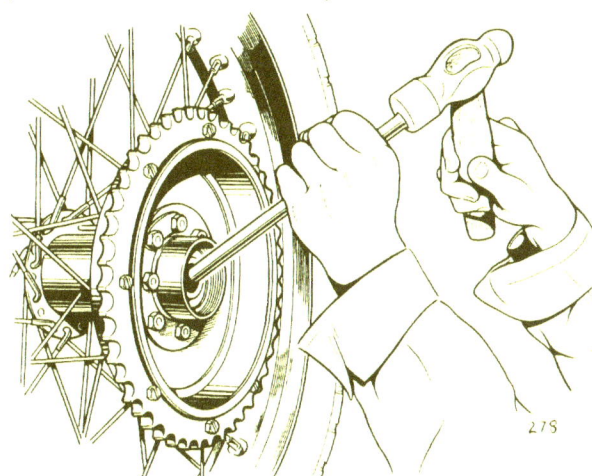

Fig. F11. Collapsing the left bearing grease retainer shim

The rear wheel is fitted with a brake drum to which a detachable steel sprocket is retained by eight bolts. Earlier wheels could be fitted with this sprocket and brake drum as a direct replacement for the original part.

REAR WHEEL (QUICKLY DETACHABLE)

Having removed the wheel from the swinging fork as described in Section F3, the wheel hub can then be dismantled. Hold the bearing sleeve by the slot at the tapered end and unscrew the nut on the right side. Use service tool Z76 (left hand thread) to unscrew the locking ring and then lift off the distance piece, felt washer and locating disc. The bearing sleeve is a sliding fit and is easily withdrawn. In order to remove the right bearing the central distance piece has to be displaced radially to allow a drift to be located on the inner ring of the right bearing. This is done by inserting a drift from the right and moving the centre distance piece radially so that the grease retainer shim collapses. Then insert a soft metal drift from the left and drive out the right bearing. Withdraw the backing ring, damaged grease retainer and distance piece; then using a drift, drive out the left bearing and withdraw the other grease retainer. Thoroughly clean all parts in paraffin (kerosene) and fully dry the bearings. Inspect the ball races for any signs of indentation or pitting and renew if necessary.

Removal of the brake drum and sprocket assembly from the swinging fork is achieved by first disconnecting the rear chain, torque stay and brake operating rod, and then unscrewing the large nut from the spindle sleeve.

Remove the brake shoes and anchor plate assembly as described in Section F6. To remove the ball bearing from the brake drum, first press out the spindle sleeve and then remove the circlip from the brake drum. The retainer and felt washer can then be levered out to enable the bearing to be driven out. Care should be taken to avoid damage to the inner grease retainer when removing the bearing. Clean the bearing in paraffin (kerosene) and check that there is not excessive play or that the race tracks are not indented or pitted. If in doubt, renew the bearing. On reassembly pack the bearings with grease and do not forget to dip the felt washer in oil.

Reassembly is a reversal of the above procedure referring to Fig. F12 for order of assembly and Section F3 for refitting the wheel to the swinging fork.

WHEELS, BRAKES AND TYRES

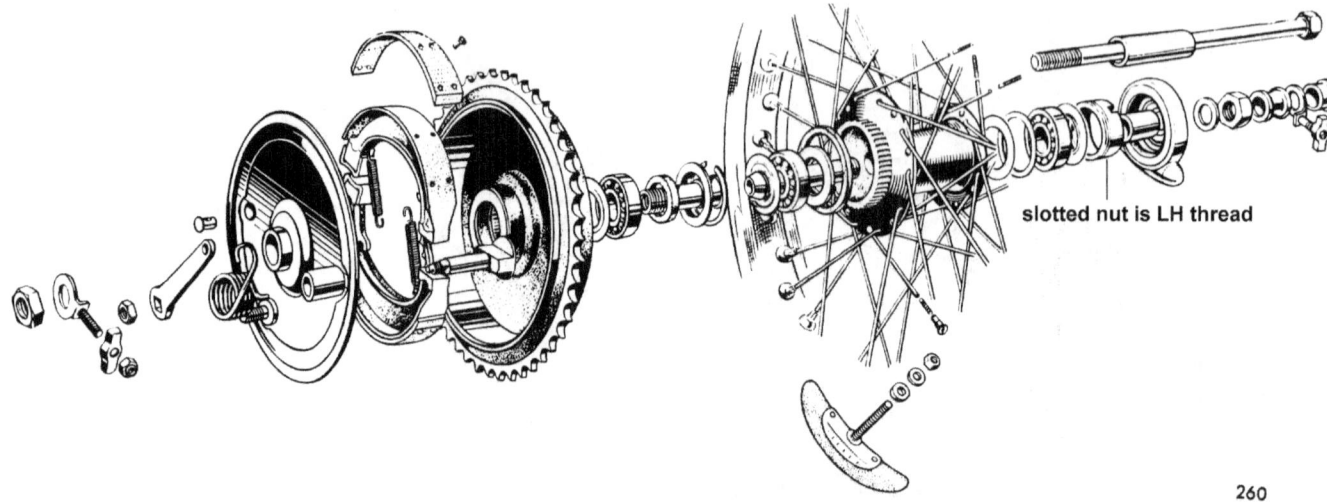

Fig. F12. Exploded view of the quickly detachable rear wheel

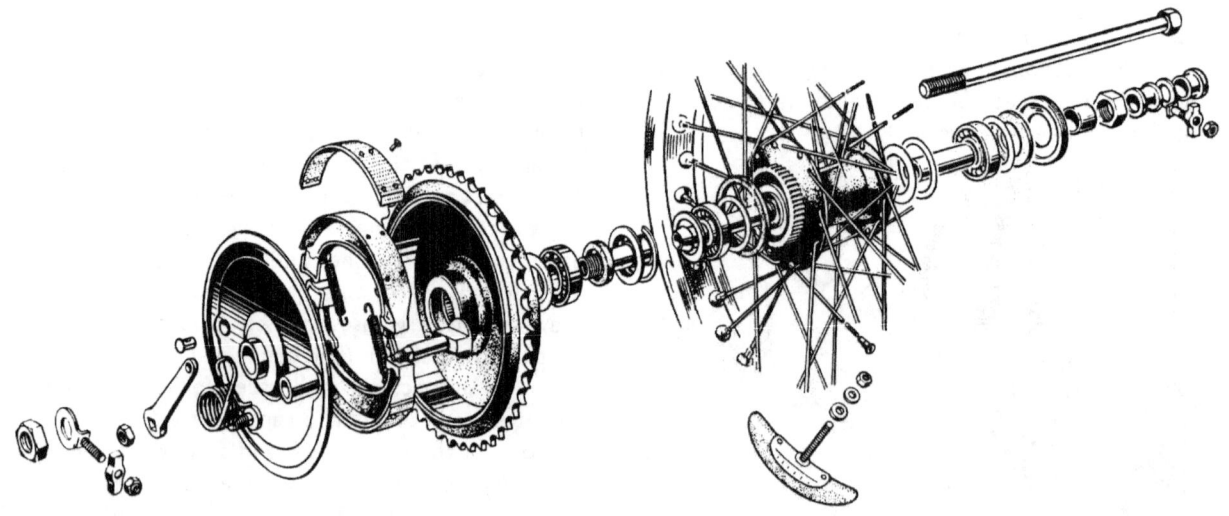

Fig. F13. Exploded view of Q.D. rear wheel (without speedometer drive)

Between engine numbers DU.13375 and DU.24875 the ball journal bearing type of wheel had no speedometer drive gearbox. The order of assembly is shown in Fig. F13.

Q.D. WHEEL PRIOR TO DU.13375
Prior to engine number DU.13375 the taper roller bearing arrangement was used. Removal of the wheel is as described in Section F3. Unscrew the two locknuts on the right hand side of the spindle sleeve (see Fig. F14) and then push the sleeve out of the bearings from the right. Extract the inner roller races and dust cover. The outer races are a press fit and should be driven out from the opposite side with a soft metal drift. Care should be taken not to damage the bearing backing rings, and inner grease retaining shims.

Thoroughly clean all parts in paraffin (kerosene) and fully dry the bearings. Check the roller bearing surfaces for pitting and pocketing. Renew the bearings if there is any indication of this.

To reassemble the wheel bearings, first press the left and right backing rings and grease retainers into the wheel hub and then press the left and right outer races into the hub. Smear the rollers and inner races with grease (see Section A2) and refit them to their respective outer races. Offer the threaded end of the spindle sleeve to the roller

WHEELS, BRAKES AND TYRES

bearings and then fit the right dust excluder cap with felt washer and left dust excluder cap. (Refer to Fig. F14).

Refit the right side distance piece and inner and outer locknuts to the spindle sleeve, then tighten the inner locknut, slacken it off one flat ($\frac{1}{6}$) turn and lock it in position by tightening the outer locknut. The sleeve and inner races should then rotate freely without any "play" in the rollers being in evidence. Reassembly is a reversal of the above. The order of stripping and reassembly of the brake drum and sprocket assembly is the same as for the later type of Q.D. wheel.

Fig. F14. Exploded view of Q.D. rear wheel (earlier taper roller bearing type)

SECTION F9
WHEEL BUILDING

Wheel building, or adjustment to the spokes to realign the wheel rim should only be undertaken by a specialist and these notes are for the specialist, to enable him to follow Triumph practice. The main point to remember is that all Triumph wheels are built with the inside spokes on the brake drum side taking the braking strain. This means the inside spokes on the drum side are in tension when the brake is applied in the direction of forward motion.

The front wheel has 40 straight 8/10 gauge butted spokes and is single cross-laced, whilst the rear wheel has 40 8/10 gauge butted spokes, and is double cross-laced.

A checking gauge suitable for Triumph wheels can be made from two pieces of mild steel bar as shown in Fig. F15 and this should be used to register from the edge of the hub or brake drum onto the wheel rim edge giving the relation indicated in the table.

This ensures the correct relation between the hub and rim centre lines.

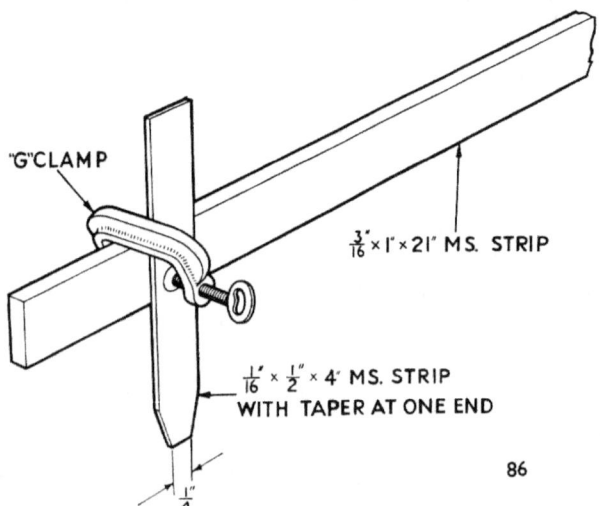

Fig. F15. Sketch of wheel building gauge

Wheel	Rim type	Location	Dimensions	
			Inches	m.m.
Front: Standard	WM2	Drum	$-\frac{1}{64}$	-0.4
Rear: Standard	WM2	Hub	$1\frac{7}{8}$	47.6
	WM3	Hub	$1\frac{3}{4}$	44.4
Q.D.	WM2	Hub	$1\frac{1}{16}$	27
	WM3	Hub	$\frac{7}{8}$	22.2

Table of "Dish" Dimensional Settings for Front and Rear Wheels

SECTION F10
WHEEL BALANCING

Wheel balancing can be achieved by fitting standard one ounce and half ounce weights which are readily available, as required. All front wheels are balanced complete with tyre and tube before leaving the factory and if for any reason the tyre is removed it should be replaced with the white balancing "spot" level with the valve. If a new tyre is fitted, existing weights should be removed and the wheel re-balanced, adding weights as necessary until it will remain in any position at rest. Make sure that the brake is not binding while the balancing operation is being carried out.

For normal road use it is not found necessary for the rear wheel to be balanced in this way.

WHEELS, BRAKES AND TYRES

SECTION F11
REMOVING AND REPAIRING TYRES

To remove the tyre first remove the valve cap and valve core, using the valve cap itself to unscrew the core. Unscrew the knurled valve securing nut and then place all parts where they will be free from dirt and grit. It is recommended that the cover beads are lubricated with a little soapy water before attempting to remove the tyre. The tyre lever should be dipped in this solution before each application. First, insert a lever at the valve position and whilst carefully pulling on this lever, press the tyre bead into the well of the rim diametrally opposite the valve position (see Fig. F16). Insert a

Fig. F17. Removing the first bead of the tyre, using two tyre levers

REFITTING THE TYRE

First place the rubber rim band into the well of the rim and make sure that the rough side of the rubber band is fitted against the rim and that the band is central in the well. Replace the valve core and inflate the inner tube sufficiently to round it out without stretch, dust it with french chalk and insert it into the cover with the valve located at the white "balancing spot" leaving it protruding outside the beads for about four inches either side of the valve. At this stage it is advisable to lubricate the beads and levers with soapy water (see Fig. F18).

Fig. F16. Removing the first bead of the tyre—Lever inserted close to valve whilst bead is pressed into well on opposite side of wheel

second lever close to the first and prise the bead over the rim flange. Remove the first lever and reinsert a little further round the rim from the second lever. Continue round the bead in steps of two to three inches until the bead is completely away from the rim. Push the valve out of the rim and then withdraw the inner tube. To completely remove the tyre first stand the wheel upright and then insert a lever between the remaining bead and the rim. The tyre should be easily removed from the rim as shown in Fig. F17.

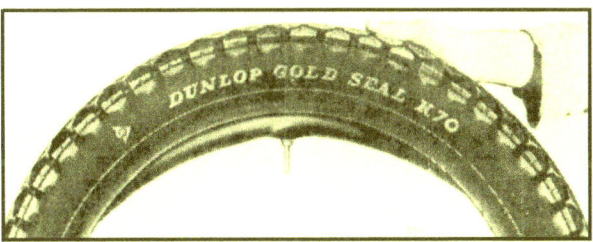

Fig. F18. Cover and tube assembled ready for refitting to the wheel

Squeeze the beads together at the valve position to prevent the tube from slipping back inside the tyre and offer the cover to the rim, as shown in Fig. F19, at the same time threading the valve through the valve holes in the rim band and rim. Allow the first bead to go into the well of the rim and the other bead to lie above the level of the rim flange.

F WHEELS, BRAKES AND TYRES

Fig. F19. Refitting the tyre to the wheel. Note valve engaged in rim hole

Press the second bead into the well of the rim diametrally opposite the valve. Insert a lever as close as possible to the point where the bead passes over the flange and lever the bead into the flange, at the same time pressing the fitted part of the bead into the well of the rim. Repeat until the bead is completely over the flange, finishing at the valve position (see Fig. F21).

Working from the valve, press the first bead over the rim flange by hand, moving forward in small steps and making sure that the part of the bead already dealt with, lies in the well of the rim. If necessary use a tyre lever for the last few inches, as shown in Fig. F20. During this operation continually check that the inner tube is not trapped by the cover bead.

Fig. F21. Refitting the second bead over the wheel rim. Care must be taken not to trap inner tube

Fig. F20. Levering the first bead onto the rim

Push the valve inwards to ensure that the tube near the valve is not trapped under the bead. Pull the valve back and inflate the tyre. Check that the fitting line on the cover is concentric with the top of the rim flange and that the valve protrudes squarely through the valve hole. Fit the knurled rim nut and valve cap. The tyre pressure should then be set to the figure given in General Data.

SECTION F12
SECURITY BOLTS

Security bolts are fitted to the rear wheel to prevent the tyre "creeping" on the rim when it is subjected to excessive acceleration or braking. Such movement would ultimately result in the valve being torn from the inner tube. There are two security bolts fitted to the rear wheel, which are equally spaced either side of the valve and thereby do not affect the balance of the wheel.

Note: The security bolt nuts must not be overtightened, otherwise excessive distortion may occur.

WHEELS, BRAKES AND TYRES

Where a security bolt is fitted the basic procedure for fitting and removing the tyre is the same, but the following instruction should be followed:—

(1) Remove the valve cap and core as described.

(2) Unscrew the security bolt nut and push the bolt inside the cover.

(3) Remove the first bead as described.

(4) Remove the security bolt from the rim.

(5) Remove the inner tube as described.

(6) Remove the second bead and tyre.

For refitting the tyre and inner tube:—

(1) Fit the rim band.

(2) Fit the first bead to the rim without the inner tube inside.

(3) Assemble the security bolt into the rim, putting the nut onto the first few threads (see Fig. F1).

(4) Partly inflate the inner tube and fit it into the the tyre.

(5) Fit the second bead but keep the security bolt pressed well into the tyre, as shown in Fig. F23, and ensure that the inner tube does not become trapped at the edges.

(6) Fit the valve stem nut and inflate the tyre.

(7) Bounce the wheel several times at the point where the security bolt is fitted and then tighten the security bolt nut.

Fig. F22. Placing the security bolt in position

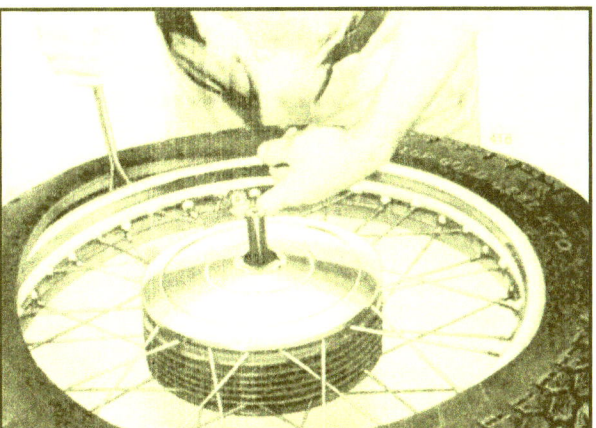

Fig. F23. Refitting the second bead with the security bolt in position

SECTION F13
TYRE MAINTENANCE

To obtain optimum tyre mileage and to eliminate irregular wear on the tyres it is essential that the recommendations governing tyre pressures and general maintenance are followed. The following points are laid out with this in mind.

(1) Maintain the correct inflation pressure as shown in "General Data". Use a pressure gauge frequently. It is advisable to check and restore tyre pressures at least once per week. Pressures should always be checked when tyres are cold and not when they have reached normal running temperatures.

(2) When a pillion passenger or additional load is carried, the rear tyre pressure should be increased appropriately to cater for the extra load.

(3) Unnecessary rapid acceleration and fierce braking should always be avoided. This treatment invariably results in rapid tyre wear.

(4) Regular checks should be made for flints, nails, small stones etc, which should be removed from the tread or they may ultimately penetrate and damage the casing and puncture the tube.

(5) Tyres and spokes should be kept free of oil, grease and paraffin. Regular cleaning should be carried out with a cloth and a little petrol (gasoline).

(6) If tyres develop irregular wear, this may be corrected by reversing the tyre to reverse its direction of rotation.

(7) If a sidecar is fitted then correct alignment should be maintained. The method for testing sidecar alignment is given in Section F14.

SECTION F14

SIDECAR ALIGNMENT

In order that the tyres of a motorcycle and sidecar combination are not subject to rapid tread wear and to provide the best steering characteristics they should be aligned as shown in the diagrams below.

First, align the front and rear wheels of the motorcycle as described in Section F4, and then, when it is ascertained that this alignment is correct, the sidecar wheel should be set using two straight test bars to the figure given in Fig. F24. Two battens about 6 feet long, 5 inches wide and 1 inch thick with one edge on each of the boards planed perfectly straight and square, would be suitable.

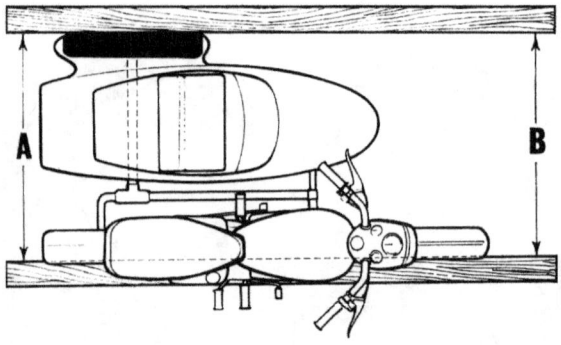

Fig. F24. Aligning the sidecar wheel to the correct amount of "toe-in"

With the combination standing on a flat, smooth floor place one of the long boards about 4 inches from the floor (i.e. using spacers), alongside the rear tyre with its straight edge touching the sides of the tyres. Straighten the front wheel until the board is parallel with the sides of the front tyre, an equal distance from both sides of the front wheel centre line. Place the other long board also about 4 inches from the floor level with its straight edge touching the sides of the sidecar tyre. Front and rear dimensions should then be measured, and the sidecar fixings adjusted until the front distance B is between $\frac{3}{8}$ inch (10 mm.) to $\frac{3}{4}$ inch (20 mm.) smaller than the rear distance A. This distance is referred to as the amount of "toe-in".

The motorcycle itself should also "lean out" and the method for making this adjustment is shown clearly in Fig. F25. To do this, attach a plumb line to the handlebar and measure the distances at the top and bottom as shown. On the inner side of the handlebar (i.e. nearer the sidecar) the plumb line should be approximately 1 inch nearer the wheel centre line at the bottom than at the top.

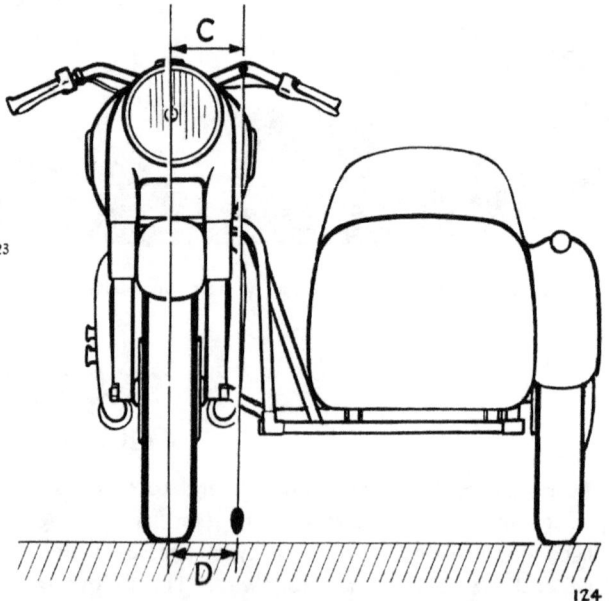

Fig. F25. Setting the amount of "lean-out" by using a plumbline

SECTION G
TELESCOPIC FORKS

DESCRIPTION	Section
REMOVING AND REFITTING THE NACELLE TOP COVER (6T)	G1
REMOVING THE TELESCOPIC FORK UNIT	G2
DISMANTLING THE TELESCOPIC FORK	G3
INSPECTION AND REPAIR OF FORK COMPONENTS	G4
RENEWING THE STEERING HEAD RACES	G5
RENEWING THE FRONT FORK OIL SEALS	G6
REASSEMBLING AND REFITTING THE FORK UNIT	G7
TELESCOPIC FORK ALIGNMENT	G8
ADJUSTING THE STEERING HEAD RACES	G9
CHANGING THE FRONT FORK MAIN SPRINGS	G10
THE HYDRAULIC DAMPER UNIT	G11

G

TELESCOPIC FORKS

DESCRIPTION

The Triumph telescopic hydraulically controlled front forks requires little attention other than an occasional check of the external nut and bolts etc. and the routine oil changes given in Section A1.

The fork uses short external main springs. Before engine number DU.5825 an earlier type of fork with internal springs and different damping characteristics was used. The capacity differs between the two types of fork, so that it is essential that the appropriate quantity of oil is poured into each fork leg when an oil change is to be carried out. The current fork utilising shuttle valve damping is illustrated below.

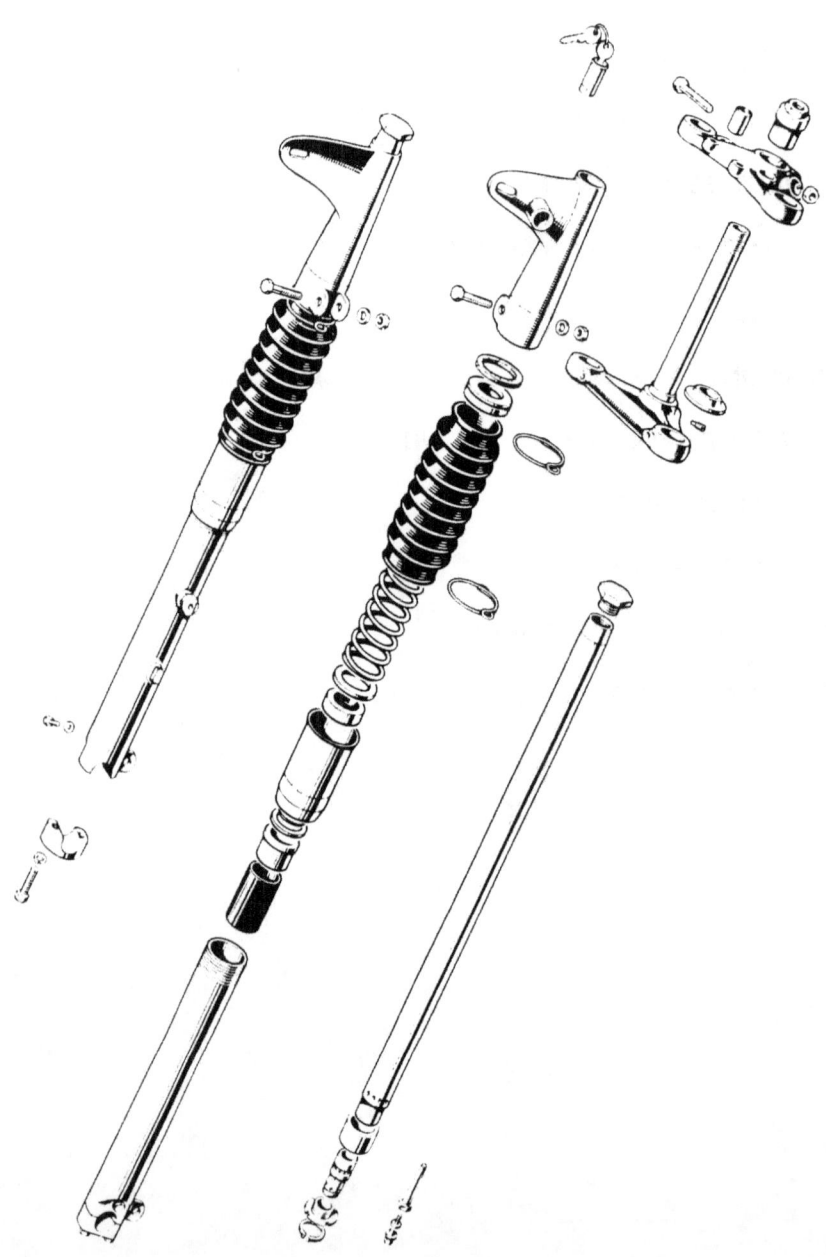

Fig. G1. Exploded view of telescopic fork (shuttle valve type)

TELESCOPIC FORKS

SECTION G1
REMOVING AND REFITTING THE NACELLE TOP COVER (6T)

Disconnect the leads at the battery terminals.

Unscrew and remove the steering damper knob.

Slacken the headlamp securing screw adjacent to the speedometer dial and lever off the headlamp. Disconnect the lead from the main bulb, pilot bulb and dip-switch (four snap connectors) and disconnect the headlamp earthing lead.

Remove the two adaptor rim securing screws and square nuts and withdraw the rims. Unscrew the two front and two rear top cover securing bolts and unscrew the left and right flash rear mounting screws.

Disconnect the front brake cable at the handlebar and thread it through the nacelle cover. Slacken off the clutch cable adjuster at the handlebar and lift the rubber sleeve at the gearbox and remove the slotted cable adaptor, then disconnect the clutch cable at the handlebar and thread it through the nacelle top cover. The nacelle cover can then be lifted to allow the drive cable and bulbholder to be disconnected from the speedometer.

Disconnect the ammeter terminal leads and detach the lighting switch and the ignition switch bakelite connection plugs. The nacelle top cover is then free to be removed.

Refitting the cover is the reversal of the above instructions but reference must be made to the relevant wiring diagram in Section H19 to avoid incorrect connections being made. The blue/brown lead from the battery —ve terminal should be connected to the ammeter +ve terminal. To check that the ammeter is correctly connected, turn the ignition switch to "IGN". The ammeter needle should deflect to discharge (—). If it does not, reverse the ammeter terminal connections.

Finally, when the headlamp adaptor rim and light unit are refitted the head main beam should be set as described in Section H12.

SECTION G2
REMOVING THE TELESCOPIC FORK UNIT

Removal of the front forks is best achieved by detaching the fork as a unit, removing the top lug only whilst the stanchions and middle lug assembly is lowered from the frame.

First, unscrew the small drain plugs at the bottom of the fork adjacent to the wheel spindle lug and drain the oil out by pumping the fork up and down a few times.

Place a strong wooden box underneath the engine so that the front wheel is about six inches clear of the ground, then remove the wheel and mudguard as shown in Section F1. Detach the headlamp unit Section H12 and then detach the throttle cable and air control cable. Detach the ignition lock and switch on current models. The handlebar can be removed by unscrewing the two self locking nuts which secure the eye bolts underneath the top lug, or, on machines without resilient mountings, by removing the clamps.

Remove the steering damper plate pivot bolt, if fitted, and then slacken the top lug pinch bolt and unscrew the sleeve nut, or blind nut, with a suitable tommy bar. Unscrew the left and right stanchion cap nuts using spanner No. D779 (D220 on earlier models) and on earlier models withdraw the two cap-nut-and-guide-tube assemblies.

Support the fork and then give the top lug a sharp tap on the under-side until it is released from the stanchion locking tapers. The stanchion and middle lug assembly can then be lowered from the frame headlug. If care is taken, the top ball race can be left un-disturbed and the lower race balls collected when the clearance is sufficient.

ALTERNATIVE METHOD
Alternatively the fork stanchions can be removed whilst the middle lug, top lug and head races are left un-disturbed. To facilitate extraction of the stanchions from the top and middle lugs in this

case service tool Z169 will be required (Z19 before DU.68363. Remove the cap nuts, slacken the middle lug pinch bolts and then unscrew the two small hexagonal headed oil filler plugs (if fitted) from the stanchion. Screw in the adaptor plug (Z169 or Z19) and drive the stanchion until it is free to be withdrawn from the middle lug, as shown in Fig. G3. It should be noted that if the stanchions are removed this way on the later models (frame No. DU.5825 onwards) a special service tool will be required to refit them (see Section G8 Part 2).

HANDLEBAR EYEBOLT ASSEMBLIES

Eyebolts are employed for fixing the handlebars on TR6, T120 and U.S.A. TR6R and T120R. There are three different types of fixing for the eyebolts. The first two use the metalastic bushes fitted in the fork top lug. The third type dispenses with these. See Fig. G2.

(A) STANDARD RUBBER MOUNTED HANDLEBAR (TR6 AND T120)

Note the hemispherical washer 'A' is fitted with the rounded side towards the head lug. The washer 'B' is radiused internally on one side only. The radius **must** be towards the head of the eyebolt.

(B) U.S.A. RUBBER MOUNTED HANDLE-BAR (TR6R AND T120R)

It will be noted that this arrangement uses an additional support rubber with cup and inner distance piece (C.D.E.) beneath the head lug. Again note the radiused washer (A) **must** have the radius towards the eyebolt head.

(C) RIGIDLY MOUNTED HANDLEBARS (FOR USE WITH HANDLEBAR WINDSCREENS)

This arrangement dispenses with the metalistic bushes in the head lug. These are replaced by pairs of rigid bushes. There is no necessity to use the radiused washers since both rigid bushes are radiused in a similar manner. It is not possible to fit the bushes into the head lug incorrectly

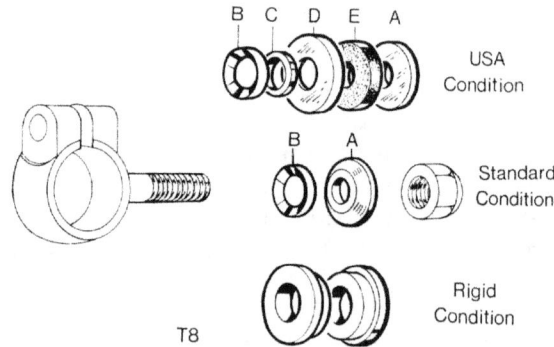

Fig. G2. Handlebar eyebolt order of assembly

SECTION G3
DISMANTLING THE TELESCOPIC FORK

There have been three types of forks fitted to unit construction models, the earliest of the inside main spring type, the second the redesigned outer main spring type and the third the shuttle valve type. To avoid confusion between the three basic types this section is divided into three parts.

PART 1. FRAME DU.101 TO DU.5824

Remove the front fork as shown in Section G3 then firmly grip the middle lug stem horizontally in a vice and unscrew the hexagon headed oil filler plugs and stanchion pinch bolts. Screw service tool Z19 into the stanchion and drive it out of the middle lug assembly. Alternatively, refit the stanchion cap nuts and use a hide mallet. When the stanchions are removed withdraw the nacelle bottom covers and collect the two spring sealing washers. On models fitted with gaiters slacken the top and bottom gaiter securing clips and withdraw them.

Removal of the dust excluder sleeve nuts is facilitated by spanner D220 which should be used when the stanchion and bottom member assembly is firmly gripped in a vice by means of the wheel spindle lug. The sleeve nut will be easily unscrewed when it has been slackened initially by giving the spanner a sharp knock with a hide or copper mallet. Withdraw the stanchion, top bush and damping sleeve from the bottom member, if necessary, by giving the stanchion a few sharp pulls to release the bush. If the stanchion cannot be freed from the bottom member due to some form of damage, service tool No. Z127 will be required to extract the stanchion. The tool should be attached to the stanchion as shown in Fig. G4 ensuring that maximum thread engagement of the adaptor cap nut is achieved.

The oil restrictor rod assembly is secured within the bottom member by means of a hexagonal headed bolt counter-bored into the wheel spindle lug. When this bolt is unscrewed the restrictor rod assembly can be withdrawn.

The bolt is sealed by means of an aluminium washer which should be removed from the counter bore and placed in safe keeping.

The bottom fork bearing bush is secured to the stanchion by means of a special slotted nut. Removal of this nut is facilitated by spanner D220.

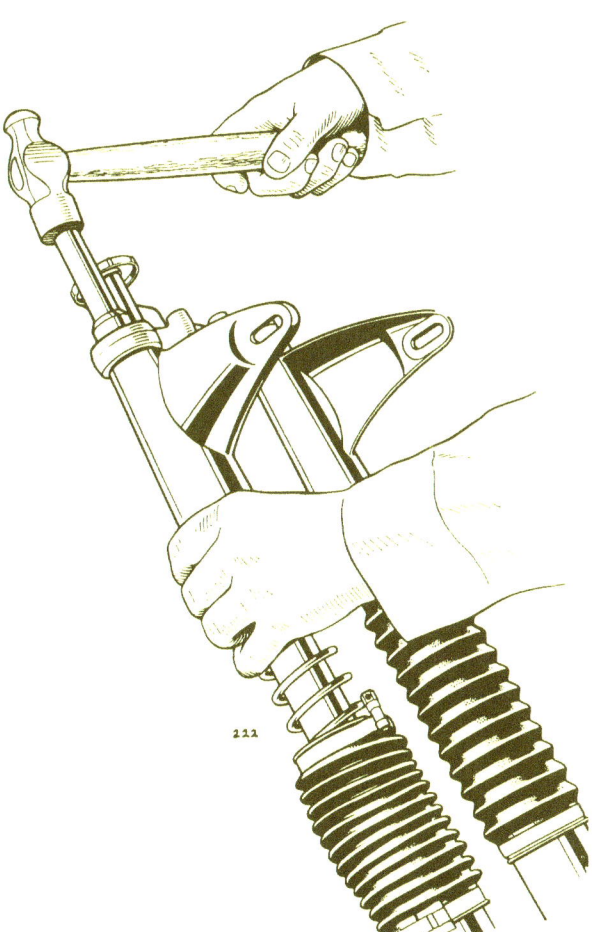

Fig. G3. Dismantling the telescopic fork using service tool Z19.

PART 2. FRAME NO. DU.5825 TO DU.66245
Remove the front fork from the frame headlug by the method shown in Section G2 and then grip the middle lug stem firmly in a vice and unscrew the two small hexagon headed oil filler plugs (if fitted) from the stanchion. Unscrew the two middle lug pinch bolts, the top and bottom gaiter securing clips if fitted, and, on earlier models (6T) withdraw the lower nacelle shrouds.

Screw in service tool Z19, or an old cap nut and drive the stanchions out of the middle lug. When the stanchions are removed, detach the spring covers, springs and top and bottom washers.

At this stage the fork top shrouds can be removed. It is advisable to renew the felt sealing washer when reassembling the forks.

Removal of the dust excluder sleeve nut is facilitated by service tool D527 which should be attached to the sleeve nut whilst the wheel spindle lug is held firmly in a vice. The sleeve nut has a right hand thread and should unscrew easily once the nut has been initially loosened by giving the spanner a sharp tap with a hide mallet.

Note: If the hydraulic damping units shown in Fig. G15 are fitted, it will be necessary to remove them before the stanchions can be withdrawn from the bottom members. To do this, unscrew the hexagon headed bolt which can be seen counter bored into the wheel spindle lugs.

When the dust excluder nut is removed, a few sharp pulls should release the stanchion, bush and damper sleeve assembly from the bottom member.

The restrictor rod securing bolt, the hexagon headed restrictor securing bolt, seen counter-bored into the wheel spindle lug, is sealed by means of an aluminium washer which should be withdrawn from the counter bore when the bolt is removed and placed in storage and refitted on assembly.

PART 3. FRAME NO. DU.66245 ONWARDS
Remove the front fork from the frame headlug as described in Section G1. Grip the middle lug stem firmly in a vice and unscrew the two middle lug pinch bolts and the top and bottom gaiter securing clips. Screw service tool Z169 for machines after DU.68363 (and Z19 prior to this number) into the top of the stanchion (use an old cap nut in the

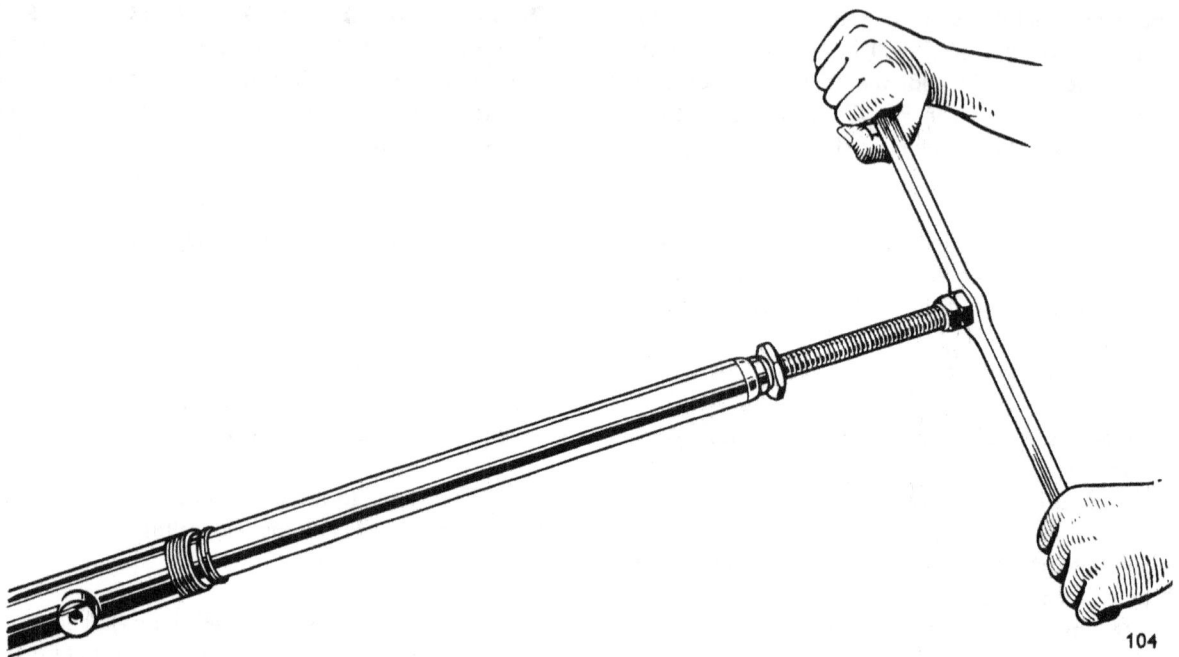

Fig. G4. Extracting the stanchion from the bottom member using service tool Z127

absence of the correct tool) and drive the stanchions out of the middle lug. When the stanchions are removed, collect the spring abutments, springs, gaiters and clips.

At this stage the fork top shrouds can be removed. It is advisable to renew the felt sealing washer when reassembling the forks.

Removal of the dust excluder sleeve nut is facilitated by service tool D527 which should be attached to the sleeve nut whilst the wheel spindle lug is held firmly in a vice. The sleeve nut has a right hand thread and should unscrew easily once the nut has been initially loosened by giving the spanner a sharp tap with a hide mallet.

When the dust excluder nut is removed, a few sharp pulls should release the stanchion, bush and shuttle valve assembly from the bottom member.

If it is required to remove the cone shaped restrictor from the bottom member, merely release the securing bolt.

The hexagon headed restrictor securing bolt, seen counter-bored into the wheel spindle lug, is sealed by means of an aluminium washer which should be withdrawn from the counter bore when the bolt is removed and placed in storage and refitted on assembly.

The shuttle valves are retained in the bottom end of each stanchion by the bottom bearing retaining nuts. Circlips are also fitted to prevent the shuttle valves recessing into the stanchions (see Fig. G5). Note that the shuttle valve fork type of stanchions can be recognised immediately by the 8 bleed holes just above the bottom bearing.

Fig. G5. Shuttle valve in position—note stanchion bleed holes

SECTION G4
INSPECTION AND REPAIR OF FORK COMPONENTS

Telescopic fork components which have received minor damage may possibly be repaired without the need of new parts. The stanchions are the most vulnerable part to damage and correction is often possible if the damage is within the limits described below. The top lug and middle lug are malleable stampings and slight misalignment can be corrected as described in the paragraphs below. The tools required in order that a thorough check of the various alignments can be made are an engineer's checking table, set square, adjustable calipers and a height gauge.

(1) Check the stanchions for truth by rolling them slowly on a flat checking table. A bent stanchion may be realigned if the bow does not exceed $\frac{5}{32}$ in. maximum. To realign the stanchion, a hand press is required. Place the stanchion on two swage "V" blocks at either end and apply pressure to the raised portion of the stanchion. By means of alternately pressing in this way and checking the stanchion on a flat table the amount of bow can be reduced until it is finally removed.

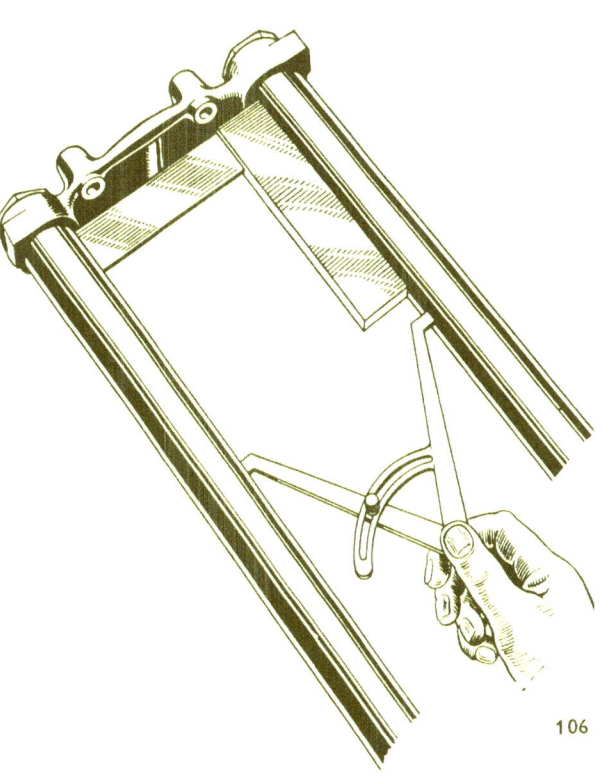

Fig. G6. Checking the top lug for alignment

(2) Inspect the top lug by fitting both stanchions (if true) with the cap nuts tightened in position as shown in Fig. G6. Check that the stanchions are parallel to each other in both planes by laying the assembly on a checking table and taking caliper readings as shown. Using a set square, check that the stanchions are at right angles to the top lug.

Check the middle lug and stem for alignment by inserting the stanchions until $6\frac{1}{2}$ in. (16·5 cm.) of the top of the stanchion protrudes above the top surface of the middle lug as shown in Fig. G5. Fit and tighten the pinch bolts in position and then lay the assembly on the checking table and with calipers check that the stanchions lie parallel in the middle lug.

The stanchions should also be checked for being parallel in the other plane by sighting along the checking table top. A set square should be used to check that the stanchions are at right angles to the middle lug.

The middle lug stamping is malleable and provided that the lug is not excessively distorted, it can be trued quite easily. Each time a distortion correction is carried out check that the assembly is true in both planes.

Fig. G7. Checking the stanchions and middle lug for alignment

(3) When the stanchions and middle lug assembly has been trued, the top lug can be used to check the position of the stem relative to the middle lug. For this purpose, the distance between the middle lug and top lug should be the same on either side and to achieve this the stanchions should be set in the middle lug to the figure given in Fig. G8. When the top lug is fitted the stem should be central in the top lug hole. If it is not a long tube can be placed over the stem and used to press the stem in the correcting direction. When this is achieved, re-check the fork assembly to ensure that the original alignment has not been adversely effected.

Check the stanchion bearing surfaces for wear, particularly in forks where grey sintered iron bushes have been used. It is permissable to polish the stanchions with fine emery cloth to remove roughness.

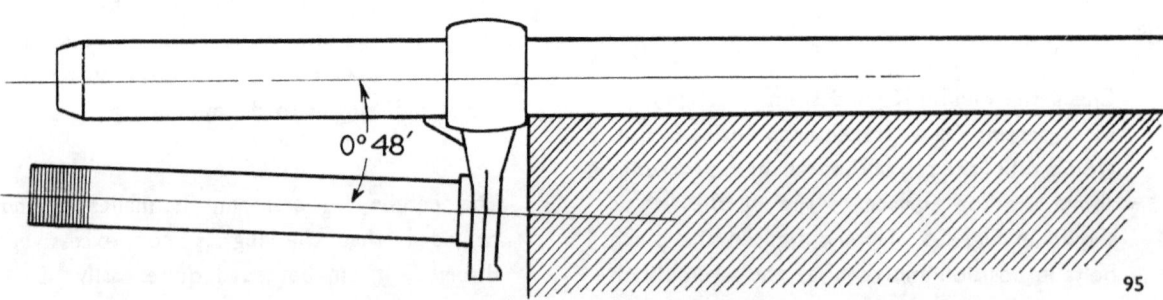

Fig. G8. Showing the correct angle between stanchion and stem centre lines

TELESCOPIC FORKS

(4) Check that the bottom members are not dented or damaged in any way by inserting the stanchion and bottom bush assembly and feeling the amount of clearance of the bush within the bore of the bottom member. Any restriction on movement indicates that the bottom member is damaged and requires renewing. The wheel spindle lug can be checked for being at right angles to the bottom member by machining a one $\frac{1}{4}$ in. wide groove in a $\frac{11}{16}$ inch diameter bar and bolting it in position in the wheel spindle lug. A square may then be used to check that the bar is perpendicular to the bottom member. If the degree of error is excessive, no attempt should be made to realign the wheel spindle lug, the bottom member should be renewed.

(5) Examine the top and bottom bushes for wear by measuring the bore diameter of the top bush and the outside diameter of the bottom bush and comparing them with the figures given in General Data. Also, the bushes can be checked against their respective mating surfaces: put the top bush over the stanchion and at about eight inches from the bottom of the stanchion check the diametral clearance at the bush. An excessive clearance indicates that the bush requires renewing. As described above, the bottom bush can only be checked by fitting it to the stanchion and inserting the stanchion into the bottom member to a depth of about eight inches whilst the diametral clearance is estimated from the amount of "play".

As a matter of course, replace any grey sintered iron fork bushes with the sintered bronze type bushes for improved wear.

(6) Examine the main springs for fatigue and cracks and check that both springs are of approximate equal length and within $\frac{1}{2}$ in. (1·3 cm.) of the original length on the earlier long type main spring, and within $\frac{1}{4}$ in. of the original length in the case of the later short main spring. The figures for the original length are given in "General Data".

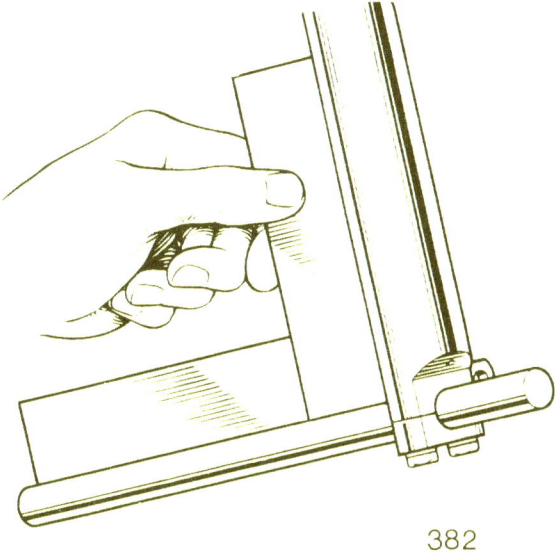

Fig. G9. Checking the bottom member wheel spindle lug for truth

(7) Inspect the cups and cones for wear in the form of pitting or pocketing. This will appear as a series of small indentations in the ball tracks and indicates that both the races and the balls require renewing.

The cups should be a tight interference fit into the frame headlug. Slackness there usually indicates that the headlug cup seatings are distorted. The bottom cone should be a tight fit onto the middle lug stem and the top cone and dust cap assembly should be a close sliding fit over the stem. Slackness of the cone on the stem indicates that the steering races have not been in correct adjustment. In this case, if the new cone is not a tight fit over the stem, then either the stem and middle lug assembly should be renewed or in certain cases a proprietary sealant may be used to secure the cone in position.

SECTION G5
RENEWING THE STEERING HEAD RACES

The cups can be driven out of the headlug from the inside by inserting a long narrow drift and locating it on the inner edge of the cups. When the cups are removed the bore of the headlug should be cleaned thoroughly and the new cups driven in by using a hammer and aluminium drift or a piece of hard wood interposed to check the blow. Care should be taken to ensure that the cup enters into the headlug squarely and that no burrs are set up due to misalignment.

The bottom cone can easily be removed from the stem by inserting levers on either side and prising the cone upwards. When it has been removed, clean the stem and remove any burrs with a fine grade file before fitting the new cones. To ensure that the new cone is driven on squarely service tool number Z24 should be used. To assist in the assembly of the cone a small amount of grease may be smeared on the middle lug stem. If the service tool is not available a suitable drift can be made from a piece of $1\frac{1}{16}$ in. (2·7 cm.) inside diameter tube 9 inches long. Note that when new cups and cones are fitted, new balls must also be used. The correct quantity is 40 off $\frac{1}{4}$ in. diameter balls—20 top race and 20 bottom race.

SECTION G6
RENEWING THE FRONT FORK OIL SEALS

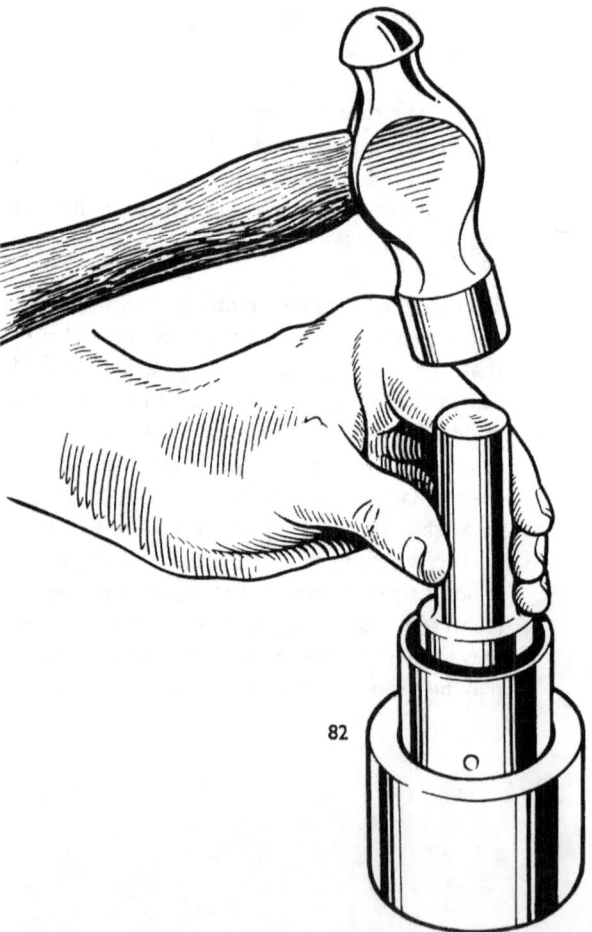

On the current front fork the oil seal is pressed into the dust excluder sleeve nut and is freely accessible from both sides. The oil seal can be driven out by inserting a suitable drift and locating it on the oil seal at one of the peripheral slots.

The new oil seal should be pressed in with the lip and spring side facing the threaded end of the sleeve nut and a check should be made to ensure that it is fully and squarely engaged.

Removal of the oil seal from the dust excluder sleeve assembly on the earlier type front fork is achieved by means of service tool Z137. The dust excluder nut should be fitted to the holder as shown in Fig. G10 and the drift inserted and used to drive the sleeve out. This will enable the oil seal to be driven out in the same direction.

When fitting the new oil seal, ensure that it is pressed in with the spring and lip side towards the threaded end of the bore and press the sleeve in until it is flush with the rear face of the oil seal.

A rubber 'O' ring seal is fitted on late machines into the thread of the chrome dust excluder. It is advisable to remove the 'O' ring which will almost certainly be compressed and to fit a new one to each dust excluder.

Fig. G10. Removing the oil seal from the earlier dust excluder sleeve assembly using service tool Z137

SECTION G7

REASSEMBLING AND REFITTING THE TELESCOPIC FORK UNIT

To cater for the three basic types of telescopic forks fitted to Triumph machines this section is divided into three parts—part one deals with the earlier type front fork, part two deals with the external spring type front fork, the assembly of which requires service tool Z161, and part three deals with the current fork with shuttle valve damping.

PART 1. FRAME NO. DU.101 TO DU.5824

First, offer the stanchion and bottom bush assembly into the bottom member and refit the damper sleeve and top bush. Offer the dust excluder sleeve nut and oil seal assembly over the stanchion using a smear of oil to assist assembly, and then tighten the sleeve nut in position using spanner D220. With the stanchion in its lowest position offer the restrictor rod assembly to the stanchion and refit the hexagonal restrictor rod securing bolt and aluminium washer until all but a few threads are engaged in the restrictor rod.

Work the restrictor rod round until the location slot in its base is level with the location plug hole then refitting the plug, tighten the restrictor rod securing bolts. Do not forget that a fibre washer is fitted under each of the location plugs.

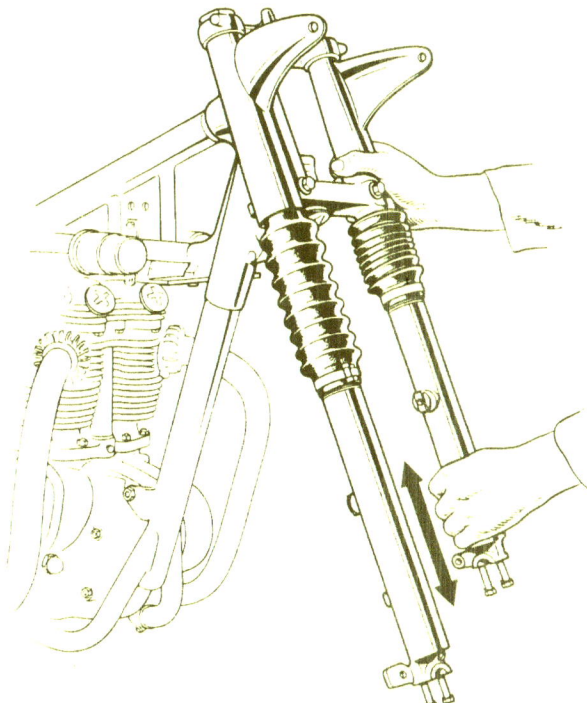

Fig. G11. Reassembling the telescopic fork

Thoroughly clean the head race cups and cones and smear the ball tracks with the recommended grease (see Section A2). Place the ball bearings in the cups (20 top, 20 bottom) using grease to hold them in position. Offer the middle lug and stem assembly to the headlug and lower the top cone and dust cover assembly into position. Refit the top lug and sleeve nut, tighten the sleeve nut until all the slack is taken up. Refit the sleeve nut pinch bolt finger tight and align the middle lug and top lug. Assemble the left and right bottom nacelle covers to the middle lug and insert the pinch bolts, but only screw on the nuts finger tight.

Offer the right stanchion (with brake anchor plate locating boss fitted) to the middle lug and rotate it until the oil filler plug hole is accessible to the headlamp aperture. Force the stanchion upwards using the bottom member as an impulse driver (see Fig. G11). When the taper is engaged in the top lug, temporarily tighten the pinch bolt then repeat the procedure for the left stanchion. Finally, pour $\frac{1}{4}$ pint (150 c.c.) of the recommended grade of oil into each fork leg and then refit the main springs. Screw in the left and right cap nuts and guide tube assemblies until several threads are engaged, then slacken the middle lug pinch bolts and then return to fully tighten the cap nuts using spanner No. D220. When this is achieved, adjust the steering head races as described in Section G10 and retighten the middle lug pinch bolts and sleeve nut pinch bolts Refit the oil filler plugs (if fitted) not forgetting the two sealing fibre washers. Reposition the handlebar but do not forget to refit the washers and self-locking nuts where the handlebars are rubber mounted.

Reassembly then carries on as a reversal of the removal instructions but reference should be made to the relevant wiring diagram in Section H19 when refitting the nacelle unit.

PART 2. FRAME NO. DU.5825 TO DU.66245

Assemble the stanchion to the bottom member and fit the damper sleeve and top bush. Then screw on the dust excluder sleeve nut and oil seal assembly having used jointing compound on the outer member threads and hold the bottom member in a vice by means of the wheel spindle lug whilst the sleeve nut is tightened using service tool D527.

G TELESCOPIC FORKS

'O' Ring Seals are fitted between the dust excluder sleeves and the bottom members on later forks. If not already fitted it would be worthwhile incorporating these 'O' Rings on any External Spring Fork ('O' Ring Part Number H2119).

Note.—From engine number DU.13375 the damper sleeve is stepped and when reassembling, the sleeve is pressed in with the thick end pointing downwards.

To refit the oil restrictor rod first slide the rod down inside the stanchion and then use a piece of tubing about 2 feet long and $\frac{1}{2}$ in. (1·3 cm.) inside diameter, to grip the restrictor rod whilst several threads of the hexagon headed securing bolt are engaged. Do not forget to replace the aluminium sealing washer which fits over the securing bolt.

Screw in the small location plug and with the tubing rotate the restrictor rod until the location slot is aligned with the plug, then tighten the securing bolt. Do not forget to fit new fibre washers under each of the two location plugs. When both stanchions are assembled in this way, fit the plain thrust washer, main spring, cover and felt washer over each stanchion. On models fitted with nacelle type headlamp there is also a plain steel washer fitted underneath the felt washer to give additional clearance. On models fitted with a headlamp unit the gaiters should be fitted over the springs and clamped up top and bottom on to the thrust washer and sleeve nut respectively.

Align the middle lug and top lug and position the left and right lower nacelle cover and then insert the middle lug pinch bolt and fit the nuts finger tight.

Offer the right stanchion assembly (with welded boss for front brake anchor plate location) and engage as much of the stanchion as possible in the middle lug. To pull the stanchion up to the top lug, service tool Z161 is required which should be inserted into the top lug and the plug adaptor screwed into the stanchion top. The stanchion can then be drawn easily up to the required level and when this is achieved, temporarily tighten the pinch bolt, remove the tool and screw in the cap nut until several threads are engaged. Repeat this procedure for the left stanchion assembly and then remove both cap nuts and pour $\frac{1}{3}$ pint (190 c.c.) of the recommended grade of oil (see Section A2) into each fork leg.

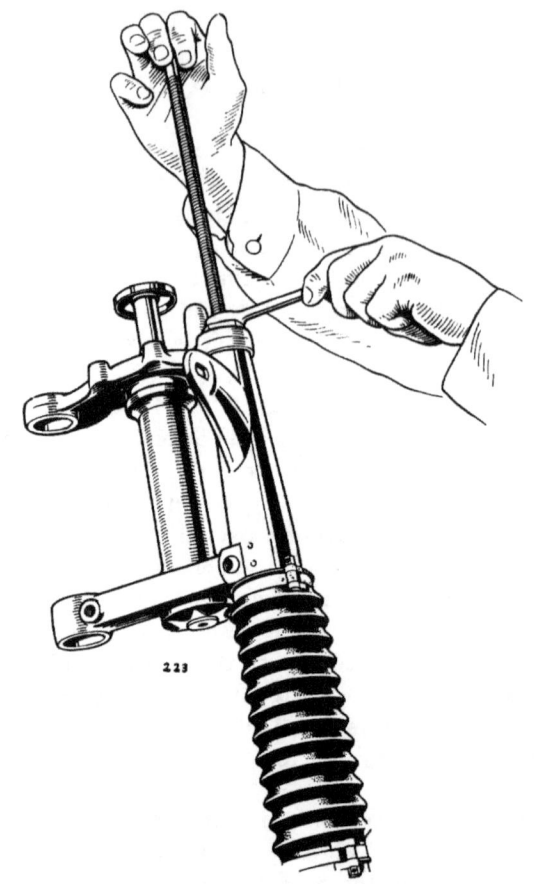

Fig. G12. Reassembling the telescopic fork, using service tool No. Z161

Refit the cap nuts until several threads are engaged then slacken off the middle lug pinch bolt and fully tighten the cap nuts. On models with nacelle type front forks the stanchions will require turning prior to tightening the cap nuts so that the oil filler plug holes are accessible through the headlamp aperture. When this is achieved, adjust the steering head races as described in Section G10 and then tighten the sleeve nut pinch bolt and two middle lug pinch bolts, to the torque figures given in "General Data"

Reassembly continues as the reversal of the dismantling procedure, referring to Section H19 for the relevant wiring diagram and Section H12 to set the headlamp main beam.

PART 3. FRAME No. DU.66246 ONWARDS
Before reassembly remember that machines after DU.68363 use unified threads on the stanchions, cap nuts and bottom bearing nuts. Machines between DU.66246 and DU.68363 though also using shuttle valve damping have C.E.I. threads. It will

TELESCOPIC FORKS　G

be noted that the parts involved are not interchangeable except as a set.

Assemble the bottom bush to the stanchion, fit the shuttle valve, large diameter uppermost and secure with the bearing retaining nut. Fit the circlip to prevent the shuttle valve sliding back into the stanchion.

If the cone shaped restrictor has been removed, it must be refitted to the bottom member at this stage, being retained by the hexagon headed bolt and aluminium sealing washer fitted into the wheel spindle cutaway recess. To hold the restrictor in position whilst the bolt is fitted, use the stanchion complete with shuttle valve as a guide.

Offer the stanchion and bottom bush assembly into the bottom member and refit the top bush. Offer the dust excluder sleeve complete with 'O' ring and seal over the stanchion which should be lightly smeared with oil. Tighten the dust excluder in position over the bottom member using spanner D527. Drop the spring into position over the stanchion followed by the gaiter and clips, top spring abutment and cork washer. The gaiters should be secured top and bottom with the clips over the top abutment and dust excluder. Align the top and middle lug. Fit the left and right fork top shrouds, and insert the middle lug pinch bolts and nuts finger tight.

Offer the right stanchion assembly (with welded boss for front brake anchor plate location) and engage as much of the stanchion as possible in the middle lug. To pull the stanchion up to the top lug, service tool Z170 for U.N.F. threads or Z161 for C.E.I. threads is required which should be inserted into the top lug and the plug adaptor screwed into the stanchion top. The stanchion can then be easily drawn up to the required level and when this is achieved temporarily tighten the pinch bolt, remove the tool and screw in the cap nut until several threads are engaged. Repeat this procedure for the left stanchion assembly and then remove both cap nuts and pour $\frac{1}{3}$ pint (200 c.c.) of the recommended grade of oil (see Section A2) into each fork leg.

Refit the cap nuts until several threads are engaged then slacken off the middle lug pinch bolt and fully tighten the cap nuts with spanner D779. When this is achieved, adjust the steering head races as described in Section G10 and then tighten the sleeve nut pinch bolt and two middle lug pinch bolts, to the torque figures given in "General Data".

Reassembly continues as the reversal of the dismantling procedure, referring to Section H19 for the relevant wiring diagram and Section H12 to set the headlamp main beam.

SECTION G8
TELESCOPIC FORK ALIGNMENT

To facilitate checking the alignment of the telescopic fork legs there is available service tool Z103 the dimensions of which are shown in Fig. G13.

To check the front fork alignment, the front wheel and mudguard must be removed and a spare wheel spindle bolted in position. If a spare spindle is not available use the one removed from the front wheel as described in Section F8.

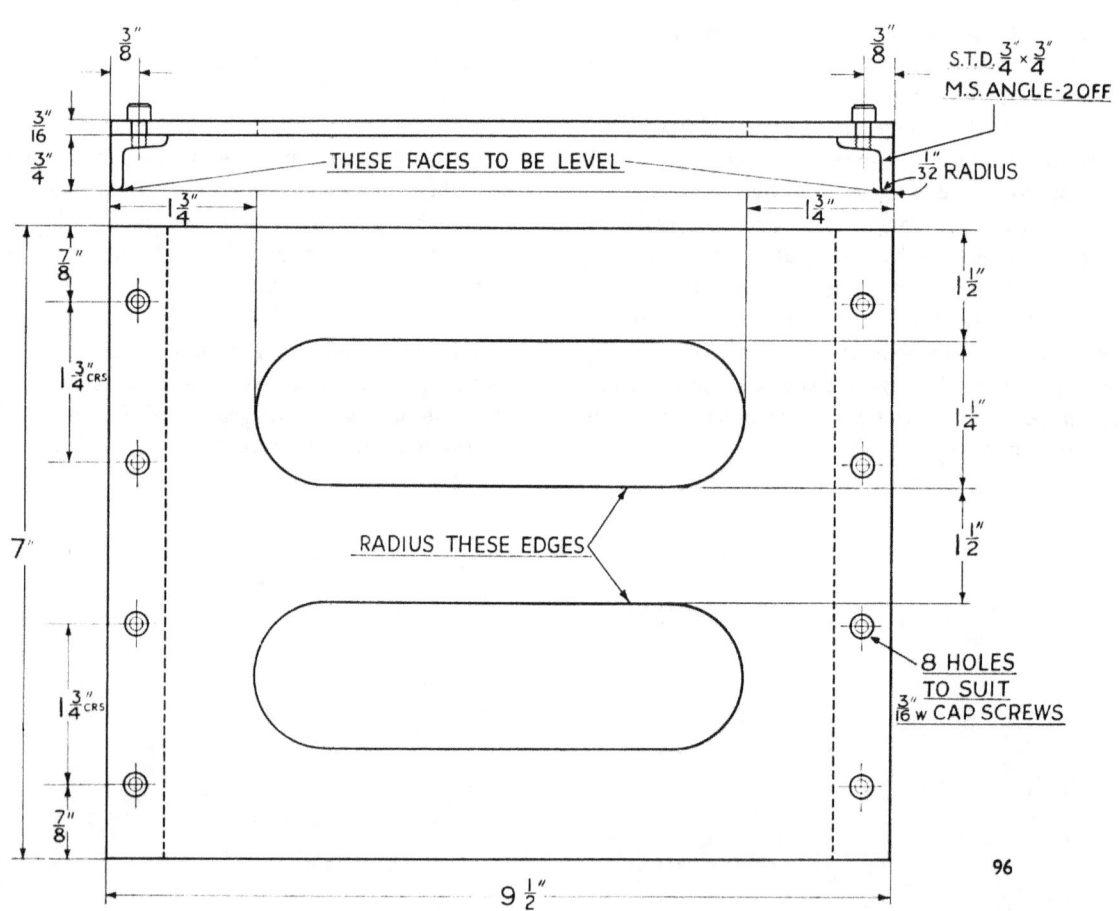

Fig. G13. Telescopic fork leg alignment gauge service tool Z103

TELESCOPIC FORKS

Hold the alignment gauge firmly against the fork legs as shown in Fig. G14 and check that the gauge contacts at all four corners. If the gauge does not make contact at point A then this indicates that point B is too far forward. To remedy this, slacken off the two middle lug pinch bolts and the stem sleeve nut pinch bolt and give point C a sharp blow using a hide mallet or a hammer used in conjunction with a soft metal drift.

Check the alignment again with the gauge and again give correcting blows in the above mentioned manner until the amount of rock at any one corner does not exceed $\frac{1}{64}$ inch. When this is achieved, tighten all three pinch bolts and then finally apply the gauge to check that tightening has not caused distortion.

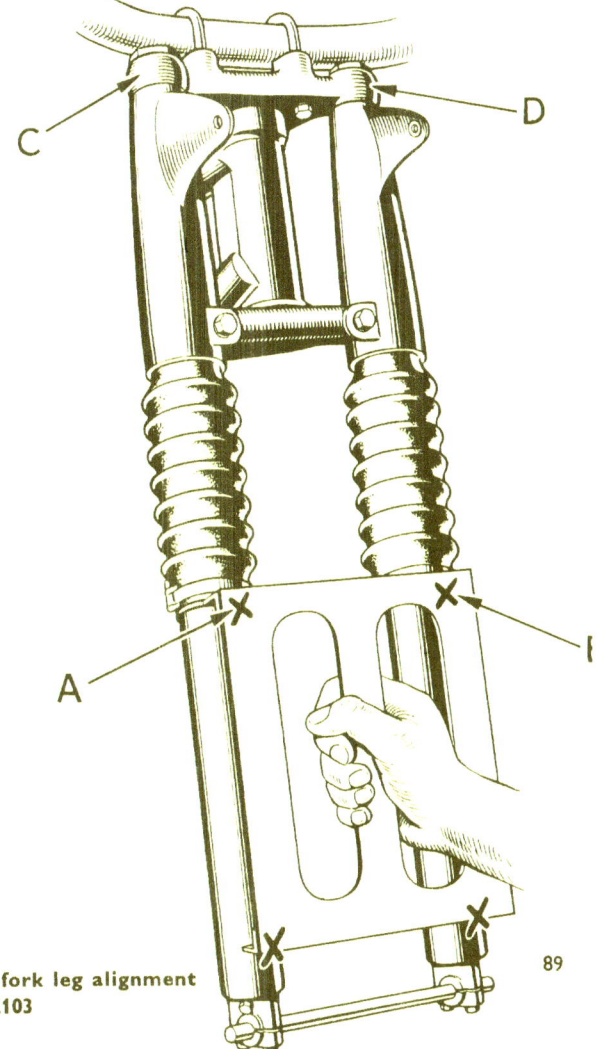

Fig. G14. Checking the telescopic fork leg alignment with service tool Z103

SECTION G9
ADJUSTING THE STEERING HEAD RACES

When a new machine has covered the 500 miles (running-in period) it will be necessary to check the steering head races for excessive play due to the balls, cups and cones bedding down.

Also, after long periods, the head races may require adjusting to compensate for any wear that may have taken place. The working clearance of the balls in the tracks of the cups and cones is controlled by the fork stem sleeve nut which is locked in position by means of a pinch bolt at the rear of the top lug. When the pinch bolt is slackened the sleeve nut can be turned to increase or decrease the head race working clearance.

Mount the machine with the front wheel clear of the ground and balance the front fork so that both the front and rear wheels are aligned. When the fork is tilted to either side of its central position it should just fall to its full lock position. If the fork will do this then the head races are not over tight and conversely to check that they are not too loose, hold the top lug with the left hand (with the headlamp unit removed on models fitted with nacelle type front forks) and hold the top portion of the front mudguard in the right hand and then attempt to "rock" the fork. If there is any "rock" in evidence, then tighten the stem sleeve nut $\frac{1}{4}$ turn and check again. Continuing this way until the fork will not rock but will turn from lock to lock easily. When this is achieved, re-tighten the stem sleeve nut pinch bolt.

SECTION G10
CHANGING THE FRONT FORK MAIN SPRINGS

First, place a strong box underneath the engine so that the motorcycle is mounted with the front wheel off the ground.

Removing the springs necessitates withdrawing the complete fork leg assemblies, leaving the top and middle lugs in the frame (see Fig. G11). This is accomplished by removing the top nuts using spanner D779 or D220 before DU.68363. The pinch bolts should be slackened and the leg assemblies driven out with tool Z169 or tool Z19 before DU.68363. The springs can then be lifted off over the stanchions. Reassembly can then be undertaken by offering up the stanchions as in Section G8 Part 2.

Removing the main springs on models fitted with the inside-spring type front fork i.e. frame No. DU.101 to DU.5824, necessitates removal of the nacelle top cover (if fitted) and handlebars.

When the cap nut-and-guide-tube assemblies are removed the main springs can be withdrawn and the new ones fitted.

When the cap nuts are refitted, they must be fully retightened. If necessary use a piece of tubing which will increase the leverage to about 12 in. to finally tighten the nuts. Reassembly then continues as a reversal of the dismantling procedure.

The table below shows the spring rates and colour codes for the purposes designated.

MODEL	SPRING RATE lb./in.	LOAD at FITTED LENGTH lbs.	COLOUR CODE
All models after DU.13374			
Solo	26½	22	Yellow/Blue
Sidecar	32½	26½	Yellow/Green
All models DU.5825 to DU.3374			
Solo	30	50	Unpainted
Sidecar	37	60	Yellow/White
ENGINE No. DU.101 to DU.5824			
6T/T120 Solo	32	85	Black/Green
6T/T120 Sidecar*	37	98	Red/White
TR6 Solo	30	46	Black/White
TR6 Sidecar	37	56	Black/Red

* With longer sidecar outer members

SECTION G11
THE HYDRAULIC DAMPING UNIT

Fig. G13 shows an exploded view of the damping unit which may be fitted to certain types of telescopic front forks. To fit these units, two alternative stanchion cap nuts are required with a threaded hole into which the top of the damper unit rod screws. Locknuts are provided to secure the cap nut to the rod. Note that on a machine fitted with these damper units, if the rod should become detached from the cap nut for any reason, it must be remembered that it will fall back into the stanchion. Therefore when fitting the fork to the frame a check should be made to ensure that the operation of fitting the damper unit rod to the cap nut has not been forgotten.

The bottom of the damper unit is secured in the same way as the restrictor rod on standard machines (Section G8), i.e. by means of a hexagon headed bolt countersunk into the wheel spindle recess. To dismantle the unit, first grip the body carefully in a vice, then unscrew the adaptor nut (two flats) and withdraw the rod assembly. The cap is removed by unscrewing the locknut from the end of the rod and withdrawing the sliding fit oil restrictor cup.

When reassembling the damper, ensure that the pin is in position and when the locknut is tight, use a centre punch to prevent the nut subsequently unscrewing.

Ensure that the oil holes in the stem are free from blockage and refit the rod assembly to the body.

After assembly, test the unit for damping efficiency by immersing the lower end of the unit into oil and pumping the centre rod a few times. There should be little or no resistance on the down stroke and a good resistance on the up stroke.

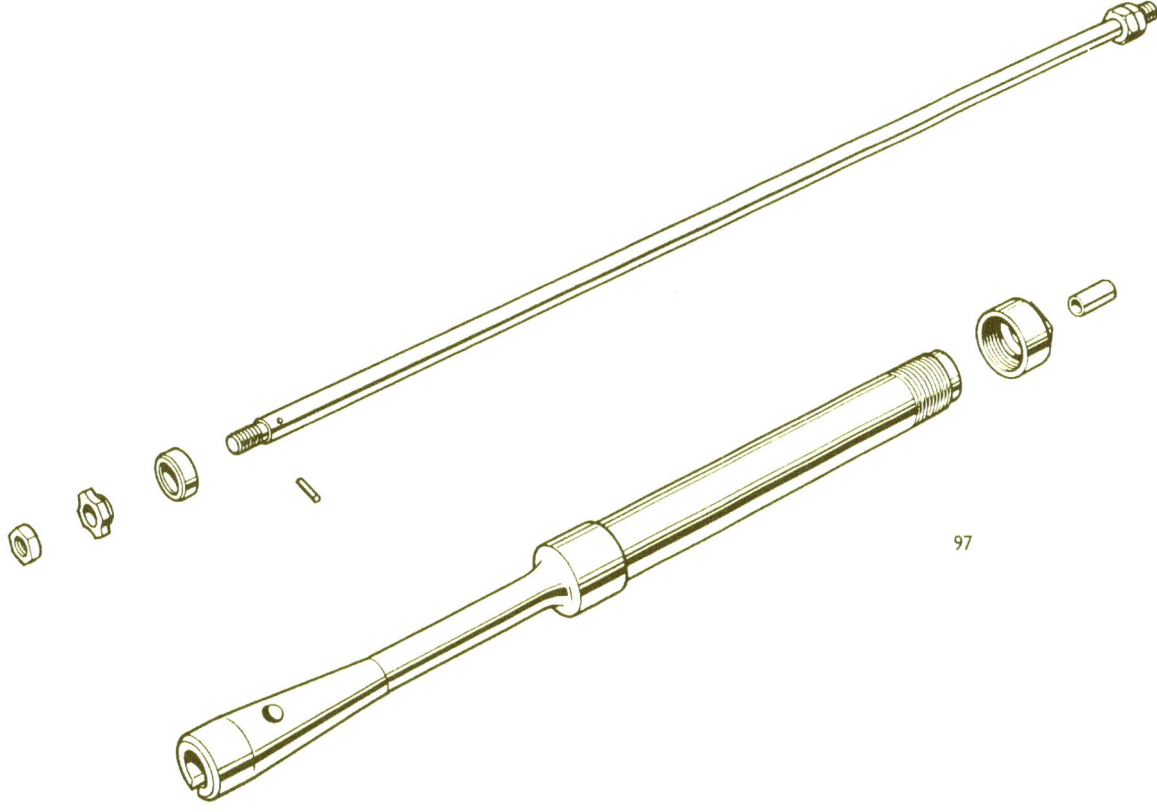

Fig. G15. Exploded view of telescopic fork internal hydraulic damper unit assembly Before DU.66246 (Alternative equipment)

NOTES

SECTION H
ELECTRICAL SYSTEM

INTRODUCTION

BATTERY INSPECTION AND MAINTENANCE ... H1
    DESCRIPTION
    (a) ROUTINE MAINTENANCE
    (b) MAXIMUM PERMISSABLE ELECTROLYTE TEMPERATURES DURING CHARGING

BATTERY CONNECTIONS—TWO 6 VOLT BATTERIES IN SERIES ... H2

COIL IGNITION SYSTEM ... H3
    DESCRIPTION
    (a) CHECKING THE LOW TENSION CIRCUIT FOR CONTINUITY
    (b) FAULT FINDING IN THE LOW TENSION CIRCUIT
    (c) IGNITION COILS
    (d) CONTACT BREAKER
    (e) CONTACT BREAKER FROM DU.66246
    (f) CHECKING THE HIGH TENSION CIRCUIT
    (g) CHECKING THE EMERGENCY STARTING CIRCUIT

SPARKING PLUGS ... H4

CHARGING SYSTEM ... H5
    DESCRIPTION
    (a) CHECKING THE D.C. INPUT TO BATTERY
    (b) CHECKING THE ALTERNATOR OUTPUT
    (c) RECTIFIER MAINTENANCE AND TESTING
    (d) CHECKING THE CHARGING CIRCUIT FOR CONTINUITY
    (e) MAKING A 1 OHM LOAD RESISTOR

ZENER DIODE CHARGE CONTROL AND TEST PROCEDURE ... H6

ZENER DIODE LOCATION ... H7

A.C. IGNITION (E.T.) AND A.C. LIGHTING SYSTEMS ... H8
    DESCRIPTION
    (a) A.C. IGNITION
    (b) TESTING THE A.C. IGNITION SYSTEM
    (c) CHECKING THE A.C. ALTERNATOR OUTPUT
    (d) DIRECT LIGHTING SYSTEM

ALTERNATOR AND STATOR DETAILS (Specifications and Output Figures) ... H9

ELECTRIC HORN ... H10

HEADLAMP ... H11
    DESCRIPTION
    BEAM ADJUSTMENTS

HEADLAMP REMOVING AND REFITTING ... H12

TAIL AND STOPLAMP UNIT ... H13

FUSES ... H14

IGNITION SWITCH ... H15

IGNITION CUT-OUT BUTTON ... H16

WARNING LAMPS ... H17

CAPACITOR IGNITION (Model 2MC) ... H18
    HEAT SINK REQUIREMENTS
    IDENTIFICATION OF CAPACITOR TERMINALS
    TESTING
    WIRING AND INSTALLATION
    SERVICE NOTES

WIRING DIAGRAMS ... H19
    ALL MODELS FROM DU.66246 (HOME)
    ALL MODELS FROM DU.66246 (EXPORT)
    COIL IGNITION—12 VOLT MODELS WITH SEPARATE HEADLAMP (FROM DU.24875) HOME
    COIL IGNITION—12 VOLT MODELS WITH SEPARATE HEADLAMP (FROM DU.24875) EXPORT USA
    E.T. IGNITION—(A.C. MAGNETO) MODELS
    COIL IGNITION—12 VOLT MODELS WITH NACELLE (FROM DU.24875)
    COIL IGNITION—12 VOLT MODELS (BEFORE DU.24875)
    COIL IGNITION—6 VOLT MODELS
    COIL IGNITION—6 VOLT POLICE MODELS WITH BOOST SWITCH

ELECTRICAL SYSTEM

INTRODUCTION

The electrical system is supplied from an alternating current generator contained in the primary chaincase and driven from the crankshaft. The generator output is then converted into direct current by a silicon diode rectifier. The direct current is supplied to a 12 volt 8 ampere/hour battery with a Zener diode in circuit to regulate the battery current.

The current is then supplied to the ignition system which is controlled by a double contact breaker driven direct from the exhaust camshaft. The contact breaker feeds two ignition coils, one for each cylinder.

On 6 volt coil ignition machines prior to DU24875 in the case of a discharged battery the emergency position of the ignition switch supplies output direct from the generator through one pair of contacts and one ignition coil to enable the engine to be started. As soon as the engine has been started the ignition switch must be returned to the normal position or burning of the contact breaker points will take place.

The routine maintenance needed by the various components is set out in the following sections. All electrical components and connections including the earthing points to the frame of the machine must be clean and tight.

No emergency start facility is provided on current 12 volt machines. On these models there is however sufficient voltage to start the machine when a discharged battery is in circuit.

Earlier models used a single 6 volt battery on 6T up to engine number DU.5824 and T120 or TR6 up up engine number DU.24874. Between DU.5824 and DU.24874 the 6T only used a 12 volt electrical system. On these models and on certain machines before DU.44394 two MKZ9E 6 volt batteries were fitted in series (see Fig. H1) to give 12 volts.

Before engine number DU.24875 the generator was connected to give alternative charge rates, governed by the positions of the lighting switch.

SECTION H1
BATTERY INSPECTION AND MAINTENANCE

The battery containers are moulded in translucent polystyrene through which the acid level can be seen. The battery top is so designed that when the cover is in position, the special anti-spill filler plugs are sealed in a common venting chamber. Gas from the filler plugs leaves this chamber through a vent pipe union at the side of the top. The vent at the other side of the top is sealed off. Polythene tubing is attached to the vent pipe union to lead corrosive fumes away from parts of the machine which may otherwise suffer damage.

To prepare a dry-charged battery for service, first discard the vent hole sealing tape and then pour into each cell pure dilute sulphuric acid of appropriate specific gravity to THE COLOURED LINE. (See table a). Allow the battery to stand for at least one hour for the electrolyte to settle down, thereafter maintain the acid level at the coloured line by adding distilled water.

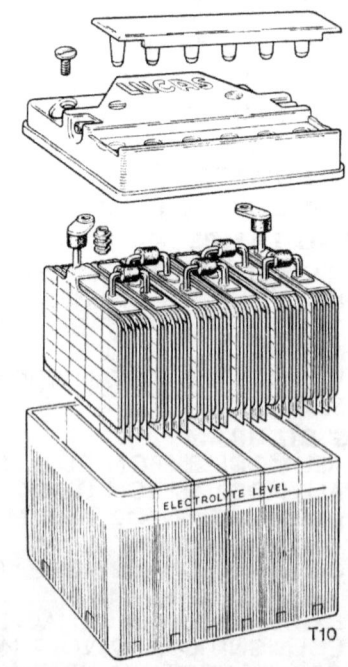

Fig. H1. Exploded view of battery

ELECTRICAL SYSTEM

H1. PART A. ROUTINE MAINTENANCE

Every week examine the level of the electrolyte in each cell. Lift the battery out of the carrier so that the coloured filling line can be seen. Add distilled water until the electrolyte level reaches this line.

Note.—On no account should batteries be topped up to the separator guard but only to the coloured line.

With this type of battery, the acid can only be reached by a miniature hydrometer, which would indicate the state of charge.

Great care should be taken when carrying out these operations not to spill any acid or allow a naked flame near the electrolyte. The mixture of oxygen and hydrogen given off by a battery on charge, and to a lesser extent when standing idle, can be dangerously explosive.

The readings obtained from the battery electrolyte should be compared with those given in table (a). If a battery is suspected to be faulty it is advisable to have it checked by a Lucas Depot or Agent.

SPECIFIC GRAVITY OF ELECTROLYTE FOR FILLING THE BATTERY

U.K. and Climates normally below 90°F (32·2°C)		Tropical Climates over 90°F (32·2°C)	
Filling	Fully charged	Filling	Fully charged
1·260	1·280/1·300	1·210	1·220/1·240

Every 1,000 miles (1,500 k.m.) or monthly, or more regularly in hot climates the battery should be cleaned as follows. Remove the battery cover and clean the battery top. Examine the terminals: if they are corroded scrape them clean and smear them with a film of petroleum jelly, such as vaseline. Remove the vent plugs and check that the vent holes are clear and that the rubber washer fitted under each plug is in good condition. Note that current batteries have the plugs en bloc and no washers are used on this type.

H1. PART B. MAXIMUM PERMISSABLE ELECTROLYTE TEMPERATURE DURING CHARGE

Climates normally Below 80°F (27°C)	Climates between 80–100°F (27–38°C)	Climates frequently above 100°F (38°C)
100°F (38°C)	110°F (43°C)	120°F (49°C)

Notes.

The specific gravity of the electrolyte varies with the temperature. For convenience in comparing specific gravities, they are always corrected to 60°F., which is adopted as a reference temperature. The method of correction is as follows:

For every 5°F. below 60°F. deduct ·020 from the observed reading to obtain the true specific gravity at 60°F. For every 5°F. above 60°F., add ·020 to the observed reading to obtain the true specific gravity at 60°F.

The temperature must be indicated by a thermometer having its bulb actually immersed in the electrolyte and not the ambient temperature. To take a temperature reading tilt the battery sideways and then insert into the electrolyte.

SECTION H2
BATTERY CONNECTIONS—TWO 6 VOLT BATTERIES IN SERIES

Early machines in the 12 volt series were fitted with two six volt batteries connected as shown. Later machines incorporated a single 12 volt battery Lucas type PUZ5A.

On machines where two six volt batteries are fitted, these are connected in series to provide a twelve volt source of power.

It is extremely important that the batteries are correctly connected into the circuit to avoid damage to the electrical equipment. All machines use a positive (+ve) earth system. Refer to Fig. H2 which shows the correct method of connecting the batteries.

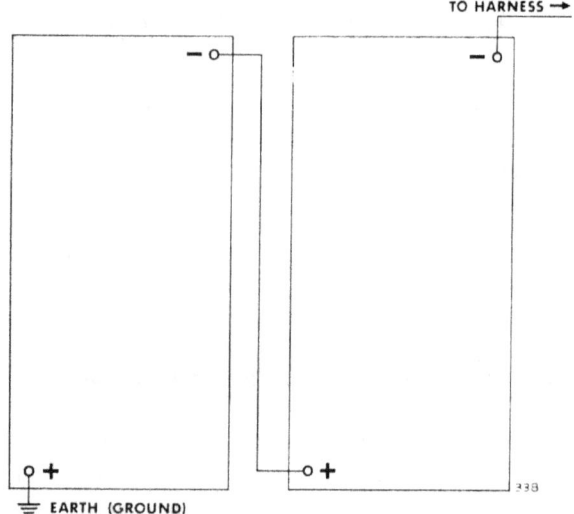

Fig. H2. Schematic diagram of 2 six volt batteries in series. (Note:—a 35 amp fuse is usually incorporated between battery positive and earth (ground))

SECTION H3
COIL IGNITION SYSTEM

DESCRIPTION
The coil ignition system comprises two ignition coils and a contact breaker fitted in the timing cover and driven by the exhaust camshaft. The ignition coils are mounted underneath the petrol tank one either side of the main tank tube. Access to the coils is achieved by removing the fuel tank as shown in Section E1. Apart from cleaning the coils, in between the terminals and checking the low tension and high tension connections, the coils will not require any other attention. Testing the ignition coils is amply covered in H3 Part C below whilst testing the contact breaker is described in H3 Part D. From DU.66246 the 6CA type of contact breaker is used. The condensers no longer comprise part of the contact breaker but are housed seperately in a rubber covered pack below the front of the fuel tank. Access to the condensers is gained by detaching the pack from the front tank mounting bracket on the frame, removing the cover and detaching the condensers individually from the mounting plate.

The best method of approach to a faulty ignition system, is that of first checking the low tension circuit for continuity as shown in H3 Part A, and then following the procedure laid out in H3 Part B to locate the fault(s).

Failure to locate a fault in the low tension circuit indicates that the high tension circuit or sparking plugs are faulty, and the procedure detailed in H3 Part E must be followed. Before commencing any of the following tests, however, the contact breaker and sparking plugs must be cleaned and adjusted to eliminate this possible source of fault.

ELECTRICAL SYSTEM

H3 PART A. CHECKING THE LOW TENSION CIRCUIT FOR CONTINUITY

To check whether there is a fault in the low tension circuit and to locate its position, the following tests should be carried out:—

Disconnect and remove the fuel tank (Section E1) removing the white lead which connects the "SW" terminals of the left and right ignition coils. Then, with the wiring harness white lead connected to the SW terminal of the left ignition coil only, turn the ignition switch to the "IGN" position. Slowly crank the engine and at the same time observe the ammeter needle, which should fluctuate between zero and a slight discharge, as the contacts open and close respectively.

Disconnect the wiring harness white lead from the left ignition coil and connect it to the S.W. terminal of the right ignition coil and then repeat the test. If the ammeter needle does not fluctuate in the described way then a fault in the low tension circuit is indicated.

First, examine the contact breaker contacts for pitting, piling or presence of oxidation, oil or dirt etc. Clean and ensure that the gap is set correctly to ·014 in.–·016 in. (·35–·40 m.m.) as described in Section B31.

H3 PART B. FAULT FINDING IN THE LOW TENSION CIRCUIT

To trace a fault in the low tension wiring, turn the ignition switch to "IGN" position and then crank the engine until both sets of contacts are opened, or alternatively, place a piece of insulating material between both sets of contacts whilst the following test is carried out.

For this test, it is assumed that the fuel tank is removed and the wiring is fully connected as shown in the appropriate wiring diagram, Section H17. With the aid of a D.C. voltmeter and 2 test-prods (Voltmeter 0–10 volts for 6 volt machines, and 0–15 volts for 12 volt electrical systems), make a point to point check along the low tension circuit starting at the battery and working right through to the ignition coils, stage by stage, in the following manner, referring to the relevant wiring diagram in Section H17.

Note. On 12V machines it will be necessary to disconnect the Zener Diode before the test is carried out. To do this remove the white lead from the Diode centre terminal.

(1) First, establish that the battery is earthed correctly by connecting the volt meter across the battery negative terminal and the machine frame earth. No voltage reading indicates that the red earthing lead is faulty (or the fuse blown, where fitted). Also, a low reading would indicate a poor battery earth connection

(2) Connect the voltmeter between the left ignition coil S.W. terminal and earth and then the right ignition coil S.W. terminal and earth. No voltage reading indicates a breakdown between the battery and the coil S.W. terminal, or that the switch connections or ammeter connections are faulty.

(3) Connect the voltmeter between both of the ammeter terminals in turn and earth. No reading on the "feed" side indicates that either the ammeter is faulty or there is a bad connection along the brown and blue lead from the battery, and a reading on the "battery" side only indicates a faulty ammeter.

(4) Connect the voltmeter between ignition switch input terminal and earth. No reading indicates that the brown and white lead has faulty connections. Check for voltage at the brown/white lead connections at rectifier, ammeter and lighting switch terminals No's 2 and 10.

(5) Connect the voltmeter across ignition switch output terminal and earth. No reading indicates that the ignition switch is faulty and should be replaced. Battery voltage reading at this point but not at the ignition coil S.W. terminals indicates that the white lead has become "open circuit" or become disconnected.

(6) Disconnect the black/white, and black/yellow leads from the C.B. terminals of each ignition coil. Connect the voltmeter across the C.B. terminal of the left coil and earth and then the C.B. terminal of the right coil and earth. No reading on the voltmeter in either case indicates that the coil primary winding is faulty and a replacement ignition coil should be fitted.

(7) With both sets of contacts open reconnect the ignition coil leads and then connect the voltmeter across both sets of contacts in turn. No reading in either case indicates that there is a faulty connection or the internal insulation has broken down in one of the condensers (capacitors).

If a capacitor is suspected then a substitution should be made and a re-test carried out.

(8) Finally, on machines with 12V electrical systems, reconnect the Zener Diode white lead and then connect the volt meter between the Zener Diode centre terminal and earth (with ignition "ON"). The volt meter should read battery volts. If it does not the Zener Diode is faulty and a substitution should be made. Refer to Section H6 (page H15) for the correct procedure for testing a Zener Diode on the machine. Ignition coil check procedure is given in Section H3, part C (page H6).

H ELECTRICAL SYSTEM

H3 PART C. IGNITION COILS

The ignition coils consist of primary and secondary windings wound concentrically about a laminated soft iron core, the secondary winding being next to the core. The primary winding usually consists of some 300 turns of enamel covered wire and the secondary some 17,000–26,000 turns of much finer wire—also enamel covered. Each layer is paper insulated from the next in both primary and secondary windings.

To test the ignition coil on the machine, first ensure that the low tension circuit is in order as described in H3 Part A above then disconnect the high tension leads from the left and right sparking plugs. Turn the ignition switch to the "IGN" position and crank the engine until the contacts (those with the black/yellow lead from the ignition coil) for the right cylinder are closed. Flick the contact breaker lever open a number of times whilst the high tension lead from the right ignition coil is held about $\frac{3}{16}$ in. away from the cylinder head. If the ignition coil is in good condition a strong spark should be obtained. if no spark occurs this indicates the ignition coil to be faulty.

Fig. H3. Ignition coils in position on machine

Repeat this test for the left high tension lead and coil by cranking the engine until the contacts with the black/white lead from the left ignition coil are closed.

Before a fault can be attributed to an ignition coil it must be ascertained that the high tension cables are not cracked or showing signs of deterioration, as this may often be the cause of mis-firing etc. It should also be checked that the ignition points are actually making good electrical contact when closed and that the moving contact is insulated from earth (ground) when open. It is advisable to remove the ignition coils and test them by the method described below.

BENCH TESTING AN IGNITION COIL

Connect the ignition coil into the circuit shown in Fig. H4 and set the adjustable gap to 9 mm. for MA12 types (12 volt) or 8 mm. for MA6 types (6 volt). With the contact breaker running at 100 r.p.m. and the coil in good condition, not more than 5% missing should occur at the spark gap over a period of 15 seconds. The primary winding can be checked for short-circuit coils by connecting an ohmeter across the low tension terminals. The reading obtained should be within the figures quoted below (at 20°C).

Coil	Primary Resistance	
	Min.	Max.
MA6	1·8 ohms.	2·4 ohms.
MA12	3·0 ohms.	3·4 ohms.

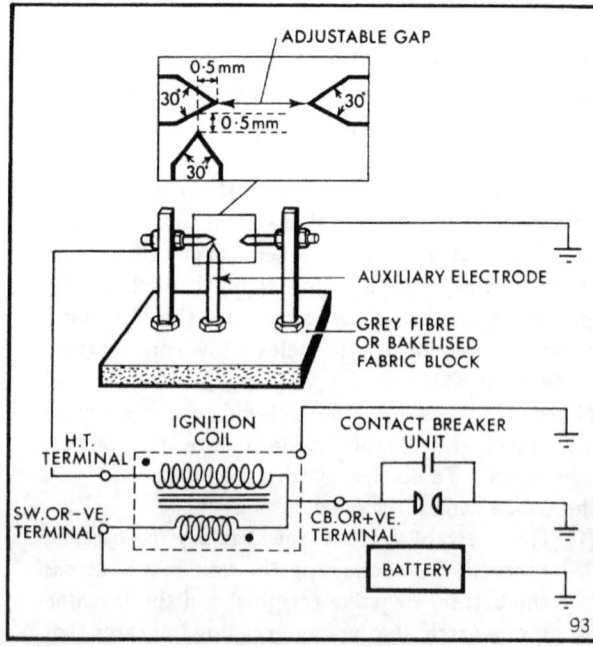

Fig. H4. Ignition coil test rig

ELECTRICAL SYSTEM

H3 PART D. CONTACT BREAKER

Faults occurring at the contact breaker are in the main due to, incorrect adjustment of the contacts or the efficiency being impaired by piling, pitting or oxidation of the contacts due to oil etc. Therefore, always ensure that the points are clean and that the gap is adjusted to the correct working clearance as described in Section B 28.

To test for a faulty condenser, first turn the ignition switch to "IGN" position and then take voltage readings across each set of contacts with the contacts open. No reading indicates that the condenser internal insulation has broken down. Should the fault be due to a condenser having a reduction in capacity, indicated by excessive arcing when in use, and overheating of the contact faces, a check should be made by substitution.

Particular attention is called to the periodic lubrication procedure for the contact breaker which is given in section A10. When lubricating the parts ensure that no oil or grease gets onto the contacts.

clean petrol (gasoline) moistened cloth. The contact faces should be slightly domed to ensure point contact. There is no need to remove the pitting from the fixed contact. When re-fitting the moving contacts do not forget to refit the insulating shields to the condenser terminals and apply a smear of grease to the C.B. cam and moving contact pivot post. Lubricate the one felt pad.

H3 PART E CONTACT BREAKER FROM DU.66246

Section H3 part D applies to the 6CA type contact breaker except for removal of the contact points. The moving contact points are removed by unscrewing the nut which secures the low tension lead, removing the lead and nylon bush. The spring and contact point can be removed from the pivot spindle. Repeat this procedure for the other contact point.

When reassembling, the nylon bush is fitted through the low tension connection tab, and through the spring location eye.

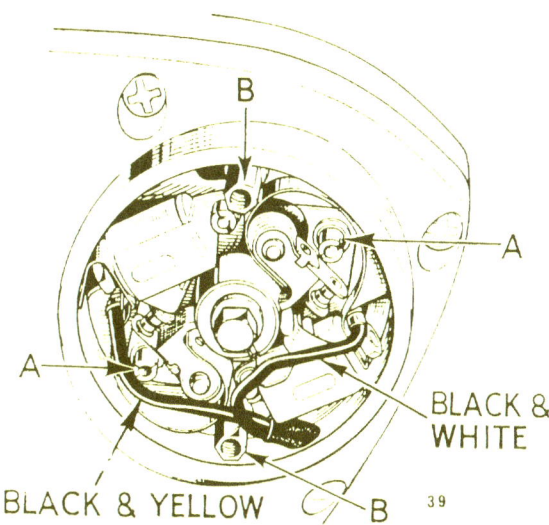

Fig. H5. Contact breaker and condenser assembly Type 4CA

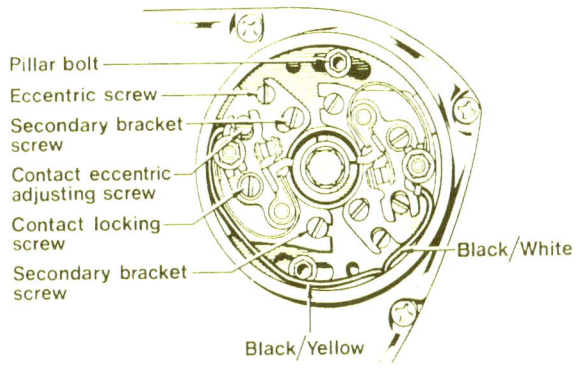

Fig. H6. Contact breaker—Type 6CA

H3 PART F. CHECKING THE HIGH TENSION CIRCUIT

If ignition failure or mis-firing occurs, and the fault is not in the low tension circuit, then check the ignition coils as described in Part C. If the coils prove satisfactory, ensure that the high tension cables are not the cause of the fault.

If it is felt that the contacts require surface grinding then the complete contact breaker unit should be removed as described in Section B28 and the moving contacts disconnected by unscrewing the securing nuts from the condenser terminals. Grinding is best achieved by using a fine carborundum stone or very fine emery cloth, afterwards wiping away any trace of dirt or metal dust with a

ELECTRICAL SYSTEM

If a good spark is available at the high tension cable, then the sparking plug suppressor cap or the sparking plug itself may be the cause of the fault. Clean the sparking plug and adjust the electrodes to the required setting as described in Section H3 below and then re-test the engine for running performance. If the fault recurs then it is likely the suppressor caps are faulty and these should be renewed.

H3 PART G. CHECKING THE EMERGENCY STARTING CIRCUIT—ONLY PRIOR TO ENGINE NUMBER DU.24875

First, ensure that the contact breaker and sparking plug gap settings are satisfactory and then remove the contact breaker cover and place a small piece of insulating card between each set of contacts.

Connect a D.C. voltmeter (0-15V) with the positive lead to earth and negative lead to the moving contact spring of the front set of contacts. A resistor is not required for this test.

Turn the ignition switch to "IGN" position. The voltmeter should indicate battery voltage. Repeat the test with the voltmeter negative lead connected to the rear moving contact spring.

Disconnect the green/yellow (green/black on 12V models) lead from the alternator (underneath the engine) and connect the voltmeter positive to green/yellow harness lead (green/black on 12V) and negative lead to frame. Turn the ignition switch to "EMG" position. The voltmeter should indicate battery voltage. If it does not the green/yellow lead (green/black on 12V) to No. 17 ignition switch terminal, and black/white lead connecting ignition coil C.B. (+) terminal to ignition switch terminal No. 15 should be checked. Reconnect alternator lead.

Finally, disconnect the battery, and then connect an A.C. voltmeter (0–15V) between the front moving contact spring and frame. With ignition switch in "EMG" position, (both contacts still insulated with card) attempt to kickstart the engine. The A.C. voltmeter should deflect to about 7 to 10 volts. If it does not, the alternator should be checked as shown in Section H5 Part B.

ELECTRICAL SYSTEM

SECTION H4
SPARKING PLUGS

It is recommended that the sparking plugs be inspected, cleaned and tested every 3,000 miles (4,800 k.m.) and new ones fitted every 12,000 miles (20,000 k.m.).

To remove the sparking plugs a box spanner ($\frac{13}{16}$ in. (19·5 m.m.) across flats) should be used and if any difficulty is encountered a small amount of penetrating oil (see lubrication chart Section A2) should be placed at the base of the sparking plug and time allowed for penetration. When removing the sparking plugs identify each plug with the cylinder from which it was removed so that any faults revealed on examination can be traced back to the cylinder concerned.

Due to certain features of engine design the sparking plugs will probably show slightly differing deposits and colouring characteristics. For this purpose it is recommended that any adjustments to carburation etc., which may be carried out to gain the required colour characteristics should always be referred to the left cylinder.

Examine both plugs for signs of oil fouling. This will be indicated by a wet, shiny, black deposit on the central insulator. This is caused by excessive oil in the combustion chamber during combustion and indicates that the piston rings or cylinder bores are worn.

Next examine the plugs for signs of petrol (gasoline) fouling. This is indicated by a dry, sooty, black deposit which is usually caused by over-rich carburation, although ignition system defects such as a discharged battery, faulty contact breaker, coil or condenser defects, or a broken or worn out cable may be additional causes. To rectify this type of fault the above mentioned items should be checked with special attention given to carburation system. Again, the left plug should be used as the indicator. The right plug will almost always have a darker characteristic.

Over-heating of the sparking plug electrodes is indicated by severely eroded electrodes and a white, burned or blistered insulator. This type of fault is usually caused by weak carburation, although plugs which have been operating whilst not being screwed down sufficiently can easily become over-heated due to heat that is normally dissipated through to the cylinder head not having an adequate conducting path. Over-heating is normally symptomised by pre-ignition, short plug life, and "pinking" which can ultimately result in piston crown failure. Unecessary damage can result from over-tightening the plugs and to achieve a good seal between the plug and cylinder head a torque wrench should be used to tighten the plugs to the figure quoted in "General Data".

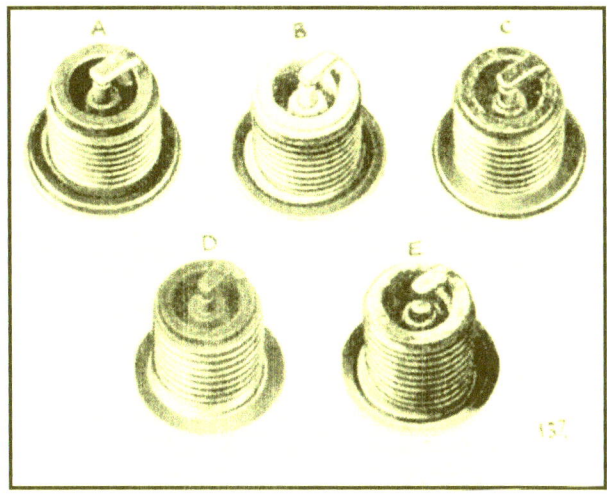

Fig. H7. Sparking plug diagnosis

A plug of the correct grade will bear a light flaky deposit on the outer rim and earth electrode, and these and the base of the insulator will be light chocolate brown in colour. A correct choice of plug is marked A. B shows a plug which appears bleached, with a deposit like cigarette ash; this is too 'hot-running' for the performance of the engine and a cooler-running type should be substituted. A plug which has been running too 'cold' and has not reached the self-cleaning temperature is shown at C. This has oil on the base of the insulator and electrodes, and should be replaced by a plug that will burn off deposits and remove the possibility of a short-circuit. The plug marked D is heavily sooted, indicating that the mixture has been too rich, and a further carburation check should be made. At illustration E is seen a plug which is completely worn out and badly in need of replacement.

To clean the plugs it is preferable to make use of a properly designed proprietary plug cleaner. The maker's instructions for using the cleaner should be followed carefully.

When the plugs have been carefully cleaned, examine the central insulators for cracking and the centre electrode for excessive wear. In such cases the plugs have completed their useful life and new ones should be fitted.

Finally, before re-fitting the sparking plugs the electrodes should be adjusted to the correct gap setting of ·020 in. (·5 mm.). Before refitting sparking plugs the threads should be cleaned by means of a wire brush and a minute amount of graphite grease smeared onto the threads. This will prevent any possibility of thread seizure occurring.

If the ignition timing and carburation settings are correct and the plugs have been correctly fitted, but over-heating still occurs then it is possible that carburation is being adversely affected by an air leak between the carburetter, manifold and the cylinder head. This possibility must be checked thoroughly before taking any further action. When it is certain that none of the above mentioned faults are the cause of over-heating then the plug type and grade should be considered.

Normally the type of plugs quoted in "General Data" are satisfactory for general use of the machine, but in special isolated cases, conditions may demand a plug of a different heat range. Advice is readily available to solve these problems from the plug manufacturer who should be consulted.

Note.—If the machine is of the type fitted with an air filter or cleaner and this has been removed it will affect the carburation of the machine and hence may adversely affect the grade of sparking plugs fitted.

SECTION H5

CHARGING SYSTEM

DESCRIPTION

The charging current is supplied by the alternator, but due to the characteristics of alternating current the battery cannot be charged direct from the alternator. To convert the alternating current to direct current a full wave bridge rectifier is connected into the circuit. The alternator gives full output, all the alternator coils being permanently connected across the rectifier. For this reason latest alternators have only 2 output leads.

Excessive charge is absorbed by the Zener Diode which is connected across the battery. On earlier machines the Zener Diode may be connected to the battery, through the ignition switch. Always ensure that the ignition switch is in the "OFF" position whilst the machine is not in use, to prevent overheating of the ignition coils, and discharging the battery.

On machines prior to engine number DU.24875 all the alternator coils are not permanently connected. The varying outputs are achieved by inter-connecting the generating coils and switch terminals as shown in the diagram in Figs. H9 and H10.

With the lighting switch in "OFF" position the coils A and B are short circuited and flux induced interacts with the rotor flux maintaining minimum output. With the switch in PILOT position the coils A and B are open circuited and the flux interaction is thereby reduced causing coil C to give increased "medium" out-put. With the switch in HEAD position the coils A, B and C are connected in parallel, giving maximum output.

On machines prior to engine number DU.24875 with a 12 volt electrical system and Zener Diode charge control, the alternator leads are connected differently in the low out-put connection (i.e. lighting switch in "OFF" position). The alternator gives "medium" out-put for the lighting switch in both the "OFF" and PILOT positions, the four coils B and C being permanently connected across the rectifier. Switching to "HEAD" position connects the two remaining coils, A. (See Fig. H9). Excessive charge is absorbed by the Zener Diode which is connected across the battery.

To locate a fault in the charging circuit, first test the alternator as described in H5 Part B. If the alternator is satisfactory, the fault must lie in the charging circuit, hence the rectifier must be checked as given in Section H5 Part C (page H11) and then the wiring and connections as shown in Section H5 Part D (page H13).

In the case of a machine prior to engine number DU.24875, first check the charging rate in the three switch positions as shown above.

ELECTRICAL SYSTEM H

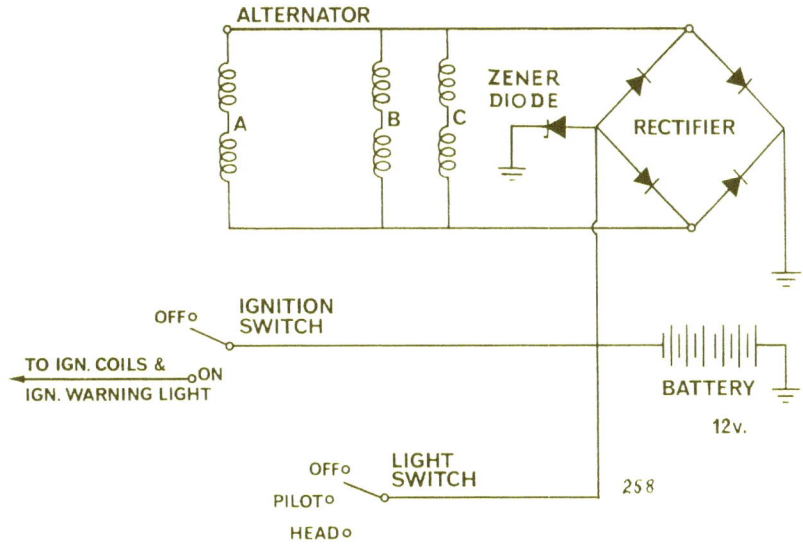

Fig. H8. Schematic diagram of 12 volt charging circuit with single charge rate and Zener Diode
All models coil ignition from DU.24875

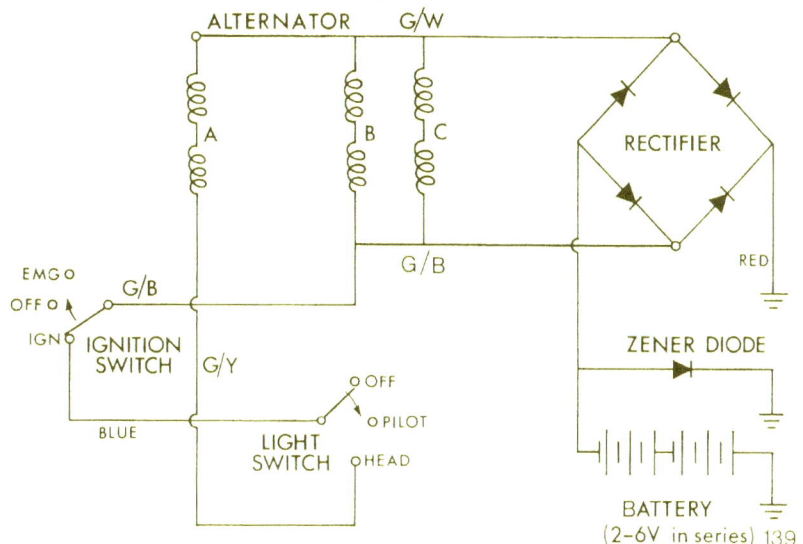

Fig. H9. Schematic illustration of 12 volt charging circuit (6T up to engine No. DU.24874)

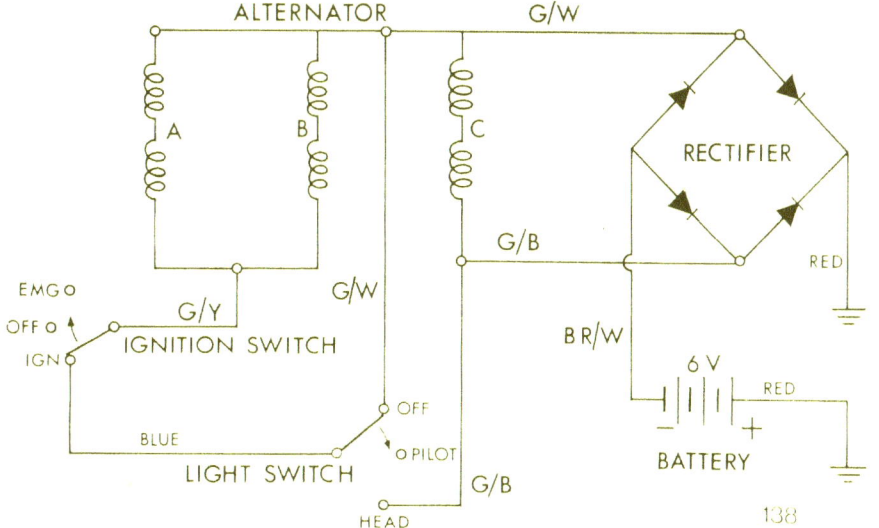

Fig. H10. Schematic illustration of 6 volt charging circuit
6T up to engine No. DU.5824 TR6 and T120 up to engine No. DU.24874

H11

H5 PART A. CHECKING THE D.C. INPUT TO BATTERY

For this test the battery must be in good condition and a good state of charge, therefore before conducting the test ensure that the battery is up to the required standard, or alternatively fit a good replacement battery.

Connect D.C. ammeter (0–15 amp.) in series between the battery main lead (brown/blue) and battery negative terminal and then start the engine and run it at approximately 3,000 r.p.m. (equivalent to 45 m.p.h. in top gear).

Note.—Ensure that the ammeter is well insulated from the surrounding earth points otherwise a short circuit may occur.

Operate the lighting switch and observe the ammeter readings, for each position of the switch. The observed figures should not be less than those tabulated in Fig. H20 for the particular model. If the readings are equal to or higher than those given, then the alternator and charging circuit are satisfactory. If the readings are lower than those quoted, then the alternator must be tested as described in Part B below.

H5 PART B. CHECKING THE ALTERNATOR OUTPUT

Disconnect the three alternator output cables underneath the engine and run the engine at 3,000 r.p.m. (equivalent to 45 m.p.h. in top gear).

Connect an A.C. voltmeter (0–15 volts) with 1 ohm load resistor in parallel with each of the alternator leads in turn as shown in the table, Fig. H20, and observe the voltmeter readings. A suitable 1 ohm load resistor can be made from a piece of nichrome wire as shown in Section H4 Part E.

From the results obtained, the following deductions can be made:—

(i) If the readings are all equal to or higher than those quoted for the particular model then the alternator is satisfactory.

(ii) A low reading on any group of coils indicates either that the leads concerned are chafed or damaged due to rubbing on the chains or that some turns of the coils are short circuited.

(iii) Low readings for all parts of the test indicates either that the green/white lead has become chafed or damaged due to rubbing on the chain(s) or that the rotor has become partially demagnetised. If the latter case applies, check that this has not been caused by a faulty rectifier or that the battery is of incorrect polarity, and only then fit a new rotor.

(iv) A zero reading for any group of coils indicates that a coil has become disconnected, is open circuit, or is earthed.

(v) A reading obtained between any one lead and earth indicates that coil windings or connections have become earthed.

If any of the above mentioned faults occur, always check the stator leads for possible chain damage before attempting repairs or renewing the stator.

It is beyond the scope of this manual to give instruction for the repair of faulty stator windings. However, the winding specification is given in the table, Fig. H20 for those obliged to attempt repair work.

H5 PART C. RECTIFIER MAINTENANCE AND TESTING

The silicon bridge rectifier requires no maintenance beyond checking that the connections are clean and tight, and that the nut securing the rectifier to the frame is tight. It should always be kept clean and dry to ensure good cooling, and spilt oil washed off immediately with hot water.

Note.—The nuts clamping the rectifier plates together must not be disturbed or slackened in any way.

When tightening the rectifier securing nut, hold the spanners as shown in Fig. H11, for if the plates are twisted, the internal connections will be broken. Note that the circles marked on the fixing bolt and nut indicate that the thread form is $\frac{1}{4}$ in. U.N.F.

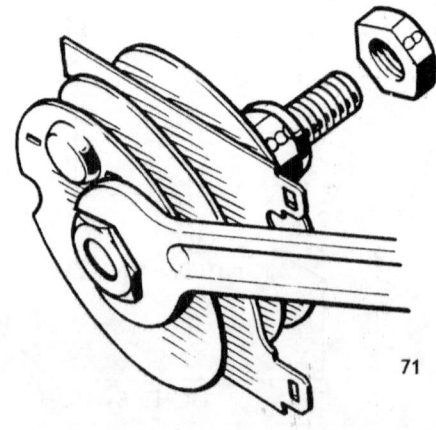

Fig. H11. Refitting the rectifier

ELECTRICAL SYSTEM H

TESTING THE RECTIFIER

For test purposes disregard the end earth (ground) terminal on latest rectifiers

To test the rectifier, first disconnect the brown/white lead from the rectifier centre terminal and insulate the end of the lead to prevent any possibility of a short circuit occurring, and then connect a D.C. voltmeter (with 1 ohm load resistor in parallel) between the rectifier centre terminal and earth.

Disconnect the alternator green/yellow lead (green/black on 12V) and reconnect to rectifier green/black terminal (green/yellow on 12V) by means of a jumper lead.

Note. Voltmeter positive terminal to frame earth (ground) and negative terminal to centre terminal on rectifier.

Ensure that all the temporary connections are well insulated to prevent a short circuit occurring then turn the ignition switch to "IGN" position and start the engine.

With the engine running at approximately 3,000 r.p.m. (approximately 45 m.p.h. in top gear) observe the voltmeter readings. The reading obtained should be at least 7·5V minimum on 12V and 6V machines.

(i) If the reading is equal to or slightly greater than that quoted, then the rectifier elements in the forward direction are satisfactory.

(ii) If the reading is excessively higher than the figures given, then check the rectifier earthing bolt connection. If the connection is good then a replacement rectifier should be fitted.

(iii) If the reading is lower than the figures quoted or zero readings are obtained, then the rectifier or the charging circuit wiring is faulty and the rectifier should be disconnected and bench tested so that the fault can be located.

Note that all of the above conclusions assume that the alternator A.C. output figures were satisfactory. Any fault at the alternator will, of course, reflect on the rectifier test results. Similarly any fault in the charging circuit wiring may indicate that the rectifier is faulty. The best method of locating a fault is to disconnect the rectifier and bench-test it as shown below:

BENCH TESTING THE RECTIFIER

For this test the rectifier should be disconnected and removed. Before removing the rectifier, disconnect the leads from the battery terminals to avoid the possibility of a short circuit occurring.

Connect the rectifier to a 12 volt battery and 1 ohm load resistor, and then connect the D.C. voltmeter in the V2 position, as shown in Fig. H12. Note the battery voltage (should be 12V) and then connect the voltmeter in V1 position whilst the following tests are conducted.

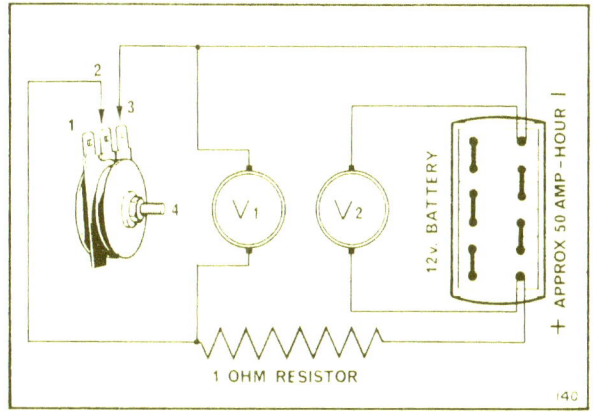

Fig. H12. Bench testing the rectifier

A voltmeter in position V1 will measure the volt drop across the rectifier plate. In position V2 it will measure the supply voltage to check that it is the recommended 12 volts on load.

Fig. H13. Rectifier—showing terminal connections for bench tests 1 and 2

H13

ELECTRICAL SYSTEM

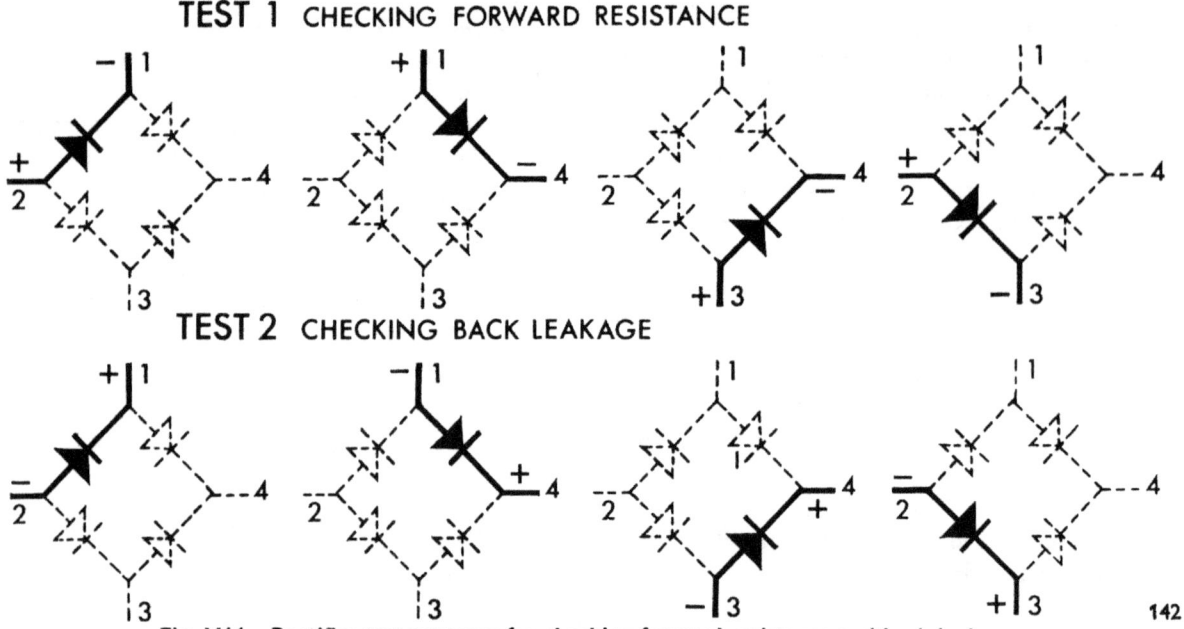

Fig. H14. Rectifier test sequence for checking forward resistance and back leakage

Test 1. With the test leads, make the following connectings but keep the testing time as short as possible to avoid overheating the rectifier cell: (a) 1 and 2, (b) 1 and 4, (c) 3 and 4, (d) 3 and 2. Each reading should not be greater than 2·5 volts with the battery polarity as shown.

Test 2. Reverse the leads or battery polarity and repeat Test 1. The readings obtained should not be more than 1·5 volts below battery voltage (V_2) (i.e. 10·5 volts minimum.)

If the readings obtained are not within the figures given, then the rectifier internal connections are shorting or aged and the rectifier should be renewed.

H5 PART D. CHECKING THE CHARGING CIRCUIT FOR CONTINUITY

On later 12 volt machines the electrical circuit is so arranged that all six alternator coils are connected in parallel so that the full alternator output is available irrespective of the lighting switch position. This also makes an emergency start system unnecessary and it is therefore possible to use a simplified wiring circuit.

First check that there is voltage at the battery and that it is correctly connected into the circuit +ve earth (ground). Ensure that the fuse has not blown.

(i) First, check that there is voltage at the rectifier centre terminal by connecting a D.C. voltmeter, with 1 ohm load resistor in parallel, between the rectifier centre terminal (not the end terminal on latest rectifiers) and earth (remember (+ve) positive earth (ground)). The voltmeter should read battery volts. If it does not, disconnect the alternator leads (green/black, green/white and green/yellow) at the snap connectors under the engine unit.

(a) Fit a jumper lead across the brown/white and green/yellow connections at the rectifier, and check the voltage at the snap connector. This test will indicate whether the harness alternator lead is open circuit.

(b) Repeat this test at the rectifier for the white/green lead.

(2) If no voltage is present at the rectifier central terminal (brown/white), check the voltage at the ammeter terminal. If satisfactory, it indicates that the brown/white wire is open circuit. If not, the ammeter is open circuit.

(3) If no voltage is present at either ammeter terminal, then the brown/blue wire from the battery (−ve) is open circuit.

On machines prior to engine number DU.24875 after checking for battery voltage at the rectifier centre terminal, proceed as follows:

(ii) *This test does not apply to machines with 12 volt systems.* Connect the green/yellow lead from the wiring harness (underneath the engine) to the rectifier centre terminal lead (brown/white), by means of a jumper lead, and turn the ignition switch to "IGN" position.

ELECTRICAL SYSTEM H

Connect a D.C. voltmeter with load resistor in parallel between the green/white lead at the rectifier and earth (frame). With the lighting switch at "OFF" position, the voltmeter should read battery volts. If it does not the leads to ignition switch terminals 16 and 18 should be checked and also the leads to lighting switch terminals 4 and 5 must be checked.

(iii) Connect the green/yellow lead (green/black lead for 12 volt system) from the wiring harness (underneath the engine) to the rectifier centre terminal, by means of a jumper lead, as in test (ii). Turn the ignition switch to "IGN" position and the lighting switch to HEAD position, and connect a D.C. voltmeter (with 1 ohm resistor in parallel) between green/black lead (green/yellow lead on 12 volt models) at rectifier and earth. The voltmeter should read battery voltage. If it does not, the leads to ignition switch terminals 16 and 17 should be checked and the leads to the lighting switch terminals 5 and 7 should also be checked. With the lighting switch in 'Pilot' position no reading should be obtained between green/black (green/yellow on 12 volt models) and earth or green/white and earth at the rectifier.

H5 PART E. CONSTRUCTING A ONE-OHM LOAD RESISTOR

The resistor used in the following tests must be accurate and constructed so that it will not overheat otherwise the correct values of current or voltage will not be obtained.

A suitable resistor can be made from 4 yards (3¾ metres) of 18 S.W.G. (·048 in. (i.e. 1·2 m.m.) dia.) NICHROME wire by bending it into two equal parts and calibrating it as follows:—

(1) Fix a heavy gauge flexible lead to the folded end of the wire and connect this lead to the positive terminal of a 6 volt battery.

(2) Connect a D.C. voltmeter (0–10V) across the battery terminals and an ammeter (0–10 amp) between the battery negative terminal and the free ends of the wire resistance, using a crocodile clip to make the connection.

(3) Move the clip along the wires, making contact with both wires until the ammeter reading is numerically equal to the number of volts shown in the voltmeter. The resistance is then 1 ohm. Cut the wire at this point, twist the the two ends together and wind the wire on an asbestos former approximately 2 inches (5 cm.) dia. so that each turn does not contact the one next to it.

SECTION H6
ZENER DIODE CHARGE CONTROL (12 VOLT MACHINES ONLY)

DESCRIPTION

The Zener Diode output regulating system uses all the coils of the 6-coil alternator connected permanently across the rectifier, provides automatic control of the charging current. It will only operate successfully on a 12 volt system where it is connected in parallel with the battery as shown in the wiring diagram (Section H19 Fig. H33). The Diode may be connected through the ignition switch or direct to the centre terminal of the rectifier.

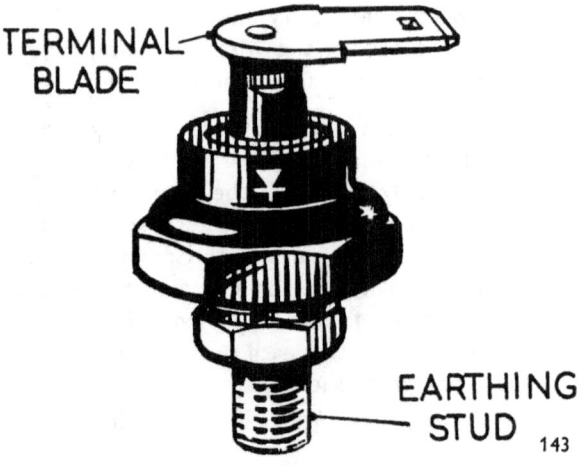

Fig. H15. Zener Diode

Assuming the battery is in a low state of charge its terminal voltage (the same voltage is across the Diode) will also be low, therefore the maximum charging current will flow into the battery from the alternator. At first none of the current is by-passed by the Diode because of it being non-conducting due to the low battery terminal volts. However, as the battery is quickly restored to a full state of charge, the system voltage rises until at 14 volts the Zener Diode becomes partially conducting, thereby providing an alternative path for a small part of the charging current. Small increases in battery voltage result in large increases in Zener conductivity until, at approximately 15 volts about 5 amperes of the alternator output is by-passing the battery. The battery will continue to receive only a portion of the alternator output as long as the system voltage is relatively high.

Depression of the system voltage, due to the use of headlamp or other lighting equipment, causes the Zener Diode current to decrease and the balance to be diverted and consumed by the component in use.

If the electrical loading is sufficient to cause the system voltage to fall to 14 volts, the Zener Diode will revert to a high resistance state of non-conductivity and the full generated output will go to meet the demands of the battery.

Provided an adequate heat sink is employed, the Zener Diode is able to absorb the full output of the alternator. Machines previously employing 6 volt systems and subsequently converted to 12 volts retain some form of charge control through the lighting switch. This is achieved by permanently connecting four charging coils across the rectifier (green/white — green/yellow) and bringing in the other two coils (green/black) in the lighting switch head lamp position (Fig. H8).

ELECTRICAL SYSTEM

MAINTENANCE

The Zener Diode is mounted on an aluminium heat sink. Providing the Diode and the heat sink are kept clean, and provided with an adequate airflow, to ensure maximum efficiency, and provided a firm flat "metal to metal" contact is mantained between the base of the Diode and the surface of the heat sink, to ensure adequate heat flow, no maintenance will be necessary.

ZENER DIODE—
CHARGING REGULATOR

TEST PROCEDURE

(Procedure for Testing on the Machine)

The test procedure given below can be used when it is required to check the performance of the Zener Diode type ZD715 whilst it is in position on the machine.

Good quality moving coil meters should be used when testing. The voltmeter should have a scale 0–18, and the ammeter 0–5 amps min. The test procedure is as follows:-

(A) Disconnect the cable from the zener diode and connect ammeter (in series) between the diode Lucar terminal and cable previously disconnected. The ammeter red or positive lead must connect to the diode Lucar terminal.

(B) Connect voltmeter across zener diode and heat sink. The red or positive lead must connect to the heat sink which is earthed to the frame of the machine by its fixing bolts and a separate earth lead. The black lead connects to the zener Lucar terminal.

(C) Start the engine, ensure that all lights are off, and gradually increase engine speed while at the same time observing both meters:—

(i) the series connected ammeter must indicate zero amps, up to 12.75 volts, which will be indicated on the shunt connected voltmeter as engine speed is slowly increased.

(ii) increase engine speed still further, until zener current indicated on ammeter is 2.0 amp. At this value the zener voltage should be 13.5 volts to 15.3 volts.

TEST CONCLUSIONS:—

If the ammeter in test (i) registers any current at all before the voltmeter indicates 13.0 volts, then a replacement zener diode must be fitted.

If test (i) is satisfactory but in test (ii) a higher voltage than that stated is registered on the voltmeter, before the ammeter indicates 2.0 amp, then a replacement zener diode must be fitted.

SECTION H7
ZENER DIODE LOCATION

FROM DU.66246
The Zener diode is mounted below the headlamp, being bolted to the fork middle lug. The aluminium heatsink is finned to assist cooling and is secured to the fork by a bracket and bolts. See Fig. below.

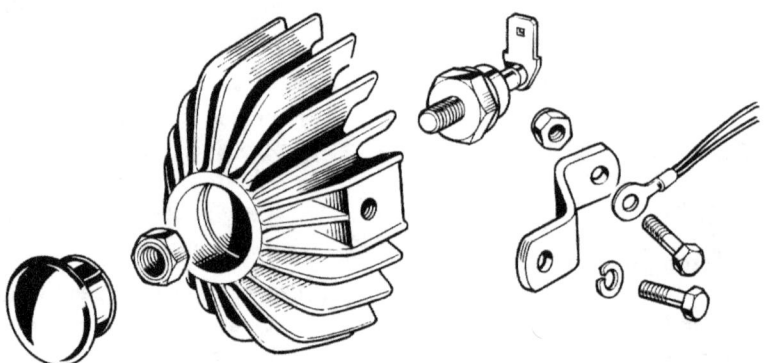

Fig. H16. Finned heatsink (from DU.66246)

To remove diode only, disconnect the brown/white double "Lucar" connector from the diode. Remove the black plastic plug from the heat sink (See Fig. H16) and unscrew the "nyloc" nut which secures the diode. When refitting, the diode nut must be tightened with extreme care.

To remove the finned heat sink, remove the front bolt from the retaining bracket. A double red earth (ground) wire is attached at this point.

DO NOT ATTACH THE EARTH (GROUND) LEADS BETWEEN THE DIODE BODY AND HEATSINK

The Zener Diode is fitted to a heat sink which is located behind the left hand switch panel.
To enable the Zener Diode to be removed from its heat sink, the left hand switch panel must first be removed as described in Section E3. Disconnect and remove the batteries so that the two bolts, nuts and washers securing the heat sink can be removed. The Zener securing nut and earthing strap should be carefully removed from beneath the heat sink and the Zener lifted clear after disconnecting the Lucar connector securing the feed cable to the top of the Zener.

NOTE: When refitting the Zener to the heat sink, it is essential that the earthing strap is refitted correctly, i.e., between the heat sink and Zener securing nut. It must NOT be placed between the Zener body and heat sink as this could cause a heat build up possibly resulting in a Zener Diode failure.

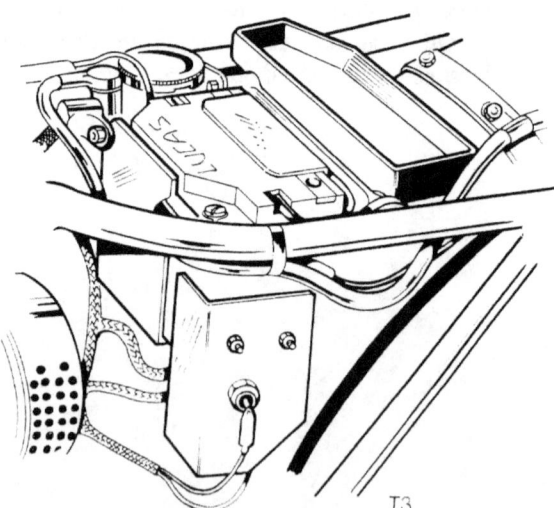

Fig. H17. Zener diode location (before DU.66246)

Before DU.24875. The heatsink on 6T machines was fitted to the front petrol tank mounting bolts but removal and refitting of the diode is as for later machines.

SECTION H8

A.C. IGNITION (E.T.) AND A.C. LIGHTING SYSTEMS

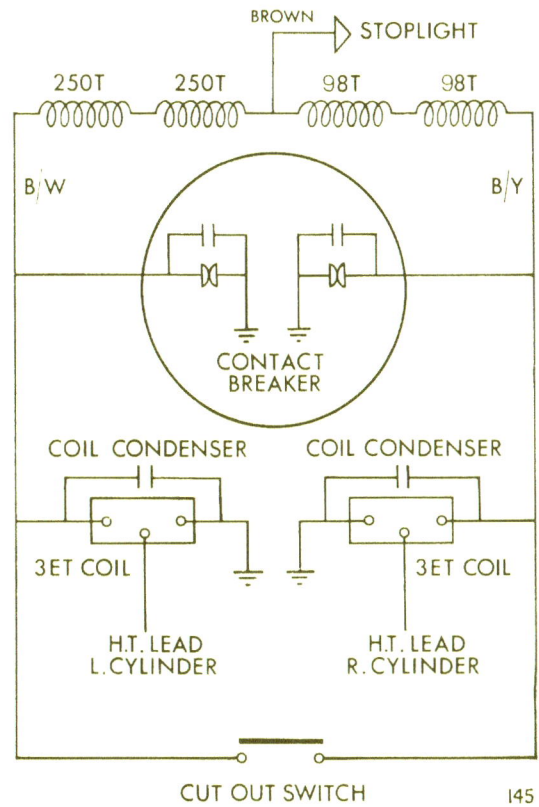

Fig. H18. Schematic illustration of A.C. ignition (E.T.) system

DESCRIPTION

The A.C. magneto (energy transfer) system consists of two 3 E.T. ignition coils, a contact breaker and an alternator specially wound for A.C. ignition and lighting. There are five leads from the alternator, two for ignition purposes and three for direct lighting purposes. The circuit diagram, Fig. H35 in Section H19 illustrates the stator coil connections.

The main features of the A.C. ignition system for twin cylinder machines is that the ignition coil and contact breaker points are connected in parallel. In practice this means that when the contacts are closed the current can flow directly to earth. When one set of contacts open, the current has to pass through the ignition coil primary winding to earth through the second set of contacts which are arranged to be closed at the same instant. From this it can be seen that the availability of a spark at either cylinder is dependent upon both contacts being clean and adjusted correctly (see Fig. H18).

Another feature is that the E.T. system operates on a rising current in the ignition coil primary winding and not falling primary current as in the conventional coil ignition system.

H8 PART A. A.C. IGNITION

The accurate and efficient working of the A.C. ignition system is dependent not only upon the piston/spark relationship that is involved but also the rotor/stator relationship at the instant of ignition. The stator is fixed to the left crankcase and requires no maintenance other than to check that the leads are not rubbing on either of the chains.

The rotor is located on the crankshaft by means of a dowel fitted to the engine sprocket. When the rotor is removed care should be taken to refit it in the appropriate position with the rotor hole located as shown in the tabel below, in accordance with ignition timing requirements.

Dowel Location	Ignition Timing Full-Advanced	Dowel Remarks
"S"	37° B.T.C.	Standard
"R"	41° B.T.C.	Racing
"M"	39° B.T.C.	"Mid" position

It is beyond the scope of this Manual to advise on a deviation from the standard setting, as so many factors are involved. If it is required to alter the settings from standard, then advice should be sought from a local Triumph Dealer or the Triumph Engineering Co. Ltd., Service Department.

The 3 E.T. coil, condensers (capacitors), and high tension leads must be kept clean and free from dirt or water. Also, it is important that the sparking plug is maintained at the correct gap setting and that the centre electrode is kept clean.

ELECTRICAL SYSTEM

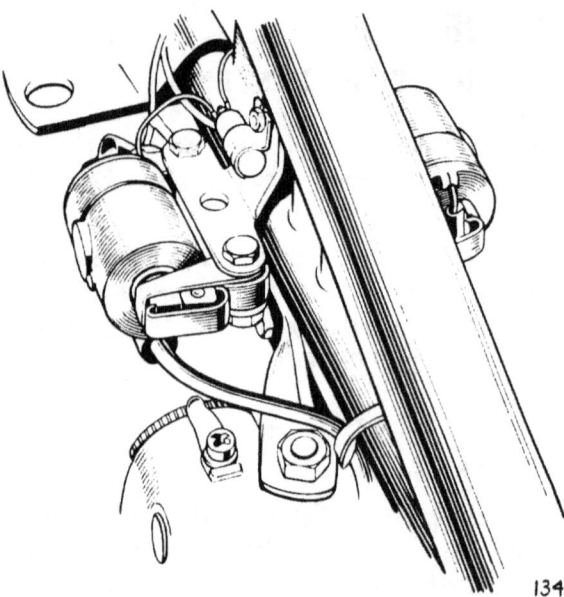

Fig. H19. A.C. ignition coils fitted on machine

Both sets of contact breaker contacts must be kept clean and adjusted correctly to the gap setting given in General Data. A fault at either set of contacts will adversely affect the ignition spark at BOTH cylinders.

H8 PART B. TESTING THE A.C. IGNITION SYSTEM

First, ensure that the timing, contact breaker and plug gaps are satisfactory, and then disconnect both H.T. leads and check that a spark is available by holding each of the cables about $\frac{3}{16}$ inches (4 mm.) from the cylinder head in turn and operate the kickstarter. A good spark should be produced. If it is not, then the 3 E.T. coil and alternator ignition supply are suspect.

As it is not possible to test the 3 E.T. coils accurately on the machine, the following test procedure should be adopted.

Two 6 volt external batteries are used for the next two tests, in conjunction with the A.C. ignition coils on the machine.

A.C. ignition coils are not designed to run under such conditions, overheating occurring in the primary windings.

Each test should be undertaken in as short a time as possible, and the batteries connected in circuit only when actually necessary to run the test.

(1) Disconnect the five alternator leads under the engine.

(2) Unplug the black/yellow lead from the condenser at the right hand side coil (under the petrol (gasolene) tank.

(3) Connect the black/yellow lead to the positive (+ve) terminal of a (6V) test battery.

(4) Connect the negative (—ve) battery lead to the condenser terminal.

(5) Unplug the black/white lead from the condenser at the left hand side coil (under the petrol (gasolene) tank).

(6) Connect the black/white lead to the positive (+ve) terminal of a second (6V) test battery.

(7) Connect the negative (—ve) terminal of the second test battery to the left hand condenser terminal.

(8) Remove the sparking plug wire from each plug in turn and with battery wires connected, open and close the contact breaker points. If the coils and condensers are satisfactory, a good spark will jump from the plug lead to earth (ground).

(9) If a poor spark (or no spark) is noted, check all wiring connections, and repeat (8) above. If the system still does not spark, instal new condensers and repeat (8). If still there is no spark, check the ignition coils by substitution.

ELECTRICAL SYSTEM

H8 PART C. CHECKING THE ALTERNATOR OUTPUT (A.C. Ignition Models)

To facilitate a check to be made on the alternator output, a separate ignition circuit must be used as given in Section H8 Part B above, so that the engine can be run at 3,000 r.p.m. (approximately 45 m.p.h. in top gear).

Pay careful regard to the warning given in the previous section (H8 part B) concerning the possible overheating of the A.C. ignition coil primary windings.

The preferred alternative method is to use two MA6 ignition coils, bolted together, with the machines C.B. leads, BLACK/WHITE, BLACK/YELLOW connected to the appropriate C.B. terminals on the test ignition coils. The test coil S.W. terminals are linked together and fed to a test battery (−ve) negative terminal and the battery (+ve) positive connected to the ignition coils cases. A jumper lead is also required between battery (+ve) positive, and motorcycle frame earth (ground). The H.T. leads are connected to the appropriate sparking plugs.

With all five alternator leads disconnected under the engine start up the engine and run at 3,000 r.p.m. (equivalent to approximately 45 m.p.h. in top gear). Connect an A.C. voltmeter (0-10V) with a 1 ohm resistor in parallel between the pairs of alternator leads given in table, Fig. H20 Section H9.

(i) If the readings are equal to or higher than the figures quoted for the particular model, then the alternator is satisfactory.

(ii) A low reading on any group of coils indicates either that the leads concerned are chafed through or damaged due to rubbing on the chains or that some of the coil turns are short circuited.

(iii) Low readings from all parts of the test indicates a partially demagnetized rotor. In this case the rotor must be renewed.

(iv) A zero reading for any group of coils indicates that a coil has become disconnected and is open circuit, in which case the stator should be replaced.

(v) A reading obtained between any one stator lead and earth (ground) indicates that some coil turns have become earthed (grounded) to the engine. In this case, brush the stator with paraffin (kerosene) or petrol (gasoline). DO NOT LEAVE TO SOAK. Retest on the machine. If still faulty, replace the stator.

If any fault does occur always check the stator leads for possible chain damage before attempting repair or renewing the stator. It is beyond the scope of this manual to give instruction for repair of faulty stator windings. However the winding specification is given in table, Fig. H19 to provide the required information for local repair work, should a correct replacement stator not be immediately available.

H8 PART D DIRECT LIGHTING SYSTEM

The electrical power for the direct lighting system is supplied by three of the five alternator leads, namely the red, brown and brown/blue. The leads are connected as shown in the wiring diagram (Fig. H35 in Section H19). In order that no one pair of coils is overloaded, the electrical loads are connected as shown and no deviation from the standard arrangement shown should be made.

An apparent loss or reduction of power at any of the lights may well be due to a high resistance caused by a loose or faulty connection. In the event of a fault occuring, always check the wiring connections, giving particular attention to the red earth (ground) lead from the alternator and headlamp. Note that a short circuit in the brown stop lamp lead will result in the ignition system failing, hence the stop lamp switch connections should be always kept clean and dry.

In the event of a fault occuring which cannot be traced to the circuit connections the alternator should be checked as described in Section H8, Part C above.

SECTION H9

ALTERNATOR AND STATOR DETAILS—SPECIFICATIONS AND OUTPUT FIGURES

Machines subsequent to DU.24875

MODELS	System voltage	Ignition type	Alternator type	Stator No.
T120, TR6, 6T T120R, TR6R	12 V.	Coil	RM.19	47162 After DU.58565 47204
T120TT, TR6 c.	6 V.	A.C. IGN	RM.19	47188

Fig. H21. Electrical system details

Stator number	System voltage	D.C. input to battery amp. @ 3,000 r.p.m.			Alternator Output minimum A.C. volts @ 3,000 r.p.m.			Stator coil details		
		Off	Pilot	Head	A	B	C	No of coils	Turns per coil	S.W.G.
47162	12 V.	1·5* 6·5†	1·0* 4·3†	1·0* 2·0†	4·0	6·5	8·5	6	140	22
47188	6 V.	Not applicable			5·0	1·5	IGN. { 3·5 LIGHT {	2 2 1 1	250 98 98 98	25 20 20 21
47204	12 V.	Not applicable			—	—	8·5	6	140	22

Coil Ignition Machines
    A = Green/White and Green/Black
    B = Green/White and Green/Yellow
    C = Green/White and { Green/Black / Green/Yellow } connected

*Zener in Circuit
†Zener disconnected

From DU.58565 2 stator leads only are used i.e. Green/White and Green/Yellow.

A.C. Ignition Machines
    A = Red and Brown/Blue
    B = Black/Yellow and Black/White
    C = Black/Yellow and Brown

Fig. H20. Alternator—minimum output and stator details

ELECTRICAL SYSTEM   H

ALTERNATOR AND STATOR DETAILS—SPECIFICATIONS AND OUTPUT FIGURES

Before engine number DU.24875

MODELS	System voltage	Ignition type	Alternator type	Stator No.
6T	12 V.	Coil	RM.19	47162
TR6SR, T120R, T120C, 6T.U.S.A	6 V.	Coil	RM.19	47162
6T, TR6, T120	6 V.	Coil	RM.19	47164
6T (Police)	6 V.	Coil	RM.19/20	47167
TR6SC, T120TT Special	6 V.	A.C. IGN	RM.19	47188

Fig. H23. Electrical system details

Stator number	System voltage	D.C. input to battery amp. @ 3,000 r.p.m.			Alternator Output minimum A.C. volts @ 3,000 r.p.m.			Stator coil details		
		Off	Pilot	Head (Main beam)	A	B	C	No of coils	Turns per coil	S.W.G.
47162	6 V.	2·75	2·0	2·0	4·0	6·5	8·5	6	140	22
	12 V.	2·0*	2·1*	1·5*						
		4·8†	3·8†	1·8†						
47164	6 V.	2·7	0·9	1·6	4·5	7·0	9·5	6	122	21
47167	6 V.	6·6‡	6·6‡	13·6‡	7·7	11·6	13·2	6	74	19
47188	6 V.	Not applicable			5·0	1·5	IGN. 3·5 LIGHT	2	250	25
								2	88	20
								1	88	20
								1	98	21

Coil Ignition Machines
  A = Green/White and Green/Black
  B = Green/White and Green/Yellow
  C = Green/White and { Green/Black / Green/Yellow } connected

A.C. Ignition Machines
  A = Red and Brown/Blue
  B = Black/Yellow and Black/White
  C = Black/Yellow and Brown

* Zener in Circuit
† Zener disconnected
‡ With Boost Switch in Circuit

Fig. H22. Alternator—Minimum output and stator details

SECTION H10
ELECTRIC HORN

DESCRIPTION
The horn is of a high frequency single note type and is operated by direct current from the battery. (On A.C. models a similar horn specifically designed for A.C. current is fitted.) The method of operation is that of a magnetically operated armature, which impacts on the cone face, and causes the tone disc of the horn to vibrate. The magnetic circuit is made self interrupting by contacts which can be adjusted externally.

If the horn fails to work, check the mounting bolts etc., and horn connection wiring. Check the battery for state of charge. A low supply voltage at the horn will adversely effect horn performance. If the above checks are made and the fault is not remedied, then adjust the horn as follows.

HORN ADJUSTMENT
When adjusting and testing the horn, do not depress the horn push for more than a fraction of a second or the circuit wiring may be overloaded.

A small serrated adjustment screw situated near the terminals (see Fig. H24), is provided to take up wear in the internal moving parts of the horn. To adjust, turn this screw anticlockwise until the horn just fails to sound, and then turn it back (clockwise) about one quarter to half a turn.

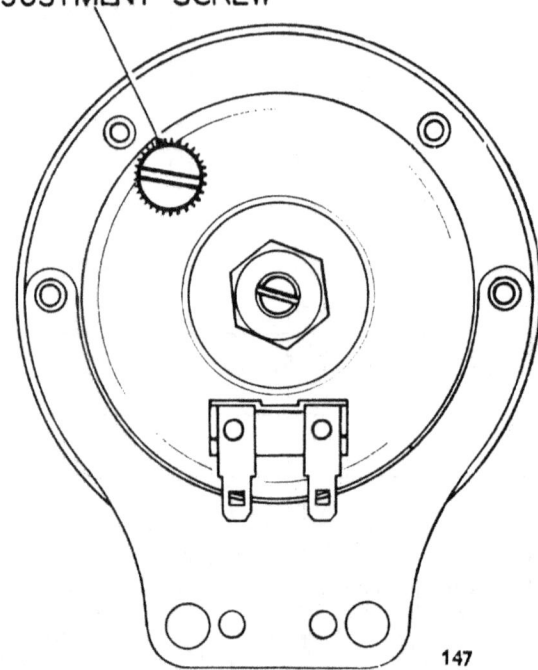

Fig. H24. Horn adjustment screw

SECTION H11
HEADLAMP

DESCRIPTION
The headlamp is of the sealed beam unit type and access is gained to the bulb and bulb holder by withdrawing the rim and beam unit assembly. To do so on the T120 or TR6, slacken the screw at the top of the headlamp or on the earlier 6T, slacken the screw at the top of the nacelle cover adjacent to the speedometer and in each case prise off the rim and beam unit assembly.

The bulb can be removed by first pressing the cylindrical cap inwards and turning it anticlockwise. The cap can then be withdrawn and the bulb is free to be removed.

When fitting a new bulb, note that it locates by means of a cutaway and projection arrangement. also note that the cap can only be replaced one way, the tabs being staggered to prevent incorrect reassembly. Check the replacement bulb voltage and wattage specification and type before fitting. Focusing with this type of beam unit is unnecessary and there is no provision for such.

BEAM ADJUSTMENTS
The beam must in all cases be adjusted as specified by local lighting regulations. In the United Kingdom the Transport Lighting Regulations reads as follows:—

A lighting system must be arranged so that it can give a light which is incapable of dazzling any person standing on the same horizontal plane as the vehicle at a greater distance than twenty five feet from the lamp, whose eye level is not less than three feet—six inches above that plane.

The headlamp must therefore be set so that the main beam is directed straight ahead and parallel with the road when the motorcycle is fully loaded. To achieve this, place the machine on a level road pointing towards a wall at a distance of 25 feet away, with a rider and passenger, on the machine, slacken the two pivot bolts at either side of the headlamp and tilt the headlamp until the beam is focused at approximately two feet six inches from the base of the wall. Do not forget that the headlamp should be on "full beam" lighting during this operation. On machines with the nacelle slacken the two small screws on the adaptor rim at either side to tilt the beam unit.

ELECTRICAL SYSTEM

SECTION H12
REMOVING AND REFITTING THE HEADLAMP

Disconnect the leads from the battery terminals then slacken the light unit securing screw at the top of the headlamp. Prise the top of the light unit free.

Detach the pilot bulbholder from the light unit and disconnect the main bulbholder leads at the snap connector. Disconnect the 4 spade terminals from the lighting switch and the terminals from the ammeter. On earlier models merely disconnect the snap connector terminals at the wiring harness. The red leads for the warning lights should be parted at the snap connectors and then the harness complete with warning light bulbholders can be withdrawn with the grommet from the back of the headlamp shell. Finally remove the pivot bolts to release the shell and collect the spacers.

Refitting is the reversal of the above instruction but reference should be made to the wiring diagram in Section H19. Finally, set the headlamp main beam as shown in Section H11.

Do not tighten the headlamp pivot bolts over the torque setting given in "General Data".

SECTION H13
TAIL AND STOP LAMP UNIT

Access to the bulbs in the tail and stop lamp unit is achieved by unscrewing the two slotted screws which secure the lens. The bulb is of the double-filament offset pin type and when a replacement is carried out, ensure that the bulb is fitted correctly.

Check that the two supply leads are connected correctly and check the earth (ground) lead to the bulb holder is in satisfactory condition.
When refitting the lens, do not overtighten the fixing screws or the lens may fracture as a result.

SECTION H14
FUSES

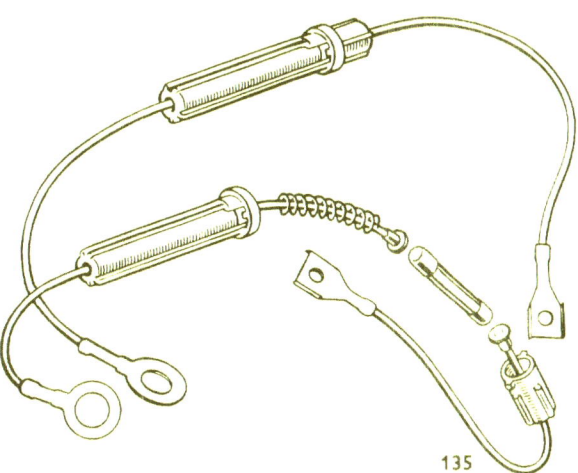

Fig. H25. Exploded view of fuseholder assembly

The fuse is to be found on the brown/blue live lead from the battery negative terminal after DU.66246 and on the red earth lead from battery positive before this number. It is housed in a quickly detachable shell and is of 35 amp fuse rating.
Before following any fault location procedure always check that the fuse is not the source of the fault. A new fuse-cartridge should be fitted if there is any doubt about the old one.
A fuse can be fitted to any Triumph coil ignition model and all that is required is a small proprietary fuse holder obtainable from most Triumph Dealers. In all cases the fuse rating must not under any circumstances be below 35 amp. rating and must be fitted on the earth lead between earth (ground) and the battery positive terminal.

SECTION H15
IGNITION SWITCH

Coil ignition editions of the TR6 and T120 models are fitted with an ignition switch incorporating a "barrel" type lock. These locks use individual "Yale" type keys and render the ignition circuit inoperative when the switch is turned off and the key removed. It is advisable for the owner to note the number stamped on the key to ensure a correct replacement in the event of the key being lost.

Three Lucar connectors are incorporated in the switch and these should be checked from time to time to ensure good electrical contact. The switch body can be released from the headlamp bracket or switch panel by removing the large nut retaining the switch in the panel and the switch pushed out. The battery leads should be removed before attempting to remove the switch to avoid a short circuit.

The lock is retained in the body of the switch by a spring loaded plunger. This can be depressed with a pointed instrument through a small hole in the side of the switch body and the lock assembly withdrawn after the lock and switch together have been detached from the machine.

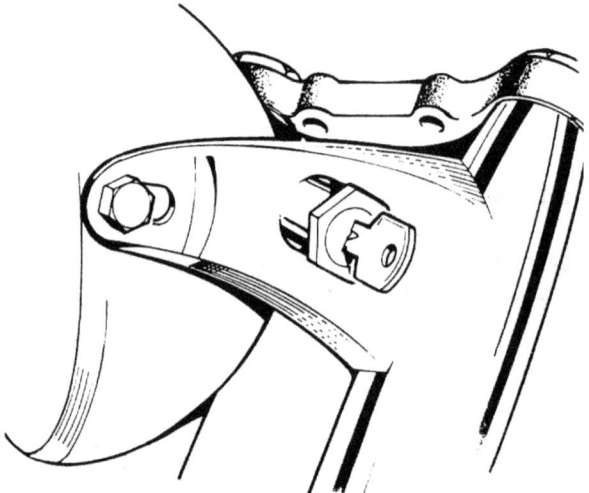

Fig. H26. Showing the ignition switch
(TR6 and T120 models)

SECTION H16
IGNITION CUT-OUT ("KILL") BUTTON

An emergency cut-out (kill) button is provided on TR6 and T120 models. This is mounted on the handlebar and can be used to stop or "kill" the engine.

NOTE: Two types of cut-out buttons are in current use, one for coil ignition machines and one for A.C. magneto equipped machines. Although both cut-out buttons appear identical externally, the internal connections are arranged differently. They must not be interchanged and if a replacement is required, refer to the appropriate replacement parts list.

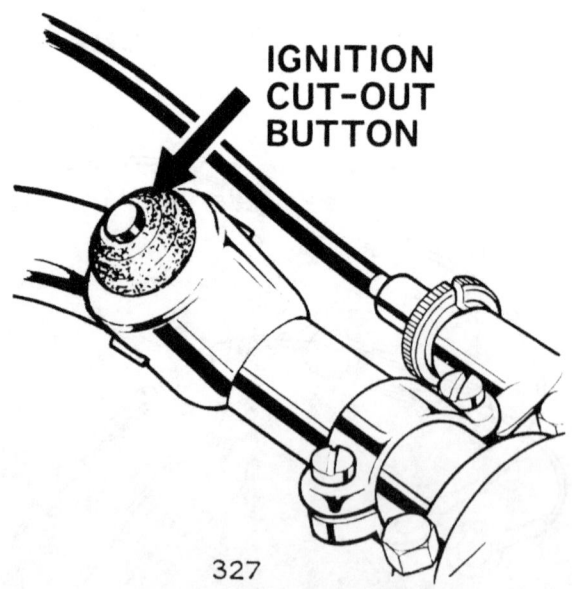

Fig. H27. Ignition cut-out button
(TR6 and T120 models)

SECTION H17
WARNING LAMPS

Warning lamps have been incorporated in the TR6 T120 electrical systems in recent years, the lamps being mounted in the headlamp shell. On earlier machines having only a warning light for the ignition, this is coloured red. On all machines with two warning lights, red is used for the main beam and green for the ignition warning.

A.C. Magneto models have a single red warning light for main beam.

The ignition warning light is not intended to act as a "no charge" lamp as in automobile practice. Its function is to warn a rider that he has omitted to switch off the ignition with the key provided.

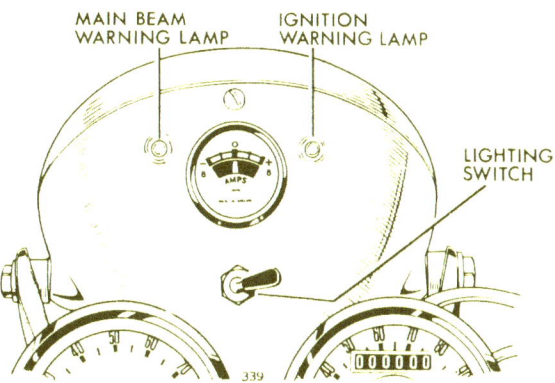

Fig. H28. Location of ignition and main beam warning lamps (TR6 and T120 only)

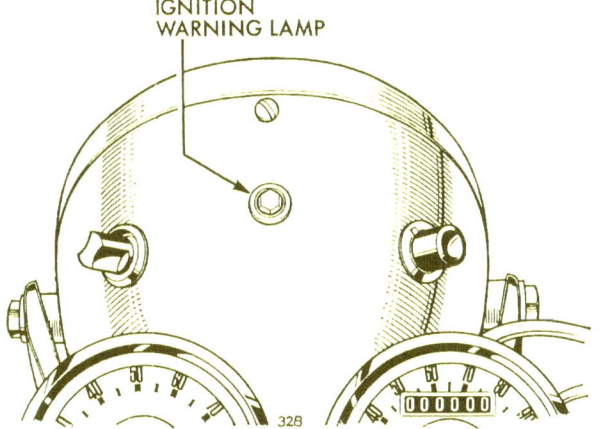

Fig. H29. Location of main beam warning lamp (A.C. magneto models only) (up to DU.66246)

SECTION H18
CAPACITOR IGNITION (MODEL 2MC)

The Lucas motor cycle capacitor system has been developed to enable machines to be run with or without a battery. The rider therefore has the choice of running with normal battery operation or running without battery if desired (e.g. competing in trials or other competitive events) and for emergency operation in case of battery failure.

Machines can readily be started without the battery and run as normal with full use of standard lighting. When stationary, however, parking lights will not work unless the battery is connected. The capacitor system also has the advantage of being much less critical with regard to alternator timing.

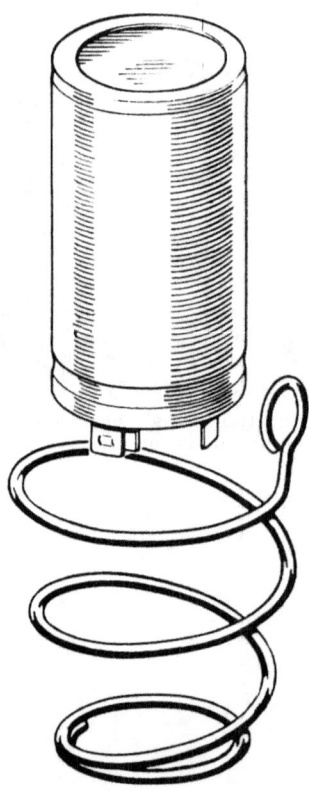

Fig. H30. Capacitor and spring

The system utilises the standard 12-volt battery-coil ignition equipment with the Zener diode charging regulator mounted on an efficient heat sink, plus a spring mounted high capacity electrolytic capacitor (Model 2MC), of a special shock-resistant type.

The energy pulses from the alternator are stored by the capacitor to ensure that sufficient current flows through the ignition coil at the moment of contact opening, thus producing an adequate spark for starting. When running, the capacitor also helps to reduce the d.c. voltage ripple.

Also with this system alternator timing is much less critical. Provided the centres of the rotor and stator poles are roughly in line in the fully retarded position (i.e. as normal battery) emergency start condition which is 30° past magnetic neutral) satisfactory starting will be obtained. Furthermore any auto-advance angle and speed characteristics may be used and perfect running ignition performance achieved.

HEAT SINK REQUIREMENTS
With the diode centrally mounted flat on its base in metal to metal contact with the plate, the assembly should be mounted on the machine so that the heat sink is in an unobstructed air stream, and in a position to avoid as far as possible any dirt or water thrown up by the wheels.

Earlier machines wired to give only part generator output in the "off" and "pilot" positions will not have heat sinks of sufficient size. These must, therefore, be replaced with one of the latest finned type. It is essential that the heat sink is properly earthed.

IDENTIFICATION OF CAPACITOR TERMINALS
The 2MC capacitor is an electroclytic (polarised) type and care must be taken to see that the correct wiring connections are made when fitting. Spare Lucar connectors are supplied to assist in connecting up. Looking at the terminal end of the unit it will be seen that there are two sizes of Lucar connector. The small $\frac{3}{16}$ in. Lucar is the *positive* (earth) terminal the rivet of which is marked with a spot of red paint. The double $\frac{1}{4}$ in. Lucar forms the *negative* terminal.

The illustration on the previous page shows the spring and capacitor. The capacitor should be positioned with its terminals pointing downwards. When fitting the spring to the capacitor, insert the capacitor at the widest end of the spring and push it down until the small coil locates in the groove on the capacitor body.

ELECTRICAL SYSTEM

STORAGE LIFE OF MODEL 2MC CAPACITOR

The life of the 2MC is very much affected by storage in high temperatures. The higher the temperature the shorter its shelf life. At normal temperature i.e. 20°C. (68°F.) it will have a shelf life of about 18 months. At 40°C. (86°F.) about 9 to 12 months. Therefore, storing in a cool place will maintain their efficiency.

TESTING

The efficiency of a stored capacitor can be determined fairly accurately with the aid of a voltmeter (scale 0-12 volts) connected to the terminals of a charged capacitor and the instantaneous reading on the meter noted. The procedure is as follows:—

(a) Connect the capacitor(s) to a 12-volt supply and leave connected for 5 *minutes*. Observe carefully the polarity of connections, otherwise the capacitor may be ruined.

(b) When charging time has been completed, disconnect the supply leads and allow the charged capacitor(s) to stand for at least 5 *minutes*.

(c) Then connect the voltmeter leads to the capacitor and note the instantaneous reading. This should not be less than 8·0 volts for a serviceable unit.

If a voltmeter is not available a rough check can be made by following the procedures in (a) and (b) and using a single strand of copper wire instead of the voltmeter to short-circuit the capacitor terminals. A good spark will be obtained from a serviceable capacitor at the instant the terminals are shorted together.

WIRING AND INSTALLATION

The capacitor is fitted into the spring and should be mounted with its terminals downwards. The capacitor negative terminal *and* Zener diode must be connected to the rectifier centre (d.c.) terminal (brown/white), and the positive terminal must be connected to the centre bolt earthing terminal (see capacitor ignition terminal Fig. H30).

The mounting spring should be attached to any convenient point under the twin seat.

Note.—Check to see if the Zener diode heat sink is of the latest finned type. If not it must be replaced with one that is (Service bulletin 288 describes heat sink conversion, refer to Section H7).

The alternator should be reconnected to give full output in all lighting switch positions. This can be done by joining together the alternator external green/black and green/yellow leads with the aid of a double snap-connector. Machines after DU.66246 are thus arranged.

SERVICE NOTES

Before running a 2MC equipped machine with the battery disconnected it is essential that the *battery negative lead be insulated* to prevent it from reconnecting and shorting to earth (frame of machine). Otherwise, the capacitor will be reuined. This can be done by removing the fuse from its holder and replacing it with a length of $\frac{1}{4}$ in. dia. dowel rod or other insulating medium.

A faulty capacitor may not be apparent when used with a battery system. To prevent any inconvenience arising, periodically check that the capacitor is serviceable by disconnecting the battery to see if the machine will continue to run in the normal manner, with full lighting also available.

A capacitor kit is available under part number C.P.210.

ELECTRICAL SYSTEM

SECTION H19
WIRING DIAGRAMS

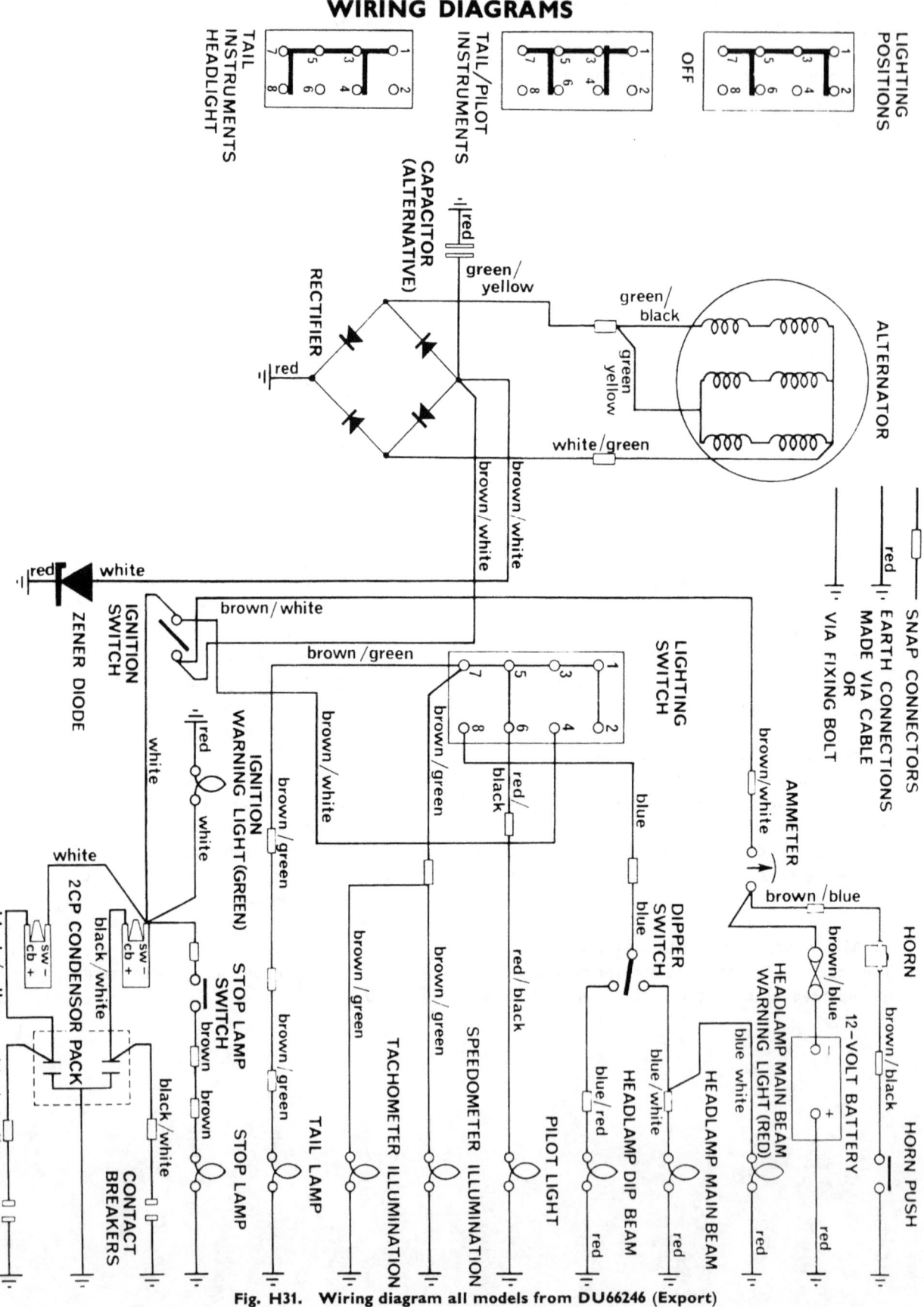

Fig. H31. Wiring diagram all models from DU66246 (Export)

ELECTRICAL SYSTEM

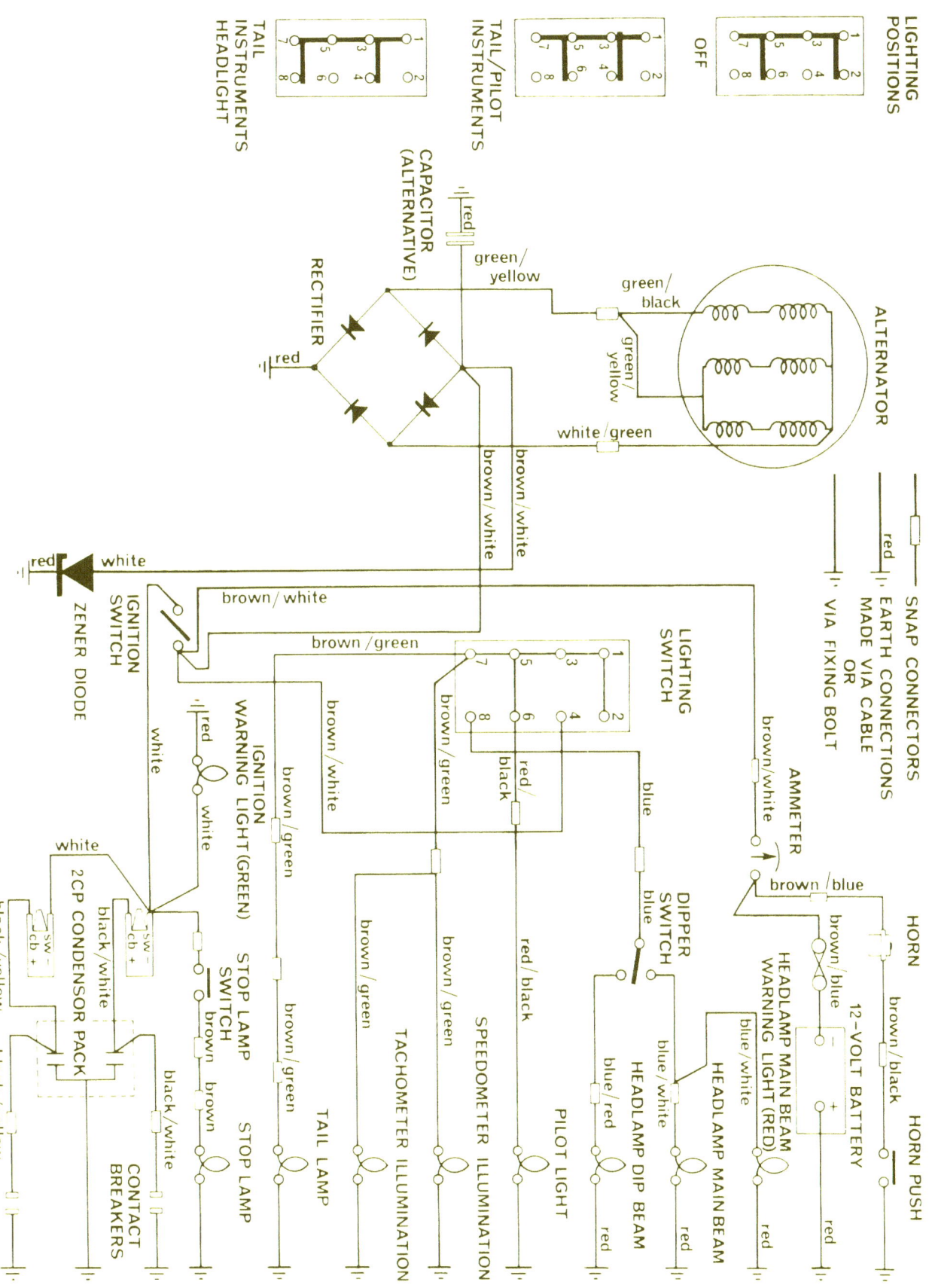

Fig. H32. Wiring diagram all models from DU66246 (Home)

ELECTRICAL SYSTEM

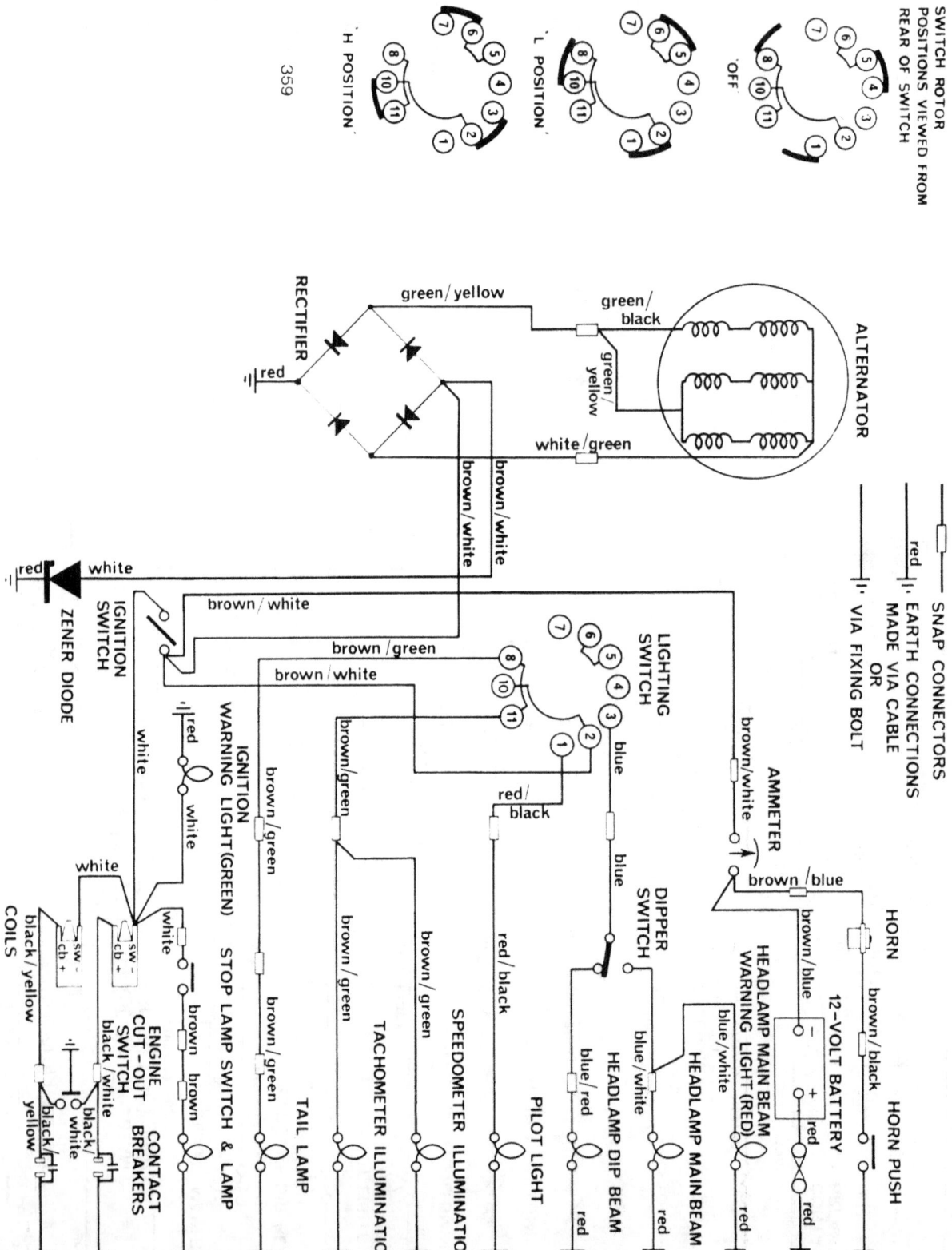

Fig. H33. Wiring diagram—Coil ignition 12 volt models with separate headlamp from engine number DU.24875(Home)

Note. The main beam warning lamp (where fitted) is connected to the headlamp main beam wire (blue/white) by a double snap connector. The ignition warning lamp is connected to an ignition coil by a white wire incorporated in the wiring harness.

ELECTRICAL SYSTEM H

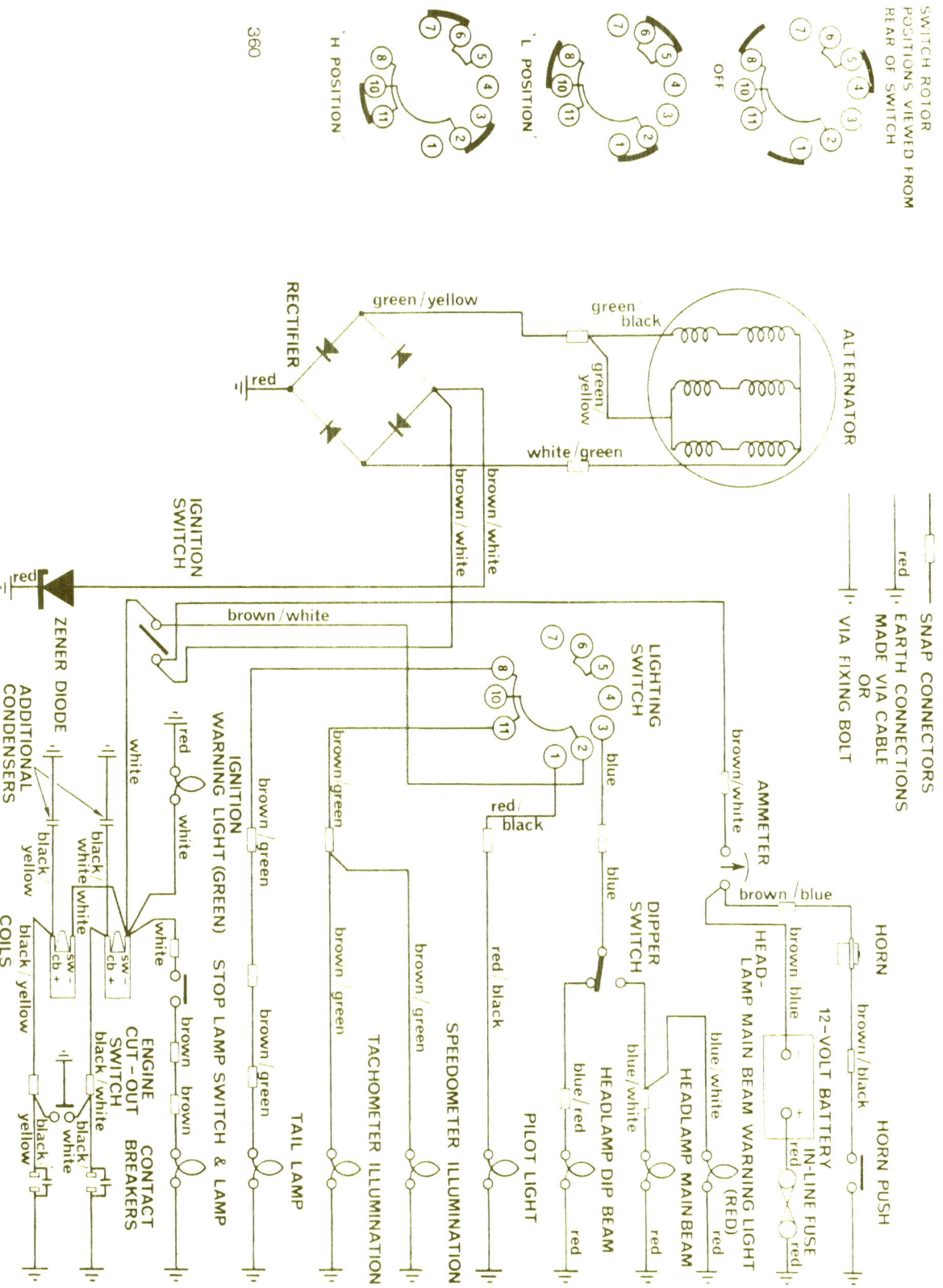

Fig. H34. Wiring diagram—Coil ignition 12 volt models with seperate headlamp engine no. DU44394-66245 (Export-USA)

ELECTRICAL SYSTEM

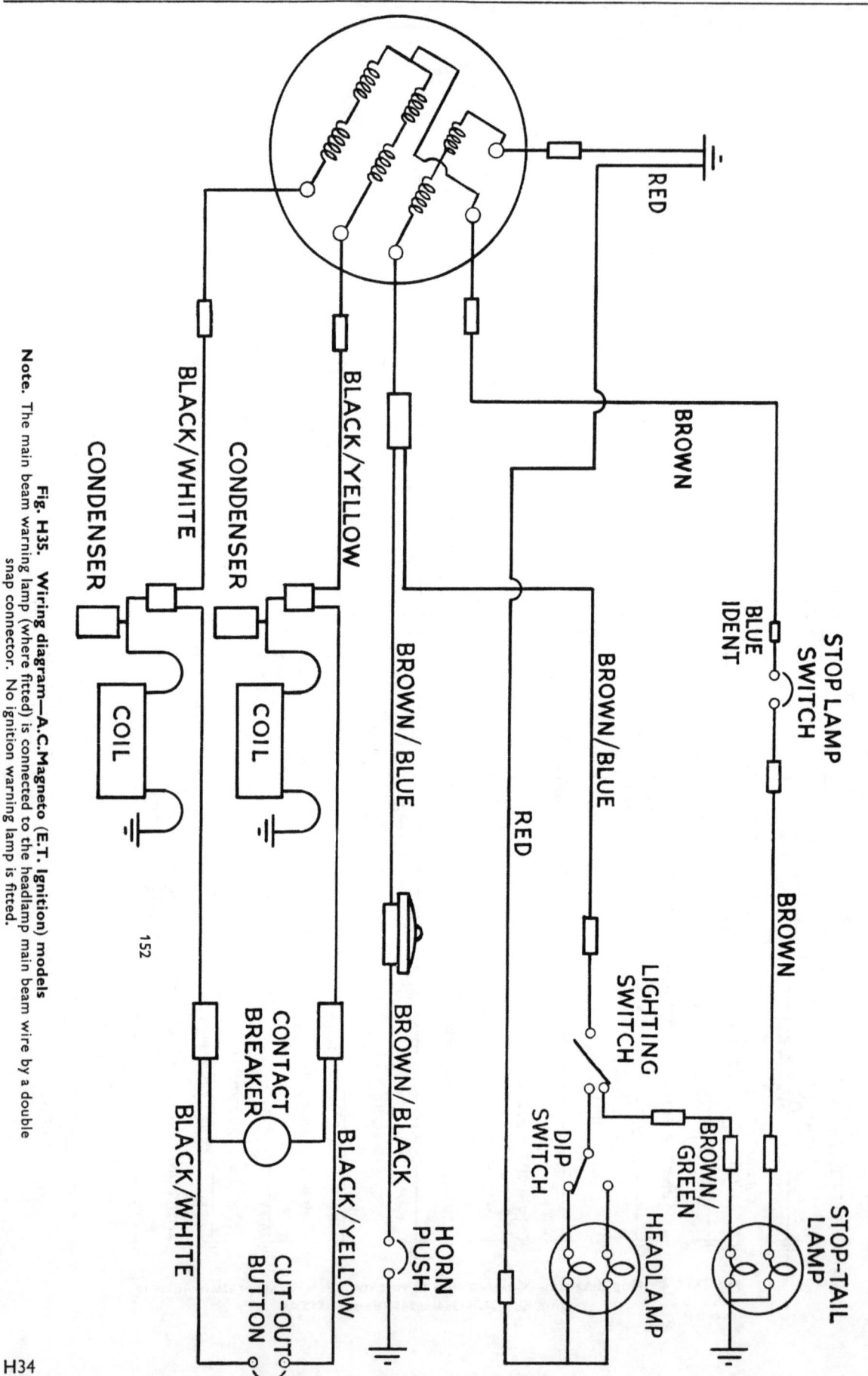

Fig. H35. Wiring diagram—A.C. Magneto (E.T. Ignition) models

Note. The main beam warning lamp (where fitted) is connected to the headlamp main beam wire by a double snap connector. No ignition warning lamp is fitted.

ELECTRICAL SYSTEM H

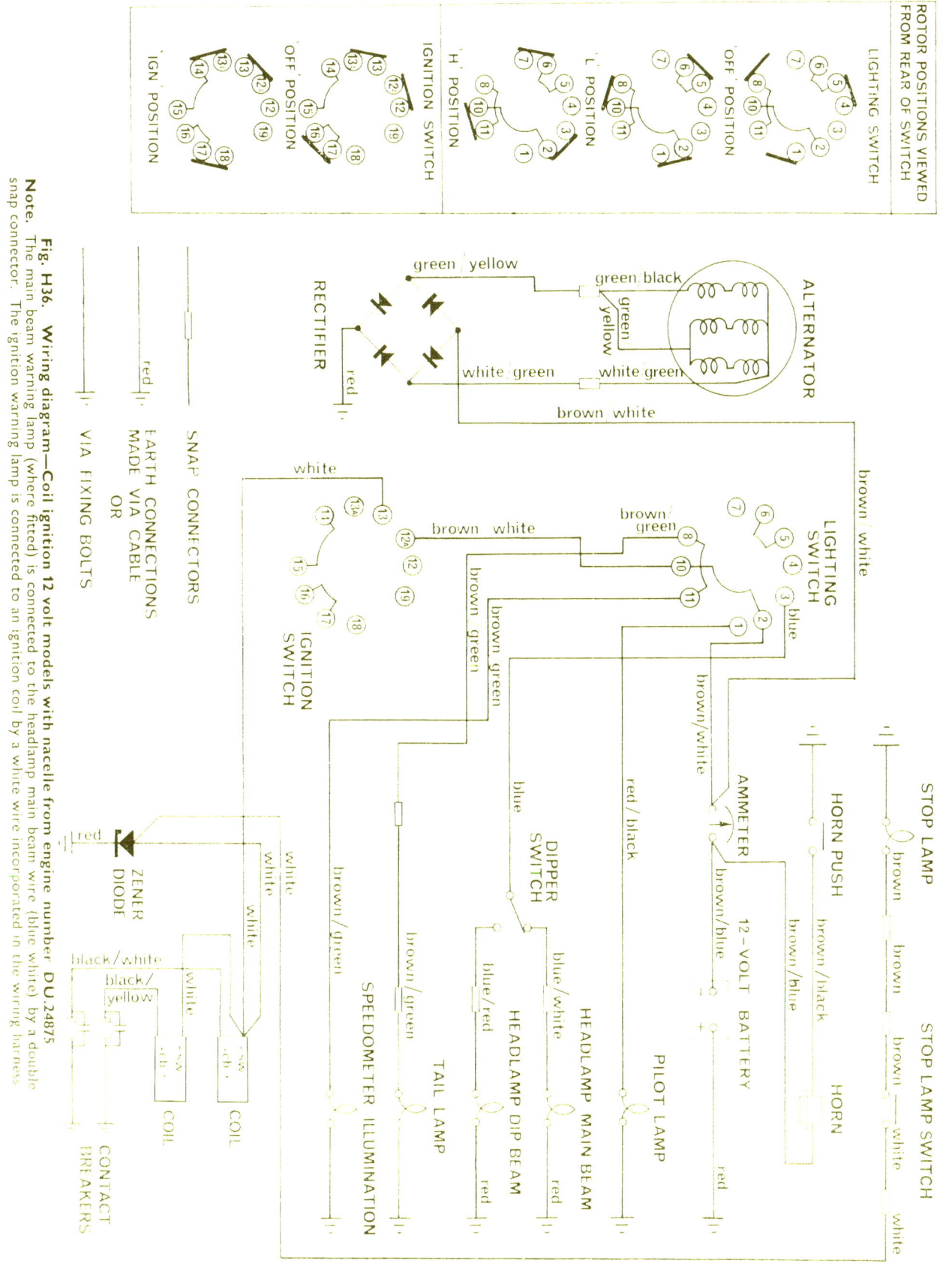

Fig. H36. Wiring diagram—Coil ignition 12 volt models with nacelle from engine number DU.24875

Note. The main beam warning lamp (where fitted) is connected to the headlamp main beam wire (blue white) by a double snap connector. The ignition warning lamp is connected to an ignition coil by a white wire incorporated in the wiring harness.

H35

H ELECTRICAL SYSTEM

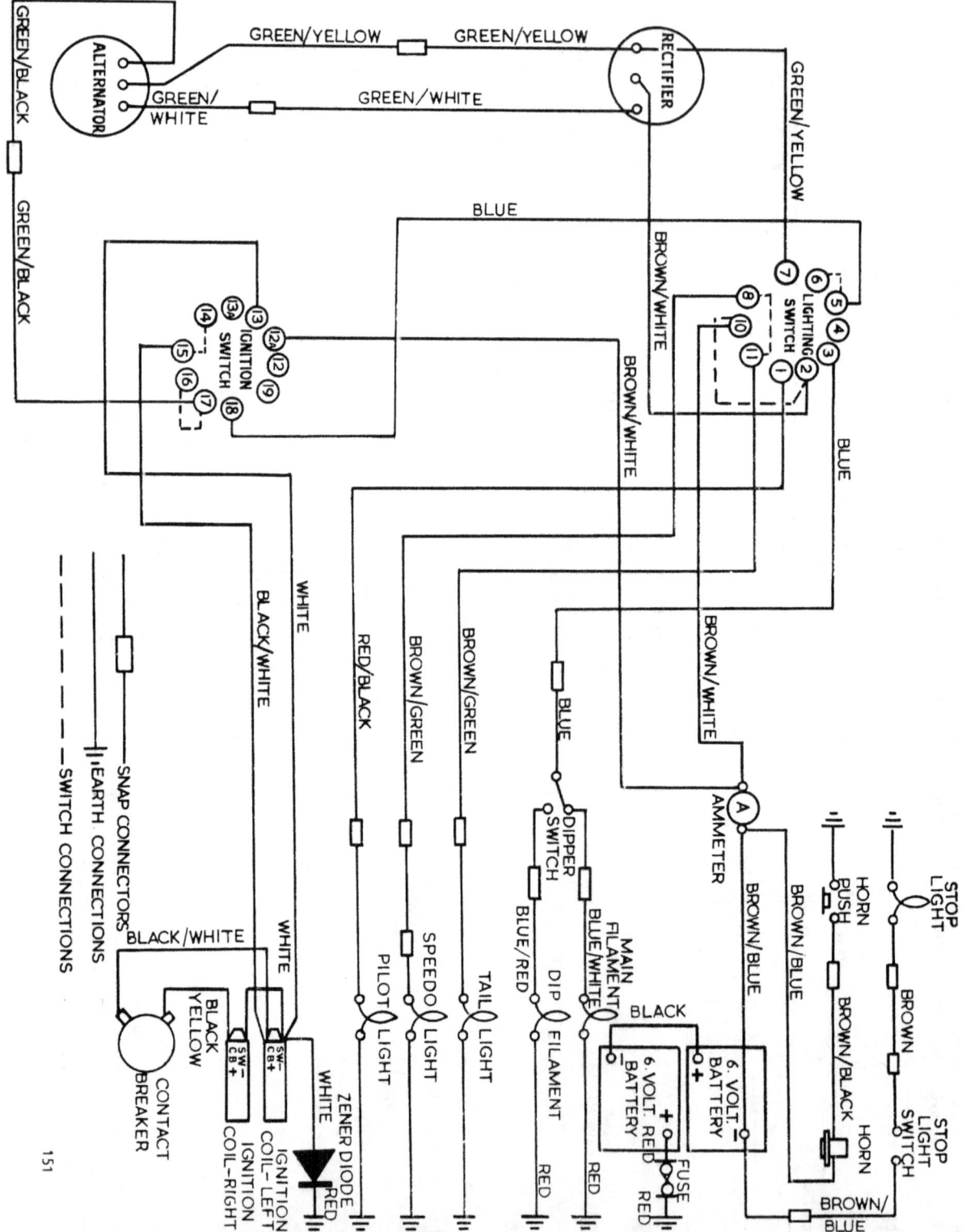

Fig. H37. Wiring diagram—Coil ignition 12V models with Zener Diode and 2 rate charge control Before engine number DU.24875

ELECTRICAL SYSTEM H

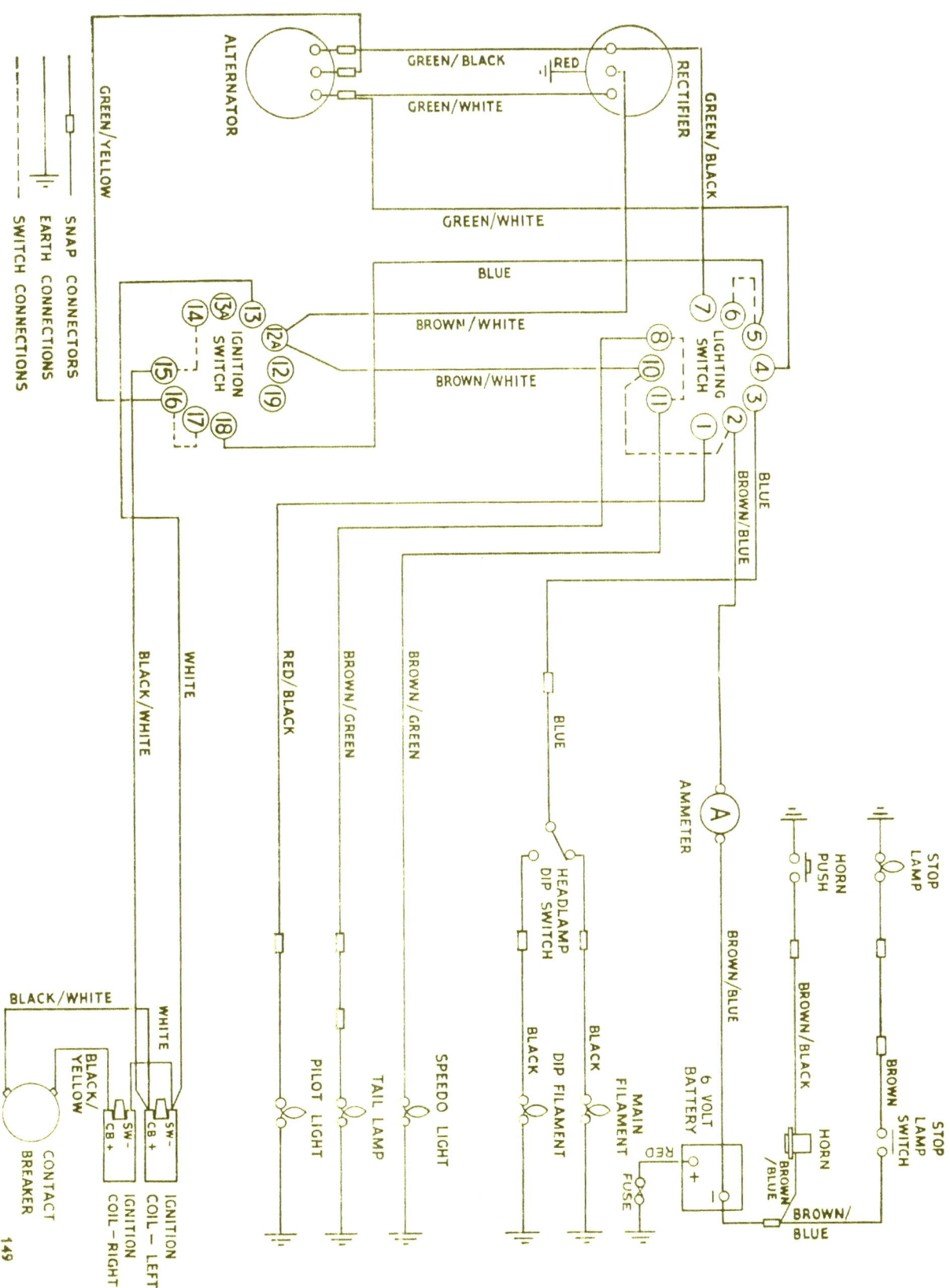

Fig. H38. Wiring diagram—Coil ignition 6V models

ELECTRICAL SYSTEM

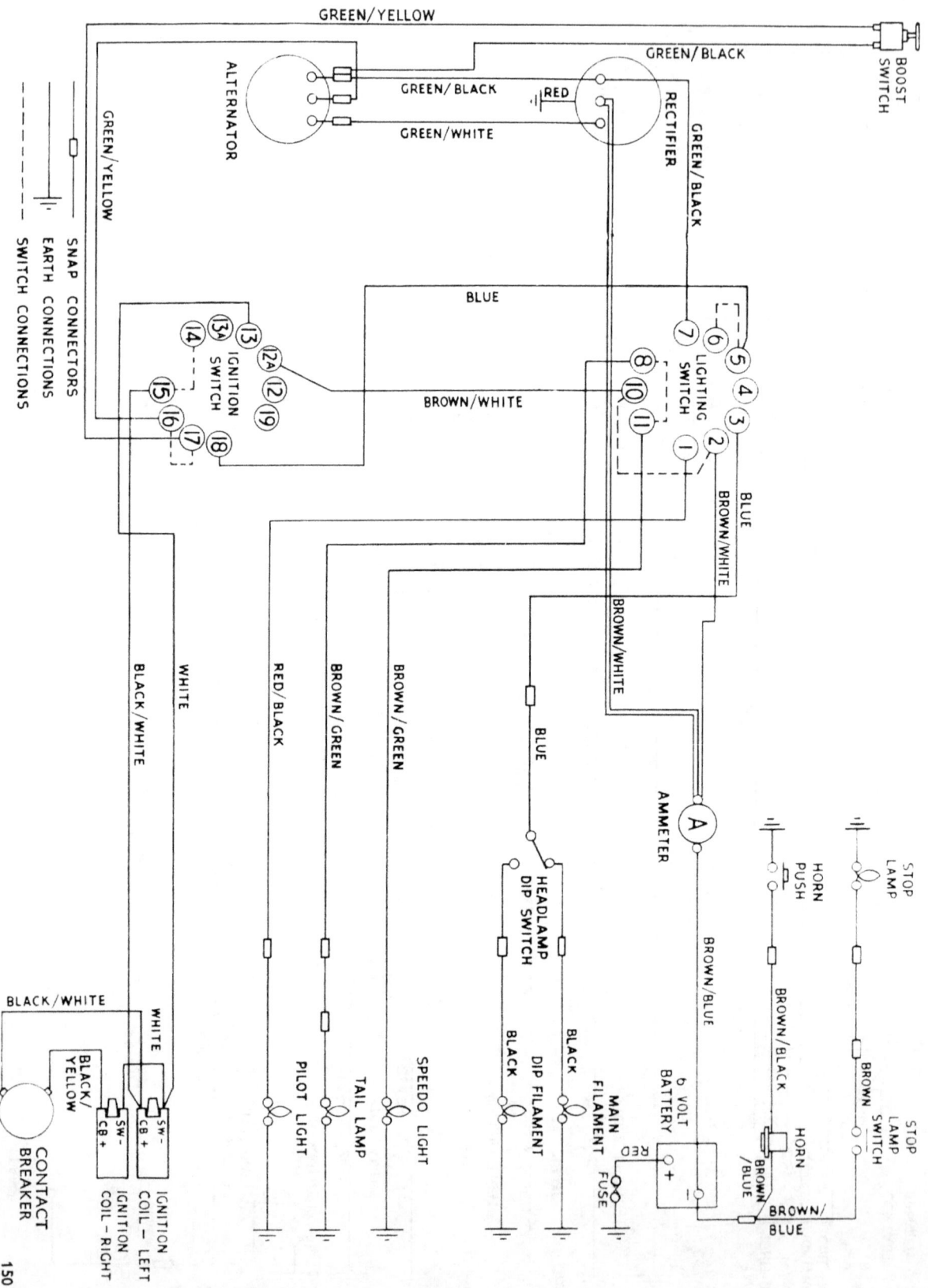

Fig. H39. Wiring diagram—Coil ignition 6V Police models with boost-switch

SECTION J

WORKSHOP SERVICE TOOLS

INTRODUCTION

This section of the Workshop Manual illustrates pictorially the workshop service tools that are available for carrying out the major dismantling and re-assembly operations on the UNIT CONSTRUCTION 650 c.c. Triumph Motorcycle.

The section is divided into sub-sections relating to the main section headings in this manual, illustrating those tools mentioned and used in the appropriate section text.

	Section
ENGINE… … … … … … … … … … … … … …	J1
TRANSMISSION … … … … … … … … … … … …	J2
GEARBOX … … … … … … … … … … … …	J3
WHEELS … … … … … … … … … … … …	J4
FRONT FORKS … … … … … … … … … … … …	J5

SECTION J1
ENGINE

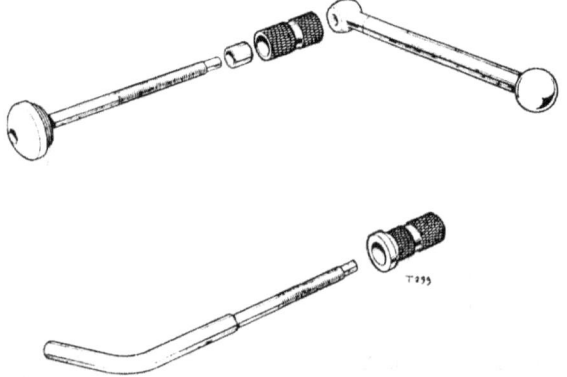

61-6063. Valve guide removal and replacement tool

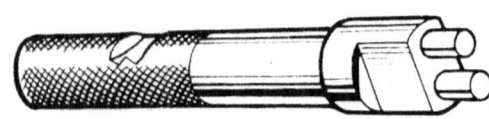

61-6008. Tappet guide block punch

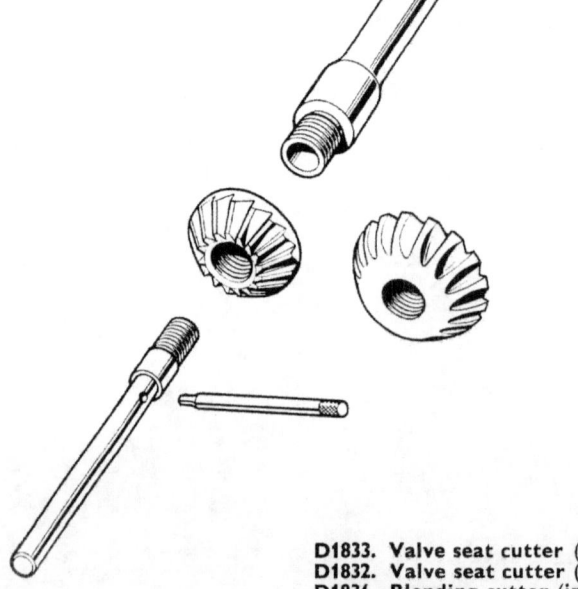

D1833. Valve seat cutter (inlet)
D1832. Valve seat cutter (exhaust)
D1836. Blending cutter (inlet)
D1835. Blending cutter (exhaust)
D1863. Arbor, pilot and tommy bars

SERVICE TOOLS   J

ENGINE (CONTINUED) J1

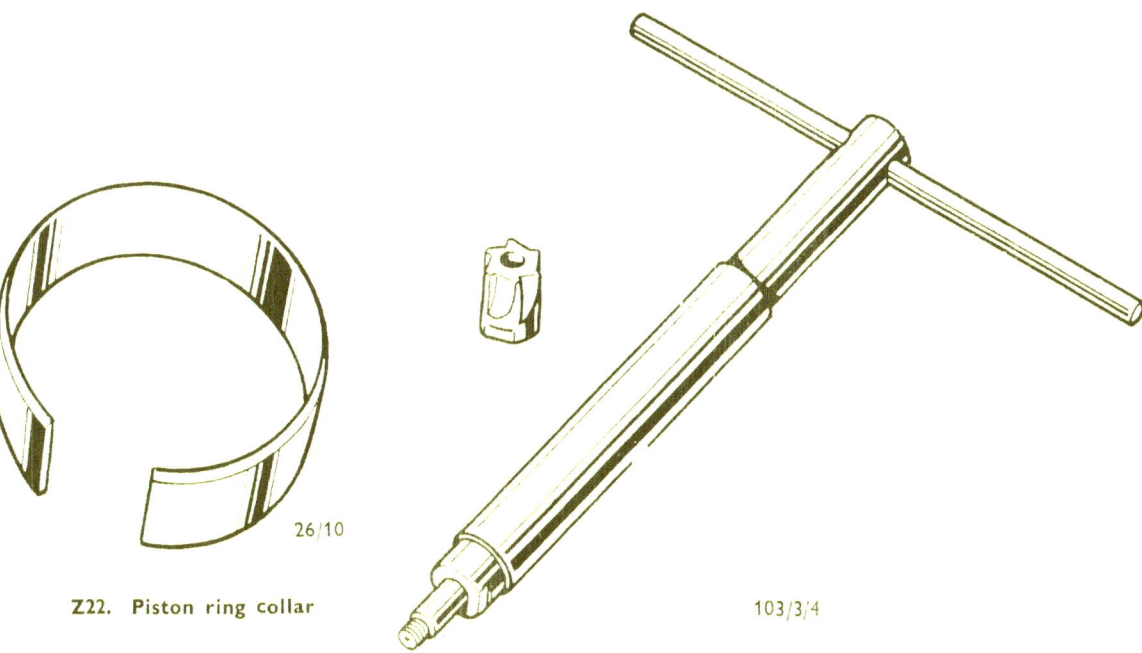

Z22. Piston ring collar

Z55. Left side reamer, camshaft bushes
Z56. Arbor for left side reamer, camshaft bushes

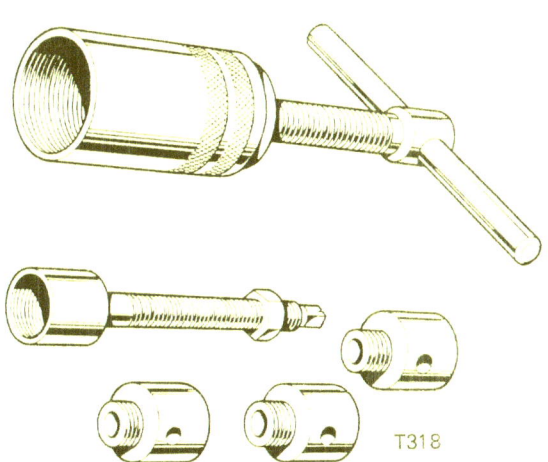

D2213. Camshaft pinion extractor and replacer with adaptors

D782. Contact breaker cam extractor

D486. Pilot for contact breaker oil seal when replacing timing cover

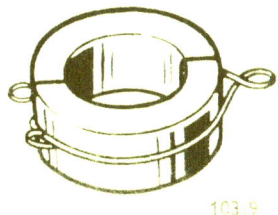

Z138. Crankshaft balance weight (689 gms.) with Z107 spring

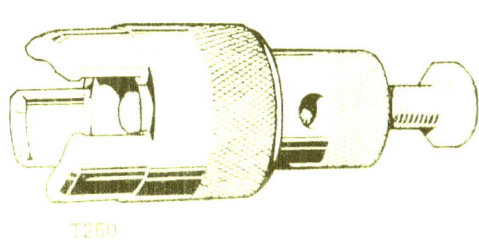

61-6019. Crankshaft pinion extractor

J3

SERVICE TOOLS

ENGINE (CONTINUED) J1

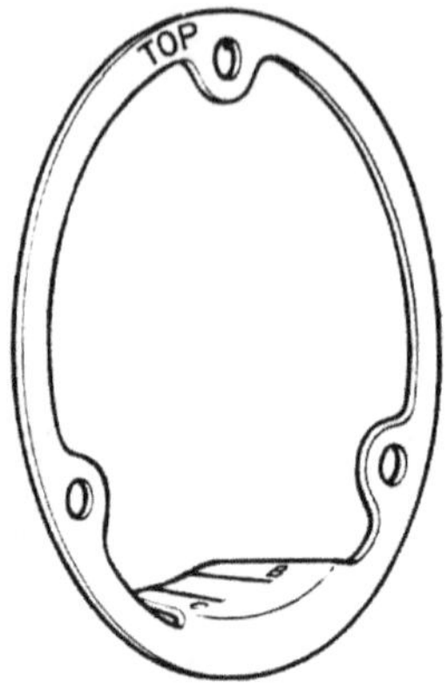

D2014. Stroboscope timing plate

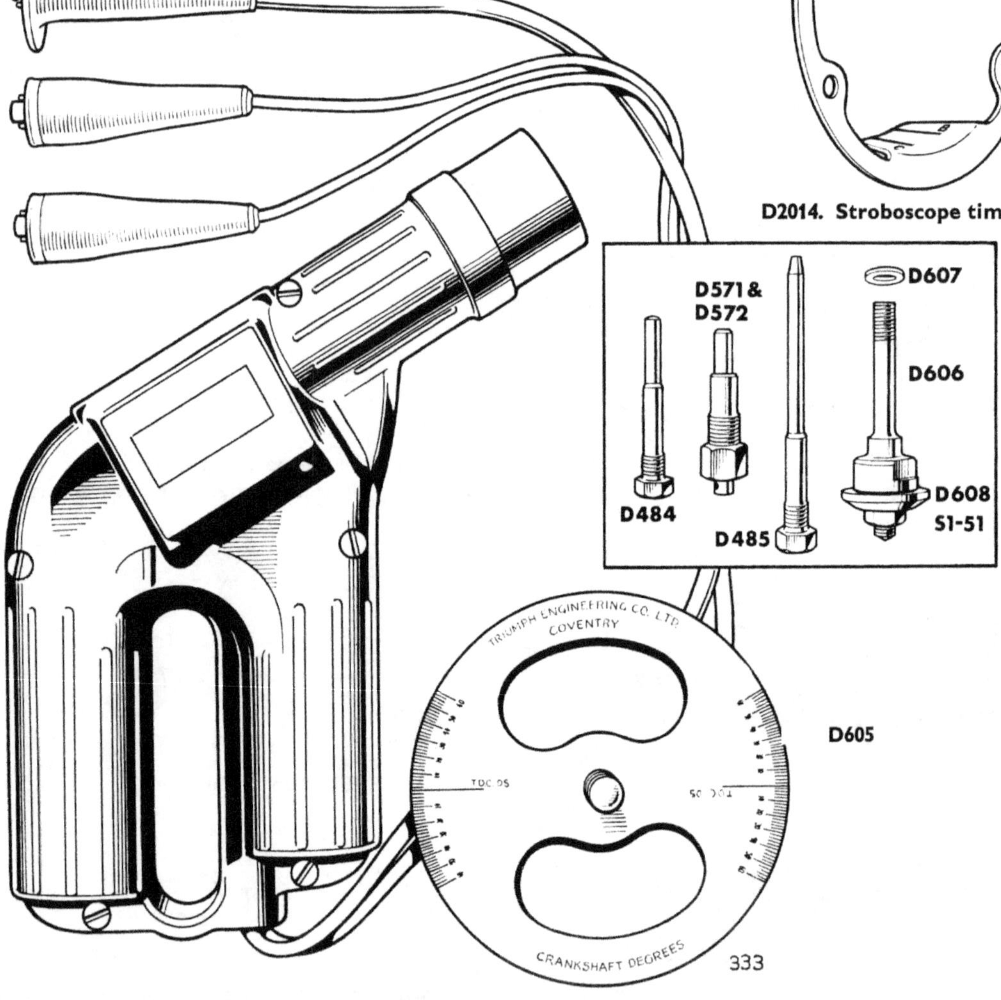

D571 & D572
D607
D484
D485
D606
D608 S1-51

CP207. Stroboscope timing kit

D605

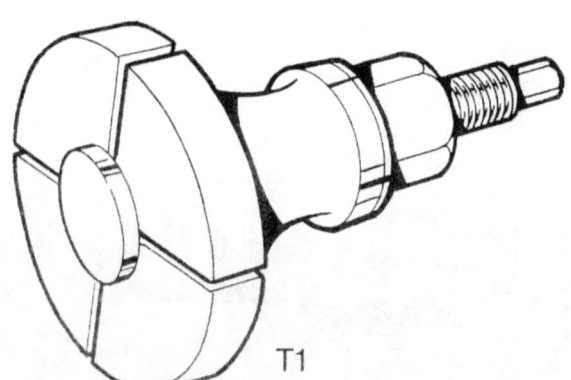

Z162. Roller bearing outer race removal tool

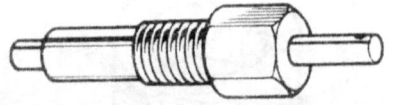

D1859. Flywheel locating body and plunger

SERVICE TOOLS J

ENGINE (CONTINUED) J1

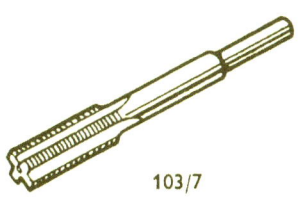

103/7

Z73. 14 mm. tap

D2221. Oil seal compressor for replacing the rocker spindle

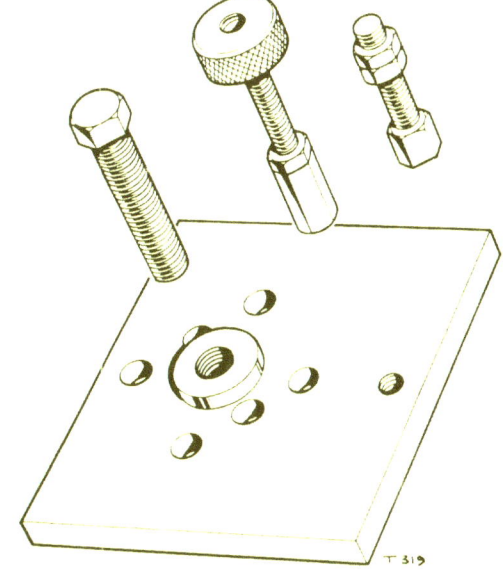

61-6014. Crankcase parting tool and sprocket extractor

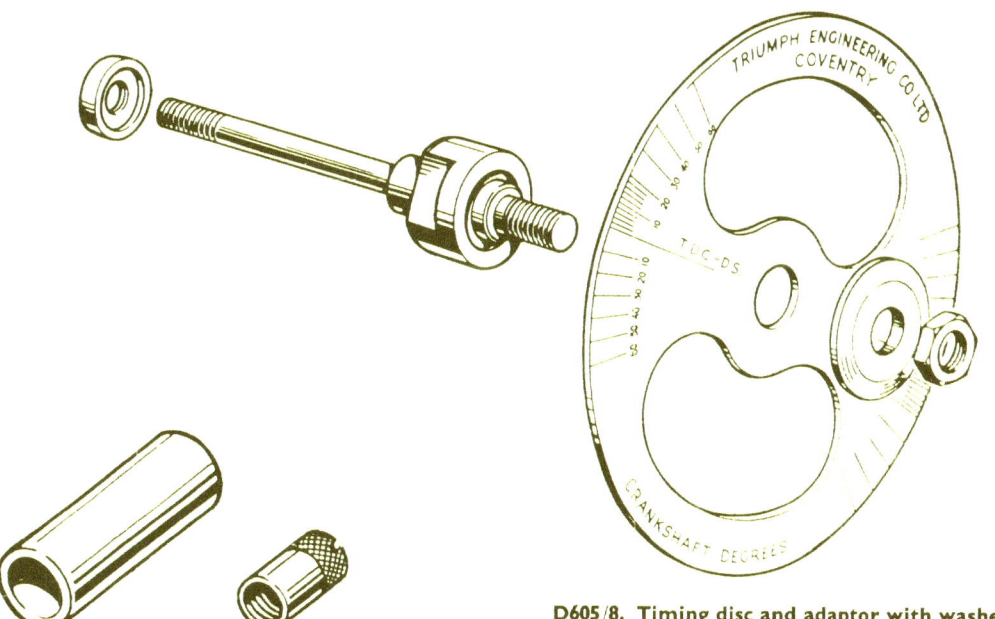

103/7

Z79. Crankshaft pinion punch and guide

D605/8. Timing disc and adaptor with washers
S1—51 Nut (see page J4 for separate Part Nos.)

J5

SECTION J2
TRANSMISSION

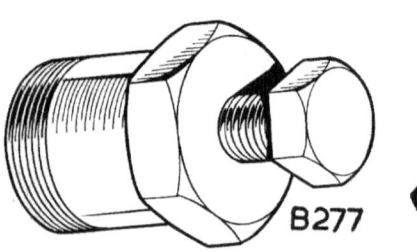
D1861. Clutch hub extractor

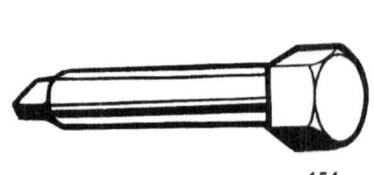
D496. Chain tensioner adjuster plug

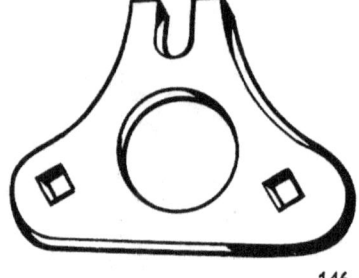
DA70. Clutch nut screwdriver

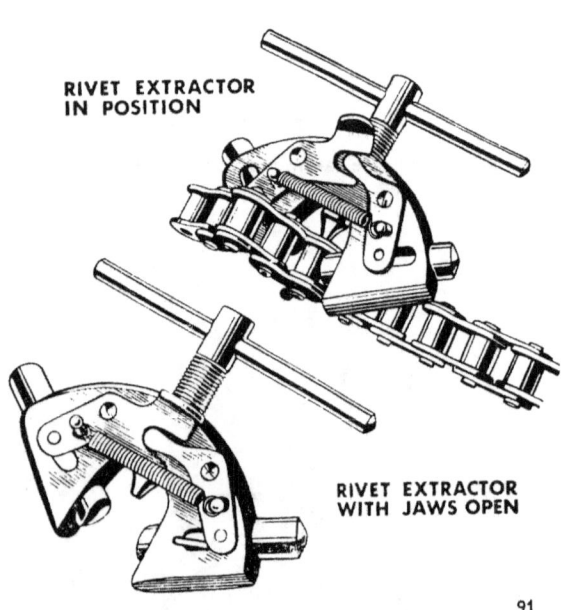
167. Rear chain rivet extractor

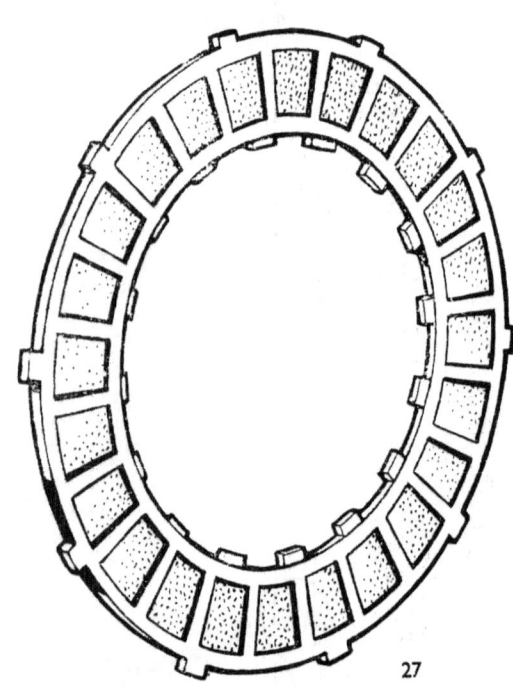
Z13. Clutch locking plate

SECTION J3
GEARBOX

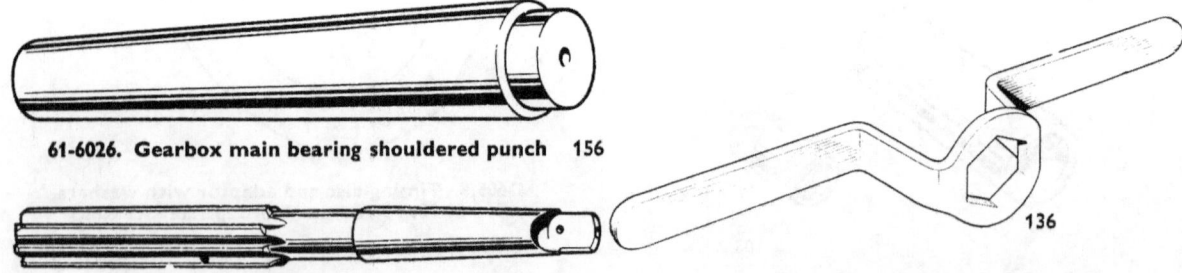

61-6026. Gearbox main bearing shouldered punch

61-6010. Reamer for gearbox high gear bush

Z63. Gearbox nut box spanner

SECTION J4
WHEELS

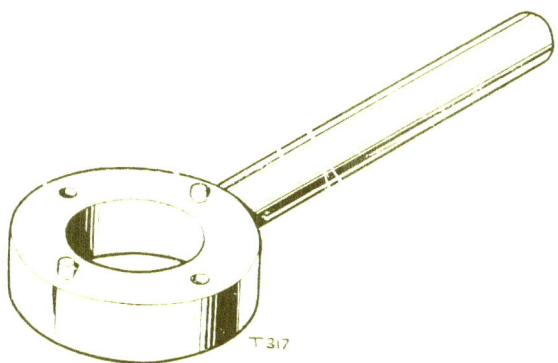

61-3694. Wheel bearing locking ring spanner

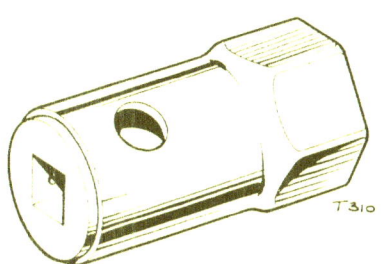

61-6062. Anchor plate nut box spanner for twin leading shoe brake

SECTION J5
FRONT FORKS

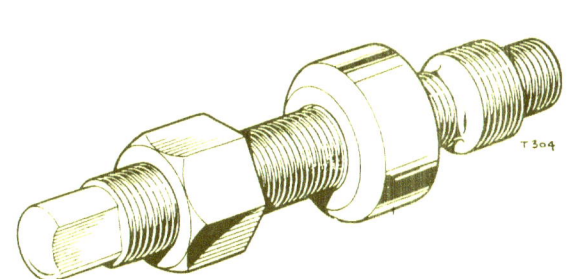

61-3824. Fork stanchion removal and refitting tool

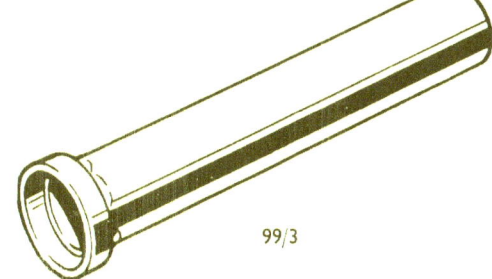

D2218. Drift for crown and stem bottom steering race

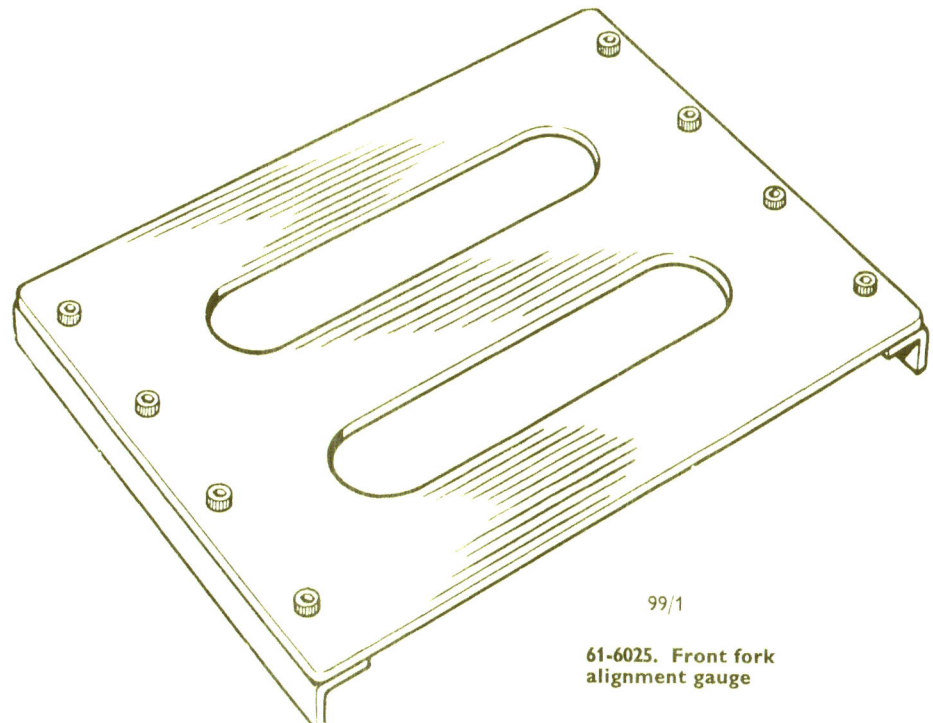

61-6025. Front fork alignment gauge

SERVICE TOOLS

FRONT FORK (CONTINUED) J5

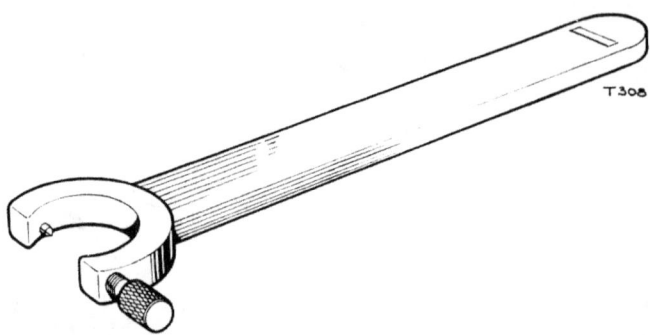

61-6017. Fork sleeve nut spanner

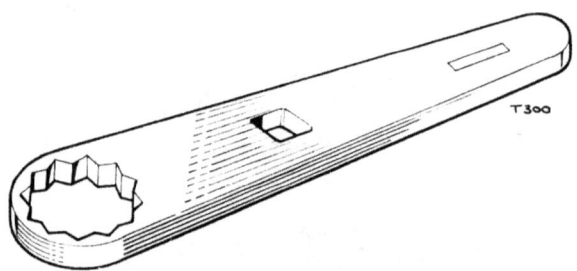

D779. Fork cap spanner

CONVERSION TABLES

INCHES TO MILLIMETRES—UNITS

Inches	0	10	20	30	40
0		254·0	508·0	762·0	1016·0
1	25·4	279·4	533·4	787·4	1041·4
2	50·8	304·8	558·8	812·8	1066·8
3	76·2	330·2	584·2	838·2	1092·2
4	101·6	355·6	609·6	863·6	1117·6
5	127·0	381·0	635·0	889·0	1143·0
6	152·4	406·4	660·4	914·4	1168·4
7	177·8	431·8	685·8	939·8	1193·8
8	203·2	457·2	711·2	965·2	1219·2
9	228·6	482·6	736·6	990·6	1244·6

One Inch—25·399978 millimetres

One Metre—39·370113 inches

One Mile—1·6093 kilos

One Kilo—·62138 miles

DECIMALS TO MILLIMETRES—FRACTIONS

1/1000	
inches	mm.
·001	·0254
·002	·0508
·003	·0762
·004	·1016
·005	·1270
·006	·1524
·007	·1778
·008	·2032
·009	·2286

1/100	
inches	mm.
·01	·254
·02	·508
·03	·726
·04	1·016
·05	1·270
·06	1·524
·07	1·778
·08	2·032
·09	2·286

1/10	
inches	mm.
·1	2·54
·2	5·08
·3	7·62
·4	10·16
·5	12·70
·6	15·24
·7	17·79
·8	20·32
·9	22·86

CONVERSION TABLES

FRACTIONS TO DECIMALS AND MILLIMETRES

Fractions			Decimals	mm.	Fractions			Decimals	mm.
		1/64	·015625	·3969			33/64	·515625	13·0969
	1/32		·03125	·7937		17/32		·53125	13·4937
		3/64	·046875	1·1906			35/64	·546675	13·8906
1/16			·0625	1·5875	9/16			·5625	14·2875
		5/64	·078125	1·9844			37/64	·578125	14·6844
	3/32		·09375	2·3812		19/32		·59375	15·0812
		7/64	·109375	2·7781			39/64	·609375	15·4781
1/8			·125	3·1750	5/8			·625	15·8750
		9/64	·140625	3·5719			41/64	·640625	16·2719
	5/32		·15625	3·9687		21/32		·65685	16·6687
		11/64	·171875	4·3656			43/64	·671875	17·0656
3/16			·1875	4·7625	11/16			·6875	17·4625
		13/64	·203125	5·1594			45/64	·703125	17·8594
	7/32		·21875	5·5562		23/32		·71875	18·2562
		15/64	·234375	5·9531			47/64	·734375	18·6531
1/4			·25	6·3500	3/4			·75	19·0500
		17/64	·265625	6·7469			49/64	·765625	19·4469
	9/32		·28125	7·1437		25/32		·78125	19·8437
		19/64	·296875	7·5406			51/64	·796875	20·2406
5/16			·3125	7·9375	13/16			·8125	20·6375
		21/64	·328125	8·3344			53/64	·828125	21·0344
	11/32		·34375	8·7312		27/32		·84375	21·4312
		23/64	·359375	9·1281			55/64	·859375	21·8281
3/8			·375	9·5250	7/8			·875	22·2250
		25/64	·390625	9·9219			57/64	·890625	22·6219
	13/32		·40625	10·3187		29/32		·90625	23·0187
		27/64	·421875	10·7156			59/64	·921875	23·4156
7/16			·4375	11·1125	15/16			·9375	23·8125
		29/64	·453125	11·5094			61/64	·953125	24·2094
	15/32		·46875	11·9062		31/32		·96875	24·6062
		31/64	·484375	12·3031			63/64	·984375	25·0031
1/2			·5	12·7000	1				25·4000

MILLIMETRES TO INCHES—UNITS

mm.	0	10	20	30	40
0		·39370	·78740	1·18110	1·57480
1	·03937	·43307	·82677	1·22047	1·61417
2	·07874	·47244	·86614	1·25984	1·65354
3	·11811	·51181	·90551	1·29921	1·69291
4	·15748	·55118	·94488	1·33858	1·73228
5	·19685	·59055	·98425	1·37795	1·77165
6	·23622	·62992	1·02362	1·41732	1·81103
7	·27559	·66929	1·06299	1·45669	1·85040
8	·31496	·70866	1·10236	1·49606	1·88977
9	·35433	·74803	1·14173	1·53543	1·92914

mm.	50	60	70	80	90
0	1·96851	2·36221	2·75591	3·14961	3·54331
1	2·00788	2·40158	2·79528	3·18891	3·58268
2	2·04725	2·44095	2·83465	3·22835	3·62205
3	2·08662	2·48032	2·87402	3·26772	3·66142
4	2·12599	2·51969	2·91339	3·30709	3·70079
5	2·16536	2·55906	2·95276	3·34646	3·74016
6	2·20473	2·59843	2·99213	3·38583	3·77953
7	2·24410	2·63780	3·03150	3·42520	3·81890
8	2·28347	2·67717	3·07087	3·46457	3·85827
9	2·32284	2·71654	3·11024	3·50394	3·89764

MILLIMETRES TO INCHES—FRACTIONS

1/1000	
mm.	inches
0·001	·000039
0·002	·000079
0·003	·000118
0·004	·000157
0·005	·000197
0·006	·000236
0·007	·000276
0·008	·000315
0·009	·000354

1/100	
mm.	inches
0·01	·00039
0·02	·00079
0·03	·00118
0·04	·00157
0·05	·00197
0·06	·00236
0·07	·00276
0·08	·00315
0·09	·00354

1/10	
mm.	inches
0·1	·00394
0·2	·00787
0·3	·01181
0·4	·01575
0·5	·01969
0·6	·02362
0·7	·02756
0·8	·03150
0·9	·03543

CONVERSION TABLES

DRILL SIZES

Letter	Size	Letter	Size
A	·234	N	·302
B	·238	O	·316
C	·242	P	·323
D	·246	Q	·332
E	·250	R	·339
F	·257	S	·348
G	·261	T	·358
H	·266	U	·368
I	·272	V	·377
J	·277	W	·386
K	·281	X	·397
L	·290	Y	·404
M	·295	Z	·413

Number	Size	Number	Size	Number	Size	Number	Size
1	·2280	14	·1820	27	·1440	40	·0980
2	·2210	15	·1800	28	·1405	41	·0960
3	·2130	16	·1770	29	·1360	42	·0935
4	·2090	17	·1730	30	·1285	43	·0890
5	·2055	18	·1695	31	·1200	44	·0860
6	·2040	19	·1660	32	·1160	45	·0820
7	·2010	20	·1610	33	·1130	46	·0810
8	·1990	21	·1590	34	·1110	47	·0785
9	·1960	22	·1570	35	·1100	48	·0760
10	·1935	23	·1540	36	·1065	49	·0730
11	·1910	24	·1520	37	·1040	50	·0700
12	·1890	25	·1495	38	·1015	51	·0670
13	·1850	26	·1470	39	·0995	52	·0635

WIRE GAUGES

No. of Gauge	Imperial Standard Wire Gauge		Brown and Sharpe's American Wire Gauge	
	Inches	Millimetres	Inches	Millimetres
0000	·400	10·160	·460	11·684
000	·372	9·448	·410	10·404
00	·348	8·839	·365	9·265
0	·324	8·299	·325	8·251
1	·300	7·620	·289	7·348
2	·276	7·010	·258	6·543
3	·252	6·400	·229	5·827
4	·232	5·892	·204	5·189
5	·212	5·384	·182	4·621
6	·192	4·676	·162	4·115
7	·176	4·470	·144	3·664
8	·160	4·064	·128	3·263
9	·144	3·657	·114	2·906
10	·128	3·251	·102	2·588
11	·116	2·946	·091	2·304
12	·104	2·641	·081	2·052
13	·092	2·336	·072	1·827
14	·080	2·032	·064	1·627
15	·072	1·828	·057	1·449
16	·064	1·625	·051	1·290
17	·056	1·422	·045	1·149
18	·048	1·219	·040	1·009
19	·040	1·016	·035	·911
20	·036	·914	·032	·811
21	·032	·812	·028	·722
22	·028	·711	·025	·643
23	·024	·609	·023	·573
24	·022	·558	·020	·511
25	·020	·508	·018	·454
26	·018	·457	·016	·404
27	·0164	·416	·014	·360
28	·0148	·375	·012	·321
29	·0136	·345	·011	·285
30	·0124	·314	·010	·254

FOOT POUNDS TO KILOGRAMETRES

	0	1	2	3	4	5	6	7	8	9	
—		0·138	0·227	0·415	0·553	0·691	0·830	0·968	1·106	1·244	—
10	1·383	1·521	1·659	1·797	1·936	2·074	2·212	2·350	2·489	2·627	10
20	2·765	2·903	3·042	3·180	3·318	3·456	3·595	3·733	3·871	4·009	20
30	4·148	4·286	4·424	4·562	4·701	4·839	4·977	5·116	5·254	5·392	30
40	5·530	5·668	5·807	5·945	6·083	6·221	6·360	6·498	6·636	6·774	40
50	6·913	7·051	7·189	7·328	7·466	7·604	7·742	7·881	8·019	8·157	50
60	8·295	8·434	3·572	8·710	8·848	8·987	9·125	9·263	9·401	9·540	60
70	9·678	9·816	9·954	10·093	10·231	10·369	10·507	10·646	10·784	10·922	70
80	11·060	11·199	11·337	11·475	11·613	11·752	11·890	12·028	12·166	12·305	80
90	12·443	12·581	12·719	12·858	12·996	13·134	13·272	13·411	13·549	13·687	90

MILES TO KILOMETRES

	0	1	2	3	4	5	6	7	8	9	
—		1·609	3·219	4·828	6·437	8·047	9·656	11·265	12·875	14·484	—
10	16·093	17·703	19·312	20·922	22·531	24·140	25·750	27·359	28·968	30·578	10
20	32·187	33·796	35·406	37·015	38·624	40·234	41·843	43·452	45·062	46·671	20
30	48·280	49·890	51·499	53·108	54·718	56·327	57·936	59·546	61·155	62·765	30
40	64·374	65·983	67·593	69·202	70·811	72·421	74·030	75·639	77·249	78·858	40
50	80·467	82·077	83·686	85·295	86·905	88·514	90·123	91·733	93·342	94·951	50
60	96·561	98·170	99·780	101·389	102·998	104·608	106·217	107·826	109·436	111·045	60
70	112·654	114·264	115·873	117·482	119·092	120·701	122·310	123·920	125·529	127·138	70
80	128·748	130·357	131·967	133·576	135·185	136·795	138·404	140·013	141·623	143·232	80
90	144·841	146·451	148·060	149·669	151·279	152·888	154·497	156·107	157·716	159·325	90

POUNDS TO KILOGRAMS

	0	1	2	3	4	5	6	7	8	9	
—		0·454	0·907	1·361	1·814	2·268	2·722	3·175	3·629	4·082	—
10	4·536	4·990	5·443	5·987	6·350	6·804	7·257	7·711	8·165	8·618	10
20	9·072	9·525	9·079	10·433	10·886	11·340	11·793	12·247	12·701	13·154	20
30	13·608	14·061	14·515	14·968	15·422	15·876	16·329	16·783	17·237	17·690	30
40	18·144	18·597	19·051	19·504	19·953	20·412	20·865	21·319	21·772	22·226	40
50	22·680	23·133	23·587	24·040	24·494	24·948	25·401	25·855	26·308	26·762	50
60	27·216	27·669	28·123	28·576	29·030	29·484	29·937	30·391	30·844	31·298	60
70	31·751	32·205	32·659	33·112	33·566	34·019	34·473	34·927	35·380	35·834	70
80	36·287	36·741	37·195	37·648	38·102	38·855	39·009	39·463	39·916	40·370	80
90	40·823	41·277	41·731	42·184	42·638	43·091	43·545	43·998	44·452	44·906	90

MILES PER GALLON (IMPERIAL) TO LITRES PER 100 KILOMETRES

10	28·25	15	18·83	20	14·12	25	11·30	30	9·42	35	8·07	40	7·06	50	5·65	60	4·71	70	4·04
10½	26·90	15½	18·22	20½	13·78	25½	11·08	30½	9·26	35½	7·96	41	6·89	51	5·54	61	4·63	71	3·98
11	25·68	16	17·66	21	13·45	26	10·87	31	9·11	36	7·85	42	6·73	52	5·43	62	4·55	72	3·92
11½	24·56	16½	17·12	21½	13·14	26½	10·66	31½	8·97	36½	7·74	43	6·57	53	5·33	63	4·48	73	3·87
12	23·54	17	16·61	22	12·84	27	10·46	32	8·83	37	7·63	44	6·42	54	5·23	64	4·41	74	3·82
12½	22·60	17½	16·14	22½	12·55	27½	10·27	32½	8·69	37½	7·53	45	6·28	55	5·13	65	4·35	75	3·77
13	21·73	18	15·69	23	12·28	28	10·09	33	8·56	38	7·43	46	6·14	56	5·04	66	4·28	76	3·72
13½	20·92	18½	15·27	23½	12·02	28½	9·91	33½	8·43	38½	7·34	47	6·01	57	4·96	67	4·22	77	3·67
14	20·18	19	14·87	24	11·77	29	9·74	34	8·31	39	7·24	48	5·89	58	4·87	68	4·16	78	3·62
14½	19·48	19½	14·49	24½	11·53	29½	9·58	34½	8·19	39½	7·15	49	5·77	59	4·79	69	4·10	79	3·57

CONVERSION TABLES

PINTS TO LITRES

	0	1	2	3	4	5	6	7	8
	—	·568	1·136	1·705	2·273	2·841	3·841	3·978	4·546
1/4	·142	·710	1·279	1·846	2·415	2·983	3·552	4·120	4·688
1/2	·284	·852	1·420	1·989	2·557	3·125	3·125	4·262	4·830
3/4	·426	·994	1·563	2·131	2·699	3·267	3·836	4·404	4·972

GALLONS (IMPERIAL) TO LITRES

	0	1	2	3	4	5	6	7	8	9	
—		4·546	9·092	13·638	18·184	22·730	27·276	31·822	36·368	40·914	—
10	45·460	50·005	54·551	59·097	63·643	63·189	72·735	77·281	81·827	86·373	10
20	90·919	95·465	100·011	104·557	109·103	113·649	118·195	122·741	127·287	131·833	20
30	136·379	140·924	145·470	150·016	154·562	159·108	163·645	168·200	172·746	177·292	30
40	181·838	186·384	190·930	195·476	200·022	204·568	209·114	213·660	218·206	222·752	40
50	227·298	231·843	236·389	240·935	245·481	250·027	254·473	259·119	263·605	268·211	50
60	272·757	277·303	281·849	286·395	290·941	295·487	300·033	304·579	309·125	313·671	60
70	318·217	322·762	327·308	331·854	336·400	340·946	245·492	350·038	354·584	359·130	70
80	363·676	368·222	372·768	377·314	381·860	386·406	390·952	395·498	400·044	404·590	80
90	409·136	413·681	418·227	422·773	427·319	431·865	436·411	440·957	445·503	450·049	90

POUNDS PER SQUARE INCH TO KILOGRAMS PER SQUARE CENTIMETRE

	0	1	2	3	4	5	6	7	8	9	
—		0·070	0·141	0·211	0·281	0·352	0·422	0·492	0·562	0·633	—
10	0·703	0·773	0·844	0·914	0·984	1·055	1·125	1·195	1·266	1·336	10
20	1·406	1·476	1·547	1·617	1·687	1·758	1·828	1·898	1·969	2·039	20
30	2·109	2·179	2·250	2·320	2·390	2·461	2·531	2·601	2·672	2·742	30
40	2·812	2·883	2·953	3·023	3·093	3·164	3·234	3·304	3·375	3·445	40
50	3·515	3·586	3·656	3·726	3·797	3·867	3·937	4·007	4·078	4·148	50
60	4·218	4·289	4·359	4·429	4·500	4·570	4·640	4·711	4·781	4·851	60
70	4·921	4·992	5·062	5·132	5·203	5·273	5·343	5·414	5·484	5·554	70
80	5·624	5·695	5·765	5·835	5·906	5·976	6·046	6·117	6·187	6·257	80
90	6·328	6·398	6·468	6·538	6·609	6·679	6·749	6·820	6·890	6·960	90

U.N.E.F. SCREW THREADS

Dia.	No. of thds.	Core dia.	Tap drill	Dia.	No. of thds.	Core dia.	Tap drill
1/4 in.	32	·2162 in.	5·60 mm.	1 in.	20	·9459 in.	61/64 in.
5/16 in.	32	·2787 in.	7·20 mm.	1-1/16 in.	18	1·0024 in.	1·010 in.
3/8 in.	32	·3412 in.	11/32 ins	1-1/8 in.	18	1·0649 in.	1·072 ins.
7/16 in.	28	·3988 in.	10·20 mm.	1-3/16 in.	18	1·1274 in.	1·135 in.
1/2 in.	28	·4613 in.	11·80 mm.	1-1/4 in.	18	1·1899 in.	1·196 in.
9/16 in.	24	·5174 in.	13·30 mm.	1-5/16 in.	18	1·2524 in.	32·00 mm.
5/8 in.	24	·5799 in.	14·75 mm.	1-3/8 in.	18	1·3149 in.	33·50 mm.
11/16 in.	24	·6424 in.	·6480 in.	1-7/16 in.	18	1·3774 in.	1·385 ins.
3/4 in.	20	·6959 in.	45/64 in.	1-1/2 in.	18	1·4399 in.	1·447 in.
13/16 in.	20	·7584 in.	49/64 in.	1-9/16 in.	18	1·4948 in.	1-1/2 in.
7/8 in.	20	·8209 in.	53/64 in.	1-5/8 in.	18	1·5649 in.	1·572 in.
15/16 in.	20	·8834 in.	57/64 in.	1-11/16 in.	18	1·6274 in.	41·50 mm.

B.A. SCREW THREADS

No.	Dia. of bolt	Thds. per inch	Dia. tap drill	Core dia.
0	·2362	25·4	·1960	·1890
1	·2087	28·2	·1770	·1661
2	·1850	31·4	·1520	·1468
3	·1614	34·8	·1360	·1269
4	·1417	38·5	·1160	·1106
5	·1260	43·0	·1040	·0981
6	·1102	47·9	·0935	·0852
7	·0984	52·9	·0810	·0738
8	·0866	59·1	·0730	·0663
9	·0748	65·1	·0635	·0564
10	·0669	72·6	·0550	·0504
11	·0591	81·9	·0465	·0445
12	·0511	90·9	·0400	·0378
13	·0472	102·0	·0360	·0352
14	·0394	109·9	·0292	·0280
15	·0354	120·5	·0260	·0250
16	·0311	133·3	·0225	·0220

B.S.W. SCREW THREADS

Dia. of bolt (inch)	Threads per inch	Dia. tap drill (inch)	Core dia.
1/4	20	·1968	·1860
5/16	18	1/4	·2412
3/8	16	5/16	·2950
7/16	14	23/64	·3460
1/2	12	13/32	·3933
9/16	12	15/32	·4558
5/8	11	17/32	·5086
11/16	11	37/64	·5711
3/4	10	41/64	·6219
13/16	10	45/64	·6844
7/8	9	3/4	·7327
15/16	9	13/16	·7952
1	8	55/64	·8399

B.S.F. SCREW THREADS

Dia. of bolt (inch)	Threads per inch	Dia. tap drill (inch)	Core dia.
7/32	28	·1770	·1731
1/4	26	·2055	·2007
9/32	26	·238	·2320
5/16	22	·261	·2543
3/8	20	·316	·3110
7/16	13	3/8	·3664
1/2	16	27/64	·4200
9/16	16	·492	·4825
5/8	14	35/64	·5335
11/16	14	39/64	·5960
3/4	12	21/32	·6433
13/16	12	23/32	·7058
7/8	11	25/32	·7586
1	10	57/64	·8719
1-1/8	9	1	·9827
1-1/4	9	1-1/8	1·1077
1-3/8	8	1-15/64	1·2149
1-1/2	8	1·358	1·3399
1-5/8	8	1-31/64	1·4649

U.N.C. SCREW THREADS

Dia.	No. of thds.	Core dia.	Tap drill
1/4 in.	20	·1959 in.	5·20 mm.
5/16 in.	18	·2524 in.	6·60 mm.
3/8 in.	16	·3073 in.	8·00 mm.
7/16 in.	14	·3602 in.	9·40 mm.
1/2 in.	13	·4167 in.	10·80 mm.
9/16 in.	12	·4723 in.	12·20 mm.
5/8 in.	11	·5266 in.	13·50 mm.
3/4 in.	10	·6417 in.	16·50 mm.
7/8 in.	9	·7547 in.	49/64 in.
1 in.	8	·8647 in.	22·25 mm.
1-1/8 in.	7	·9704 in.	63/64 in.
1-1/4 in.	7	1·0954 in.	1-7/64 in.
1-3/8 in.	6	1·1946 in.	1-13/64 in.
1-1/2 in.	6	1·3196 in.	1-21/64 in.
1-3/4 in.	5	1·5335 in.	1-35/64 in.
2 in.	4-1/2	1·7594 in.	1-25/32 in.

U.N.F. SCREW THREADS

Dia.	No. of thds.	Core dia.	Tap drill
1/4 in.	28	·2113 in.	5·50 mm.
5/16 in.	24	·2674 in.	6·90 mm.
3/8 in.	24	·3299 in.	8·50 mm.
7/16 in.	20	·3834 in.	9·90 mm.
1/2 in.	20	·4459 in.	11·50 mm.
9/16 in.	18	·5024 in.	12·90 mm.
5/8 in.	18	·5649 in.	14·50 mm.
3/4 in.	16	·6823 in.	11/16 in.
7/8 in.	14	·7977 in.	0·804 in.
1 in.	12	·9098 in.	23·25 mm.
1-1/8 in.	12	1·0348 in.	26·50 mm.
1-1/4 in.	12	1·1598 in.	29·50 mm.
1-3/8 in.	12	1·2848 in.	1·290 in.
1-1/2 in.	12	1·4098 in.	36·00 mm.

VELOCEPRESS MANUALS – MOTORCYCLE BY MAKE

AJS 1932-1948 SINGLES & TWINS 250cc THRU 1000cc (BOOK OF)
AJS 1945-1960 SINGLES 350cc & 500cc MODELS 16 & 18 (BOOK OF)
AJS 1955-1965 SINGLES 350cc & 500cc (BOOK OF)
AJS 1957-1966 FACTORY WSM - ALL SINGLES & TWINS
ARIEL UP TO 1932 (BOOK OF)
ARIEL 1932-1939 PREWAR MODELS (BOOK OF)
ARIEL 1933-1951 (WORKSHOP MANUAL)
ARIEL 1939-1960 4 STROKE SINGLES (BOOK OF)
ARIEL 1958-1964 LEADER & ARROW (BOOK OF)
BMW R26 R27 (1956-1967) FACTORY WORKSHOP MANUAL
BMW R50 R50S R60 R69S (1955-1969) FACTORY WORKSHOP MANUAL
BRIDGESTONE 90 SERIES FACTORY WSM & PARTS CATALOGUE
BRIDGESTONE 175 SERIES FACTORY WSM & PARTS CATALOGUE
BRIDGESTONE 350 SERIES FACTORY WSM & PARTS CATALOGUES
BSA SERVICE SHEETS MASTER CATALOGUE ALL MODELS 1945-1967
BSA BANTAM D1 TO D7 1948-1966 FACTORY SERVICE SHEETS MANUAL
BSA BANTAM ALL MODELS FROM 1948 ONWARDS (BOOK OF)
BSA DANDY FACTORY WORKSHOP MANUAL (COMPILATION)
BSA SINGLES & V-TWINS UP TO 1927 (BOOK OF)
BSA SINGLES & V-TWINS UP TO 1930 (BOOK OF)
BSA SINGLES & V-TWINS UP TO 1935 (BOOK OF)
BSA SINGLES & V-TWINS 1936-1939 (BOOK OF)
BSA C10, C11 & C12 1945-1958 FACTORY SERVICE SHEETS MANUAL
BSA OHV & SV SINGLES 250-600cc 1945-1959 (BOOK OF)
BSA C15 & B40 1958-1967 FACTORY SERVICE SHEETS MANUAL
BSA OHV & SV SINGLES 250cc (ONLY) 1954-1970 (BOOK OF)
BSA B31, B32, B33 & B34 1945-60 FACTORY SERVICE SHEETS MANUAL
BSA OHV SINGLES 350 & 500cc 1955-1967 (BOOK OF)
BSA M20, M21 & M33 1945-1963 FACTORY SERVICE SHEETS MANUAL
BSA TWINS A7 & A10 1948-1962 FACTORY SERVICE SHEETS MANUAL
BSA TWINS A7 & A10 1948-1962 (BOOK OF)
BSA TWINS A50 & A65 1962-1965 FACTORY WORKSHOP MANUAL
BSA TWINS A50 & A65 1962-1969 (SECOND BOOK OF)
DOUGLAS 1929-1939 PREWAR ALL MODELS (BOOK OF)
DOUGLAS 1948-1957 POSTWAR ALL MODELS FACTORY SHOP MANUAL
DUCATI 160cc, 250cc & 350cc OHC MODELS FACTORY SHOP MANUAL
HONDA 50 ALL MODELS UP TO 1970 INC MONKEY & TRAIL (BOOK OF)
HONDA 90 ALL MODELS UP TO 1966 (BOOK OF)
HONDA 50-65-70-90cc OHC SINGLES 1959-1983 FACTORY WSM
HONDA 125-150cc TWINS C/CS/CB/CA FACTORY WORKSHOP MANUAL
HONDA 125-160-175-200cc TWINS 1964-1980 WORKSHOP MANUAL
HONDA 250-305 TWINS C/CS/CB 1959-1967 FACTORY WSM
HOHDA 250-350 TWINS CB/CL/SL 1968-1973 FACTORY WSM
HONDA 450 CB/CL 1965-1974 K0 TO K7 WORKSHOP MANUAL
HONDA C100 SUPER CUB FACTORY WORKSHOP MANUAL
HONDA C110 SPORT CUB 1962-1969 FACTORY WORKSHOP MANUAL
HONDA TWINS & SINGLES 50cc THRU 305cc 1960-1966 (BOOK OF)
HONDA TWINS ALL MODELS 125cc THRU 450cc UP TO 1968 (BOOK OF)
INDIAN PONYBIKE, BOY RACER & PAPOOSE ILL PARTS LIST & SALES LIT
J.A.P. ENGINES 1927-1952 & MOTORCYCLES 1934-1952 (BOOK OF)
MATCHLESS 1931-1939 ALL MODELS 250cc THRU 990cc (BOOK OF)
MATCHLESS 1945-1956 350 & 500cc SINGLES (BOOK OF)
MATCHLESS 1955-1966 350 & 500cc SINGLES (BOOK OF)
MATCHLESS 1957-1966 FACTORY WSM - ALL SINGLES & TWINS
NEW IMPERIAL ALL SV & OHV FROM 1935 ONWARDS (BOOK OF)
NORTON 1932-1939 PREWAR MODELS (BOOK OF)
NORTON 1932-1947 (BOOK OF)
NORTON 1938-1956 (BOOK OF)
NORTON 1955-1963 MODELS 19, 50 & ES2 (BOOK OF)
NORTON 1955-1965 DOMINATOR TWINS (BOOK OF)
NORTON 1960-1970 TWIN CYLINDER FACTORY WORKSHOP MANUAL
NORTON 1970-1975 COMMANDO 850 & 750cc FACTORY WSM
NORTON 1975-1978 MK 3 COMMANDO 850 cc FACTORY WSM
PANTHER 1932-1958 LIGHTWEIGHT MODELS 250 & 350cc (BOOK OF)
PANTHER 1938-1966 HEAVYWEIGHT MODELS 600 & 650cc (BOOK OF)
RALEIGH MOTORCYCLES 1919-1933 (BOOK OF)
ROYAL ENFIELD 1934-1946 SINGLES & V TWINS (BOOK OF)
ROYAL ENFIELD 1937-1953 SINGLES & V TWINS (BOOK OF)
ROYAL ENFIELD 1946-1962 SINGLES (BOOK OF)
ROYAL ENFIELD 1958-1966 250cc & 350cc SINGLES (SECOND BOOK OF)
ROYAL ENFIELD 736cc INTERCEPTOR FACTORY WORKSHOP MANUAL
RUDGE 1933-1939 (BOOK OF)
SUNBEAM 1928-1939 (BOOK OF)
SUNBEAM 1946-1957 S7 & S8 (BOOK OF)
SUZUKI 50cc & 80cc UP TO 1966 (BOOK OF)
SUZUKI T10 1963-1967 FACTORY WORKSHOP MANUAL
SUZUKI T20 & T200 1965-1969 FACTORY WORKSHOP MANUAL
SUZUKI TWINS 1962 ONWARDS 125-500cc WORKSHOP MANUAL
TRIUMPH 1935-1949 SINGLES & TWINS (BOOK OF)
TRIUMPH 1937-1951 (WORKSHOP MANUAL)
TRIUMPH 1945-1955 FACTORY WORKSHOP MANUAL
TRIUMPH 1945-1959 TWINS (BOOK OF)
TRIUMPH 1956-1969 TWINS (BOOK OF)
TRIUMPH 1963-1970 UNIT CONSTRUCTION 650cc FACTORY WSM
VELOCETTE 1925-1970 ALL SINGLES & TWINS (BOOK OF)
VILLIERS ENGINE UP TO 1959 INC. 3 WHEELERS (BOOK OF)
VILLIERS ENGINE UP TO 1969 (BOOK OF)
VINCENT 1935-1955 (WORKSHOP MANUAL)
YAMAHA 1961-1967 YA5 & YA6 (WORKSHOP MANUAL & ILL PARTS LIST)
YAMAHA 1971-1972 JT1& JT2 (WORKSHOP MANUAL & ILL PARTS LIST)

VELOCEPRESS TECHNICAL BOOKS – MOTORCYCLE

1930'S BRITISH MOTORCYCLE CARBS & ELEC COMPONENTS (BOOK OF)
1930'S BRITISH MOTORCYCLE ENGINES (OVERHAUL & MAINTENANCE)
1930'S BRITISH MOTORCYCLE GEARBOXES & CLUTCHES (BOOK OF)
CATALOG OF BRITISH MOTORCYCLES (1951 MODELS)
LUCAS ELECTRONICS BRITISH M/CYCLES REPAIR & PARTS (1950-1977)
MOTORCYCLE ENGINEERING (P.E. Irving)
MOTORCYCLE ROAD TESTS 1949-1953 (Motor Cycle Magazine UK)
SPEED AND HOW TO OBTAIN IT (Motor Cycle Magazine UK)
TUNING FOR SPEED (P.E. Irving)
WIPAC (COMBO) MANUAL NUMBER 3 + M/CYCLE & SCOOTER MANUAL

VELOCEPRESS MANUALS – SCOOTERS BY MAKE

BSA SUNBEAM SCOOTER WORKSHOP MANUAL 1959-1965
BSA SUNBEAM SCOOTER 1959-1965 (BOOK OF)
LAMBRETTA 1947-1957 ALL 125 & 150cc MODELS (BOOK OF)
LAMBRETTA 1957-1970 LI & TV MODELS (SECOND BOOK OF)
NSU PRIMA 1956-1964 ALL MODELS (BOOK OF)
TRIUMPH TIGRESS SCOOTER WORKSHOP MANUAL 1959-1965
TRIUMPH TIGRESS SCOOTER (BOOK OF)
VESPA 1951-1961 (BOOK OF)
VESPA 1955-1963 125 & 150cc & GS MODELS (SECOND BOOK OF)
VESPA 1955-1968 GS & SS (BOOK OF)
VESPA 1963-1972 90, 125 & 150cc (THIRD BOOK OF)

VELOCEPRESS MANUALS – MOPEDS & MOTORIZED BICYCLES

CYCLEMOTOR (BOOK OF)
NSU QUICKLY 1953-1963 ALL MODELS (BOOK OF)
PUCH MAXI N & S MAINTENANCE & REPAIR (3 MANUAL COMPILATION)
RALEIGH MOPEDS 1960-1969 (BOOK OF)

VELOCEPRESS MANUALS - THREE WHEELER'S

BOND MINICAR THREE WHEELER 1948-1967 (BOOK OF)
BMW ISETTA FACTORY WORKSHOP MANUAL
BSA THREE WHEELER (BOOK OF)
RELIANT REGAL THREE WHEELER 1952-1973 (BOOK OF)
VINTAGE MORGAN THREE WHEELER (BOOK OF)

VELOCEPRESS MANUALS – AUTOMOBILE BY MAKE

ALFA ROMEO GIULIA WORKSHOP MANUAL 1300 TO 2000cc 1962-1975
ALFA ROMEO GIULIA TECH MANUAL CARBURETED CARS FROM 1962
ALFA ROMEO GIULIA TECH MANUAL FUEL INJECTED CARS FROM 1969
ALFA ROMEO GIULIETTA & GIULIA 750 & 101 SERIES 1955-1965 WSM
AUSTIN-HEALEY SPRITE & MG MIDGET WORKSHOP MANUAL 1958-1971
BMW 600 LIMOUSINE FACTORY WORKSHOP MANUAL
BMW 600 LIMOUSINE OWNERS HAND BOOK & SERVICE MANUAL
BMW 2000 & 2002 1966-1976 WORKSHOP MANUAL
CORVAIR 1960-1969 WORKSHOP MANUAL
CORVETTE V8 1955-1962 WORKSHOP MANUAL
FIAT 500 FACTORY WORKSHOP MANUAL 1957-1973
FIAT 600, 600D & MULTIPLA FACTORY WORKSHOP MANUAL 1955-1969
JAGUAR E-TYPE 3.8 & 4.2 SERIES 1 & 2 WORKSHOP MANUAL
JAGUAR MK 7, 8, 9 & XK120, 140, 150 WORKSHOP MANUAL 1948-1961
METROPOLITAN FACTORY WORKSHOP MANUAL
MGA & MGB OWNERS HANDBOOK & WORKSHOP MANUAL
MG MIDGET TC, TD, TF & TF1500 WORKSHOP MANUAL
PORSCHE 356 1948-1965 WORKSHOP MANUAL
PORSCHE 911 2.0, 2.2, 2.4 LITRE 1964-1973 WORKSHOP MANUAL
PORSCHE 911 2.7, 3.0, 3.2 LITRE 1973-1989 WORKSHOP MANUAL
PORSCHE 912 WORKSHOP MANUAL
TRIUMPH TR2, TR3, TR4 1953-1965 WORKSHOP MANUAL
VOLKSWAGEN TRANSPORTER, TRUCKS & WAGONS 1950-1979 WSM
VOLVO 1944-1968 ALL MODELS WORKSHOP MANUAL

VELOCEPRESS TECHNICAL BOOKS - AUTOMOBILE

FERRARI OWNER'S HANDBOOK
HOW TO BUILD A FIBERGLASS CAR
HOW TO BUILD A RACING CAR
HOW TO RESTORE THE MODEL 'A' FORD
MASERATI OWNER'S HANDBOOK
PERFORMANCE TUNING THE SUNBEAM TIGER
SOUPING THE VOLKSWAGEN
SOLEX CARBURETORS (EMPHASIS ON UK & EU AUTOMOBILES)
SU CARBURETORS (EMPHASIS ON UK AUTOMOBILES)
WEBER CARBURETORS (EMPHASIS ON ALFA & FIAT)

VELOCEPRESS BOOKS & GUIDES - AUTOMOBILE

COMPLETE CATALOG OF JAPANESE MOTOR VEHICLES
FERRARI 308 SERIES BUYER'S AND OWNER'S GUIDE
FERRARI BROCHURES AND SALES LITERATURE 1968-1989
FERRARI SERIAL NUMBERS PART I - ODD NUMBERS TO 21399
FERRARI SERIAL NUMBERS PART II - EVEN NUMBERS TO 1050
HENRY'S FABULOUS MODEL "A" FORD
MASERATI BROCHURES AND SALES LITERATURE

VELOCEPRESS BOOKS – RACING

CARRERA PANAMERICANA - MEXICAN ROAD RACE (BOOK OF)
DIALED IN - THE JAN OPPERMAN STORY
VEDA ORR'S NEW REVISED HOT ROD PICTORIAL

AUTOBOOKS WORKSHOP MANUALS

FOR A COMPLETE LISTING OF THE AUTOBOOKS WORKSHOP MANUALS THAT WE CURRENTLY HAVE AVAILABLE, PLEASE VISIT OUR WEBSITE.

www.VelocePress.com

www.ingramcontent.com/pod-product-compliance
Lightning Source LLC
Chambersburg PA
CBHW060248240426
43673CB00047B/1890